GEOFFREY CHAPMAN THEOLOGY LIBRARY

The Spirit of Love

GEOFFREY CHAPMAN THEOLOGY LIBRARY

General editor: Michael Richards

GEOFFREY CHAPMAN THEOLOGY LIBRARY

THE SPIRIT OF LOVE
Theology of the Holy Spirit

Brian Gaybba

GEOFFREY CHAPMAN
LONDON

A Geoffrey Chapman book published by
Cassell Publishers Limited
Artillery House, Artillery Row, London SW1P 1RT

First published 1987

ISBN 0 225 66500 X

Nihil obstat: Father Anton Cowan, *Censor*
Imprimatur: Rt Rev. John Crowley,
Bishop in Central London
Westminster, 19 October 1987

The *Nihil obstat* and *Imprimatur* are a declaration that a book or pamphlet is considered to be free from
doctrinal or moral error. It is not implied that those who have granted the *Nihil obstat* and *Imprimatur*
agree with the contents, opinions or statements expressed.

British Library Cataloguing in Publication Data
Gaybba, Brian
  The spirit of love : theology of the
  Holy Spirit. — (Geoffrey Chapman
  Theology Library).
  1. Holy Spirit
  I. Title   II. Series
  231'.3   BT121.2

Typeset by Inforum Ltd, Portsmouth

Printed and bound in Great Britain
by Biddles Ltd, Guildford

Contents

Foreword

The welcome given to this series by reviewers and readers has confirmed those who planned it in their conviction that they are meeting a real need of the present generation in the Church. The appraisal and revision of Catholic life that was undertaken and set in motion by the Second Vatican Council called for a fresh approach to the study of Christian doctrine: one which would continue to observe the classical norms and scope of the systematic teaching of the Gospel as practised from the beginning, while benefiting from the new methods and instruments of study that are now available.

The series sets out to communicate the essentials of each chosen area of study through the personal reflection of an experienced scholar and teacher who has made his mark in his own particular field. Each volume attempts to survey the documentary materials needed in the investigation of its theme, the special problems and topics of interest that centuries of study have thrown up, and the questions asked in the controversies of the present. As far as possible, Catholic beliefs are expounded and discussed in relation to the established and contemporary teaching of other Christian bodies and of other religious faiths, so that some indication at least is given of the doctrinal dialogue necessary for the understanding and reconciliation in faith which is the purpose of the Christian mission.

The Spirit of Love, built on Brian Gaybba's university teaching experience, provides a thorough survey of the reflection on the work of the Holy Spirit that has been a marked feature of recent years. The Christian revelation of the nature of God, the manner in which the Church is led and is given a coherent living pattern by the Spirit, the 'charismatic' renewal of the personal life of the individual as of the corporate life of the Church: all these areas of intellectual exploration and practical pastoral policy received particular attention at the Council, and research has been intensified since that time. Pope Paul VI greatly encouraged this renewed awareness of the presence of the Spirit in the world and in the Church, and expressed his concern that the mistakes and deviations all too recurrent in previous centuries should be avoided. Brian Gaybba's book reminds us of the wasted opportunities of the past, but is in itself an indication, both searching and systematic, of the way in which the Church, having learnt many lessons, now finds itself able to respond with greater boldness to the guidance of the Spirit.

Michael Richards

To Monika, Jenny and Richard

This book is an elaboration of tutorial material I prepared for my students at the University of South Africa. I am grateful to the University for enabling me to make liberal use of that material here.

Part One

The historical development of the doctrine of the Holy Spirit

To understand well any Christian doctrine, one must know something about its history. It is only such a knowledge that will both liberate from the mentally enslaving idea that a doctrine's present form is its only possible one, and provide the necessary guidelines for reformulating it in a way that remains true to all its essentials.

The history that follows has been written to provide the necessary data for a deeper understanding of the Church's belief in the Holy Spirit. What follows is not the sort of history a professional historian would write, though I hope any historical scholar will not find excessive fault with what I am about to produce. The present book is a work of *theology*, and this historical section is unabashedly a looking-back by a theologian over the centuries in order to understand as best he can the origins of a particular belief he holds. Only those developments are focused on, therefore, that will provide some insight into how various aspects of belief in the Holy Spirit came about. This entails inevitably the fact that the often confused, groping, quite unsystematic reality of history is not really reflected. Instead, clear lines are drawn which would not necessarily have been all that clear to people at the time. Indeed, on occasion lines have to be drawn that in reality hardly existed except in a very broken and confused way. This is particularly true of the biblical testimony, where the rich complexity of the evidence has to

1

be sacrificed in order to highlight certain recurrent ideas and their inter-relationship.

One final word of introduction. Some may find it rather odd that the Bible is dealt with here as a historical source rather than as the norm of faith. However, its very character as a norm can only operate properly when one sees it as the (albeit inspired) product of history. As Rahner once observed (1966:6–7), we find in the scriptures normative *developments*, historical developments that reach a point where they take on a normative character for all subsequent doctrine. Hence the normative character of scripture and its historicity are not contradictory.

1

The Old Testament

A. THE SPIRIT'S NAME

To a great extent we have lost the interest the ancients had in the meaning of names. For an Israelite of old, a name was not simply a convenient label for distinguishing someone, but the revelation of a person's character.

As regards the three persons constitutive of the Trinity, two of them ('Father' and 'Son') have names that immediately mean something to us. Moreover, the incarnate Son's name, 'Jesus Christ', also means something. 'Jesus' means 'saviour', 'Christ' means the anointed one, the Messiah.

When one turns to the Spirit, here too the name has a meaning. However, it is at first sight a very odd meaning, one that seems rather out of keeping with the dignity of a divine person. Certainly, it initially affords little understanding of the distinctive character of this at one time rather neglected person of the Trinity.

The English word 'spirit' comes from the Latin *spiritus*, which means 'breath' or 'breathing'. *Spiritus* was the Latin word used for translating the Hebrew *ruach* (and its Greek equivalent, *pneuma*). *Ruach* has two basic meanings: 'wind' and 'air'. However, in both the emphasis is on the power present in them (Westermann 1981:224). *Ruach*'s root meaning is 'a stream of air' (Koch 1970:869) — not a static, but a dynamic reality.

Often enough in the Old Testament, the word refers simply to a powerful wind and to life-giving breath. For example, in Gen 8:1 and 1 Kings 19:11, the meaning is simply 'wind'. Several scholars would add that in Gen 1:2, usually translated as 'God's Spirit hovered over the waters', *ruach* simply means 'a mighty wind sent by God'. In Gen 45:27 and Judg 15:19 *ruach* simply means 'breath'.

There are other, transferred, meanings of the term. For example, the inability of people to understand or control the wind led to the use of *ruach* as a term for all that is empty or useless (Koch 1970:870; Albertz and Westermann 1976:731). We too use air in this sense — we speak of people talking so much 'hot air'. Well-known examples of this use of *ruach* are Eccles 1:14 and Jer 5:13. Another transferred meaning, this time derived from the basic meaning of 'breath', was to describe emotions. Since emotions can affect a person's breathing pattern, emotions came to be described as 'spirits', that is to say, 'breaths' (see Koch 1970:872). Examples of this use are: anger (Job 4:9), despair (Ez 3:14), patience (Prov 17:27). These emotions are called 'spirits' of anger, despair, etc. A further, connected, meaning is that of an impersonal force that can grip one, producing depression (1 Sam 16:14), jealousy (Num 5:14), deception (1 Kings 22:22; see Albertz and Westermann 1976:739–740 and Heron 1983:4–5).

However, these and still other meanings (see especially those in Lys 1962) are not as relevant to our theme as the basic ones of 'wind' and 'breath'. It is these that are at the origin of the concept of 'the Spirit of the Lord', since the word 'spirit' means here 'wind', 'breath'. 'The Spirit of the Lord' originated as a way of describing God's powerful, mysterious activity, using the imagery of wind and breath. 'The Spirit of the Lord' was 'the wind of the Lord', 'the breath of the Lord'.

For the people of the ancient East, 'wind' was a very mysterious thing. It seemed to them to be something divine, something they could not control, but which controlled them instead. The wind was therefore widely worshipped as a god of nature. However, for the people of Israel there was only one God, and all things were under that God's control. For them the wind was something made by (Amos 4:13) and under the control of (Jer 10:13) the one true God, who used it for whatever purposes God wished. Thus, God might use the wind to prepare the chaos for the divine creative word (Gen 1:2), just as the wind in nature brings clouds which fertilize the earth with life-giving rain. Or God could use wind to end the flood (Gen 8:1), to provide a route through the sea (Ex 14:21ff.), food for the people (Num 11:31), as a punishment (Is 57:13), and so on (more details can be found in Koch 1970:870–871). For the Israelites, the power and mysterious character of wind (see Eccles 11:5) made it a perfect symbol of the power and mysterious ways of God's actions (see Jn 3:8).

'Breath', too, was a mysterious and awesome thing to them. It was the sign of life, the very presence of life. Life was widely seen as the gift of the gods. For Israel it was the gift of Yahweh, the one true God. It was a gift God could give or take away at will (Ps 104:29–30). God, too, was pictured as having a breath. The wind was often portrayed as such. Thus, the wind that opened the sea for the escaping Israelites (Ex 14:21) becomes (in Ex 15:8) a 'blast' from God's nostrils. And two verses further on we are told that God's 'breath' caused the sea to close again.

Similar images are found in Ps 33:6 and 2 Sam 22:16, Is 11:15, Job 4:9 and elsewhere (see Albertz and Westermann 1976:731).

The 'Spirit of the Lord' originated therefore as a distinctive way of picturing God's actions. Elsewhere, for example, God is spoken of as having 'hands' (e.g., Deut 11:2) or 'fingers' (e.g., Deut 9:10) with which God performs certain actions. The 'Spirit of the Lord' portrays God as acting through wind.

However, Albertz and Westermann (1976:733) warn that the imagery of God's breath is more than a metaphor like God's 'hands' or 'fingers'. Wind and breath were often seen, it seems, as a sort of manifestation of the divine presence, an outward sign of a real presence, as was the pillar of cloud that led the Israelites to freedom (Ex 13:21). Possibly God was so intimately associated with wind that a danger to the divine transcendence needed to be counteracted with the sort of experience narrated in 1 Kings 19:11 ('. . . but Yahweh was not in the wind').

The 'Spirit of the Lord', therefore, was a very distinctive way indeed of portraying God's activity. Albertz and Westermann's observation also implies the added element of God's presence. God's 'Spirit' — that is to say, God's 'wind' or 'breath' — are not realities manipulated by God from a distance. Very often they imply God's presence, as in Ps 139:7 (Schmidt 1984:171).

However, it is also necessary to point out that God's breath or wind can, by the inner logic of the symbol, be pictured as going forth from, and therefore as distinct from God. Thus, God can be said to 'put' God's Spirit 'into' people (e.g., Is 63:11), to 'pour' it out (Joel 2:28), to 'clothe' people with it (Judg 6:34), and so on. This of course does not contradict the idea that God is often seen as being in some sense *in* the divine 'wind' or 'breath'. It simply looks at the symbol from another angle and sees it as something that can go out from God to rest on an individual.

The idea of God's 'Spirit' therefore began its life as a way of portraying God's actions, God's active, powerful presence. Even after the word ceased to be thought of as a wind or a breath — as is the case today — 'the Spirit of the Lord' still retained the basic meaning of God-in-action, the way in which God was actively present to people.

The Spirit's name is indeed revealing, then. It reveals to us the powerful, mysterious way in which God acts and is present to us.

B.   THE ACTIVITIES ASCRIBED TO GOD'S SPIRIT, GOD'S 'WIND'

What activities were ascribed to God's 'wind'? To begin on a more general note, Koch (1970:873) observes that the earliest descriptions of the Spirit attribute to it 'transitory phenomena in the physical or psychological order, all of which have an element of the tempestuous and the violent in them'. Note the words 'transitory', 'tempestuous', 'violent'. They describe well-known characteristics of wind. Since the idea of the Spirit originated as a way of portraying God's actions as God's 'wind', it is not surprising that the earliest conceptions of the Spirit's actions are precisely those that recall a wind suddenly hitting people, showing immense strength (Judg 14:6), even carrying people away (1 Kings 18:12; 2 Kings 2:16).

Thus conceived, the Spirit was seen as active in two areas particularly: charismatic leadership in pre-monarchical Israel; and early prophecy (Albertz and Westermann 1976:763).

As regards charismatic leadership, God gives individuals the Spirit for a specific task, after which it is removed. Thus the Spirit 'comes on' Othniel (Judg 3:10), Gideon (Judg 6:34), Jephthah (Judg 11:29). It 'seizes' Samson (Judg 15:14; see also 14:6, 19) and Saul (1 Sam 11:6).

As regards prophecy, it needs to be recalled that the earlier meaning of 'prophecy' was not the delivery of a clear message in the manner of the later prophets, but rather the experience of being caught up in a state of ecstasy or religious frenzy. Attributing such states to a divine 'spirit' (as is done in 1 Sam 10:5–13, 19:20–24) was not unique to Israel. Indeed, it is quite likely that the Israelites simply took over this idea from the Canaanites. Partial evidence of this is the fact that when connected with ecstatic prophecy, the Spirit is usually described as the Spirit of *Elohim*, rather than as the Spirit of Yahweh (Albertz and Westermann 1976:745). *Elohim* means 'God' or 'gods' and of itself could be used of any god — unlike 'Yahweh'. This may also explain the references to an 'evil' (1 Sam 18:10) or 'lying' Spirit (1 Kings 22:21–22, where the portrayal of the Spirit as a power that can converse with Yahweh may be another hangover of polytheistic ideas — see Heron 1983:9).

In short, any behaviour that went beyond the normal (even interpreting dreams — see Gen 41:16, 38) was seen as a sign of the Spirit's presence. The association of unusual, ecstatic behaviour with the Spirit will remain a permanent feature of Christian thought.

With the establishment of the monarchy we see a change taking place (Albertz and Westermann 1976:749). A king is a more permanent leader than one raised up to deal with a specific need. The Spirit was believed to remain with the king, as God's anointed, throughout his reign. Thus, only when Saul's kingship ceased did the Spirit leave him (1 Sam 16:14), to remain henceforth with the new king, David (1 Sam 16:13). We have here the origins of the institutionalization of the Spirit's presence, that is to say the establishment of a permanent link between the Spirit and a particular office.

Part and parcel of this incipient institutionalization was the conferring of the Spirit through symbolic actions, such as the anointing of David (1 Sam 16:13). A parallel development occurs when a particular individual is seen as having a permanent and not just an *ad hoc* prophetic role. Thus, Elijah had the Spirit in a continuous way and the habitual possession of the Spirit passed on to his successor Elisha through the symbolic action of his taking up Elijah's cloak (2 Kings 2:12–13).

With this incipient institutionalization of the Spirit's presence we also have the beginnings of criteria to establish it that go beyond the merely abnormal. For the kingly office was a sign of where the Spirit's presence could be found.

However, far more important was the development of ethical criteria for the Spirit's presence. An early example of this can be found in the prophet Micah. In Micah 3:8 he — alone of the new breed of prophets of the Word (see below) — appeals to the Spirit as the one moving him to declare to God's people their crimes. Other early examples of the link between the Spirit and right living can be found in Isaiah. In Is 11:2–3 the Spirit is said to be a Spirit of 'fear of the Lord'. And in Is 32:15–17 righteousness is seen as an effect of the pouring out of the Spirit. This, incidentally, is a prophecy of future salvation. It is the earliest reference we have to the Spirit regarded as the bringer of future salvation.

During and after the exile in Babylon the link between the Spirit and righteous living became a prominent theme. Only then was the Spirit clearly and frequently viewed as the source of moral and religious renewal in God's people. The earliest example of this is found in Ezekiel. In Ez 36:23–31 the purpose of the gift of the Spirit is the purification of the people in order that they may live in accordance with God's decrees (see especially verse 27). In Is 44:3 the pouring out of the Spirit involves a renewal of the covenant between God and the people (see verse 5). Another example is the famous text about God's mysterious servant, who, having received the Spirit, will bring justice to the nations (Is 42:1; see also Is 61:1–3).

More specifically, in Old Testament times the Spirit came to be associated with two things especially: prophecy, and Israel's hopes for salvation.

To begin with *prophecy*, from the eighth century B.C. onwards, conceptions of 'prophecy' and 'prophet' began to change. Increasingly they were thought of as the delivery and the deliverer, respectively, of a clear message from God, unaccompanied by frenzies or ecstasies. Indeed, frenzies and ecstasies fell into some disrepute. They were not sure signs of the Spirit's presence at all, and therefore no authentication of any messages delivered in such a state. Jeremiah could reject them as empty air, empty *ruach* (Jer 5:13).

Pre-exilic practitioners of this new style of prophecy, such as Amos, Hosea, Isaiah, Jeremiah, clearly wished to avoid being confused with the ecstatic prophets of old. As a result they avoided appealing to the Spirit to justify their messages. They appealed simply to God's Word, to the fact that God spoke to them. Moreover, a message was not the sort of activity that traditionally had been associated with the Spirit. This was quite likely a further reason for their not appealing to it in such a transitional stage (Westermann 1981:226). Micah was the only exception among the pre-exilic prophets of the Word. The reason is interesting: in the very place where he appeals to the Spirit, he brings in the moral dimension — God's condemnation of wickedness. This moral dimension distinguished his conception of the Spirit's role from that of the ecstatic prophet.

After the exile, however, Micah's link between the Spirit and prophetic messages — especially of divine displeasure — became the norm. Not only did prophets like Ezekiel claim that the Spirit enabled them to hear God's message (Ez 2:2), or even brought the message to them (Ez 11:5), but the earlier prophets of the Word are now said to have spoken through the Spirit (Zech 7:12; Neh 9:30).

This link between God's Word and God's Spirit eventually gave rise to another criterion of the Spirit's presence: viz., whether or not something conforms to what God has revealed, to what God is believed to be like.

As regards *Israel's hopes for the future*, the earliest role attributed to the Spirit in this respect was that of guiding the king. The king was seen as God's instrument in bringing blessings to the people. But corrupt kings led to disillusionment, and this in turn led to a belief in a future ideal king, an ideal 'anointed one' or 'messiah' (see 1 Sam 16:13). Is 11:2, a famous text, pictures this ideal king as being endowed in an especially full way with the Spirit: 'on him the spirit of Yahweh rests, a spirit of wisdom and insight, a spirit of counsel and power, a spirit of knowledge and of the fear of Yahweh'. The qualities listed in this text (wisdom, insight, etc.) are those needed by a ruler (see verses 3–4). These qualities will enable him to rule so perfectly that a veritable paradise will result (verses 6–9).

One of the qualities or gifts mentioned is that of wisdom. The idea that the Spirit brings wisdom is developed also in the Wisdom literature. In Proverbs 1:20–23 wisdom is personified as a goddess who will 'pour out her Spirit on people'. Strictly speaking, there is no mention here of *God's* Spirit. But since the wisdom is God's own wisdom, the Spirit referred to is clearly God's. In the book of Wisdom, this personification is more marked and the qualities of the Spirit that is in wisdom are spelt out (Wis 1:1–15, and 7:22 – 8:1).

Not only the Messiah-king, but also his collaborators will be endowed with the Spirit so that they can pass judgement with justice. In Is 28:5–6 we see the magistrates of messianic times and even the soldiers defending the gate of God's city as being endowed with the Spirit so that the peace and justice of messianic times may not be disturbed.

The prophet who announces salvation is another one said to be endowed with the Spirit. 'The Spirit of the Lord Yahweh has been given to me, for Yahweh has anointed me. He has sent me to bring good news to the poor, to bind up hearts that are broken; to proclaim liberty to captives, freedom to those in prison; to proclaim a year of favour from Yahweh . . .' (Is 61:1–2). Jesus applied this text to himself in Lk 4:16–22.

But the really outstanding thing about the blessings of the future is that not only those who have some active role to play in bringing about salvation (the Messiah, his helpers, the prophet announcing salvation), but everybody will receive the Spirit. The Spirit will be 'poured out' on God's people. The theme is indeed an old one. In Num 11:29 Moses is said to have expressed the wish that all the people would receive the Spirit and 'prophesy' (i.e., experience the ecstasy of the Spirit's presence). And Isaiah spoke of the Spirit being poured out on the people (Is 32:15). But it is only after the exile that this theme became prominent (see Is 44:3; Ez 39:29; and most especially Joel 3:1–2, or as it is numbered in some versions of the Bible, Joel 2:28–29). The text from Joel, probably written about the fourth century B.C., is the best known.

Towards the end of the Old Testament period the conviction developed that the Spirit had been withdrawn from Israel until the Messiah came. As a result, the expectation of a future outpouring of the Spirit became even more a sign of messianic times. The reason for the conviction of the Spirit's withdrawal seems to have been the increasing role of the Law and its interpretation in the lives of the Jewish people (see Montague 1976:111–115). The conviction grew that what God required of each generation could be ascertained by studying the Law. The Spirit-inspired prophet as someone who brought God's Word to his generation had died out. Instead, the influential leaders were those who knew and could interpret the Law: the 'rabbis', as they came to be known. They believed that the age of the great works of the Spirit was past, that the Spirit had departed from Israel after the last prophets (Haggai, Zechariah and Malachi) had died. The present age was regarded as unworthy of the Spirit which, as a result, came to be associated exclusively with the future messianic age.

When that age came, the pouring out of the Spirit on all people would not only enable them to 'prophesy', but also purify them of sin, making new creatures of them. It would give them new hearts to live new lives

(Ez 36:25–27). Here the Spirit is seen as responsible for what was later called justification and sanctification. This particular role of the Spirit was fully developed only in New Testament times.

All the above means that God's Spirit was seen as having a creative function. The Spirit creates new life. The result will be a new world. Because of this, and because of texts such as Gen 1:2, Ps 104:30, Ps 33:6, Job 33:4, the Spirit came to be called 'creator Spirit'. There is a famous Latin hymn that begins *Veni creator spiritus* — 'Come, Holy Ghost, Creator, come'. We are therefore accustomed to think of the Spirit as the creator of the world and all that is in it. Theologically, such an idea is unobjectionable. However, it is worth noting that it is not one that is stressed in biblical times. There are only four places (see above) in the Old Testament where the Spirit is connected with the work of creation, and even those four places are disputed by scholars. In Gen 1:2 *ruach* may simply mean 'a mighty wind', not the symbol of God's action normally meant by 'the Spirit of the Lord'. Then in Ps 104:30 *ruach* probably means the breath of life that God gives to a being so that it will live (see also Gen 2:7). Job 33:4 may well have the same meaning. Ps 33:6 is stronger evidence, but *ruach* there could simply be another way of saying God 'breathed' the creative Word, for breath is needed in order to speak a word. In other words, it could just be another way of saying 'God spoke a word — and it was so'.

It is instructive to try and ascertain the reason why there are no unambiguous references to the Spirit as the creator of the world. I believe the reason was that 'the Spirit of the Lord' was used as a way of expressing God's action towards God's *people* and *through them* on the world around us. 'The Spirit of the Lord' seems mainly to be a way of describing God's active presence to people. This is instructive because it gives us an insight into the 'nature' of the Spirit. Its nature is to be a means of contact between persons, to be a means of unity, an idea developed very fully in Christian times.

C. THE 'HOLY SPIRIT'

In the New Testament it is usual to refer to the Spirit as the 'holy' Spirit. However, the phrase 'holy Spirit' is rare in the Old Testament. It occurs in Is 63:10 and in Ps 51:11, and also occurs in the book of Wisdom (see Wis 1:5). The expression 'holy Spirit' became more widespread among the rabbis towards the end of the Old Testament period. They repeatedly said that not only the prophets, but also the words of the Torah were 'inspired' by the 'holy Spirit'. Here we have the origins of the idea that the scriptures were inspired by the Spirit. The Dead Sea Scrolls also have several references to the 'holy Spirit'.

In Is 63:10 and Ps 51:11 the whole point of stressing that the Spirit was a *holy* Spirit was to contrast the holiness of God with the sinfulness of people. Both these texts are about sinners, sinners who have violated the Law of the all-holy God. In Isaiah they are therefore said to have grieved God's *holy* Spirit (this expression — 'grieving' the holy Spirit — is found also in Eph 4:30). In Ps 51 the sinner begs to be made clean and enjoy the presence of God's *holy* Spirit. By calling the Spirit 'holy', the psalmist is acknowledging the contrast between himself and the God he has offended (see verses 3–4).

However, as I have mentioned, it was only towards the end of the Old Testament period that the expression 'the holy Spirit' became very widespread. Why only then? A very likely reason is that people by then had ceased to pronounce God's name ('Yahweh') out of reverence. Believing it to be too holy to pronounce, they found roundabout ways of referring to God. They would therefore no longer talk of *God's* Spirit, but rather of the *holy* Spirit. The word 'holy' made it clear that the Spirit spoken about belonged to God.

The late development of the custom of referring to the Spirit as 'the Holy Spirit' is not, therefore, an indication that at last people were beginning to look upon the Spirit as a distinct person. Certainly, the practice of speaking of the Spirit *as though* a person became widespread during the end period of Old Testament times. God's 'wind' was personalized. But so too was God's wisdom. This did not mean that either God's wind or wisdom were regarded as being really distinct from God, or as intermediaries of some sort between God and humanity (see on this Isaacs 1976:52–58).

QUESTIONS

Check questions

1 What is the basic meaning of 'spirit', *ruach*?
2 What is the link between that meaning and the theological concept 'the Spirit of God'?
3 What activities were amongst the oldest to be ascribed to 'the Spirit of God'?
4 How did the association of the Spirit with institutional structures begin?
5 What was meant originally by 'prophesying', and how did the term's meaning change?
6 Why were the prophets of the Word originally unwilling to appeal to the Spirit as the source of their inspiration?
7 How did ideas about the signs of the Spirit's presence begin to change?
8 What was the original role given to the Spirit as regards the achievement of Israel's future hopes?
9 What further roles developed?

10 When did the term 'holy Spirit' become widespread and what was the purpose of
    describing the Spirit as 'holy'?
11 What effect on ideas about the Spirit's activity in Israel did the late Old Testament
    emphasis on the Law and its interpretation have?

Discussion question

In older theological textbooks assertions are repeatedly found to the effect that the Holy
Spirit's existence was revealed only in New Testament times. Is that a valid standpoint?

RECOMMENDED READING

A detailed and very useful commentary on the principal texts dealing with the Spirit in the
Old Testament can be found in Montague 1976. For a more general survey, Koch 1970 is
still well worth reading. A useful summary account of the history can also be found in
Heron 1983, ch. 2 of which deals with issues barely touched on here, such as the changing
meaning of the Greek word for Spirit (*pneuma*) under the influence of Jewish ideas.

2

The New Testament

My aim in this chapter is to trace the main features of the doctrine of the Spirit that developed in New Testament times. Unlike the case of the Old Testament, I shall not attempt to trace stages in the development of beliefs about the Spirit. The New Testament period is too short. Instead, I shall concentrate on highlighting the similarities and differences between New and Old Testament conceptions of the Spirit. This also has the advantage of being a more modest task than trying to deal with all that the New Testament has to say on the subject, an attempt that would be impossible here. The subject is far too vast. Moreover, it is complicated by the fact that there is no one single concept of the Spirit running throughout the documents.

The main focus of this chapter will therefore be on the principal ways in which the Spirit was conceived of in New Testament times. However, it is necessary to begin with a brief examination of the conviction that the early Christians had that the days of the outpouring of the Spirit had arrived.

A.   HOPE FULFILLED: THE OUTPOURING OF THE SPIRIT

When one turns to the New Testament, it is immediately obvious that one is faced with people who are convinced that the longed-for day of the outpouring of the Spirit on all had arrived. This is particularly evident in Paul's letters (or those traditionally ascribed to him) and the Acts of the Apostles.

In these documents the Spirit is mentioned constantly, as can be seen merely by paging through them. Moreover, the way the Spirit is referred to makes it clear that the early Christians regarded the Spirit as permanently present in the community. In both Acts and Paul's letters, the community is Spirit-filled and its individuals enjoy the permanent presence of the Spirit. In its ordinary peaceful life, the Church is 'filled with the consolation of the Holy Spirit' (Acts 9:31). The Church is a house in which God dwells in the Spirit (Eph 2:22), and Christians are temples of the Spirit (1 Cor 6:19).

The conviction of the early Church that the days of the Spirit's outpouring had arrived is made explicit in the story of Pentecost (Acts 2:1–21). 'They [the disciples] heard what sounded like a powerful wind ['wind' again!] from heaven, the noise of which filled the entire house in which they were sitting; and something appeared to them that seemed like tongues of fire; these separated and came to rest on the head of each of them' (Acts 2:1–4). Then came the decisive experience, described as their being 'filled with the Holy Spirit', an event that is immediately manifested in speaking 'foreign languages' (Acts 2:4).

There is a controversy as to the meaning of 'foreign languages'. Did the disciples actually *speak* the languages or (according to some scholars) dialects of their hearers? Or did the disciples speak their own language but were heard by each listener in his or her dialect? Was it a miracle of speech or of hearing? In trying to resolve this debate, a significant clue may be the fact that many thought the disciples were drunk (Acts 2:13). This seems to indicate that what really happened was a sort of ecstatic speech, an ecstatic form of glossolalia or speaking in tongues (see 1 Cor 14:23). Some would have heard this babbling as a language familiar to them, others simply as babbling.

As was seen in Chapter 1, one of the oldest ideas about the Spirit was that it induced a state of religious fervour that was called 'prophecy'. The Pentecost experience would therefore understandably have convinced the group of disciples that what had happened to them was what Israel had longed for: the outpouring of the Spirit. And that is the explanation of the event given by Peter in Acts 2:14–21.

However, the story of the 'foreign languages' also serves to make the point that with the coming of the Spirit the division between people caused by sin is beginning to be overcome. According to Gen 11:5–9, humanity's pride resulted in its being divided by language. In the story of Pentecost the sign that the Spirit overcomes humanity's divisions is that language does not divide people on that day. Instead, each hears her or his own language being spoken (Acts 2:6, 8, 11). Pentecost reverses Babel.

For the author of Acts, the Pentecost event is obviously a unique one, and one that created the Spirit-filled community, the Church. From Jerusalem, where Pentecost occurred, this community then spread out to the rest of the world (see Lk 24:47). However, there are scholars who wonder whether this is not an oversimplification of what really happened. They suspect that there was more than one 'Pentecost' (see on this Dunn 1975:136ff.). In other words, they believe that the experience of receiving the Spirit was one that occurred in other places and created the Church there *independently of what happened in Jerusalem*. One of the reasons for this opinion is that in Acts Luke deliberately concentrates entirely on events in Jerusalem, so as to present a picture of Christianity spreading from there to the whole world.

Some of these scholars believe that the Jerusalem happening was neither more nor less spectacular or significant than the other cases, while others (such as Dunn 1975:139) are of the opinion that the Jerusalem happening was a much more influential one, so much so that it can rightly be regarded as the beginning of the Church.

Then there are scholars who believe that the Pentecost story is really a 'dogmatic creation', that is to say a fictional story designed to emphasize the theological meaning of experiences of the Spirit that were widespread in the early Christian community (see Haenchen 1961:137–139). In support of this view, there is the fact that Luke is the only one who says that the Spirit came on Pentecost day. This is rather odd if Pentecost was the clear-cut moment of the dramatic origin of the Church's mission that Acts makes it out to be (compare the frequent references in the New Testament to Christ's resurrection). Further support can be found in the fact that the Pentecost story in Acts not only affirms *that* the Spirit came, but also has much to say about the *meaning* of the Spirit's coming. For example, the mere fact that Spirit is said to have come on *Pentecost* day is highly significant. Originally Pentecost was a harvest festival (see Ex 23:14–17). It was celebrated fifty days (*pentēkostos* is the Greek for fiftieth') after the feast of Unleavened Bread or Passover (the two are identified in several texts, e.g., Ex 23:14–17). Pentecost was also known as the feast of Weeks (Ex 34:22), being the culmination of the seven-week period of Unleavened Bread that began with Passover. However, Pentecost eventually took on a new meaning for the Jews which was quite probably widespread even in Jesus' time. It came to be seen as the celebration of the giving of the Law on Mount Sinai, and the ratification of the covenant. Legends also arose about people hearing God's voice in a miraculous way, amid signs of fire and spirit (see Montague 1976:277–279).

The link between all this and the account of Pentecost in Acts is not hard to see. The Spirit — God's presence — comes in the form of fire (verse 4), and the result is that people hear a message in a miraculous way (verses 6–8). In addition, Pentecost was the completion of festivities that began with the Passover fifty days previously. Passover celebrated the occasion when the Israelites were delivered from slavery and formed into God's people. Pentecost celebrated the Law given to them on Mount Sinai as part of the Covenant that made them such. Paralleling this, the Church is God's new people, saved by Jesus on the feast of Passover (Lk 22:14–20). Christians are the beneficiaries of a new covenant, a covenant based on a new law, that of love. What could be more appropriate, then, than that his new people should begin its life filled with God's presence, filled with the Spirit that pours love into believers' hearts (Rom 5:5), on the very day that the giving of the Law and the formation of the old covenant was being celebrated (see also 2 Cor 3:6)?

Hence, one can ask whether Luke did not deliberately construct the Pentecost story with the intention of teaching us that the Church's experience of the Spirit is the sign of the creation of God's new people, who are bound by a new covenant, based on a new law, that of love (Luke's emphasis on love can be seen from texts such as Acts 2:44–45 and 4:32).

I must confess that I find the arguments for regarding the account in Acts purely as a theological creation inadequate. In fact, I find inadequate the arguments for even doubting that Luke is indeed reporting at least the substance of something that occurred on Pentecost day. By 'substance' I mean an overwhelming experience of the presence of God in their midst on that day and the effects this had on them (e.g., glossolalia). There is no reason why the disciples should not have been given so eventful an experience on Pentecost day. If such an experience is all the more significant because of the connections that can be found between it and the later meaning of Pentecost or the Sinai legends, then so much the better. Why deny God a sense of the dramatic, the ability to choose the appropriate moment? And, if Luke did know of the legends and the meaning of the feast of Pentecost in the Judaism of his time (Dunn 1975:140 doubts whether he did), why should he not design his narrative so as to emphasize the appropriateness of the event occurring on that day?

At any rate, whether or not Luke's account of Pentecost is regarded as a report of something that actually happened, it is clear that New Testament Christians were convinced that the promised outpouring of the Spirit had occurred. This conviction rested not simply on the Pentecost story but also and especially on the experience that various local communities and individuals had had of the Spirit's presence (see, e.g., 1 Cor 2:4; Gal 3:5; Acts 10:44).

The fact that the Spirit had been lavishly poured out on them was, for the early Christians, a sign that the 'last days' had come. This too is shown by the deliberate insertion in the quotation from Joel (Acts 2:17) of the words 'in the last days' (translated in some Bibles as 'in those days' or 'in the days to come'). The insertion may or may not have been made by Luke. But he used it, and this use did not imply that for him the last days in the Old Testament sense of the actual end of the world's history had come. He could hardly have meant that, since his aim in Acts was to show his readers that they were now living in an age characterized by the expansion of the Church through the power of the

Spirit. The Church was living in 'the last days' in the sense that the major events associated with those days (such as the resurrection and the outpouring of the Spirit) had already begun to happen.

B. NEW TESTAMENT CONCEPTIONS OF THE SPIRIT: CONTINUITY AND DEVELOPMENT

How was the Spirit conceived in New Testament times, and what activities were ascribed to that Spirit?

The documents do not display one viewpoint, universally subscribed to. Instead, the reader is confronted with different ideas — reconcilable, but nevertheless different. Three in particular can be mentioned. First of all, there is the viewpoint associated especially with Acts: the Spirit is a power that the Church needs for its mission, and which is manifested especially in extraordinary phenomena. In contrast to this is the second viewpoint, represented especially by Paul: the Spirit as the giver of inner, spiritual life, the Spirit that is revealed in ordinary virtue, above all love. Thirdly, there is the gospel of John, which stresses the knowledge brought about by the Spirit, who is referred to as the 'Spirit of truth'. John also has Jesus speak of the Spirit as a person, one who is, like Jesus, a Paraclete (see C (iii) below).

However, in the midst of such differences there is a common factor: the Old Testament idea of the Spirit as the way in which God is present to people. It is incorrect to imagine, therefore, that *the* difference between Old and New Testament conceptions of the Spirit is that for the latter the Spirit is a person, the third of three divine persons. Certainly, one of the new elements in the New Testament is a marked tendency, especially in John, to regard the Spirit as a distinct person. Nevertheless, the average Christian of those times would most likely have thought of the Spirit as the way in which God's (and, as will be seen, Christ's) presence was experienced.

There was then a basic continuity between Old and New Testament conceptions of the Spirit. This continuity also manifests itself in the fact that the sort of actions ascribed to the Spirit in Old Testament times are found also in the New Testament, even if different authors emphasize different ones. Here are just a few examples.

Just as in the Old Testament, so too in the New, behaviour that went beyond the normal was ascribed to the Spirit: e.g., 'prophecy' (Num 11:24–30; Acts 2:17), being 'carried away' by the Spirit (1 Kings 18:12; Acts 8:39), being 'seized by the Spirit', and thereby enabled to perform unusual feats (Judg 14:6; Acts 11:28).

In Old Testament times one of the gifts of the Spirit was wisdom (see

Is 11:2). In New Testament times, the Spirit is called the Spirit of truth (Jn 14:17) who will enable the disciples to say the right things in times of persecution (Mt 10:19–20).

In the Old Testament, moral and religious renewal was attributed to the Spirit's presence. Similarly, in New Testament times rebirth to a new life is attributed to the Spirit (Jn 3:5–6) and the fruits of the Spirit's presence are a complete moral renewal (Rom 8:13 and Gal 5:22–23).

In Old Testament times the Spirit was connected with the promised salvation of the future. For obvious reasons, this link is very much stressed in the New Testament. The mere presence of the Spirit is the sign of the presence of salvation, the sign of the arrival of the last days. To share in the Spirit is to share already in salvation (Rom 8:9–11; Gal 6:8). The Spirit poured out on us is described as the 'down payment' or deposit, a 'pledge' given by God guaranteeing our complete sharing in salvation (2 Cor 5:5). Another description of the Spirit that means the same thing is found in Rom 8:23, where the Spirit is described as the 'first-fruits' of the harvest of salvation.

The New Testament conception of the Spirit is therefore built on that of the Old Testament. However, there are also new elements. The most startling one is the close link forged between Jesus and the Spirit. This in turn leads to further developments in the doctrine of the Spirit.

C.   THE LINK BETWEEN CHRIST AND THE SPIRIT

In the New Testament Christ and the Spirit are so closely related that one gets at times the impression that they are identified. This close link between the two is the most important of all the New Testament's additions to the concept of the Spirit and is, in my opinion, a central factor in the development of the idea of the Spirit as a distinct person.

The connection between Christ and the Spirit is manifested in various ways, of which four can be mentioned here. Firstly, during his lifetime on earth Jesus appears as a unique bearer of the Spirit. Secondly, the Spirit is only given to others after Jesus' death and resurrection. Thirdly, even then the Spirit's task will be to glorify Christ, as Jn 16:14 puts it. This is but an aspect of a broader role of the Spirit: to be the way in which the risen Lord is actively present in the community's midst. Fourthly, the link between the risen Lord and the Spirit is so close that the former becomes the giver of the Spirit to others: Jesus the bearer becomes Christ the giver of the Spirit. In short, while in the Old Testament the Spirit was *God's* Spirit, in the New Testament the Spirit is clearly also *Christ's* Spirit.

(i) Jesus the unique bearer of the Spirit

The early Christians evidently believed that after the death and resurrection of Jesus the promised outpouring of the Spirit had taken place. However, they also clearly believed that this was not the first manifestation of the Spirit after the long period of its absence. For them, the Spirit became active once again when Jesus and John the Baptist appeared on the scene (see Mt 1:20, Lk 1:15, 35). Of these two, it is Jesus who is uniquely endowed with the Spirit. Or to say the same thing another way, God was acting in Jesus in a unique way. John is only Jesus' precursor (Lk 7:18, 27–28), being filled with the Spirit precisely in order to witness to Jesus (Mt 3:11).

We are told that the Spirit descended on Jesus at the beginning of his ministry — that is to say, at his baptism by John (Mk 1:9–11, Mt 3:13–17, Lk 3:21–22, Jn 1:32–34). The early Christians regarded this event as an immensely important one in Jesus' life, one that marked him out as God's Son, filled with God's Spirit.

The Holy Spirit is said to have descended on him in the form of a dove. Precisely why a dove was chosen to serve as the sign of the Spirit's presence is uncertain. However, some interesting suggestions have been made. One is that since a dove was used as an image of Israel in the Bible (e.g., Hos 11:11, Ps 74:19) and in non-biblical Jewish writings of the time, the Spirit descended on Jesus in that form in order to show that in him we see the representative and the beginnings of God's new people. Another suggestion (and one which I find more convincing) is based on the explicit use of the dove as an image of the Spirit in extra-biblical writings (for an example see Montague 1976:240–241).

The Spirit's descent can therefore be seen as a sign that with Jesus' appearance the new age, the new creation, the longed-for last days have begun to dawn. This idea is supported by the fact that a voice is heard from heaven. For it means that once again God speaks to men — directly (Montague 1976:241). Moreover, the voice makes it clear that Jesus is the mysterious Servant upon whom God put the Spirit (Is 42:1). The difference is that the Servant is here addressed as God's Son.

Filled with the power of the Spirit, Jesus is now led by that same Spirit into the desert (Mt 4:1–11, Mk 1:12–13, Lk 4:1–13). There we see him doing battle with Satan and emerging victorious. The story reminds us of how Israel spent forty days in the desert after being led out of Egypt, was tempted, and fell. God's Spirit is portrayed as bringing about something totally new in Jesus: a human life that is completely victorious over Satan — yet another sign of the dawning of the final age. The stage is set for the story of Jesus' Spirit-filled life.

'Jesus, with the power of the Spirit in him, returned to Galilee' (Lk 4:14).

Jesus' power over evil, thanks to the presence of the Spirit, is seen dramatically in his healings and exorcisms. That exorcisms demonstrate a power over evil is obvious. But for the Jews not only exorcisms but healing too was a victory over the forces of evil, since it was believed that sickness was the result of sin (see, e.g., Jn 9:2), a sign that a person was to some extent under the power of Satan (Lk 13:16). Therefore, Jesus' cures were signs of his power over Satan. Because of this power he could tell people with absolute certainty that their sins were forgiven (notice the connection between healing and forgiveness in Mt 9:6–7).

In Matthew's gospel, Jesus himself attributes his power over evil to the Holy Spirit (Mt 12:28). Moreover, for Jesus the power at work in him was so clearly a sign of the Spirit's presence that to attribute his power to the devil was deliberately to blind oneself to the truth. It was to 'blaspheme' against the Holy Spirit (Mt 12:30–32). Many theologians have regarded sinning against the Spirit as unforgivable not because God refuses to forgive it, but because the sinner is excluding God's forgiveness by refusing to see the truth. To attribute Jesus' power to Satan is deliberately and culpably to avoid admitting that God's Spirit is at work in him. This in turn means deliberately and wilfully rejecting not only Jesus, not only God, but also the forgiveness God is offering through Jesus.

Jesus' whole life, then, was one filled with the Spirit and with the joy the Spirit brings (Lk 10:21).

The final event of Jesus' life was his death. Here we see his final and greatest struggle with the powers of evil. His death seemed to be a victory for those powers (Lk 22:53). But it was in fact the moment when he triumphed (Jn 12:23–24), for the Spirit-filled man rose from the dead and became himself a life-giving Spirit (1 Cor 15:45).

As is clear, the writings of the apostolic Church present Jesus as a unique bearer of the Spirit. However, strangely enough he himself seems to have said very little about the Spirit. Scholars have noted and puzzled over the paradox that a reality so important to the infant Church as the Spirit is hardly mentioned by Jesus in the gospels. In fact, the only gospel in which Jesus discusses the Spirit is that of John, and even in John the most extensive teaching about the Spirit is given by Jesus the night before he died (see Jn 3:5–8; 7:39; 4:23–24; 14:15–17, 25–26; 16:7–15).

How much or how little Jesus actually did say about the Spirit is something we do not know. We also do not know for certain why, if Jesus did teach his disciples about the Spirit, there are hardly any references to the Spirit by him in the Synoptics (and the references that do exist scarcely amount to much information). Scholars differ in their explanations of this phenomenon. G. S. Hendry (1965:19) gives the following one: 'Their [the synoptic gospels] primary concern is to present Jesus not merely as a teacher of the Spirit, but as the unique bearer of the Spirit'. C. K. Barrett's explanation (1966:117–118) is that the non-Christian world of those days had so many people who claimed to be bearers of a divine spirit that another such claim would hardly attract attention. Therefore the Synoptics focused rather on the divine and exalted aspects of Jesus.

Personally, I believe that Jesus may well have said very little about the Spirit. However, this does not mean that he was not aware of the Spirit's power at work in him. The text in which he attributes his casting out of demons to 'the Holy Spirit' (Mt 12:28) is widely regarded as Jesus' own words (Lk 4:18ff., by contrast, is widely regarded as an apt quotation put into Jesus' mouth in order to make it clear that he fulfilled that prophecy).

In his fascinating book *Jesus and the Spirit* Dunn argues very strongly that 'Jesus thought of himself as God's Son and as anointed by the eschatological Spirit, because in prayer he experienced God as Father and in ministry he experienced a power to heal which he could only understand as the power of the end-time and an inspiration to proclaim a message which he could only understand as the gospel of the end-time' (Dunn 1975:67). I find Dunn's arguments convincing. Jesus may well have said little about the Spirit, but that he was conscious of the Spirit's presence within him seems to me to be clear. This means that he must have expected prophecies such as Joel's to be fulfilled soon — and why should he not have led his disciples to expect the same?

However, Joel's prophecy could not be fulfilled until after Jesus died. Here we have another important aspect of the link between Jesus and the Spirit: the Spirit is only poured out after Jesus' death and resurrection.

(ii) Jesus' death and resurrection as the condition of the Spirit's outpouring

In Jn 7:39 we read that during Jesus' lifetime 'there was no Spirit as yet because Jesus had not yet been glorified'. This does not mean that the Spirit was not believed to have been active before that event. On the contrary, the Spirit was seen as very much active in Jesus' own ministry, something John's gospel itself records in 1:32. Moreover, in Old Testament times the Spirit had been active. But the promised outpouring of the Spirit, the permanent gift of the Spirit to God's people, did not take place during Jesus' lifetime (Barrett 1978:329). It happened only after his glorification. The same point is made in an even stronger way in Jn 16:7. In this text Jesus stresses that if he does not go back to the Father, then the Paraclete (i.e., the Spirit) will not come.

In these texts can be seen a still closer link between Jesus and the Spirit: the Spirit's outpouring in the last days was conditional upon Jesus' death and resurrection.

Why was this so? Why could the Spirit not be poured out on all prior to Jesus' death and resurrection? Since no clear answers are given in the text, they must be supplied either from theological presuppositions or, if one wishes to remain within the ambit of a historical approach, from an interpretation of other passages.

An example of a straight theological answer would be that Jesus had first to complete the work of redemption before the fruits thereof could be distributed. What appears to me as a more sophisticated version of this is C. K. Barrett's explanation: 'The Spirit is the agent of the creation of the Church and the salvation of the world; in this sense the coming of the Spirit depends upon the completion of the work of Christ' (Barrett 1978:486). I believe that this remains too much within later theological categories, even though Barrett can indeed appeal to the biblical idea of the Spirit as the eschatological gift (1978:329).

An explanation which has a truer ring as far as I am concerned, and which is in no way dependent on later ideas for its viability, is that the Spirit was to take the place of Jesus. Hence the Spirit could only be given after Jesus had departed this life (see, e.g., Hunter 1965:85; Brown 1971:711). What I find most interesting about this explanation is that it grants the Spirit a role remarkably similar to the one we have seen hitherto: being a means whereby someone was present. Of course, traditionally it was God's active presence that the Spirit mediated. Now it is, in addition, Jesus' presence. Needless to say, this has enormous implications for Jesus' status. To say that God's Spirit is Jesus' Spirit, God's way of being present is Jesus' way of being present, is to elevate Jesus to God's level, make him a participant in God's own life. New Testament pneumatology, its theology of the Spirit, is really Christology, a theology of Christ. But this observation goes beyond our concerns here.

The above explanation finds support in John's idea of the Spirit as a Paraclete. But it is not limited to the Johannine tradition, being very much part of the Pauline one too, so much so that the theme of the Spirit as the way in which the risen Lord is present to his people deserves a separate section.

(iii) The Spirit as the way in which the risen Christ is actively present in the midst of his people

One of the most startling New Testament ideas is that God's Spirit is also that of a man — Jesus. So close is the connection forged at times between Jesus and the Spirit that many scholars have wondered whether or not they are being identified. The idea has even been mooted — and gained some currency — that Pentecost was a resurrection appearance (Dunn 1975:142–146). As will be seen, I believe that Jesus and the Spirit are in fact not identified. However, I do also believe that their close association implies that the Spirit is the way in which not only God but also the Jesus who promised to be with his disciples for all time (Mt 28:20) are actively present in the midst of what is *their* people.

As noted in the previous section, the clearest evidence for this is found in John's gospel (the Paraclete sayings) and the Pauline writings. As regards the former, the relevant sayings are found in Jn 14:15–18, 25–27; 15:26; 16:7–11, 13–15. Some scholars have argued that 'the Paraclete' originally referred to something or someone other than the Holy Spirit and that later the two were confused and eventually identified with each other (Brown 1966:113). Whether this is so or not, it is clear that in John they are identified (Jn 14:26). The Spirit is clearly spoken of in Jesus' farewell discourse as a Paraclete. Since this is the only place where this happens, one must assume that this strange title is meant to teach us something about the Spirit. What is that something?

To begin with the name 'paraclete', this is simply a transliteration of the Greek *paraklētos*. There is no agreement, unfortunately, about its meaning. Some have said it means a comforter, others an intercessor, others an interpreter, others a preacher, others a prosecuting counsel, others a defence counsel. Raymond Brown believes that with one exception *all* these ideas — and not just a particular one — are meant to be part of John's meaning of 'paraclete'. The one exception is the idea of 'defence counsel', which Brown believes is a role attributed indeed to the Spirit in Mt 10:20 and Acts 6:10, but not in John's gospel (Brown 1966:115–119). A widely favoured translation of 'paraclete' is 'helper'. This could serve as a basic meaning, so that being a comforter, intercessor and so on would be the various ways in which the Spirit is seen in the Gospel as a helper. However, Brown (1966:117) believes its vagueness does not do justice to the more concrete meanings of 'paraclete'.

More important for the present theme, however, is the idea that the Spirit will be *'another* Paraclete'. Calling the Spirit 'another' Paraclete implies that Jesus was a Paraclete for his disciples during his lifetime. In another piece of Johannine writing — 1 Jn 2:1 — the risen Lord is explicitly called a *paraklētos*. As Brown points out, this means that the Spirit will be for the disciples all that Jesus was for them during his lifetime (for a detailed demonstration of the resemblances between Jesus and the Spirit see Brown 1966:126–128 or Brown 1971:1140–1141). However, the Spirit does not simply replace a Jesus who is now absent from his disciples. Rather, the Spirit is the way in which *Jesus himself* will continue to be present to them. After Jesus promises the disciples the Paraclete (Jn 14:16–17), he immediately adds (verse 18) that he will not leave them orphans but will come back to them. This seems quite clearly to imply that, as Brown puts it, 'the presence of Jesus after his return to the Father is accomplished in and through the Paraclete. Not two presences but the same presence is involved' (1971:645; for a critique of some aspects of Brown's views see Johnston 1970:92–96, 126).

This indescribably close link between the Spirit and Jesus is clearly the fundamental reason why no one can claim the Spirit's authority for anything that goes against what Jesus said, or that distinguishes between the glorious, risen Lord and the earthly Jesus, glorifying the former, disparaging the letter (1 Cor 12:3). When the Spirit 'teaches' the disciples (Jn 14:26), guides them along the way of truth (Jn 16:13), it is not a new revelation that will be given them, but the truth revealed by *Jesus* (Jn 16:14). It is of what *Jesus* taught them that they will be reminded (Jn 14:26), for the Spirit will speak only what 'he has learnt' (Jn 16:13) from *Jesus*, which is a message that comes ultimately from the Father (Jn 16:14–15). It is *Jesus* whom the Spirit will glorify (Jn 16:14), to *Jesus* that the Spirit will bear witness (Jn 15:26).

The other New Testament author who makes it clear that the Spirit is the way in which not only God but also Christ is present among believers is Paul. He does not direct our attention to the similarity between the functions of the Spirit and those of the earthly Jesus, as John did. However, he is nonetheless convinced that the Spirit experienced by the early Christians was the way in which not only God but also Christ was present in the Church.

This point is made in various ways. *One way* is by making identical statements regarding the believer's relationship to Christ, on the one hand, and the Spirit, on the other. Thus, Paul says that the Christian is 'in Christ' (Gal 2:17), but also that the Christian is 'in the Spirit' (1 Cor 6:11). He says that we are sanctified 'in Christ' (1 Cor 1:2), but he also says that we are sanctified 'in the Spirit' (1 Cor 6:11). He says that we are sealed 'in Christ' (Eph 1:13), but also that we are sealed 'in the Spirit' (Eph 4:30). He says that if Christ is in us, then we have life (Rom 8:10), but also that if the Spirit is in us, then we have life (Rom 8:11). *Another way* in which Paul makes the point clear is by saying that the Spirit is not only the Spirit of God but also the Spirit of Christ: 'Your interests, however, are not in the unspiritual, but in the spiritual, since the Spirit *of God* has made his home in you. In fact unless you possessed the Spirit *of Christ* you would not belong to him' (Rom 8:9). Since 'the Spirit of God' is a term that described the way in which God acted on and was present to people, 'the Spirit of Christ' can be seen as a term that describes the way in which Jesus Christ acts on and is present to his people.

Of course, 'the Spirit of God' and 'the Spirit of Christ' are seen as being one and the same. There are not two 'Spirits', one that God uses, and another used by Christ in order to be present to believers. The selfsame Spirit mediates God's presence as well as Christ's. To put it more accurately theologically, God is present through the presence of Christ. For just as during his lifetime Jesus was God's Word made flesh, God's image in the world, the one in whom people could see the Father (see Jn 1:14, 14:9), so too the risen Lord's presence to his people is God's presence to them.

(iv)   Christ the giver of the Spirit

That Christ is the giver of the Spirit is also clearly taught in the New Testament. In Jn 16:7 Jesus promises that *he* will send the Spirit to his disciples (note that elsewhere — Jn 14:26 — he says that the *Father* will send the Spirit, which is another way of stressing that the same Spirit is both God's and Jesus'). In Jn 20:22 he fulfils his promise by personally giving the Spirit to the disciples. Paul, on the other hand, calls the risen Lord a 'life-giving Spirit' (1 Cor 15:45). This is an apt summary of the close link between Christ and the Spirit. It means that the risen Lord is so filled with the Spirit that he himself can now also be the source of that Spirit to others. To put it another way, one could say that Jesus is so filled with and transformed by God's presence, that he can be the source of that presence to others.

D.   THE SPIRIT AND THE CHURCH

The preceding section dealt with the link between the Spirit and Christ. Because of this connection, the gift of the Spirit is also linked to the community centred on Christ: the Church. This is yet another difference between what the Old and New Testaments have to say about the Spirit: the Old Testament did not envisage the Spirit's outpouring as being linked to a fairly well-defined community distinct from the Jewish one.

The fact that the apostolic community linked Spirit and Church did not mean that it never saw the Spirit as active outside the Christian fold. But it did mean for them that any action of the Spirit outside their community had as its purpose the leading of people to Christ and his Church. A good example of this is the story about Cornelius in Acts 10. We read there how the Spirit descended on Cornelius and his household even before they were baptized. What is more, they were Gentiles — and this fact astonished the Jewish believers. However, the whole point of the Spirit's intervention was, we are told, to lead Cornelius and his household to Christ and the Christian community — and to show the Jewish believers that Christ and his community were for everybody, Jews as well as Gentiles (see verses 44–48).

Because the early Christians believed that any action of the Spirit outside the community was intended to lead people to Christ and his community, they felt justified in seeing the Spirit's action even in Old Testament times as preparing people for the day when Christ would come. This is one of the reasons why they saw the Spirit-inspired Old Testament scriptures as pointing to Christ. They also believed that their ability to interpret what they saw as the Old Testament's pointers to Christ was the gift of the risen Lord to them. Luke makes this point in his story of how Jesus appeared to the disciples *en route* to Emmaus and explained the scriptures to them (Lk 24:27). John makes the same point by relating how Jesus promised that the Spirit will lead them into the truth (Jn 16:13).

For the New Testament, all the Spirit's actions are directed towards building up Christ's Body, the Church. Moreover, the Spirit is seen as being so completely involved in the Church's life that anything that builds up the Church is seen as a gift of the Spirit. Often enough, the service a person may perform for the Church may not be spectacular. It may in fact be very ordinary — e.g., being a helper (1 Cor 12:28). But it is still a gift of the Spirit.

Seeing the Spirit's presence in even ordinary things represents a considerable change from the Old Testament's idea of the Spirit's actions. For the Old Testament, the main way in which the Spirit's presence was manifested was through unusual phenomena, so striking that a person could hardly fail to see God's hand in them. Ecstasies are an obvious example. But even the prophet with an intelligible message was a rare bird and therefore an unusual phenomenon. The moral renewal and salvation with which the Spirit was already associated in Old Testament times were, I suspect, regarded as events which would create a situation so strikingly different from our sinful, suffering world that they would be a clear sign of the Spirit's presence. In the New Testament, however, the Spirit is credited with very ordinary actions.

Moreover, the Spirit is credited with events that occur within an individual's heart and which therefore cannot on their own be signs of that Spirit's presence. Of course, the change in a person's life that results from this may in itself be quite spectacular. But then again, the change may not be so spectacular after all. The New Testament does not compel us to believe that the lives of Spirit-filled Christians were always and obviously better than the lives of others. In fact, Paul's frequent reminders to his converts that they must lead holy lives makes it clear that their lives often left much to be desired.

In short, the differences between the Spirit's actions in the Old and in the New Testaments is that in the New Testament *everything* that builds up God's people, no matter how ordinary it may be, can be seen as a gift of the Spirit. The Spirit is a permanent part of Christ and therefore of his Body, in contrast to Old Testament times, when the Spirit was not a permanent part of the scene. The Church is the Spirit's 'home', so to speak, in the New Testament (1 Cor 3:16–17), producing fruits and other effects that may and yet may not be spectacular. In fact the greatest effect of all is one that is usually quite unspectacular: love. Paul had to remind his converts that love is greater than all the Spirit's gifts. And by love he meant not just a spectacular love, like dying for one's neighbour, but the ordinary, patient kind of love that has nothing of the spectacular about it (see 1 Cor 13:4–7; see also Gal 5:22). This very ordinary love is for Paul *the* sign of the Spirit's presence. Of course this is not surprising. Jesus insisted that love fulfilled the whole Law (Mt 22:37–40), and so too did Paul (Rom 13:8–10, Gal 5:14). Therefore, the greatest sign of the presence of Jesus' Spirit is love (see how Paul connects the Spirit and love in Rom 5:5, 15:30, Gal 5:22, Col 1:8, Eph 3:16ff.).

Here, then, we see a climax in the development of the doctrine of the Spirit: God's Spirit is not to be found simply in the spectacular, but rather in every act of love. In fact love, and not the spectacular, is clearly seen as *the* sign of the Spirit's presence. God is love, as 1 Jn 4:16 put it, and therefore it makes sense that *the* sign of God's presence is love.

To end this section, let me now list briefly the more specific activities the Spirit is credited with as regards the Church.

To begin with, the Spirit is a source of the Church's unity. This is a prominent theme in the Pauline writings. When faced with dissension in the infant communities, Paul stressed the unity given by the Spirit. Phrases such as 'in the one Spirit' (Eph 2:18), 'preserve the unity of the Spirit' (Eph 4:3), 'one Body, one Spirit' (Eph 4:4), 'the same Spirit . . . this one Spirit . . . In the one Spirit' (1 Cor 12:9, 11, 13) are familiar ones.

As Dunn (1975:260) observes, the experience of the Spirit is, for Paul, a shared experience. It is an experience that makes real for the Christians he addressed the idea that they shared in one Spirit, that they had one Spirit in common (Phil 2:1). The Spirit they 'received' (Rom 8:15; see also 5:5) was a shared experiential reality, a 'fellowship' (2 Cor 13:14).

But Paul bases his appeal for unity on more than bare experience. The experience is for him the testimony to a deeper reality, the work of the Spirit within individuals, binding them to each other through the love poured into them (Rom 5:5), through uniting all to Christ so that with Christ they too could address God as their common Father (see next section).

As is well known, their unity in love was a mark of the early Christians. That its practical expression in communal living is recorded for us in the book in which the Spirit features most prominently — Acts — is no coincidence (see Acts 2:44–47; 4:32–35).

Intimately connected with the Spirit's role in creating the Church's unity is that of being a source of gifts — whether ordinary or extraordinary — that build up the Church (1 Cor 12 – 14). The individual shares in the Spirit, and so even such natural talents as may be possessed now become gifts of the Spirit to the community. The variety of these gifts, and the stress on the importance of that variety (1 Cor 12:27ff.), reveals a significant aspect of the sort of unity created by the Spirit: viz., a unity that respects individuality, not one that tries to submerge it in a sea of uniformity. Yet another aspect of unity revealed here is that it is built up through service. The variety of the gifts fosters unity through the various services they render to members of the community. Hence, Christians are *expected* to exercise their talents, are expected to allow them to be gifts of the Spirit to the community (see Dunn 1975:264). In that sense one must not 'try to suppress the Spirit' (1 Thess 5:19).

These gifts highlight the third function to be listed here, namely the leadership role attributed to the Spirit in the infant Church. The present century has witnessed a debate — still largely unresolved — on the relationship of charism and authority in the apostolic Church. Did authority derive from institutional structures, or exclusively from the inspiration of the Spirit? The very raising of the question is an indication of the prominent role attributed to the Spirit in creating what we today would call ministries within the Church. 1 Cor 12:27ff. associates apostles, teachers, good leaders, and prophets with the gifts of the Spirit discussed earlier on in the text.

I do not wish to enter into the debate here. Nor is it necessary to do so. It is sufficient to be aware of the fact that the Spirit is credited with creating such a variety of ministries that the churches of that period were more charismatic than institutionalized communities. This does not mean that there were no institutionalized elements there (e.g., the office of apostle rested for its authority on more than the inspiration of the Spirit — see on this Dunn 1975:272–280). But it does mean that, as Hasenhüttl (1969) put it, Spirit-inspired gift or charism was a principle giving the Church its specific structure.

The fourth function attributed to the Spirit is that of being the power that propagated the Church and enabled it to carry out its mission of making disciples of all nations (Mt 28:19–20). In John's gospel Jesus' gift of the Spirit is connected with his sending of the disciples to continue the mission he himself had (Jn 20:21–22). Paul makes the same point regarding his own preaching in 1 Thess 1:5 and 1 Cor 2:4. Acts makes the point in 1:8 and also in the chapters that follow the story of Pentecost. For it is the Spirit that fills Peter when he speaks (4:8), that prompts Stephen to say the right things (6:10), that initiates the mission to the Gentiles (10:19, 44), chooses missionaries (13:2), and directs Paul's way (16:6–8). And it is the Spirit that effects the response of faith on the part of the hearer of the message (1 Cor 12:3).

Fifthly, the Spirit enables the community to make important decisions about its life (Acts 15:28) and, as the Spirit of truth, guides it in its understanding and living-out of Christ's message (Jn 14:26, 16:13, 1 Cor 7:39–40).

Sixthly, it is the Spirit who inspires the sacred writings of God's people, the scriptures. This was already believed in Old Testament times, and Jesus reflects this belief in Mk 12:36. It is also reflected in 2 Tim 3:16. Towards the end of the New Testament period we see the development of a belief that Christians too have their sacred writings, their scriptures inspired by the Spirit. This is clear from the inclusion of Paul's letters with 'the rest of scripture' in 2 Pet 3:16.

E.   THE SPIRIT AND THE INDIVIDUAL

The Church is composed of individuals, united to each other in Christ. The Spirit's role is to enable such individuals to be living, productive members of the community.

Association with the community begins with faith and baptism. As regards the former, the Spirit is portrayed as being both the enabler (1 Cor 12:3) and the immediate reward (Gal 3:14, 5:5) of faith. As regards the latter, its waters are said to wash one clean thanks to the Spirit (1 Cor 6:11), whose outpouring is therefore associated with the pouring of water (Tit 3:5). Thanks to the Spirit, baptism 'renews' (Tit 3:5; see also 2 Cor 5:17, Gal 6:15, Eph 4:24), giving a new birth (Jn 3:5), so that one is now a child of God, able to address God as *abba*, in the way Jesus did

(Rom 8:15–16, Gal 4:6; see Mk 14:36). One is 'sealed', marked out, as belonging to God and Jesus, by the Spirit (2 Cor 1:22; Eph 1:13).

After the initiation, the Spirit continues to dwell in the individual (1 Cor 3:16; see Jn 14:16), who is henceforth the Spirit's temple (1 Cor 6:19; see also Eph 2:22). Constantly present to the believer, the Spirit imparts an experience that enables the believer to be sure of sharing in salvation, of being united to God (1 Jn 3:24, 4:13). The indwelling Spirit is viewed as a 'down-payment', a pledge of present unity with Christ (2 Cor 1:22) and future sharing in heavenly life (2 Cor 5:5; Eph 1:13–14). The Spirit's presence, therefore, imparts a boundless hope (Rom 15:13).

As the text just cited indicates, this hope feeds on the experience of the Spirit's power in the believer's life. For the Spirit is one not of timidity but of power (2 Tim 1:7). Thanks to that Spirit one's 'hidden self' grows strong (Eph 3:16), enabling one to speak with courage and conviction in the face of persecution (Lk 12:12). There is indeed a need to open oneself to the Spirit's influence, to be 'guided by the Spirit' (Gal 5:16, 25). The result will indeed be an experience of inner conflict, battle between the Spirit and one's former 'unspiritual' self (Rom 7:14 – 8:9; Gal 5:16–26). But alongside this will be an experience of victory, a bringing-forth of the fruits of the Spirit (Gal 5:22ff.), a sharing in Christ's freedom (Rom 8:2; Gal 5:1).

Empowered, freed, transformed by the Spirit's presence, the believer is also endowed with gifts — or finds his or her natural talents transformed by the Spirit (1 Cor 12:4ff.; see preceding section; for a discussion of each of the gifts see Chapter 15 below). These gifts exist primarily as ways of serving the community. The only exception to this is the gift of tongues, which is why Paul evaluates this as the least of the gifts (1 Cor 14:2, 4). The greatest service and therefore the greatest gift is love (1 Cor 12:31ff., 14:1).

The Spirit therefore is active in every aspect of the believer's life — enabling her or him even to pray in an inexpressible way (Rom 8:26). Above all, the Spirit produces love (Rom 5:5; Gal 5:22; Col 1:8; Eph 3:16–19), so much so that, as Koch (1970:886) observes, 'to walk in the Spirit is virtually synonymous with "to love one another" '. It is the Spirit of love, and no longer that of law, that governs our relationship to God (2 Cor 3:6).

Finally, it is the Spirit who ensures that even death loses its sting for the Christian (Rom 6:23; 1 Cor 15:55). Resurrection and transformation (1 Cor 15:39–44) are the Spirit's final, everlasting gift to the believer (Rom 8:11).

F. THE SPIRIT AND THE UNIVERSE

The salvation brought by Christ is seen by some texts as extending to the entire universe. It can be expected therefore that the Spirit would have a role to play here too. The New Testament has relatively little to say about the sharing of all creation in salvation. Nevertheless, it is significant that the one place where the theme receives the most attention — Rom 8:18–25 — is also the place where the Spirit's role is mentioned. Paul pictures the whole of creation as groaning for salvation. The whole universe — and not just humanity — is destined to share in salvation (8:21). Humanity's world will not be destroyed but transformed, gloriously so. And, Paul implies, the power that will do this is the power of the Spirit. For, he writes, the presence of the Spirit is only the 'first-fruits' (Rom 8:23) of a fuller glory yet to come, a glory in which everything will share.

G. THE SPIRIT AS 'PERSON'

The basic meaning of 'the Spirit' in the previous sections is, once again, this: the way in which God and Christ are actively present in the midst of believers. For the New Testament, the Spirit is the way in which Christ builds up his Body, the Church, by bringing people to faith in him, by uniting them in love to him, thereby enabling them to share in all that he is and has. It is the way in which Christ will eventually transform the whole of creation.

It is incorrect, therefore, to think that whenever a New Testament author mentions the Spirit he is referring to a 'third person' in a 'trinity'. It is not that such a conception is wrong, but simply that it is not the way the New Testament generally thinks of the Spirit. However, it is also true that the New Testament contains the seeds of the later doctrine of the Spirit as a clearly distinct 'person' from Christ and the Father.

The first of those seeds is the personal language used of the Spirit. This was not entirely new, since such language was already being used in late Old Testament times (see Chapter 1, C). This 'personalization' was reinforced by the transfer to God's Spirit of the personal characteristics possessed by angelic spirits (see Brown 1966:121ff.). 'Personalization' becomes still more marked in the New Testament, and the older treatises on the Trinity regularly appealed to texts attributing personal actions to the Spirit, in order to argue for the revelation of the latter's existence as a third divine person. Examples of such texts are 1 Cor 12:11, where the Spirit is spoken of as a person distributing gifts 'just as he chooses'; Rom 8:16 where we are told that 'the Spirit himself' witnesses to the believer's being a child of God; Acts 13:2, where the Spirit speaks, saying 'I want Barnabas and Saul set apart . . .'; Rev 2:7, 11, 17, 29, etc., where once again speech is attributed to the Spirit. Then there are the texts that list the Spirit alongside Father and Son in a way that suggests all three are persons (e.g., Mt 28:19, 2 Cor 13:14, 1 Cor 12:4–6). Above all, there are the Paraclete passages in John's gospel, where the masculine *paraklētos* is spoken of in so unambiguously personal a way that several scholars used this as an argument for the thesis that originally 'Spirit' and 'Paraclete' were two distinct ideas (Brown 1966:124; see C (iii) above).

However, this personalist language does not mean that Christians of that time clearly thought of the Spirit as a third divine person within a trinity. Personalist language could be explained by several factors, ranging from figures of speech reflecting forms of personification such as occurred with wisdom; through the very important fact that the Spirit was never seen simply as impersonal but rather as the way in which the persons of God and Christ were present; to conceiving of the Spirit as a 'dynamic energy immanently at work within men and women' (Johnston 1970:123).

I am not sure that personalist language on its own would have led to the later clear belief in the Spirit as a third divine person. Whatever personality the Spirit has in the New Testament seems to have been that of God or of Christ. However, there is in the documents another factor, another seed, and it was this, I suspect, that eventually provided the major impulse to the full flowering of the Spirit's distinct personality. This factor is the clear distinction made between Jesus, the Father, and the Spirit, despite the close association of all three.

To begin with Christ and the Spirit, I have argued repeatedly that the Spirit is the way in which Christ is present to us. However, this raises the question of the distinction between the Spirit and the Christ. In the Old Testament 'the Spirit of the Lord' was not conceived of as something distinct from God. Rather, it was seen as none other than God actively present in our midst. Must not the same be said about the Spirit and Christ? Must one not say that 'Christ's Spirit' is simply another name for 'Christ actively present in our midst'? Or is there a distinction between Christ and the Spirit, a distinction that would force one to say that for the New Testament God's Spirit is not *Christ*, but *the means by which* Christ becomes present and acts in the midst of believers?

In Paul, for example, Christ and the Spirit are sufficiently closely associated to give some credence to the idea that he identified the two. As was seen in C (iii), expressions such as 'in Christ' and 'in the Spirit' are used interchangeably (e.g., Rom 8:1, 9; Phil 2:1). Paul also moves from the Spirit's indwelling to that of Christ, as though they are identical realities: 'if Christ is in you . . . if the Spirit . . . is in you' (Rom 8:10–11). Then there is his famous and much discussed text, the 'Lord is the Spirit' (2 Cor 3:17; see also verse 18). Many have argued that 'Lord' here refers to Christ. And in 1 Cor 15:45 the risen Lord is called 'a life-giving Spirit'.

However, none of this amounts to a solid case that Paul identified Christ and the Spirit. As regards 2 Cor 3:17, Paul is arguing that the blindness of the Jews to the true meaning of the Old Testament can only be removed by turning to the Lord, just as the veil that covered Moses's face was removed whenever he turned to talk to the Lord (Ex 34:35). 'The Lord' that the Jews must turn to now in their blindness is the Spirit. As regards Paul's interchange of expressions, this is explicable in terms of the close association of Christ and the Spirit, without assuming their identity. A similar observation can be made about 1 Cor 15:46. Indeed, in one of the texts referred to — Rom 8:9–11 — a distinction between Christ and the Spirit is also expressed: the Spirit of Christ is also the Spirit of God, the Spirit who raised Jesus from the dead.

The distinction between Jesus and the Spirit is, in fact, quite clear from elsewhere in the New Testament. It is clear, for example, that during his lifetime Jesus was the unique *bearer* of God's Spirit. He himself was not the Spirit. Nowhere is it suggested in the New Testament that Jesus is the Spirit of God made flesh. Rather, he is said to be the *Word* made flesh (Jn 1:14). If Jesus was not the Spirit during his earthly life, then he was not the Spirit after his resurrection. For the earthly Jesus and the risen Lord are seen by the New Testament as being one and the same person. And the Spirit that rested on the earthly Jesus and the one that filled and transformed him on the day of his resurrection are one and the same Spirit. The distinction that existed between them during Christ's life on this earth therefore continues to exist in his risen state. John's gospel makes this distinction particularly clear. During the Last Supper Jesus talks of the Paraclete quite clearly as being distinct from him. The Paraclete is '*another* Paraclete' (14:16), who comes from the Father (15:26), whom the Father will give at Jesus' request (14:16) and send in Jesus' name (14:26), indeed whom Jesus himself will send (15:26, 16:7). For John's gospel the Spirit is indeed the way in which Jesus will be present to his disciples forever. But this does not mean that 'Spirit' is simply another name for 'Jesus'. John emphasizes both the distinction as well as the close relationship between Jesus and the Spirit. Thus, in Jn 20:22 we read that Jesus breathed on the disciples and said to them 'receive the Holy Spirit'. It is very difficult to avoid seeing there a distinction between the giver (Jesus) and the gift (the Spirit).

Now the fact that the Spirit is both the way in which Christ is present (the Spirit of Christ), and yet distinct from him, implies a distinction between the Spirit and the Father. Unlike the Spirit, the Father is certainly not seen as sent by Christ, given by Christ, making Christ present, and so on. Hence, Christ's relationship to the Spirit takes the Old Testament picturing of the Spirit as a distinct reality an important stage further: the distinction now becomes more than simply a figure of speech. Just as Jesus' relationship to the Father implies not only distinction but also oneness, so too does the Spirit's relationship to both.

It is not to be wondered at, therefore, that formulae are found in the New Testament documents listing Father, Son and Spirit as three distinct entities. The beginnings of this process are discernible already in 1 Thess 1, the earliest of the texts, where the first five verses mention consecutively Father, Son and Spirit (Brown 1983:227). Other well-known examples of the close naming of the three are 2 Cor 13:14 and 1 Cor 12:4–6. However, the best example is the one occurring at the end of Matthew: 'baptise them in the name of the Father and of the Son and of the Holy Spirit' (Mt 28:19).

These so-called 'trinitarian' texts not only underline the distinction between Father, Son and Spirit, but reinforce the idea that the last-mentioned is also a personal reality. Once again, the Spirit does not seem to have been conceived of as a person in the same way as Christ and the Father, and so to have constituted with them a trinity of divine persons. As stated on several occasions, whatever 'personality' the Spirit was invested with was that of Christ and the Father. The Spirit was conceived of as the way in which *those* persons were actively present and experienced in the Church. However, the distinction between Father, Son and Spirit was there. The Spirit was not regarded merely as an impersonal force. On the contrary, the late Old Testament tendency to personalize the Spirit had grown in New Testament times. These were the seeds from which grew a future theology of the Spirit as a person. The time has come to trace that and other post-biblical developments.

QUESTIONS

Check questions

1   What evidence is there that the early Church was convinced that the days of the Spirit's outpouring had arrived?

2 What purposes does the story of the 'foreign languages' spoken at Pentecost serve?
3 What are the main viewpoints regarding whether or not Pentecost was a unique event?
4 What grounds could be advanced for seeing Pentecost as a 'dogmatic creation'?
5 Why was the outpouring of the Spirit seen as a sign that the 'last times' had come?
6 In what way was there continuity and in what striking way discontinuity between New and Old Testament conceptions of the Spirit?
7 List four basic ways in which Jesus and the Spirit are linked in the New Testament.
8 Why was the Spirit's eschatological outpouring conditional on Jesus' death?
9 What evidence is there for seeing the Spirit as *the* way in which the risen Christ is actively present in the midst of his people?
10 What can be regarded as *the* sign of the Spirit's presence, and why?
11 List some specific activities with which the Spirit is credited as regards the Church.
12 What is the link between the Spirit's role in *individuals*, and in the Church?
13 List some specific activities with which the Spirit is credited as regards individuals.
14 Has the Spirit any role as regards the entire universe, and if so, what?
15 What are the New Testament seeds of the later doctrine of the Spirit as a 'person' clearly distinct from Father and Son?

Discussion question

Take up the question posed at the end of Chapter 1 and discuss it further in the light of the contents of this present chapter.

RECOMMENDED READING

The article by Koch referred to in Chapter 1 is once again a useful source of detailed information on New Testament texts and themes dealing with the Spirit (Koch 1970:877–888). Another useful source is the entry *'pneuma'* in Kittel's well-known *Dictionary of the New Testament* VI (Grand Rapids: Eerdmans, 1968), pp. 332–451, but the biblical words explained there are listed in Greek, not English. However, this article from Kittel's work is available in a small book called *Spirit of God*, by E. Schweizer and others (London: Black, 1960), which in turn is part of a series called 'Bible Key Words from Gerhard Kittel's *Theologisches Wörterbuch zum neuen Testament*'. A useful theological synthesis of the New Testament material can be found in Green 1975, chs 3–10. A much briefer but more strictly historical approach is contained in Heron 1983, ch. 3. In a more difficult, but very rewarding book, Dunn (1975) deals in turn with the Spirit-experience of Jesus (chs 2–4), of the earliest Christian communities (chs 5–7), and finally of Paul and the Pauline churches (chs 8–10). The sections on Jesus' experience of God as Holy Spirit (ch. 3) and Pentecost (ch. 6) are particularly good. As regards the Paraclete, Brown 1966 is rather technical but well worth the effort of reading. In slightly modified form it is printed as an appendix to vol. 2 of his more accessible commentary on John (Brown 1971). A later and equally technical work, which takes a different approach from Brown, is Johnston 1970. Finally, a very useful book indeed is, once again, Montague 1976. He gives a detailed exposition of all the important New Testament texts dealing with the Spirit.

3

From the Apostolic Fathers
to the time of Athanasius

The chapters that follow have a limited purpose: to show where and when the major ideas associated with the Spirit originated. They do not pretend to supply a comprehensive history of the subject.

The present chapter deals with the period up to and including Athanasius of Alexandria, that is up to about A.D. 375. Subsequent ones deal with Augustine and the Cappadocians (Chapter 4), the Middle Ages (Chapter 5) and the period from the Reformation to the present century (Chapter 6).

A. PRIOR TO THE RISE AND SPREAD OF MONTANISM

There has been a great deal of controversy about what was taught and believed concerning the Spirit in this early period (the first 170 or so years). As Kretschmar observes: 'The interpretation of practically every stage of the way is disputed, all the more so since it is not clear at the outset in what sense one can even speak of a "way" ' (1968:5–6).

There is much, then, that is unclear about these early decades. Moreover, they display a surprising lack of interest in the Spirit, by comparison with the New Testament period and that following the rise of Montanism. However, there were some significant developments.

What was striking about the New Testament was the prominence given to the Spirit as the imparter of gifts or charisms. The same prominence is absent in this period. Nevertheless, as would be expected, the earliest non-biblical references to the Spirit do testify to an interest in the latter chiefly as the source of the charisms of inspiration and prophecy. The Spirit is spoken about mainly as the inspirer of both spoken (prophecy) and written (inspired writings) words. Having inspired the prophets and biblical authors of old, the Spirit continues to inspire people today.

Examples of such a view of the Spirit can be found in *1 Clement*, the *Didache,* and the *Shepherd of Hermas* (see Swete 1912:11–25). In the latter two there is also an attempt to grapple with a problem that Paul had already experienced, and which became increasingly pressing with the passage of time: how to distinguish between true and false claims to the Spirit's inspiration. The test proposed by the *Didache* and the *Shepherd* is to examine the claimant's behaviour or way of life. 'Test the man who has the Divine Spirit by his life' (*Shepherd*, Mandate XI:7; see also *Didache*, XI:7).

The *Shepherd* is also interesting because it has two pneumatologies existing side by side in it (so Wilson 1977): The first, dualist in character, stresses the Spirit as the *Holy* Spirit in opposition to evil spirits. There is a strong element here of Jewish apocalyptic and Essene thought. The Son of God is never related to the Spirit in this first pneumatology (Wilson 1977:275). The second pneumatology, however, focuses precisely on the Son's relationship to the Spirit. But the stress is on the Son's openness to the Spirit, to the point where Son and Spirit become one (Wilson 1977:277). In this connection, Paul's assertion that Christ became a 'life-giving Spirit' springs to mind. However, according to Wilson (1977:28) the idea that the Spirit was the way in which Christ continued to be present to his disciples is totally absent from the *Shepherd* (yet there may be some evidence to the contrary — see Pernveden 1966:104).

As is well known, the early Christian apologists were a group of men with a philosophical training who attempted to defend their faith rationally, and demonstrate its harmony with the best of classical Greek thought. Hence, it is not surprising to discover in their works the first attempts to think through the relationship of the Spirit to Father and Son respectively. The first recorded attempt was made by Justin Martyr (Swete 1912:35), who died *c.* A.D. 165. The result of Justin's attempt is somewhat confusing. On the one hand he appears to distinguish between Christ and the Spirit, who is described as third in 'rank'. On the other hand he explicitly identifies the Word or pre-existent Christ with the Spirit (Swete 1912:37–38). This is a point I will return to shortly.

Athenagoras is an Apologist who belongs to a slightly later period (*c.* 180). However, his views can be more meaningfully dealt with here. He delves somewhat deeper into the inner-trinitarian relationships. What unites Father, Son and Spirit is their power. What distinguishes them is their rank. The 'ranking' of the Spirit often implies a subordinate status in the Apologists, but not always. What is more interesting is that Athenagoras may well have been the first to speak of the Spirit as the bond of unity between Father and Son — an idea that had an immense influence on subsequent trinitarian theology, especially in its western form. 'The Son', he writes, 'is in the Father and the Father in the Son by the unity and power of the Spirit' (*Legatio*, 10, as quoted by Swete 1912:43 and Lewis 1978:62; see also Swete 1967:115). The Spirit, moreover, is conceived of as an 'effluence' going forth from God so as to inspire people (Swete 1912:43).

I mentioned above that Justin rather confusingly identified the Spirit with Christ, despite also distinguishing between them. This identification was not limited to Justin. On the contrary it was sufficiently widespread in this period to stand out as its hallmark.

It is a puzzle why this is so. One reason may possibly be that the word 'spirit' was widely used at the time as a synonym for the divine. 'Spirit' would therefore have been the obvious word to use for expressing Christ's divinity. Texts that appear to identify Christ and the Spirit would simply be confusing ways of speaking of Christ as divine. Support for this idea would be the fact that it is the *pre-existent* Christ that is identified with the Spirit. However, I think there was more to the matter than a confusing synonym. It needs to be recalled that part of the culture of people like the Apologists was a cluster of philosophical ideas in which a *logos* (principle of order, reason) played a prominent role, readily adaptable to Christ, whom John called the *Logos* or Word (Jn 1:1). But within the system there was no comparable role to which the Spirit could easily be adapted (see Swete 1912:66 as regards Gnostic ideas). It is quite understandable therefore that the close link between Christ and the Spirit found in biblical times should frequently become for all practical purposes an identity (see also Swete 1967:115). Nevertheless, one cannot be certain as to the reasons for the identification, so characteristic of the period.

To conclude this section, let me turn briefly to a theme that still strikes many as rather odd, but which was widespread in an area of the Church influenced very much by the older, Aramaic culture. The theme is that of the Spirit as the female, mother principle in God (*ruach*, it should be recalled, is feminine).

In the *Shepherd of Hermas*, the Spirit is usually conceived of in feminine imagery (Wilson 1977:280). More curious, however, is the idea of the Spirit as mother, found in other texts. What is curious about it is that the Spirit is often spoken of as the mother of Christ. For example, the *Gospel of the Hebrews*, as it is called, apparently had a text in which Jesus says: 'Even so did my mother, the Holy Spirit, take me by one of my hairs and carry me away to the great mountain Tabor' (as quoted in Lewis 1978:21). Of course, the idea of the Spirit as mother of Christ could not survive an orthodox doctrine that came to see the Son as either a source of the Spirit or in some way contributing to the Spirit's identity. But at this stage such a concept must have been attractive not only because of the gender of *ruach* but also because it fitted in well with the Spirit overshadowing Mary at the Annunciation. Moreover, it provided a role for the Spirit in some Christian adaptations of Gnostic ideas, according to which masculine emanations or aeons had their counterparts in feminine ones. Curiously enough, though, in several of these Gnostic writings the identification of the Spirit and Christ referred to earlier is also found (see Lewis 1978:26, 30).

No doubt because of its close association at this early stage with heterodox ideas, the conception of the Spirit as female, as mother, never became part of the mainstream of Christian theology, even though the idea never disappeared entirely. In Catholicism one finds it resurrected, though with qualifications, by the great nineteenth-century theologian Scheeben (1948:431ff.). And in an offshoot of Christianity, such as The Association of the Holy Spirit for the Unification of World Christianity (also known as The Unification Church or, somewhat derogatorily, the Moonies), the idea of the Spirit as a female divine principle plays a central theological role.

B.   MONTANISM

The stress on the Spirit as the Spirit of inspiration and prophecy, characteristic of what little the preceding period has to offer us on the Spirit, became one of the hallmarks of the first big Spirit-oriented movement in the Church: Montanism. Another hallmark was its stress on the Spirit as the eschatological gift of God to the community — a view of the Spirit that may well have been kept alive here and there in the Church (Kretschmar 1968:29).

The movement is named after Montanus who, about 172 (Congar 1983a:66), felt himself seized by the prophetic Spirit. He apparently spoke in tongues and went into trances, in addition to uttering prophecies. He was soon joined and almost eclipsed by two disciples, Priscilla and Maximilla. Montanus and his two prophetesses gained a considerable following. There was nothing remarkable about their claim that the Spirit was speaking to the Church through them; nor that such a speaking was conceived of as taking place in the world's final days. Nor was there anything heretical about their remarkable claim that the New Jerusalem would shortly descend at Pepuza in Asia Minor, where Christ would reign for a thousand years. Knox (1950:34–37) mentions elements that could be regarded as heretical — for example, a distinction between the Spirit that came at Pentecost and that which inspired Montanus, this latter alone deserving the name 'Paraclete'. However, the real break Montanism represents with the past is not so much its contradiction of any specific doctrine, but rather the claim of Montanus and his prophetesses to be the authoritatively inspired leaders of the entire Church, the purveyors of prophecies designed to supplement the message handed over to the Church by the Apostles. Had not Jesus himself said (so they argued) that the Paraclete would introduce the Church into all truth (Jn 16:12–13)? Montanism was the first movement to set the Spirit effectively over against the Church and its tradition. In the writings of its illustrious convert, Tertullian, the movement sowed the seeds of an idea that broke out again and again in the future, namely that the final age is an age of the Spirit, *in contrast to* the previous ages of the Son and of the Father respectively. The age of the Spirit is marked by a new asceticism that was not required until then. One example of this new rigorism was a ban on marrying again after the death of one's spouse (the interested reader can find further examples from Tertullian's writings in Lewis 1978 or Burns and Fagin 1984).

The movement led to a concentration of attention not only on the Spirit and the Spirit's charisms, but also on the link between the Spirit and Christ, and the Spirit and the Church.

As regards the Spirit's charisms, Montanism brought back into relief a dimension of Church life that seemed to be dying out. Opponents of Montanism such as Irenaeus took care to point out that the charisms of the Spirit did indeed flourish in the Church. References to the continued existence of the charisms can be found throughout the two succeeding centuries (Congar 1983a:67).

As regards the Spirit's link with Christ and the Church, Montanism had drawn attention to an issue that was also raised, though not so explicitly, by the Gnostic heresies. Both Montanism and heretical Gnosticism posed a challenge to the authority of the Church's tradition, indeed to the tradition that only what was handed down was authoritative. It was Irenaeus, bishop of Lyons, who responded to this challenge.

C.   IRENAEUS

Irenaeus (*c.* 130–200) concentrated his attentions on heterodox Christian Gnostic systems. Gnosticism was a movement that sought to provide initiates with esoteric knowledge, the sort of saving knowledge the Greek mind craved for. Several Christian Gnostic systems sprang up which claimed to possess a store of information passed down secretly from the Apostles, and available only to initiates (see also Chapter 15, B (ii)).

Irenaeus's argument against such a claim (and therefore also against the Montanist one) was that all the knowledge Christians needed had been publicly revealed by Christ and publicly passed on down the ages n the Church (*Adversus Haereses* [= 'against the heresies'], III, 1, i). Anyone who seeks the truth must therefore seek it in the Church (*Adversus Haereses*, III, 4, i). It is to *that* truth that the Spirit bears witness. The Spirit preserves that truth in the *Church*, and only those who are members of the Church will share in the Spirit and in the truth. In common with others, Irenaeus identifies the Spirit with Wisdom in the Old Testament. Moreover, for him the Spirit and the Church are so closely linked that 'where the Church is, there too is the Spirit of God, and where the Spirit of God is, there is the Church and all grace; for the Spirit is truth' (*Adversus Haereses*, III, 24, i).

There is here an institutionalizing of the Spirit's activity that no doubt contributed to the relative disappearance of charisms such as prophecy in subsequent centuries. However, Irenaeus himself did not see the exclusive link of Spirit and Church as stifling the charisms. As mentioned in the previous section, he speaks warmly of Church members who possess and exercise the gift of prophecy, as well as other gifts such as tongues, healing, and exorcism (*Adversus Haereses*, II, 32, iv–v; see also V, 6, i). However, it is clear that the Spirit's relationship to the Church implies that the Spirit can never be invoked in support of a prophecy that claims to supplement the truth preached by or publicly handed down in the Church.

As can be expected, Irenaeus stresses the unifying role of the Spirit. The Spirit unites scattered peoples, moulding their differing tongues into a unified paean of praise, compacting the dry wheat that the Church would otherwise be into the solid dough that it is (*Adversus Haereses*, III, 17, ii).

This closeness is, of course, only an aspect of the close unity forged by the Spirit between believers and Christ (*Adversus Haereses*, III, 17, i). As a result they will one day be totally transformed into God's likeness, as fully transformed as Christ was when he rose from the dead (*Adversus Haereses*, V, 13, iv).

The Spirit, therefore, is also a life-giving Spirit — a favourite theme of Irenaeus's. Those who deprive themselves of the Spirit by not being one with the Church, deprive themselves of life (*Adversus Haereses*, III, 24, i).

Finally, the Spirit cannot be appealed to in order to support any Gnostic denigration of the Old Testament in favour of the New, of material creation in favour of redemption. The Spirit was one of God's 'hands' (the other 'hand' was the Word) at creation (*Adversus Haereses*, IV, 20, i). In another image, Irenaeus speaks of the Spirit as the 'ladder' to God (*Adversus Haereses*, III, 24, i).

His insistence on the exclusive relationship of Church and Spirit is understandable in the circumstances. However, the practical application of that principle will prove to be more complex. The complexity of the issue was highlighted for the early Church by Cyprian's standpoint on the validity of baptism administered by heretics or schismatics.

D. CYPRIAN

Although Cyprian lived his Christian life after Tertullian (who influenced him considerably) and Origen, it will be useful to consider his contribution at this point, as it relates directly to the issue raised so pointedly by Irenaeus.

Cyprian defended the thesis that since the Spirit operated only within the Church, all sacraments conferred by people who had broken with the Church were invalid — including baptism. The issue surfaced when, as a bishop, he was faced with requests from people baptized by schismatics to be admitted to his church. He rebaptized them, on the grounds that the Spirit operated only within the Church, and there was no valid sacrament without the Spirit's action.

Of course, all admitted that there could be no true sacrament if the Spirit were not present in it. But not all agreed with Cyprian's view that baptism administered by heretics was invalid. The African churches and many churches of the East adopted his view, but the churches of Rome and Alexandria held a contrary one. They believed that heretical baptism was valid. Rome's argument was that the personal condition of the person conferring baptism (whether saint, sinner, orthodox or heretic) did not affect the validity of the sacrament, the reason being that God, not man, conferred it. At first sight this does not seem to answer Cyprian's argument, since he would have agreed that God was the one conferring a sacrament, his point being that God was not active beyond the borders of the Church. However, Cyprian bolstered his argument by claiming that God's Spirit did not work through sinful or unorthodox people. To Rome such an argument implied that the efficacy of a sacrament was dependent on the good qualities of the person conferring it. This Rome found unacceptable since, as it saw the matter, the presence and power of God's Spirit was not dependent on people. There is here a sane balance to excessive institutionalization of the Spirit. Of course, what was also implied in Rome's position was that baptism as a ceremony was always linked to the Church and that where the Spirit was, there in some sense was the Church. But this in itself only serves to stress the dependence of the Church on the Spirit, rather than the reverse.

This refusal to straitjacket the Spirit is made explicit in a *Treatise on*

Rebaptism dating from the closing decades of the third century. In the document (extracts of which can be found in Burns and Fagin 1984:84–87) the link between the Spirit and water-baptism is broken, since the latter may or may not confer the Spirit, we are told. If conferred outside the Church, no Spirit is imparted because — and here Cyprian's argument is invoked — the Spirit is not outside the Church (X, 28). However martyrdom — a baptism of blood — can confer the Spirit, and since such martyrs are clearly those who have not yet become Christians, the document's stress that the Spirit does not operate outside the Church only serves to underline the idea that where the Spirit is, there too is the Church.

A third form of baptism (apart from water and blood) mentioned by the treatise is what it calls 'spiritual baptism'. This is an imposition of episcopal hands on someone baptized (by water) outside the Church. This 'spiritual baptism' has the effect of conferring the Spirit on such a person, thus supplementing the (as later ages would put it) valid but inefficacious water-baptism (see XV, 29).

At this early stage, therefore, the need to balance the Spirit's link with the Church against the Spirit's lordship and freedom is already surfacing. It is an issue that will recur again and again in the years to come. But let us now return to Montanism or rather to its famous convert, Tertullian.

E.   TERTULLIAN

By focusing attention on the Spirit and capturing the loyalty of a man such as Tertullian, Montanism contributed to a development of the theology of the Spirit that went far beyond the movement's own prophetic charismatic interests. For in a work dating from his Montanist period — *Against Praxeas* — Tertullian presents a picture of the Spirit as the third of three divine 'persons'. He is the first (as far as is known) to speak of Father, Son and Spirit as constituting a 'trinity' of 'persons'. By using a term ('person') hitherto reserved exclusively for Father and Son, he fixed or at least contributed enormously to fixing in western Christendom's mind the idea of the Spirit as a distinct, personal entity. As Bulgakov (1946:10) observed, Tertullian marks the third century as the one in which for the first time the question is raised: who is the Spirit?

There is some dispute as to the extent to which Montanism contributed to his theology of the Spirit as a third divine person. Certainly, his conversion to the sect gave him an intense interest in the Spirit, without which the *Adversus Praxean* might never have been written.

But did his conversion to Montanism actually contribute to his development of a trinitarian theology?

An affirmative answer has been given by several scholars, and defended recently in detail by Stegman (1979). The latter argues that in his pre-Montanist days Tertullian had a 'binitarian' theology of God, one in which only Father and Son were conceived of as divine persons. The term 'Holy Spirit' was used either to indicate Jesus' divinity (recall the widespread use of the term 'spirit' for that purpose), or to refer to the Father and Son's power to give spiritual life, to redeem, recreate humanity, etc.

The background to Tertullian's thinking here (and later) was the dualistic one of the conflict between good and evil. 'Holy Spirit' was repeatedly used by Tertullian as the contrasting pole to the *spiritus diaboli*, the spirit of the devil. Stegman (1979:91ff.) points out the influence that the *Shepherd of Hermas* had on him in this matter. Tertullian's thought underwent a major shift, she says, when he was faced with the necessity of defending the Montanist claim that the Spirit had given the Church new revelations concerning Church discipline, revelations that were equal in authority to scripture. Opponents of the Montanists accused their 'spirit' of being a spirit of the devil. It is in reply to this objection that Tertullian developed the idea of the Spirit as a third person. Stegman's explanation of this crucial step is somewhat unclear. Certainly, Tertullian needed to argue for the Spirit's divinity. But why take the additional step of transforming the Spirit into a third person? Stegman gives pointers to a very interesting answer, without developing it: because Tertullian needed to give the Spirit an authority not only equal to Father and Son (i.e., a divine authority) but also *distinct* from them (see Stegman 1979:208ff.).

The occasion for developing a theology of a distinction of divine persons within the unity of the godhead, and extending it to the Spirit, was provided by Praxeas's modalism. 'Modalism' is the name given to the heresy that Father, Son and Spirit are simply names given to three different manifestations or 'modes' of one and the same divine person. Against this viewpoint Tertullian argued that Father, Son and Spirit were three distinct persons, all of whom shared one divine substance. What Tertullian did here was to raise to the level of the inner life of the godhead the roles ascribed to the Spirit in man's salvation. Previously, those roles were seen simply as distinct activities of Christ or the Father. Now their distinction is pushed into the godhead itself. They are distinct activities, because a distinct divine person is their immediate source.

Stegman's point, then, is that Tertullian developed a theology of the Spirit as a distinct divine person in order to provide a distinct source of authority for the Montanist prophecies. If that is so, then Tertullian's contribution rests on a (no doubt unconscious) attempt to separate Christ and the Spirit. It is a separation that is, as we saw, at the heart of all Montanist-like movements. However, that Tertullian was able to draw on and develop ideas and tendencies already present in the Church can be gathered from the fact that his theology of the Spirit as a third divine person was not simply rejected as a novelty. On the contrary, the whole thrust of Christian thinking — East and West — was towards some sort of trinitarian theology.

Whatever the explanation of its origins, Tertullian's theology of the Spirit as a third distinct person is a landmark in Christian thought. But his Trinity is still not in all respects the Trinity of later Christian theology, marred as it is by subordinationist and emanationist ideas.

No thinker is uninfluenced by philosophical ideas. Those that influenced Tertullian were derived from Stoicism. Stoic philosophy saw everything as material. At the heart of all reality there was a refined kind of matter, fire being a favourite example of this. From the undifferentiated substance at the origin of all things there emerged the seeds of order and rationality in the world, the ordering of which is therefore directly linked to the emergence of such seeds. These were called *logoi spermatikoi*, literally 'reason seeds' or 'word seeds'. John's gospel calls Christ the *Logos,* the Word, through whom all things were made. There is therefore some similarity between what Scripture says about Christ as the Logos-creator and the role Stoicism ascribed to the *logoi spermatikoi.* Because of this similarity, Tertullian links Christ's emergence or emanation from the originally undifferentiated godhead with the act of creation. Before creation there was neither Father, nor Son, nor Spirit: just the original undifferentiated divinity. At creation, the differentiation between Father and Son occurred. As regards the Spirit, however, there was nothing in the Stoic system that corresponded to the role ascribed to the former by Christianity. So Tertullian took his cue from the story of Pentecost and held that the Spirit appeared as a distinct entity only after Christ's ascension.

This view of the origin of distinct persons within the godhead, which was not peculiar to Tertullian, has come to be known as belief in a purely 'economic' Trinity. The 'economic' Trinity is the Trinity viewed in relation to man's salvation. (The Greeks called our salvation a divine 'economy', hence the name 'economic Trinity'.) Belief in a purely economic Trinity is the belief that no Trinity pre-existed our creation and salvation. Such a belief was also partial to the idea that when all things have been brought to their final perfection, then the trinitarian distinction within the divinity will also cease.

For Tertullian, then, the Spirit is the third, the last in line, and therefore in a way the least of the three divine persons. It seems quite likely that the emanationist mentality that influenced him inevitably led him to subordinate Spirit to Son and Son to Father. For each emanation is subordinate to its source. Common to emanationist systems was the idea that successive emanations, like successive streams from a river, contain less and less of the original divine substance. Of course, according to our way of thinking this would mean that the Spirit was not God. But this was not the way Tertullian would have thought. If the Son and Spirit are thought of as emanating from one original divine substance, then they too are divine, even though less divine than the original substance. As Tertullian put it on one occasion, 'when a ray of light is shot from the sun . . . there will be sun in it' (*Apology*, XXI, 12).

Perhaps the emanationist background was also responsible for Tertullian being the first (it seems) to speak of the Spirit as originating not simply from the Father, but also from the Son. 'In my opinion', he writes, 'the Spirit comes from the Father through the Son' (*Adversus Praxean*, IV; *PL* 2:159). The phrase 'through the Son' will become famous. Evans (1948:203) suggests he may have got the idea from the images he uses later — and they are emanationist ones — such as that of the Spirit as the 'fruit' of a 'shoot' (the son) that grows out of the 'root' (the Father).

Finally, like Irenaeus Tertullian too affirms a very close link between the Spirit and the Church. In his pre-Montanist days he wrote a book against certain heretics called *De Praescriptione Haereticorum* ('On Prescription against Heretics'). One of his arguments against them is that the unanimous tradition of the Church is a sure sign of the presence of the true apostolic tradition, the true deposit of faith handed on to us by the apostles. The reason why unanimity was such a sign, he argued, was because the Spirit was active in the Church precisely in order to teach the truth (XXVIII; *PL* 2:40), and unanimity was the surest sign of the Spirit's activity. This link between the Spirit and the Church's tradition is increasingly emphasized as time goes on and the Church moves further away from apostolic times.

F.   ORIGEN

At roughly the same time as Tertullian, Origen, arguably the greatest of all the East's speculative minds, was formulating his views on the Trinity and therefore on the Holy Spirit. In his *Commentary on St John* and *On First Principles* he is the first to present us with a far-ranging examination of questions concerning the Spirit's nature, origin and relationship to Christ. His answers are not always consistent — no doubt because of the pioneering character of his work as well as the competing demands of middle-Platonist ideas and biblical ones.

Like that of Tertullian, Origen's cultural background was somewhat emanationist in character. However, unlike Tertullian, it was middle-Platonist rather than Stoic ideas that shaped his thinking. In his lifetime, the ideas were already current that would soon be welded by his contemporary Plotinus into what has come to be known as neo-Platonism. In contrast to the Stoics, the Platonists insisted that the divine substance from which all things originated was spirit, and not some refined form of matter. Nevertheless there was a continuity between the world of spirit and matter, the bridge being a series of intermediate beings hierarchically arranged, with each inferior being proceeding from its superior. The original undifferentiated divine substance was called the 'One'. From the One proceeds *Nous* — i.e., 'mind' or 'spirit'. *Nous* became the repository of Plato's blueprint Ideas. From *Nous* proceeds 'Soul'. Soul has two levels to it. The world is fashioned from the lower of the two.

This structure gave Origen a ready-made trinitarian framework for the Christian tradition he had received. Quite possibly the framework assisted him in conceiving of Father, Son and Spirit as being three 'hypostases', the eastern equivalent for what the West came to call 'persons' (see his *Commentarium in Ev. Joannis* ['Commentary on John's Gospel']; *PG* 14:127–130). And it seems that just as Tertullian was the first in the West to refer to the Spirit as a person like Father and Son, so too Origen (at roughly the same time!) was the first in the East to refer to the Spirit as a *hupostasis*, like Father and Son (Prestige 1952:179). Whatever the explanation for this remarkable coincidence, the salient point is that the distinction between the three and the hypostatic or 'personal' character of each is clear in Origen's work (Swete 1912:133).

The triple, emanationist-flavoured structure also gave Origen a tool for analysing the Spirit's origins. The Father took the place of the One, the Son of *Nous*, and the Spirit of Soul, even though the only real similarity between the Spirit and Soul was being the third of their respective trinities (Father and Son, by contrast, were easily assimilated to the Platonic One and *Nous*). The triple structure provided a vision of the origin of all things as being itself structured in such a way that within it there was an unoriginated source (Father); an originated source, providing rationality and order to the world (*Nous*, *logos* — the Son); and a being — the Spirit — that came from the unoriginated source via the second in the chain. The idea of the Spirit as third in line after the Son was, of course, not peculiar to Origen. Tertullian had it. Moreover, tradition always spoke of Father, Son and Spirit in that order. However, as with Tertullian so too with Origen, an emanationist philosophy no doubt assisted him in conceiving of the Son as having a role to play in the origin of the Spirit, placing the Spirit in a third position as a matter of metaphysical necessity. Origen is the first eastern theologian to use a phrase almost identical to Tertullian's 'through the Son' in order to express much the same idea (Palmieri 1913:774). Soul comes via *Nous* from the One. The Spirit comes via the Son from the Father. 'The Holy Spirit is the first of all that the Father made through Christ. . . . The Spirit seems to need the Son, because the Son communicates to the *hupostasis* that is the Spirit not only existence but also wisdom, intelligence and justice' (*Commentarium in Ev. Joannis*, II, 6; *PG* 14:129, 130). Origen is aware of the tradition that called the Spirit 'the mother of Christ' (see section A above) and sees clearly the conflict between it and his standpoint. He therefore takes the trouble to explain the sense in which the Spirit can be called that, namely in the same sense in which Jesus could say that anyone who fulfilled his Father's will was his brother, sister, mother (*Commentarium in Ev. Joannis*, II, 6; *PG* 14:133, 134; see Mt 12:50).

However, this issue of the role of the Son as a source of the Spirit provided Origen with some difficulties. Two can be mentioned here.

The first was whether the Spirit was 'made' by the Son or not. The problem arose because scripture said that all things were made by the Word. As arising after the Word, surely the Spirit must be 'made'? However, scripture nowhere talks about the Spirit as made, but rather as 'proceeding' from the Father (Jn 15:26). Here then was a conflict with the Platonist framework. In the *Commentarium in Ev. Joannis*, Origen draws the conclusion that the more pious opinion is to affirm that the Spirit was 'made' — the first and most outstanding of all that was 'made' by the Father through the Son (see the text cited above). On the other hand, in the *De Principiis* ('On first principles') he speaks of the divine 'nature' of not only the Father and Son but also the Spirit as *not* being made (IV, 28, xxxv; *PG* 11:409). Possibly the emanationist mentality here focused on the Spirit's 'substance'. However, a more likely explanation is Swete's suggestion (1967:120) that Origen did not distinguish between two senses of *genētos* (translated above as 'made'): viz., 'derived' and 'created'.

A second issue — connected to the first — concerned the reason why the Spirit was not a 'son'. Scripture said the Spirit proceeded from the Father. But why then is the Spirit too not a son? What is it that prevents the Spirit from being a son? In posing this question Origen raised an issue that thinkers would grapple with in succeeding centuries in one form or another, but which received an intellectually satisfying answer only in the Middle Ages. He himself put forward as a possible explanation the idea that the Spirit needs the Son in order to exist and to be wise etc. (*Commentarium in Ev. Joannis*, II, 6; see above). This certainly would rule out the Spirit being the immediate offspring of the Father. But Origen's problem is still not fully solved. For why could one not think of the Spirit as the Son's son, the Father's grandson? Origen does not pose such a question, as far as I know, but the question is implicit in the solution he offers, and the idea of the Spirit as a 'grandson' is mooted not long afterwards (see Gregory Nazianzen's comments quoted in Burns and Fagin 1984:128–129).

The Spirit's unity with Father and Son is very close for Origen, since the entire Trinity shares one and ·the same incorporeal nature (*De Principiis*, IV, 32; *PG* 11:406–407). In this text — which unfortunately has come down to us only in Rufinus's Latin translation — Origen also observes that to share in the Spirit is to share in Father and Son, which can (I think) be seen as Origen's version of the old idea of the Spirit as the way in which God and the risen Lord are present to people. A similar idea can be found in his *Commentary on the Epistle to the Romans* (VI, 13; *PG* 14:1099–1100).

To stress that the entire Trinity shares one and the same nature raises the issue of the equality of the three. Here Origen's philosophical framework leads him into difficulties. That very framework certainly allows him to divorce the origins of Son and Spirit from creation, in contrast to Stoicism's forcing Tertullian into such a purely 'economic' trinity. Origen is able without any difficulty to affirm the eternity of the Son — and even of the one who was 'made' by or through the Son, namely the Spirit. All three therefore stand on the same side of a line dividing God and creation. However, the Platonist emanations suffer from the same subordinationism as the Stoic ones. As a result, despite texts such as the above, and others (again only in Latin translation) such as that 'nothing in the Trinity can be said to be greater or lesser' (*De Principiis*, I, 3, vii; *PG* 11:152) — despite these texts, Origen remains trapped in the subordinationism of his framework. Soul is inferior to *Nous* and *Nous* to One. So too the Spirit is inferior in power to the Son, and the Son similarly inferior to the Father (*De Principiis*, I, 3, v; *PG* 11:151).

This inferiority is evident in the spheres of competence of each. The Father's sphere of competence is the broadest. Being the origin of all things, he gives existence to all things. The Son's competence is narrower — being the conferring of order, rationality on reality (its existence does come from the Son too, but more accurately from the Father *through* the Son). So far Origen is able to slot Father and Son into Platonism's One and *Nous*. With the Spirit, however, there is no element in Soul as malleable to Christian needs as in·the case of the other two. So Origen relies exclusively here on his Christian heritage and ascribes to the Spirit the role of sanctifier, a role that is exercised in the narrow sphere of spiritual beings either converted or being converted to God. As he puts it in the *De Principiis* (I, 3, viii; *PG* 11:154): 'that things exist they have from the Father; that they are in conformity with reason they have from the Son; that they are holy, they have from the Spirit'. Therefore, the Son's inferiority is expressed by the fact that his sphere of influence extends only to the rational, the Spirit's by the fact of having a sphere of influence limited to the area of holiness (*De Principiis*, I, 3, v; *PG* 11:151). In this last item Origen, no doubt unwittingly, is retrieving the old idea that saw the Spirit as the way in which God was present to *people*. However, Origen's Christian tradition prevents him from restricting the Spirit's action to sanctification, since he recognizes that the Spirit does not simply sanctify but also inspires and interprets the scriptures (see *De Principiis*, II, 7, ii; *PG* 11:216–217).

It is remarkable that the theology of the Spirit should take so decisive a turn in both East and West at roughly the same time. Prior to Tertullian and Origen, precious little attention was paid to the Spirit's nature or origins. With these two theologians — both viewed, though for differing reasons, as renegades in their respective communities — we have for the first time treatises in which extensive attention is devoted to the Spirit and to theological issues that could be raised concerning the theme. Subordinationism may still mar their work, but in their writings are to be found the main outlines of future developments.

G.   FROM ORIGEN TO ATHANASIUS

Origen died in the middle of the third century. The next hundred years do not offer any very significant material on the development of the doctrine of the Holy Spirit. Snippets of information can be found here and there, indicating a somewhat confused situation (for details see Swete 1912:135–171). There were those who evidently affirmed the superiority of the Spirit's teaching to that of the Son — a clear attempt to justify teachings at variance with or at least not clearly demanded by the gospels. On the other hand there were those who affirmed the Spirit to be inferior to the Son. There were the modalists who reduced Father, Son and Spirit to different names for one and the same divine person. And there were those who stressed the distinct personal character of each of the three — including the Spirit. However, the debate was not simply between trinitarians and modalists. The old idea of the Spirit as being only the way in which Father and Son are present could still be found. Lactantius apparently maintained 'that the Spirit is to be referred either to the Father or to the Son, and that His name indicates merely the sanctifying grace (*sanctificatio*) of the two other Persons', to quote Swete's translation of a comment of Jerome's (Swete 1912:150). Jerome, of course, saw only heresy here, a denial of the Spirit's personal character. However, he knew enough of the antecedents of this position to call it a 'Jewish error'!

A more consistent — albeit insufficiently explicit — picture is presented by the various liturgical expressions of faith dating from the period. Their trinitarian character bears repetitive witness to a tradition of naming the Spirit alongside Father and Son as though of equal status and distinctiveness to these other two. One is justified in seeing in this, as Swete (1912:159) does, yet another example of the Church's practice and piety being in advance of clear doctrinal formulations.

On the level of theological debate, however, there was indeed a confusing diversity of views.

The confusion was compounded and matters thereby brought to a head by the Arian-inspired view that the Spirit was really an angel, created by the Son, and one of the spirits ministering to God in heaven. Arianism was a heresy that denied the Son's divinity, the fact of the Son's being 'of one substance' with the Father. Part of the heresy's complex origins was a reaction against the sort of position espoused by Origen: viz., that the divine substance could be shared by more than one *hupostasis* through a process akin to emanation. This for many was an attempt to have one's cake and eat it. For them the divine was a simple, that is to say, an utterly indivisible, incapable-of-being-shared reality. Moreover, the divine could not suffer or experience temporal reality — as the Son did. Hence the Son could not be part of God's substance, but must be one of God's (i.e., the Father's) creatures. He was indeed the first such creature and the creator of all others, but still a creature nevertheless. Arius focused on the Son specifically, and it was concerning the Son that the battle raged. Logically the Spirit in such a scheme of things had to be a creature of the Son — the first, but still a creature produced by the Son. However, there is no record of Arius and his immediate followers having actually drawn this conclusion, though there is some evidence that they were aware that some such idea flowed logically from their standpoint (see Swete 1912:164–165). At any rate, the Arian position was condemned in 325 at the Council of Nicaea. It proclaimed that the Son was as fully God as the Father — 'of one substance with', 'one in being with' the Father, as we say to this day in the creed bearing Nicaea's name. As regards the Spirit, the council said as little as Arius appears to have done. The conciliar profession of faith simply ended with: 'and we believe in the Holy Spirit. Amen'.

A quarter of a century later, the issue of the Spirit was raised explicitly — this time by people who accepted Nicaea's judgement about the Son, but extended Arius's ideas to the Spirit. For their troubles they were dubbed Pneumatomachi, that is to say 'enemies of the Spirit'. They were also known as Macedonians, after Macedonius of Constantinopole, a leading episcopal exponent of the heresy.

An early and outstanding opponent of their views was Athanasius of Alexandria (295–373), who is better known for his opposition to the Arians. He brought forward arguments that were later taken up and developed by the Cappadocians: e.g., that Father, Son and Spirit form a divine triad, not a dyad; that the Spirit sanctifies, which is a divine activity; that the Spirit divinizes, and hence must be fully divine; that the Spirit is unchangeable and present everywhere, which are divine characteristics (see Burns and Fagin 1984:98–108). His letters To Serapion on the Holy Spirit composed in 359 mark the ending of the long post-Origen drought as regards the theology of the Spirit.

Athanasius convened a synod in Alexandria (362), at which the Spirit's full divinity was clearly acknowledged (see Burns and Fagin 1984:109–110). Other synods (e.g., Rome 369, Illyria 375 — see Swete 1912:180) supported the Alexandrian one. But others again supported the view that the Spirit was the Son's creature (Swete 1912:176, 181).

One other writer of the period can be mentioned — Hilary of Poitiers (315–367). A Latin theologian, he too defended the Spirit's full divinity. But what is of particular interest is his description of the Spirit as 'gift'. This is what he sees as distinctive of the Spirit. It is an idea with biblical roots and which became a classic theme in both eastern and western pneumatology. Hilary also spoke of the Spirit as proceeding from the Father 'through' the Son, something he acknowledges he cannot comprehend, but which his former neo-Platonism may have assisted him in formulating (see Burns and Fagin 1984:110–114).

By 380 — the year before the council met that finally condemned the Pneumatomachian position — confusion about the Spirit was widespread, despite the work of men such as Athanasius and Hilary. The main opinions, as summarized by Gregory Nazianzen (Oration XXXI, 5) were as follows: the Spirit is an energy; a creature; God but less so than Father and Son; fully God (see Swete 1912:241). And some, we are told, held these views firmly, while others professed to have an open mind on topics such as the Spirit's divinity, and therefore on whether the Spirit should be worshipped.

But the days of confusion were soon to end, thanks above all to the Cappadocians.

QUESTIONS

Check questions

1   What aspect of the Spirit do the earliest non-biblical references appear to focus on?
2   What criteria did the *Didache* and the *Shepherd of Hermas* propose for testing claims to the Spirit's inspiration?
3   Who were the first to think through the Spirit's relationship to Father and Son, and what were the results of their endeavours?
4   Who may well have been the first to have spoken of the Spirit as the bond of unity between Father and Son?
5   What possible explanations are there for the identification of Christ and the Spirit widespread in the early Church?
6   What explanations can be given for the attractiveness of the idea of the Spirit as female?
7   What was the first big Spirit-orientated movement in the Church, and what was it in the movement that provoked a strong reaction of rejection from the Church as a whole?
8   What did Irenaeus have to say about the Spirit in response to Gnostic and Montanist claims?
9   What was Cyprian's view as regards the relationship between Spirit and Church, and what reaction did it provoke?
10 What was Tertullian's major contribution to the development of the doctrine of the Spirit, and how may his Montanism have influenced him in the matter?
11 How was Tertullian's thought influenced by Stoicism? In particular, how may it have influenced his view of the relationship between Christ and the Spirit?
12 What is meant by belief in a purely 'economic' trinity?
13 What were Origen's contributions to the doctrine of the Spirit that paralleled Tertullian's? What philosophical background influenced Origen, and how did it do so? What issues did Origen raise but not resolve as a result of his speculations on the Spirit?
14 What were the various viewpoints concerning the Spirit being aired at the time of the Cappadocians? Specifically, who were the Pneumatomachi and what was their theological ancestry?

Discussion question

What answer would you give to the problem Origen posed as to why the Spirit was not also a 'son'?

RECOMMENDED READING

General surveys: Heron 1983, the relevant sections; Congar 1983a:65–69; Swete 1912, chs 1–3 (by far the best; covers over 200 pages); Swete 1967:114–124 (briefer). Specifically on Montanism: Knox 1950. But there is no substitute for reading original texts. Hence I recommend: Burns and Fagin 1984, chs 1–3; Lewis 1978:17–109.

4

The Cappadocians and Augustine

As regards the doctrine of the Trinity (and therefore of the Spirit), what the Cappadocians were for the East, Augustine was for the West. Both represent the culmination of developments in East and West respectively. Both gave the doctrine of the Spirit the shape it had ever afterwards in their respective churches.

A. THE CAPPADOCIANS

So called because they were all born in Cappadocia, the Cappadocians are: Basil, bishop of Caesarea (Basil the Great), who lived from *c.* 330 to 379; his brother Gregory, bishop of Nyssa (*c.* 330–395); and Gregory Nazianzen (329–389). These were the men who in their fight against the Pneumatomachi gave the doctrine of the Trinity, and therefore of the Spirit, 'the intellectual form which ultimately prevailed throughout the Greek-speaking East' (Swete 1912:230).

Against those who doubted, attentuated or denied the Spirit's divinity, the Cappadocians argued that the Spirit's possession of divinity in all its fullness was part of Christianity's faith. Gregory Nazianzen avoids all ambiguity by using Nicaea's term 'of one substance with' (*homoousios*) in order to assert that like the Son the Spirit too is of one substance with the Father (*Oration* XXX, 6; see Burns and Fagin 1984:130). He also (the only one of the three to do so) calls the Holy Spirit quite simply 'God'.

Amongst the arguments used by the Cappadocians were the following. First of all, there was the baptismal formula. As noted earlier, the Church's faith was implicitly trinitarian before any explicit theological formulation of it appeared on the scene. The ranking of the Spirit as a distinct and apparently equal entity alongside Christ and the Father argued for the equal divine character of all three. Basil in particular stressed this point (Basil, *Letter* 125, 3 and 189, 2; Burns and Fagin

1984:121–122; Luislampe 1981:189ff.). The formula also exhibited the order of the persons, which is something distinct from their divine equality (see Swete 1912:231). A second argument used was the inclusion of the Spirit in doxologies, that is to say formulae of praise offered to the Father and the Son. This argument, too, is particularly beloved by Basil (on the doxological structure of Basil's entire pneumatology see Luislampe 1981:32–49). He concedes that many doxological formulae are not scriptural, but he argues that the unwritten tradition of the Church is sufficient warrant. Ancient forms and customs cannot be abandoned simply because they are not found in so many words in scripture (*On the Holy Spirit*, XXVII, 66; Swete 1912:237). Another argument was drawn from the Spirit's role in salvation. Salvation is a divine work. It is God who saves us. Therefore the Spirit must be God (Basil, *Letter* 159, 2; *On the Holy Spirit*, XVIII, 44; Gregory Nazianzen, *Sermon on Pentecost* (41), 14; Gregory of Nyssa, *On the Holy Trinity*, VII; see Burns and Fagin 1984:121–137). The argument drawn from the Spirit's undisputed sanctifying role had a great appeal for the Greek mind. The Greeks saw sanctification as a divinization, a sharing in the divine nature as 2 Pet 1:4 put it. If that was so, then only God can sanctify and the *Holy* Spirit must be God (see also Pelikan 1971:215–216; Congar 1983c:30–31).

For the Cappadocians, then, the Spirit shared with Father and Son one *ousia*, one divine nature. The three theologians distinguished sharply between *ousia* and *hupostasis*, reserving the latter for the three distinct persons (Michel 1922:382–383). Of course, Origen had used *hupostasis* before then, but its usefulness had been restricted by the fact that it had not been sufficiently clearly marked off from *ousia*. Both terms could — and had been — used interchangeably. Both could be used for a particular being, *hupostasis* stressing its independence, *ousia* its nature. By distinguishing consistently between the terms, the Cappadocians enabled the East to arrive at a formula — one *ousia*, three *hupostaseis* — that paralleled the West's *una natura, tres personae* — one nature, three persons.

However, it is easy enough to use a word such as *hupostasis* consistently, less easy to define it. The basic idea contained in *hupostasis* was that of particularity. As Basil put it, the distinction between it and *ousia* was between the general (*ousia*) and the particular (*hupostasis*). A *hupostasis* was therefore the particular way in which the general existed (*Letter* 38; *PG* 32:325–329; Michel 1922:382). In short, as he put it elsewhere, a *hupostasis* was a particular 'mode of being', a particular *way in which* something existed (*On the Holy Spirit*, 46; see Fortman 1972:81).

As a particular way of existing distinct from all others, a *hupostasis* must have identifiable characteristics. The Cappadocians therefore list what they call the 'properties' (*idiotētes*) of each of the divine persons, an idea that became a permanent part of western theology. Basil describes the properties as 'paternity', 'sonship' and 'sanctifying power' (Kelly 1977:265). What is peculiar to the Spirit is being the *Holy* Spirit — holy like Father and Son, but whose specific role is to make us holy (Luislampe 1981:169). The two Gregorys use the more technical terminology of 'being ungenerated', 'being generated', 'procession' (or 'mission') (Kelly 1977:265). The Spirit's distinctive property then is that of 'proceeding' or 'being sent' as sanctifier. This latter focuses on the Spirit's distinctive character in terms of our salvation, while the former attempts to define what makes the Spirit unique within the Trinity itself.

So, for the Cappadocians the Spirit was, like the Son, 'of one substance' with the Father, and yet distinct from both. This raised two further issues.

The first was Origen's problem: why is the Spirit not also a 'son'? What is it that distinguishes the former from the latter? The distinction cannot be that the one is less divine than the other — an idea that appealed to many at the time (see Gregory Nazianzen's polemic against it in his *Oration* XXXI, 6). Instead the distinction must be based on the way in which each came forth from the Father. The Son — all admitted — came forth by means of 'generation', a term normally used for the process of begetting offspring. What about the Spirit? Basil's first step was to give the Spirit's coming forth another name — 'proceeds' (*Letter* 125, 3; Burns and Fagin 1984:121). This at least focused all attention on the manner of coming forth as the explanation of the difference. However, once again it is easy to use a word, less easy to define it. What is the difference between 'procession' and 'generation'? How do the two ways of coming forth differ? Gregory Nazianzen declines to attempt any further definition of 'procession' on the grounds that not even the Father's 'unbegottenness' can be so defined (*Oration* XXI, 6, viii; Burns and Fagin 1984:130). However, Basil and the other Gregory do attempt some further analysis, slight though it be. Basil takes up the roots of the Spirit's name and describes the Spirit's coming forth as analogous to breathing rather than generating, to breath rather than birth (*On the Holy Spirit*, XVIII, 46; Burns and Fagin 1984:124). This has within it the glimmerings of the idea that different divine faculties are involved in the issuing forth of Son and Spirit, an idea that will become central to western trinitarian theology. The glimmerings of this idea appear even stronger in Gregory of Nyssa, the most speculative of the Cappadocians. Gregory uses the analogy of breath accompanying speech to describe both the difference and the relationship between the Son and the Spirit's issuing forth from the Father. The Son issues forth as does a word. He is, of course, the divine Word. The Spirit, however, issues forth as the divine Breath accompanying the Word (*Catechetical Oration* II; *PG* 45:18; see Swete 1912:247). The use of 'breath' as a distinguishing factor in the Spirit's coming forth entered eventually into western theology, giving us the technical Latin term *spiratio* (whence 'spiration', literally a 'breathing forth'). The term *processio* then came to apply equally to Son and Spirit's coming forth, with 'generation' distinguishing the former's, 'spiration' the latter's procession.

But back to the Cappadocians. Gregory's use of the breath–word analogy also focused attention on the Son's role in giving the Spirit a distinct identity. The 'grandson' idea, raised by Origen's model of the procession, was kept at bay by not speaking of the Son as an inner divine *source* of the Spirit. Instead, the Son's mediating role is explicitly affirmed only with regard to the Spirit's activity in our salvation. We receive the Spirit from Christ. We experience the Spirit as Christ's Spirit. As regards any role the Son may have had in the inner-trinitarian production of the Spirit, the Cappadocians are mostly silent. Moreover, the few passages that touch on the matter (see Congar 1983c:30–32) are debatable as regards either their authenticity or their meaning. Gregory of Nyssa did, for example, recognize some sort of inner-trinitarian difference based on the Son being closer to the ultimate source, the Father (*That we should not think of saying there are three Gods*, XXXI; Burns and Fagin 1984:140), and which necessitates speaking of the Spirit as the Son's Spirit but not vice versa, i.e., of the Son as the Spirit's Son (*Third Sermon on the Lord's Prayer*, XXXIII; Burns and Fagin 1984:141). But this does not amount to a clear assertion of the Son being a source of the Spirit within the Trinity. The only clear inner-trinitarian role granted to the Son is that by being there as Son he somehow or other ensured that the Spirit was not a Son.

The second issue raised by the assertion that all three were distinct and yet fully God concerned the sort of thing that distinguished the persons. Each person has, as was seen, distinguishing properties. But what is the nature of those properties? Are they of such a nature that one must say that each person lacks something divine that the others possess? Such an assertion would deny their full equality as regards the divine 'substance' they all shared. What then is the character of their distinguishing properties?

The Cappadocians appealed to an idea that Augustine too would use and which eventually became the classic solution to the problem: what distinguishes Father, Son and Spirit is not some *thing* that each possesses exclusively, but rather their *relationship* to each other (see Bulgakov

1946:37; Kelly 1977:266). Their distinguishing characteristics are all relational ones (if we ignore the property of 'sanctifying' attributed by Basil to the Spirit). What distinguishes the Father is the relationship of paternity to the Son. What distinguishes the Son is the relationship of filiation he has to the Father. What distinguishes the Spirit is the relationship of proceeding from the Father, a relationship whose more precise character is also determined by the existence of the Son. In short, as later theology will put it, what distinguishes the divine persons are the way in which each possesses one and the same divine nature.

In this section on the Cappadocians I have concentrated on their analysis of the Spirit's nature, since this is where their major contribution is to be found. However, it needs to be noted that they had much to say on the workings of the Spirit: as sanctifier; as the one who illumines our minds; as the one who showers blessings on us; as the one who, living in the Church, fills and leads it to perfection; as the one who unfolds more and more of Christ's truth to the Church as time goes on; as the one who provides the Church with apostles, prophets, teachers (Damaskinos 1974:49–56; on Basil specifically see Luislampe 1981:49ff., who also stresses [23–31, 91–107] the retention in Basil's monastic background of the charismatic element; on Gregory of Nyssa see Jaeger 1966:101–121).

B.   THE COUNCIL OF CONSTANTINOPLE

The Cappadocians' efforts bore fruit at the highest level of Church life. For in 381 the Council of Constantinople, at which Gregory of Nyssa appears to have played an important part (Jaeger 1966:70), condemned the Pneumatomachi — those who denied the Spirit's divinity. Moreover, the Council's name has been associated with an expanded version of the Nicene Creed, called the Nicene-Constantinopolitan Creed. In it there was added to Nicaea's 'we believe in the Holy Spirit' these words: 'the Lord and Giver of Life, who proceeds from the Father, who together with the Father and the Son is adored and glorified, who spoke through the prophets', words familiar to us from the creed normally recited at Mass. This addition made the divinity and distinct personality of the Spirit perfectly clear.

Cappadocian terminology was also used in 382 by the same bishops, who met at a second council in Constantinople. In a letter to Pope Damasus they proclaimed their belief in one Godhead shared by three *hupostaseis* (text in Burns and Fagin 1984:150).

That same year (382) a council met in Rome endorsing Pope Damasus's *Tome*, in which the Spirit is affirmed to be of one substance with the Father and the Son, a true person, like Father and Son, equal in eternity, power, knowledge, majesty, and glory to Father and Son since they share one and the same power, knowledge, majesty, etc. The Spirit is said moreover to form with Father and Son a divine Trinity, belief in which is identified with Christian salvation (text in Burns and Fagin 1984:151–152).

In short, the Spirit is now, in both East and West, clearly viewed as one of three equal, fully divine hypostases or persons, sharing the one indivisible Godhead. An important phase of the development of the doctrine of the Trinity, and therefore of the Spirit, is over.

C. AUGUSTINE (354–430)

Augustine was baptized six years after the Cappadocians' work culminated in the decisions of Constantinople. Hence, he never had to do battle with the likes of the Pneumatomachi. Instead, he could reap the benefits of previous insights (both eastern and western — see Congar 1983c:80) and push the theology of the Holy Spirit a significant stage further. It is to Augustine above all that we owe a fully developed doctrine of the *Filioque* — the belief that the Spirit proceeds from the Father *and the Son*; of the Spirit as the bond of love uniting Father and Son; and of the Spirit's specific character as 'gift'.

Early on in his career, while still only a priest, he delivered an address on the Creed (entitled *Faith and the Creed*) to a full council of bishops at Hippo (393). In it (chapter 9) he gives what seems to be a brief survey of the point at which the theology of the Spirit was at the time. However, Augustine's choice of items already shows where his interest lies. Hence, it is worth quoting a fairly large portion of the text (the admittedly loose translation is my own):

Concerning the Holy Spirit, the learned and outstanding commentators on the sacred scriptures have not yet discussed matters so fully and deeply that one is able to see clearly what is proper to him as well as what it is that makes him the Holy Spirit and neither a Father nor a Son. They simply say that he is the gift of God, so that we may believe that God does not give us a gift inferior to himself. They take care moreover to avoid saying that the Spirit is generated, as is the Son, since Christ is the only one who is begotten. They also avoid saying that the Spirit is from the Son as if he were the Father's grandson. Nor do they regard the Spirit as owing his existence to no one, but hold rather that he owes it to the Father, from whom come all things. In asserting this they avoid the false, absurd and heretical idea that there are in the Godhead two principles without origin. However, there are those who are of the opinion that the Spirit is the communion of Father and Son, their common deity, which the Greeks call *theoteta*. . . . They call this common deity not only the Holy Spirit, but also the mutual love of Father and Son, charity, and appeal to several biblical passages to support their point of view. . . . One biblical idea appealed to is the fact that the Holy Spirit is called the gift of God [Eph 3:7].

There are those who oppose this idea. They argue that such a communion, which we call deity or love or charity, is not a substance, and the Holy Spirit must be conceived of as such. However, they do not realize that they can only profess that 'God is love' if love were a substance . . . (*PL* 40:191–192).

In this text one can see Augustine's mind already fastening on to what became key, interconnected concepts in his theology of the Holy Spirit: the Spirit as the bond of love between Father and Son, and the Spirit as gift. Later on he unites both these ideas to a third one: the procession of the Spirit from Father and Son, as their common love.

Each of these ideas is developed in his definitive work on the topic: *The Trinity*, a large work comprising fifteen books composed over a period of more than twenty years. In what follows I will confine myself to that work.

Augustine's starting-point (Book 1) is the absolute equality of the persons. All are equally divine, and yet there is but one God, one indivisible divine substance, one mind, one will, possessed fully by each. His emphasis on the unity of the persons is so strong that it blurs the sharper distinctions maintained by the East as regards the individual role played by each divine person in the work of salvation. Indeed, for Augustine, the word 'God' no longer refers directly to the Father, as *ho theos* did for the Greeks, but rather to the divinity itself, shared by three persons (Fortman 1972:141). Augustine stressed that whatever action is performed by God outside the Godhead (e.g., creation, sanctification) is done by all three. Of course, Greeks such as Basil would have agreed (Fortman 1972:141). But Augustine stresses the matter to the point where none of the persons appears to have a *distinctive* role in our salvation (apart from the Son's own life, death, and resurrection, since he alone became incarnate). Any such distinction is reduced to the level of 'appropriation' — the attribution, for reasons of fittingness, of a characteristic or activity to one person rather than another, even though all three possess that characteristic or perform the activity equally. The upshot of this is that we do not really have a distinct relationship to each of the persons, but only with the divinity as such. This inference was already beginning to influence Augustine, who suggested that since the entire Trinity regenerated us by grace we can — metaphysically — call the entire Trinity 'Father' (V, 11, xii; Hill 1985:95, 98).

Because of so strong a stress on the unity and equality of the persons, the Cappadocians' dilemma was just as acute for Augustine, if not more so. He takes over the Cappadocians' idea that the only distinguishing factor is their relationship to each other. What distinguishes the Father and Son are their respective relationships of paternity and filiation. But what about the Spirit?

In searching for the Spirit's distinguishing mark, Augustine takes up

Hilary of Poitiers's idea (see Chapter 3, G) of 'gift'. The Spirit is the gift of Father and Son to us, and is therefore related to Father and Son as gift to giver (V, 11, xiii). Father and Son are the givers, the Spirit the gift. His biblical warrant is found in texts like Acts 8:20 and Rom 5:5.

When speaking of the Spirit as gift Augustine always thinks of creatures as the recipients. The Spirit is not conceived of as the mutual gift of Father and Son to each other (Hill 1985:70). But how can one give as an identifying characteristic something linked to the contingent fact of creation? Did the Spirit have no distinct identity before creation? Augustine is aware of the problem. His answer is that a gift exists even before it is given (V, 15, xvi). The Spirit is from eternity a gift that is there to be given by Father and Son, should they so will.

On its own, this may seem rather a weak identifying characteristic — to have the ability to be given! But when linked to the second of Augustine's key ideas, that of the Spirit as love, as the love-bond uniting Father and Son, it took on a power that captured the imagination of western theology ever since.

Gifts are (normally) signs of love. What marks the Spirit as one who can be given is love. For Augustine, the Spirit is in a special way love, and for that reason gift. As an old man finishing his book, he hammers this point home. 'The Spirit', he says, 'is called gift only because of love. . . . The love that is from God and which indeed is God, is, properly speaking, the Holy Spirit. . . . What is meant by Gift, if not love. . . .?' (XV, 18, xxxii).

In pursuit of a deeper understanding of the Trinity, Augustine searches the depths of what he believes to be the best image of God available to him: the human being, especially humanity's spiritual capacities. And of these latter, Augustine singles out mind (see on this Hill 1985:122ff.). Mind is a particularly useful image because of its dynamic character. As Augustine saw the matter, our minds perform three basic activities: remembering ourselves, understanding ourselves and willing (or loving) ourselves. The first activity produces the second. Being mindful of oneself produces a mental 'word' of self-understanding, which is therefore related to 'self-mindfulness' as to its source. Augustine sees this as an image of the relationship between Father and Son, the Son being the mental 'word' or expression of the Father. The Spirit, however, issues forth not as a mental word but in the way an act of self-love does. And just as this third activity must flow from the first two, so too do the activities giving rise to Father and Son precede that which gives rise to the Spirit.

Of course, Augustine did not associate the Spirit with love because of his psychological image of the Trinity. If anything, the reverse was true. But the two ideas meshed so well that, as finally developed and polished by Aquinas, they became a virtually unquestioned part of Catholic theology to this day. Moreover, the Spirit's association with a faculty issuing forth in love provided the rudiments of an answer (to be worked out only in mediaeval times) to Origen's question: why is the Spirit not a son? Augustine, too, raises this question, but gives no really satisfactory answer. After ruminating on the way in which knowledge precedes love (which is a variation on the unsatisfactory Cappadocian idea that it is the Son's being already there that makes the Spirit not a Son), Augustine comes to within striking distance of an answer when he argues that the process of bringing forth knowledge is similar to the begetting of offspring. However, he does not explain the precise area of similarity, and as a result struggles to explain why one must rule out a similarity between loving and the bringing forth of offspring (IX, 12, xviii). In the final pages of *The Trinity* (XV, 27) he turns to the issue again, but this time he simply uses a form of *reductio ad absurdum* to explain why the Spirit is not a son: to hold this view could imply that the Spirit was either Christ's brother or the son of both Father and Son (by this stage Augustine had fully committed himself to the idea that the Spirit proceeded from both Father and Son).

But we have drifted from the Spirit as love. Augustine recognizes that Father and Son, too, love. Why then reserve 'love' for the Spirit? The answer he gives in chapter 17 of Book XV is that just as there are reasons why wisdom/word/understanding should be regarded as special to the Son, even though also the Father and the Spirit are wise and understand things, so too are there special reasons for singling out love as the Spirit's identifying characteristic. The reasons he gives are biblical: examples of the scriptures associating love in a particular way with the Spirit (e.g., Rom 5:5 again). Here Augustine remains within the categories of pure 'appropriation'.

However, he also provides the basis for an association of the Spirit with love that goes beyond mere appropriation. The basis is to be found in his idea of the Spirit as the common element between Father and Son and therefore as their *mutual love* for each other. During the course of his discussion of the Spirit's identifying characteristic, a discussion that led him to see it as gift, he ponders the paradox in the Spirit's name: 'Holy Spirit'. The paradox is that neither of the elements in that name ('holy', 'spirit') is unique to the Spirit. Father and Son, too, are holy and are spirit. But this paradox points to something that in fact *is* unique to the Spirit: to be a sort of bond, an 'inexpressible communion' between Father and Son. This, says Augustine, is the very reason why the Spirit's personal name ('Holy Spirit') is something the Father and Son have in common. It is also the reason why 'gift' is appropriate as the Spirit's identifying characteristic, since the Spirit is the gift of both to us. It is their *common* gift to us.

In this idea of the Spirit as the communion or bond between Father and Son, Augustine gave the Spirit an identifying characteristic not possessed by the other two, and one that was more basic than that of being gift. If the Spirit is gift, then this is so because of the Spirit's character as communion between Father and Son rather than vice versa. Moreover, it enables love to be seen as proper to the Spirit in the sense of the love *binding Father and Son*, that is to say their mutual love. Neither Father nor Son can be on their own the mutual love of both of them. If one regards the Spirit as in some way or other their togetherness, the way in which they are one, then one can say that the Spirit alone is their mutual love.

In chapter 19 of Book XV he uses these ideas to reinforce his argument that it is fitting that love should be identified in a special way with the Spirit. The Spirit is, he says, the mutual love of Father and Son, the love whereby they love each other. It is love that is the bond uniting them, the 'inexpressible communion' he had referred to earlier. However, even here Augustine remains within the ambit of appropriation, reminding us that it is not just the Spirit who is love (were that the case, he says, the Son would have to be the Son of the Spirit too!). He does not seem to have drawn the conclusion that if one identifies the Spirit with what is common between Father and Son, and if one sees that bond as being pre-eminently their love for each other, then being their mutual love is proper to the Spirit alone. Certainly love is common to all three. Certainly Father and Son too can love. But their very love for each other identifies and, in that sense, is proper to the Spirit — if one sees the Spirit as the 'inexpressible communion' between the two.

Whether or not love, the mutual love of Father and Son for each other, is proper to the Spirit will be debated down to the present day. But Augustine's association of the Spirit with love, with a procession from an act of loving, entered into the heart of western trinitarian theology and to this day remains enshrined there.

The third of Augustine's key ideas concerning the Spirit, and the one that has become part of Catholic dogma, is the *Filioque*, the belief that the Spirit proceeds from the Father and Son. The link between this and the preceding ideas is obvious: viz., the Spirit's character as the expression of the togetherness of Father and Son. This togetherness is reflected in Augustine's teaching that the Spirit proceeds from the Father and the Son as from one source (*principium*). Just as the entire Trinity is one undivided source of creation, so too Father and Son are one undivided source of the Spirit. Just as Father and Son are one God, not two, so also are they one source of the Spirit, not two (V, 14, xv). Moreover, their unity as source is such that the Spirit proceeds *simultaneously* from both. It is not as though the Spirit proceeded first from the Father into the Son, and then from the Son and in that sense through him (XV, 27, xlviii). Augustine's point here is that the Spirit is not a 'son', since children (as his biology understood the matter) proceed first from the father into the mother, and then from the mother into the world. Augustine is therefore ruling out the idea that the Son is merely a medium through which the fully formed Spirit passes. On the contrary, the Son contributes to the Spirit's very being. He does so, furthermore, not by contributing a part of that being, as though the Spirit came partly from the Father and partly from the Son. On the contrary, the unity of Father and Son is so total that the Spirit proceeds equally from both. Both are equally sources of the Spirit.

However, there is a difference between the two as source of the Spirit. For just as the Son has the divinity not of himself but only as received from the Father, so too does the Son possess the divinity *as the source of the Spirit* only as received from the Father. In the very act of proceeding from the Father, the Son received not simply his divinity but also his ability to be a source of the Spirit. Hence, Augustine stresses that the Spirit proceeds *principally (principaliter)* from the Father (XV, 17, xxix). In other words, the Spirit proceeds from the Father as from the unoriginated source of all reality, whereas the Son operates as an originated, a derived source. The source is one and the same undivided divinity: Father and Son are one source. But that source, that divinity is possessed by the Father as underived source and by the Son as received.

What led Augustine to this explicit doctrine of the *Filioque*? Hill (1985:111) believes it to be 'spontaneously produced from the reading of the New Testament and the whole drift of his inquiry'. Hill's point is that it was not the fruit of polemics. Moreover, Augustine's belief that the way in which the persons are sent or given to us reveals their inner-trinitarian relationships (IV, 20, xxix; on this see Hill 1985:84–90) leads him to the conclusion that the Spirit, since sent by the Son, proceeds from the Son too. However, I doubt whether this conclusion was simply the product of a spontaneous reading of the New Testament. It needs to be recalled that others had already spoken of the Spirit as 'receiving' from the Son or proceeding 'through' him. Aware of these statements, Augustine would only naturally have asked himself 'the exact meaning of these phrases and attempted to formulate in theological language the truth which lies behind them' (Swete 1912:329). His theology of the *Filioque* can therefore be seen as a coming to fruition of hints and ideas preceding him. No doubt an important factor here was the idea of the Spirit as communion, as the love-bond. The attraction of this to a theologian as obsessed with the centrality of love and unity as was Augustine, is obvious. The fact that it fitted in so well with the *Filioque* must have added powerfully to its convincing character for him. Curiously enough, Augustine does not appear to argue for the *Filioque* from the principle, subscribed to by him, that the persons are only distinguished from each other by relations of origin (Hill 1985:111). If the Son is distinct from the Spirit then — so the argument would go — there must be a relationship of origin between them. But even if Augustine did not use this argument, it became widely invoked in later times.

The Spirit then is gift, love, the inexpressible communion existing between Father and Son who form the undivided source of that gift, that love, that communion. This does not mean that the Spirit was for Augustine an 'impersonal' reality. Far from it. He saw the Spirit as being as much a 'person' as Father and Son were. However, though he used the term 'person' of them, he found it unsatisfactory as a description for the members of the Trinity. For him 'person' was not a relational term. It signified a substance, not relationship. Hence to speak of three 'persons' only too easily could mean three 'substances' (Hill 1985:100–101; see also *The Trinity*, V, 8, ix).

As with the Cappadocians so too with Augustine, the real breadth of the doctrine of the Spirit is not to be found in the above analyses of the Spirit's inner-trinitarian character and role, important though they are. One must look rather at all Augustine has to say about the Spirit's work within us. Unfortunately, there is space for only a few remarks in this connection.

It is clear that what he has to say on the Spirit's work in the Church and individuals is for the most part just the detailed application of his views of the Spirit as the love-bond, the 'inexpressible communion' between Father and Son. Indeed, it was his views on the Spirit as the one enabling us to love, the one who creates an inexpressibly close communion between Father, Son and us that affected his views on the Spirit's inner-trinitarian role and identity.

He connects the two beautifully in his *Sermon* 71: Father and Son wish to give us that which unites them so that we can be similarly united to them and each other (see Swete 1912:327). This communion is one of love, and is broken by a lack of love. To break with the Church is to demonstrate a lack of love. This love is the special gift of the Church to its members. Hence — and this is Augustine's response to Cyprian's problem — while even heretics and schismatics can confer the sacraments validly, they cannot give the love that is meant to go hand in hand with them, and in that sense cannot give the Spirit of love (*On Baptism*, III, 16, xxi; Burns and Fagin 1984:167–168). As later ages would put it, such sacraments are valid but unfruitful. The Spirit can give the sacrament, but the Spirit as love-bond will not be given (for texts see Burns and Fagin 1984:169ff.).

The Spirit, then, creates the Church through creating love. So close is the bond between Spirit and Church that the Spirit can be called the 'soul' of the Church. 'What the soul is to the members of our body, that the Spirit is to Christ's members, the members of Christ's body, the Church' (*Sermon* 268, 2; *PL* 38:1232). The description of the Spirit as the soul of the Church was one that became widespread in later theology.

The unity in love forged by the Spirit is also a guarantee of the presence of the truth in the Church (*Letter* 105, 5; *PL* 33:403–404). Hence truth is linked to love — a very important insight on Augustine's part. Indeed, Augustine regards love as essential to knowing the truth in all its fullness (see Gaybba 1985).

From the above, it is in no way surprising that for Augustine love stands out as *the* sign of the Spirit's presence. In his *Sixth Homily on the Epistle of John* (10, xii), he contrasts love with the older, extraordinary signs of the Spirit. It is clear that in his day the striking charism of tongues was no longer in evidence. He sees it as something that was useful for the original spreading of the Gospel and so has passed away for good. He then asks the question: if the Spirit's presence is no longer manifested through such extraordinary phenomena, how is a person to know he or she has received the Spirit? Augustine's answer is clear: look into your heart and see whether you love your neighbour, whether you love the Church, whether you love the peace and unity binding the Church's members to each other (text in Burns and Fagin 1984:174). He even insists that love is part of the criterion 1 Jn 4:2 gives for discerning truly divine from counterfeit spirits (confessing Jesus to have come in the flesh). Confessing Jesus to have come in the flesh is not simply a matter of words, but deeds. One confesses it by loving, since Jesus came in the flesh to die, to show us the depths of love, to create love, the love of a people drawn together thanks to his death. Moreover, as we saw, even doctrinal agreement, which can be viewed as a sign of the Spirit's presence, is for Augustine at bottom a sign of love (13, xiii; Burns and Fagin 1984:175–176).

Unity and love — these are the recurring themes in Augustine's theology of the Spirit. One could say that this theology is but the detailed and consistent application of the idea that love unites and, by uniting, transforms all it unites.

QUESTIONS

Check questions

1   Who were the Cappadocians?

2   What arguments did they use against those who doubted, attenuated or denied the Spirit's divinity?
3   What consistent meaning did they give to *ousia* and *hupostasis*?
4   Why did the Cappadocians assign 'properties' to each of the divine persons and why? What were those properties?
5   What were their views on the issue: why is the Spirit not also a 'son'? What role does the Son play, for them, in giving the Spirit a distinct identity?
6   What was their solution to the problem: how can the three *hupostaseis* be equally divine and yet distinct?
7   Is there any evidence that there was a continued presence in their Church of a charismatic element?
8   What Council endorsed the Cappadocians' views on the Spirit's full divinity and distinct character? What are its famous phrases?
9   What similar developments took place at the same time in the West?
10 What are the three key ideas interlocking Augustine's theology of the Spirit?
11 How are those key ideas related to each other?
12 What was it about Augustine's theology that blurred the distinct relationship the believer has to each member of the Trinity?
13 What for Augustine is the Spirit's distinguishing property?
14 What led Augustine to identify the Spirit with love?
15 What was Augustine's answer to the question: why is the Spirit not a son? Why was his answer unsatisfactory?
16 What basis did Augustine give for a way of associating the Spirit with love in a way that goes beyond mere appropriation?
17 Why does Augustine stress that Father and Son form a single source for the Spirit and that the Spirit proceeds *simultaneously* from both?
18 In what way does Augustine see Father and Son as *not* being equal as sources of the Spirit?
19 What led Augustine to formulate his doctrine of the *Filioque*?
20 Why did Augustine have misgivings about the suitability of calling the divine three 'persons'?
21 Give one or two examples illustrating how Augustine's theology of the Spirit's work in our lives is only the detailed practical application of the idea that the Spirit is the love-bond uniting Father and Son.

Discussion questions

1   In what way could love, and therefore the Spirit, enable one to understand the things of God?
2   The Greeks, as will be seen, rejected the *Filioque* on both biblical and rational grounds. What sort of arguments do you think they could have appealed to?

RECOMMENDED READING

As regards general surveys of the period, a brief and illuminating account can be found in the relevant sections of Heron 1983. A far more detailed and highly to be recommended account can be found in Swete 1912, chs 4 (on the Cappadocians) to 9 (Gregory the Great). Part III of Swete 1912 (359–409) is a valuable summary of the doctrine of the Spirit in the ancient Church. Another good summary, tracing the actual course of development, is to be found in Burns and Fagin 1984, ch. 5. Swete 1967:124ff. is another useful, though brief, survey. On Augustine, I highly recommend a companion volume in this series, Hill 1985, chs 7–14. A briefer account of Augustine is to be found also in Congar 1983a:73–81. On the Cappadocians Congar 1983c has a short but useful section on pp. 29–36. For texts from the period, see Burns and Fagin 1984, chs 3 and 4; Lewis 1978:110–124, 136–137.

5

The Middle Ages

The 'middle ages' comprise a vast slice of history — a thousand years stretching from 500 to 1500. They are usually treated as a unit on the grounds of their supposed homogeneity. As mediaeval studies progress, this homogeneity becomes increasingly questionable because of the ever-increasing discovery of yet further heterogeneity. In theology alone, for example, there is a clear difference between the traditional, patristic type of theology that reached its zenith in twelfth-century 'monastic theology' (as it has been called), and the scholasticism that developed from that time onwards. Moreover, scholasticism spawned systems that were basically irreconcilable. Hence to lump together a thousand years of development under the single heading of 'middle ages' is, I must agree, not the happiest of approaches. Nevertheless, there were sufficient common bonds during that period, especially theological, to justify continuing the practice of dealing with it as a unity. This is particularly true as regards our theme.

The length of the period (which is the reason for the length of this chapter) poses a further problem, however. The Middle Ages saw the development of theology into an academic discipline and therefore an explosion of theological writing not seen before. To follow the previous method of singling out authors to illustrate stages of development would lengthen the chapter intolerably, if one wished to do justice to all who contributed. As a result, I have chosen to switch now to a thematic form of treatment, in which I will outline the developments that took place regarding certain aspects of the theology of the Spirit.

Finally, from this point on the focus will be on western thought. There are two reasons for this. The first is quite simply my lack of expertise in the further development of eastern thought. The second is that henceforth the two traditions — Greek and Latin — developed in increasing isolation from each other. Hence, the historical background to our western theology of the Spirit is from mediaeval times on virtually exclusively western.

A.   PERSON

We can begin with the concept 'person'. By the end of the fifth century, both East and West confessed the Spirit to be as much a 'person' (or 'hypostasis') as were Father and Son. But what did the term mean? I have already pointed out what the Cappadocians meant by 'hypostasis': the individual concrete existent, as opposed to a nature as yet lacking individuation, lacking realization in individual existents. This remained the core idea of 'hypostasis' in Greek thought (see Michel 1922:404–406).

'Hypostasis' was therefore a broader term than 'person'. 'Person' implied a conscious, spiritual dimension. A tree could be a hypostasis, but it could not be a person. Hence Boethius (*c.* 480–524) gave the following definition of person: 'an individual substance of *a rational nature*' (*On person and two natures against the views of Eutyches and Nestorius*, chapter 3). This definition became famous in the West, being taken over by most mediaeval theologians (Michel 1922:409). However, it had its difficulties.

The first was that, as it stood, it could be applied to the divine nature itself, giving then a total of four persons! Hence the note of 'incommunicability' was added to the notion of person by the twelfth-century theologian Richard of St Victor (*The Trinity*, IV, 18, xxii). In other words, I can never be or even share in being you, nor you me. This in turn led Thomas Aquinas and several other mediaeval authors to observe that there was no essence of 'person', a sort of general nature of 'person' that each individual shared in in her or his way (Mühlen 1967:29–30). For Thomas each person's uniqueness derived from the way that person existed in and for him or herself. Individuation was therefore a dynamic reality brought about by the person's own activity (Mühlen 1967:36).

The second difficulty with Boethius's definition was that it lost sight of Augustine's objection that 'person' was not a relational term, while what constituted and distinguished the divine persons was precisely their relationship to each other. In this matter too, Richard of St Victor offered a correction. For him a divine person's individuality and incommunicability derived from that person's origins. To be a divine person was to 'ex-sist', that is to say, to 'be-from' (*The Trinity*, IV, 12; Mühlen 1967:37ff.). Aquinas, on the other hand, did not see relationality as the decisive element in the notion of a 'person'. For him its distinctiveness, its incommunicability was the decisive element. However, since distinction in God was derived solely from origin, it involved relationship. Indeed it *was* relationship. Hence, a divine person was a 'subsisting relationship' (*Summa theologiae*, Ia, 29, 4, resp.). Unlike Aquinas, John Duns Scotus (late thirteenth–early four-teenth century) believed that relationality was an essential characteristic of every person, divine or human (Mühlen 1967:55). For him too, then, the uniqueness of the divine persons derived from the uniqueness of the relations constituting them.

Scholastics — mediaeval and modern — debated the finer points of 'subsistence' — that mode of being peculiar to hypostases and therefore 'persons'. The debate ranged around the issue of what made subsistence the sort of existence it was (see Michel 1922:410–429). But these debates need not concern us. Their aim was primarily the resolution of the problems caused by affirming that Christ possessed a perfect human nature but was not a human person. Hence they did not contribute much to the notion of the Spirit as a divine person.

However, there is one debate, connected to the idea of subsistence, that does need at least a brief mention. It concerned the relationship of the divine persons to the divine essence. The issue surfaced when Gilbert of Poitiers (1076–1154) tried to express the unity and trinity of God in the following way: in God there is one *subsistence* but three *subsistents*. Rightly or wrongly, this seemed to many of his contempor-aries to be saying that the divine subsistents (the persons) are one thing, the divine subsistence (the divinity) another, and that all *four* formed one God (Fortman 1972:183–185).

The question at issue was whether or not a real distinction could be made between the divine essence (the divinity) and the divine persons. The old problem of three distinct persons who are nevertheless fully divine, while there is only one God, was raised yet again, though in a more focused way. Must we say that the divine persons are in reality (as distinct from the way we think about them) identical to the divine essence? Or is there as real a distinction between them and the divine essence as there is between each of them in their mutual relationships? The latter viewpoint seemed to posit a quaternity in God, since it gave the divine essence a subsistence distinct from the persons. Hence the Fourth Lateran Council (1215) condemned it, asserting that in God there is only a trinity, not a quaternity, since each of the divine persons is the divine essence (DS 804).

Such a statement demanded some sort of distinction to be made within a relationship itself, and Thomas Aquinas provided it in his *Summa*, Ia, 28, 2. There he distinguishes between the relativity of relation (its respect to another) and its inherence in that which is so related. The issue as to whether the persons (who, remember, are conceived of by him as subsistent relations) are identical to the essence or not concerns the second aspect of a relationship, and not its relativity as such. Now in creatures there is always a distinction between the modifications their substances undergo (the technical term for these was 'accidents') and those substances themselves. But in God there is no such distinction. Hence, as regards their 'inherence' aspect, the divine relations/persons are identical to the divine essence, their distinction being found in their relativity as such. Whether this answers the problem or not can be debated. But for our purposes it marks a high point in the development of the idea of a divine person, and therefore of the Spirit as person. A person is a subsistent relation, identical with the divine essence as regards its 'being-inness' (its *esse in*, to use what became the widespread scholastic term), yet distinct from the other persons in virtue of its 'being-towardness', its relativity (its *esse ad*).

B.   THE FILIOQUE

As western Europe moved into the Middle Ages, the *Filioque* — the belief that the Spirit proceeded from the Father *and the Son* — was already widespread. After Augustine's explicit embracing of it, we find it in his disciple Fulgentius and in the late fifth-century creed influenced by him and known as the Athanasian Creed. It is also found in the writings of Pope Leo the Great (though not as explicitly) and of several other bishops of the fifth century. It is found, furthermore, in the works of the two leading laymen of the sixth century, Boethius and Cassiodorus (Congar 1983c:51–52; for texts see Palmieri 1913:805–806).

In the sixth century, moreover, the *Filioque* was adopted by a local council: the third of Toledo (589). Here its adoption served the purpose of stressing both that the Son was in no way inferior to the Father and that the Spirit was of one substance with Father and Son (Congar 1983c:52). Subsequent councils of Toledo reaffirmed belief in the *Filioque*.

Popes, too, accepted it. Apart from Leo the Great mentioned above, there was Gregory, also called the Great, and in the ninth century Leo III, who accepted the doctrine but refused to add it to the Nicene-Constantinopolitan Creed.

The *Filioque* was probably added to that creed for the first time in Gaul and Spain, towards the end of the sixth century (Congar 1983c:53). However, it was only towards the end of the eighth century that the papacy began to be pressurized to make it an official part of the western Church's creed. The pressure came mainly from Charlemagne, but Leo III stood his ground — even to the point of engraving the original texts (that is to say, without the *Filioque*) in Greek and Latin on silver shields, and hanging them up in St Peter's for all to see. It was only in the eleventh 'century — forty years before the final break between East and West — that Pope Benedict VIII capitulated to a demand of the emperor Henry II that the creed with the *Filioque* be sung at the latter's coronation in Rome (Congar 1983c:54). By that stage the *Filioque* had already become a subject of bitter controversy between East and West. Benedict's action served only to alienate the Greeks still further, providing fuel for the fire of their rejection not only of the *Filioque* but also of a papal authority that would dare unilaterally to alter an ecumenical creed. Insult was added to injury, as far as the Greeks were concerned, when uninformed Latins began to accuse the Greeks of *deleting* the *Filioque* from the creed!

Up to the ninth century, the Latins were able to profess their *Filioque* without any serious protest from the Greeks, despite their being in communion with each other (Congar 1983c:52). The typical Greek position up to this point was certainly not one that held for the *Filioque*, but it did ascribe some role to the Son, as we saw. This role enabled Greek Fathers such as John Damascene to talk of the Spirit as proceeding from the Father *through* the Son. Once again, this did not mean what the Latins meant by the *Filioque*, since the Son's role was not conceived of as a causal one. John distinguished between 'from' the Son (which he rejects) and 'through' the Son (which he accepts — see Congar 1983c:38–40). However, there was no clearly articulated opposition to the *Filioque* in John's position. It is only with Photius that the issue became controversial to the point of being seen as justifying breaches of communion. In 867, while still Patriarch of Constantinople (he was twice deposed), he attacked the *Filioque* on several fronts.

First of all, it was, he said, an innovation, a western innovation. The fact that Fathers such as Augustine taught it was simply proof of their fallibility (Orphanos 1981:25).

Secondly, the doctrine was unbiblical. The West argued from biblical references to the Spirit as the Spirit of the Son and as being sent by the Son. But, says Photius, this does not prove that the Son is a source of the Spirit *within the divinity*. The Spirit proceeds from the Spirit only in the sense that the Son sends the Spirit to us (Orphanos 1981:24).

Thirdly, the West's position splits the divinity. To say the Spirit proceeds from Father and Son is to say that the Spirit proceeds from two principles, and this in turn implies that the Spirit's being is divided (Orphanos 1981:22–23), deriving something different from each.

Fourthly, the West's reply to the previous argument is attacked in the following way. The West stressed that Father and Son form not two sources but a single source. Moreover, this was seen as preserving the divine unity in the best way possible. But in that case, Photius argued, one is either cancelling the distinction between Father and Son (confusing the hypostases, as he put it), or the Spirit must be its own source.

Whatever is common to two divine persons is common to all three. If Father and Son have in common the property of being the source of the Spirit, then so too must the Spirit possess such a property (Orphanos 1981:23).

This last argument is important, dealing as it does with the heart of the issue: is there nothing common to Father and Son that is not also shared by the Spirit? For Photius there were, as Congar (1983c:58) noted, only two possibilities: an activity that was strictly personal, belonging to one person only; an activity that was shared by all three. Being a source or cause of a divine person was a strictly personal activity, and it belonged to the Father.

In his attack on the *Filioque* Photius retreated even from the accepted Greek idea of the Spirit proceeding *through* the Son — even though this did not necessarily imply that the Son was the source of the Spirit's being (Orphanos 1981:25; Congar 1983c:58). Instead he stressed that the Spirit proceeded from the Father alone, Son and Spirit being as two branches from a single stem (see Congar 1983c:58).

Photius's influence on subsequent Greek tradition was immense, his objections remaining to this day the major Greek ones against the *Filioque*.

Congar (1983c:58) points out that for Photius the distinction between the divine persons was adequately explained by the personal properties of each. The West, on the other hand, saw the distinction as deriving from relationships of origin. If two divine persons were distinct, then the reason must be because they were related to one another as source and derivation from source. The Spirit's distinction from the Son was explicable therefore only if the one was the source of the other.

In his *Procession of the Holy Spirit against the Greeks*, Anselm of Canterbury (see C below) develops this line of reasoning in detail. Moreover, he puts the stress on the equality of Father and Son as source, warning that Augustine's distinction between a principal source (the Father) and a derived one (the Son) means no inequality on the part of the Son as source (Congar 1983c:99).

His argument was taken up by the great thirteenth-century scholastics Albert (*Summa*, 7, 31, 3), Bonaventure (*Commentary on the Sentences*, I, d 11, a 1, q 1), Aquinas (*Summaa*, Ia, 36, 2, resp.), and used by the Council of Florence in its *Decretum pro Jacobitis* (DS 1330). However, its validity was rejected by the Franciscan theologian Duns Scotus, who saw disparate (and not just opposite) relations as being sufficient for distinguishing the persons (Fortman 1972:222). Whether any Greek theologians who lived after him held his position, I do not know. But no doubt they would have applauded. For the response formulated by the Greeks to this western argument was that what distinguished the persons was not opposing relations, but rather the different ways in which Son and Spirit proceeded from the Father (Orphanos 1981:44). These resulted in the Son and Spirit having different, though not opposed, relationships.

The *Filioque* controversy forced both East and West to sharpen the understanding and defence of their respective positions. A good example in the East is the response developed to the West's accusation that the East did not take sufficiently seriously the Son's role as regards the Spirit. Photius, as we saw, played down the traditional idea of such a role, which was conceived of as 'manifesting' the Spirit and being the reason why the Spirit was not a son. The Greek tradition may not have granted the Son any role in communicating the divine essence to the Spirit, in being a source of the Spirit's very being. But it did teach that the character of the Spirit's procession from the Father, and therefore the Spirit's own character, derived not simply from the Father but also from the fact of the Son's presence.

The distinction between the Spirit's very being on the one hand, and character or manifestation on the other, was expressed by Gregory Palamas (1296–1359) in terms of his distinction between the divine 'essence' and 'energies' (Congar 1983c:61–67; Orphanos 1981:29–35). As far as I understand the matter, this is a distinction within the Godhead between what can (viz., 'energies') and cannot (viz. 'essence') be communicated to a creature. Both essence and energies are uncreated. Both are part of the divine being. But while we can neither know nor share in the divine essence, we can both know and share in the divine energies. The term 'energy' conveys also the idea of dynamism, of a divine movement reaching out to creatures. Now the Spirit's 'essential derivation' (i.e., the Spirit's divine being) is from the Father alone, while the Spirit's 'energetic manifestation' is through the Son (Orphanos 1981:44).

As an expression, then, of the divine energy, the Spirit is dependent not only on the Father but also on the Son. The divine energies or activities flow from the Father through the Son, and reach us in the Holy Spirit. Moreover, the 'energetic manifestation' of the Spirit is not simply the Spirit's being sent to us. This energetic manifestation or energetic procession of the Spirit is eternal, part of the Godhead (Orphanos 1981:44–45). The idea that from all eternity the Spirit 'proceeds' from the Son, in the sense of receiving from him not being but a specific 'character' had already been resurrected and developed by Gregory the Cypriot (d. 1290) as a balance to Photius's limiting the Son's role to sending the Spirit to us (Orphanos 1981:25–29). Gregory Palamas's 'energetic manifestation' was therefore also an eternal procession (not of being, but of 'character'). As a result, the West's argument that one can and must see the Spirit's manifestation in our salvation as a revelation of the Spirit's procession in the Trinity was no longer simply rejected. However, our experience of the Spirit reveals not the essential but rather the energetic procession of the Spirit within the Godhead.

Palamas's theology of essence and energies became so much a part of eastern thought that some Orthodox theologians regard it as dogma. Our own theological tradition finds this further distinction within the divinity (over and above the persons) hard to accept. Some have even held it to be heretical (on this see Congar 1983c:65–67). However, it is in my view an enriching element in our common tradition, and one we need to absorb into our own western thinking.

Two attempts were made to reunite East and West in a council. Both were the result more of political pressures than genuine ecumenical concern. Both failed.

The first attempt was at the Council of Lyons (1274). Regarded by the West as ecumenical, it was attended by only a token Greek presence, who saw themselves as representing their emperor rather than their Church. The emperor in question — Michael VIII — needed union with the Latins to protect Constantinople from invasion. The council met and passed a decree in which it was said that the Spirit proceeded 'eternally from Father and Son, not as from two sources (*principiis*) but as from a single source, not as a result of two spirations but rather of one spiration' (DS 850). For the Latins the *Filioque* had become dogma. The text goes on to say that the council's assertions represented the true and unwavering view of both Latin and Greek Fathers. Sad to say, that was not the case. Within ten years the council and the union it believed it had achieved were repudiated by the East.

The second — and final — attempt was at Florence, where what the Catholic West regards as the fourteenth ecumenical council met in 1438. This time the eastern contingent was large and representative of the Orthodox Church. As regards the *Filioque*, the debate was intense. Virtually every conceivable angle of the matter was explored. The upshot was an agreement, signed on 6 July 1439, in which it was said that the Latins' 'from the Son' and the Greeks' 'through the Son' meant the same thing (DS 1301). An interesting argument was used to achieve this remarkable conclusion. It went like this: the holy Fathers were protected by the Spirit from teaching error in matters of faith; but Latin Fathers said 'and from the Son', while Greek ones said 'through the Son'; therefore they must mean the same thing. The Greeks accepted the principle of patristic infallibility in matters of faith, and that what was at issue was indeed a matter of faith. When therefore the Latin expert, John of Montenero, produced an array of texts showing that the

Fathers had used both expressions, the Greek delegation came to believe that the two formulae, despite appearances, must be saying the same thing (Gill 1982:230–231).

In fact, of course, as understood by the Latins the *Filioque* was not saying quite the same thing as the East's 'through the Son'. The Greeks interpreted the latter as referring to the Spirit's *energetic* manifestation. The Latins, however, saw the *Filioque* as referring to what for the Greeks was the Spirit's *essential* derivation. Moreover, in its explanation of how the two expressions agreed, the council took the western understanding as the norm. It then interpreted the Greek phrase in the light of the *Filioque* (Congar 1983c:187). When one reads the text one is reading the clear product of a Latin mind, not a true fusion of Greek and Latin theology. It is not surprising then that the Greeks were not very enthusiastic about the union. They did not, as is commonly believed, repudiate it on their return home. But opposition to it began to grow and found general support amongst the people (Gill 1982:349ff.). The official promulgation of the union in the East was delayed until 1452, when the Turks were threatening Constantinople. One year later, when Constantinople fell, the union ended.

It has been argued that the council failed because the Greeks were in various ways forced to reach an agreement. There was no true freedom, it has been said, to agree or disagree. Gill (1982:403ff.) refutes this belief convincingly. He himself lays a major share of the blame for the council's failure at the door of the leader of the Greek theological delegation, Mark Eugenicus (Gill 1982:395ff.). Alone of the leading Greek theologians, he did not accept the Latin position as orthodox and avoided signing the decree. His continued opposition to a council accepted at the time by the Greeks as ecumenical should, says Gill, have been punished. But he was left free to fight vigorously against the union. In Greek eyes, however, he remains one of their most trust-worthy theologians (Orphanos 1981:42). The fact that he was also a strong supporter of Palamas's distinction between the Spirit's essential derivation and energetic manifestation no doubt contributed to his refusal to assert that the Latin and Greek expressions were saying the same thing. It is also worth considering that if Mark was able to drum up support for his opposition, it was because, as Congar put it so well, 'Florence was too great a victory for the Latins — and the papacy — for it to be a full council of union' (1983c:187). There was no real fusion of minds on the topic but rather an agreement of Greeks to Latin ideas.

For Catholics, Florence remains a truly ecumenical council and its teaching of the *Filioque* binding. And I believe that the Latin position is, historically, correct. However, more attention needs to be paid to the heart of Florence's decree. This was not so much the fact that the Spirit proceeded from the Father and the Son as that the two formulae — Latin and Greek — expressed a common faith (see Congar 1983c:186). The theological interpretations of the formulae may differ, but there could be, as Florence believed, a common faith behind both. It is that common faith that needs focusing on — and recent years have seen such developments (see Chapter 7, C (i)). Congar's point is also worth repeating, viz., that the time has perhaps come to cease interpreting the Greek phrase 'through the Son' in the light of the *Filioque*, but rather to take Florence's proclamation of a common faith underlying both seriously enough to do the reverse: interpret the *Filioque* in the light of the Greek phrase. This could help us arrive at the faith we have in common despite differing theological approaches deriving from it.

C.   THE SPIRIT AS LOVE

Augustine's idea of the Spirit as love became common to all great western thinkers of the Middle Ages and beyond. However, it was developed along two major lines, both representing significant departures from Augustine's own thought.

The first line goes back to Anselm of Canterbury (1033–1109). In his *Monologion* (chapters 48–51) he uses Augustine's psychological model of the Trinity (memory, intelligence, love), but adapts it to serve as a true *explanation*, not simply a model, of the origins of the divine persons. Whereas for Augustine it was an image, a reflection of the divine, for Anselm it provided a metaphysical account of what occurred within a 'Supreme Spirit', as he put it (Congar 1983a:85). This Spirit knows itself and the resultant self-knowledge is the Son. It also (now in the dyadic form of Father and Son) loves itself, and the resultant self-love is the Holy Spirit.

What was crucial for Anselm was the *parallel* between the effect of the Supreme Spirit's self-knowledge (an act of self-knowledge) and the effect of its self-love (an act of self-love). Just as the Supreme Spirit produces the Son by an act of self-knowledge, so too does the Supreme Spirit, now existing as Father (or memory) and Son (or intelligence), produce the Holy Spirit by an act of self-love. The love that produces the Spirit is not, therefore, the mutual love of Father and Son. Anselm did not discard the idea of their mutual love. But it played no specific role in his explanation of the existence of the third person. What was crucial to his explanation was the divinity's love of itself, paralleling its knowledge of itself. It was the love Father and Son had for the divine essence, the divine goodness, rather than a mutual love between persons that was for Anselm the source of the Spirit (Bourassa 1970:63–64).

Thomas Aquinas (1225–74) developed Anselm's approach. He too sought an understanding of the Trinity by way of an insight into the very nature of spiritual reality. A spiritual being is one with two basic faculties: intellect and will. The former produces knowledge, the latter love. The Son is the product of an act of divine self-knowledge, the Spirit of an act of divine self-love. Even more than Anselm, Thomas valued the idea of the Spirit as the mutual love of Father and Son. However, for him this could neither explain the origin of, nor be identified with the Spirit. A 'bond' is a connection, something standing between two other realities. As such it is a medium and not an end product or *terminus*, a term (*Summa*, Ia, 37, 1, ad 3). For Thomas the idea of the Spirit as the mutual love of Father and Son was an attractive image. But it could only function as an image, not as a true explanation (see Congar 1983a:90).

Anselm's approach had within it the seeds of a view of the Spirit as the terminus of an act of love, paralleling the terminus of an act of understanding (unlike Thomas, Anselm did not actually distinguish between an act and its terminus — see Congar 1983c:96–97). These seeds came to full fruition in Thomas's work. Just as the divine mind produces a word, the Word, so too does the divine will produce its own term. Thomas admits that we have no way of describing this second term, but it can be regarded as some sort of impression of the loved reality within the lover (*Summa*, Ia, 37, 1, resp.). In this view the Spirit is clearly *not* to be identified with love, but rather with the *fruit* thereof. That fruit is the terminus of an act of love paralleling the mental word, which is the fruit of an act of understanding.

Thomas's theology of the Spirit's procession by way of love not only developed Anselm's line but gave it its final form. It became the typical Thomist approach and as such has been influential in Catholicism down to the present day.

The second major way in which Augustine's thought was developed had its beginnings in the work of Richard of St Victor (d. 1172). More accurately, its origins are traceable to Richard's abbot at St Victor, Achard (d. 1171), to whom the former was directly indebted (see Congar 1983c:103). However, it was through Richard's appropriating of Achard's ideas that this particular approach began its influential life.

Richard's trinitarian starting-point is an attractive one: if God is not only greater but also better than all else, then God must be love, and in a way that exceeds all our created experience thereof. Richard's whole explanation of the Trinity is in terms of love. True to the Augustinian–monastic influence on the Victorines, love predominates. The intellect's role recedes into the background. If there is trinity in God, it is not because Spirit is propelled first to know and then to love itself, but

rather because Spirit — God (Richard is not fond of Anselm's impersonal terms) — is propelled to be love in the fullest possible way.

Now to be that, there must be at least two persons in God (recall that
Richard is the one who corrects Boethius by including relationality in
his definition of a divine person). Love begins by gratuitously being
given to another (see Richard's *On the Trinity*, V, 16). Hence the initial
dyad expresses purely *gratuitous* love (the Father) and received or
indebted (*debitus*) love (the Son). However, love shared by only two is
not yet perfect. Perfect love wishes to flow beyond the intimacy of the
two so as to embrace a third loved by both. Perfect love leads lovers to
turn away from each other so as to share their love with a third. This
third is loved together with their love for each other. Hence Richard's
famous term for the third — the *condilectus* (= 'loved-together-with'; a
'co-beloved'). This third is the Holy Spirit, who is love in a third form:
love that is *purely* received, purely indebted (*debitus*). Congar sum-
marizes Richard's thought well: 'The special way of existing which
characterizes the divine Persons consists in a manner of living and
realizing Love. That Love is either pure grace, or it is received and
giving, or it is purely received' (1983c:105).

As can be seen, despite his stress on love, Richard's thought is rather
different from Augustine's. As for Anselm, so too for Richard, the
Spirit is not the mutual love of Father and Son. The love expressed by
the Spirit is not of two individuals turned to each other, but rather of
two turned to a third. Richard's position is, in that respect, even further
removed from Augustine's idea than Anselm's was, since the Supreme
Spirit's love for its divinity included a love for the two primary
possessors of it (Father and Son). However, it has been argued that
Richard was not entirely closed to the idea of the Spirit as mutual love,
nor that the latter was irreconcilable with the idea of the Spirit as
condilectus (see Congar 1983c:108).

The great Franciscan master, Alexander of Hales (d. 1245), took over
and developed Richard's ideas. He also provided a way of reconciling
Richard's *condilectus* with Augustine's position. Alexander's starting-
point is similar to Richard's, though the former expresses it in the
famous phrase, neo-Platonic in its origins, *bonum est diffusivum sui* —
'goodness is self-diffusive'. Goodness wishes to spread itself around —
what a marvellous start to any theology!

Diffusion takes place in two distinct ways (for the following see
Fortman 1972:211; Congar 1983c:109). The first is by way of nature —
a diffusion whose aim is the total sharing by the beneficiary of all that
goodness is. This occurs in the divinity through an act of knowledge.
The result is an initial dyad. However, the second mode of goodness's
diffusion is also essential to it: by way of affection or love. The relevant

faculty here is the will. Goodness needs to be enjoyed. And such enjoyment demands that its diffusion be the work not of a single individual but of at least two. Hence Father and Son are necessary for the Spirit's procession. This amounts to saying that for goodness's diffusion to be perfect, a point must come where two together produce a third who is beloved by both — a *condilectus*. And so, taking his cue from Richard, Alexander writes that for love to be perfect there must be not only *dilectio* (love) but also *condilectio* (Fortman 1972:212). This *condilectio* is a loving-together and the outcome is love loved, a *condilectus*. By speaking of the *condilectus* as a love loved, Alexander provided a way of reconciling it with Augustine's idea of the Spirit as mutual love.

Alexander's fellow Franciscan and pupil, Bonaventure (1221–74), lays great stress on the idea of the Spirit as mutual love. But he also accepts Richard's idea of the Spirit as *condilectus*, offering a synthesis of the two.

Once again, the starting-point (see Fortman 1972:213ff.) is not the divine faculties but the divine goodness. This goodness must be 'supremely diffusive', which in turn demands that from all eternity the Godhead must have experienced a movement whereby its nature is totally shared (giving rise to the Son) and one whereby its volitional capacities, its ability to love, are fully realized.

The result of the first movement (the distinction of Father and Son) obviously provides the beginnings of the realization of goodness's capacity for love. However, love is incomplete unless lover and beloved pour out their love on a third. It is at this point that the Spirit as mutual love enters the picture. The Spirit proceeds by way of the *mutual love* of Father for Son. Mutual love that does not pour itself out on a third has the imperfection of desire in it, being no longer pure giving (*I Sent.* d 10, a 1, q 1).

Moreover, Bonaventure does not simply see the Spirit as the *fruit* of mutual love (which is easily reconcilable with the idea of a *condilectus*) but as being that mutual love itself (Congar 1983c:111). The reconciliation between the two ideas is, I suspect, to be found in the shift of meaning Alexander gave to *condilectus* ('love loved'). Augustine himself spoke of the Spirit as being love loved (*The Trinity*, VIII, 7, x). It is therefore the subsistent mutual love of Father and Son that is the *condilectus*, the co-beloved, the love-loved. 'Love', in the sense of mutual love, and 'gift' are therefore names proper to the Spirit alone, expressing different aspects of the same reality (Congar 1983c:111; 1983a:88).

The mediaeval theology of the Spirit as love was a specifically western one, and was virtually unknown in the East. Orphanos (1981:27–28) says that Gregory Palamas was the first to make any use of it. Probably the main historical reason was that Augustine moved the

West's mind along the lines of faculties (intellect and will) producing the person, while the East simply thought of the Father as being the source of two different types of coming forth: generation and procession. A further reason may have been the involvement of the Son in the willing process — which supported a *Filioque* position, anathema to the mediaeval Greeks. At any rate, the idea of the Spirit as love enabled the West eventually to provide a meaningful explanation of why the Spirit was not a son, something eastern theology was unable to do.

The key to the solution of this question was in analysing the difference between a procession by way of the will on the one hand, and by way of nature or intellect on the other. The latter two alternatives (nature or intellect) represented two divergent ways of approaching the matter.

The first way can be traced back to Alexander, who spoke of a twofold manner in which goodness communicated itself: by way of nature, and by way of will. The contrast sounds strange to us and is in fact rejected by the other approach which sees will as part of nature. But the point of the contrast was between a procession whose aim was the total sharing in a nature and one whose purpose was liberality, the outpouring of love as such. A production by nature indeed took place through the intellect, but its point was the communication of the divine nature to another. If the point is put that way, one can see immediately the lines of the solution to the problem concerning the Spirit's not being a son. 'Generation' involves the communication to another of one's nature. Therefore the procession by way of nature was a generation. The same approach was adopted by Albert the Great in his *Summa* (but not in his *Commentary on the Sentences* — Fortman 1972:203), by Bonaventure and by Scotus, becoming thereby part of the Scotist or Franciscan stream of theology. Only a procession by way of nature was generation, not one by will.

The second way of resolving the issue was older, going back to Anselm. Its starting point was that Spirit had two faculties: intellect and will. In the divinity the processions are therefore by way of intellect and by way of will. The procession by way of intellect is intrinsically orientated to producing a likeness. Hence it alone deserves the name 'generation', since generation is a process directed to the production of like from like. Over a century before the idea was taken up and refined by Albert and Bonaventure, Anselm observed that the Word, who sprang from the Father's intelligence, bore an obvious likeness to the Father, while love did not of itself display any likeness to the one from whom it sprang (*Monologion*, 55). But Anselm made no real impact on theology until the thirteenth century. Perhaps he was too rationalistic for the twelfth century, even for its nascent scholasticism. At any rate, the significance of his observation was not perceived by that master compiler of theological ideas, Peter Lombard (d. 1160). Peter believed it was impossible for us in this life to distinguish between the generation of the Son and the procession of the Spirit (*IV Sent.*, I, d 13, 3). However, when he wrote his commentary on the *Sentences* Albert certainly saw Anselm's point. He later changed his mind, preferring to speak of a procession by way of nature as being the crucial factor. But he also contributed a valuable item to the final by-way-of-intellect solution in his tackling of the following form of the problem: if the Spirit too is truly God, fully like God, the production of like from like, then why was the Spirit's procession not a generation? Albert's answer was that the Spirit's likeness was a necessary *concomitant* to the Spirit's procession, but not part of the very nature of the procession itself. Unlike that of the Son, the Spirit's procession was not *directed* to producing a likeness (see Fortman 1972:203).

In Albert's pupil, Thomas, all the elements were put together in a consistent synthesis whose intellectual power made it the classic Catholic view (see his *Summa*, Ia, 27, 2 and 4). The Son's procession is a process of generation because he proceeds through an act of divine self-knowledge. It is such because the very purpose of such an act is to produce a likeness of the reality known, and 'generation' is a process directed at the production of like from the substance of like. An act of the will, by contrast, has as its purpose some sort of dynamism or movement. Hence the procession from the divine will produces not a 'son' but a 'spirit', a word that designates a vital movement or impulsion of some kind. The old meaning of 'spirit' had not disappeared entirely!

The Spirit's procession is therefore clearly distinguished now from that of the Son. But what about a name for it? Can one give it a name as illuminating as 'generation'? Thomas says that we cannot, because we have no created analogy for the communication of a nature other than by generation (a 4, ad 3). A procession from the will resulting in a third sharing in the divine nature lacks such an analogy. However, one can use the coined word 'spiration' for such a procession, so as to indicate its inner propulsion towards the production of 'spirit' as distinct from 'son'.

Where exactly the term 'spiration' originated, I do not know. But it did become the customary western term for the procession of the Spirit. It was used by the Council of Florence, which speaks of the Spirit's procession as taking place by means of a single 'spiration' (DS 1300). Henceforth, the West used 'procession' as a general term, generation and spiration being its two distinct types.

The idea of the Spirit as love may have been foreign to Greek theology, but not the idea of the Spirit as the *telos* or completion of the inner divine movements whereby the divine nature was shared by three persons. As with the distinction between the coming-forth of the Son and that of the Spirit, some sort of reason had to be provided for the Spirit's being the completion of those comings-forth. Whether Greek theology had similar difficulties here as it did with the reason for the Spirit not being a son, I do not know. But in the West the idea of the Spirit as love certainly provided an intellectually satisfying answer.

Those who opted for the idea of the Spirit as *condilectus* could argue that a *condilectus* was necessary and sufficient for love or goodness to be perfect, and that of its nature the *condilectus* had to be preceded by a dyad of lover and beloved.

Those who opted for the idea of the Spirit as the terminus of an act of volition paralleling the Word's existence as the terminus of an act of knowledge, could appeal to the fact that a spiritual being had only two faculties, intellect and will. A spiritual movement beginning in knowledge is therefore completed in love.

As to why a second, third, fourth, etc., inner-divine process should not start up, each ending with its Sons and Spirits, various answers were given that need not concern us here. Thomas's answer is worth noting: in God there can be only one perfect Word and one perfect Love, since God knows and loves in one simple eternal act (*Summa*, Ia, 27, 5, ad 3). The salient point, however, was that taking Father, Son and Spirit by themselves, the idea of the Spirit as 'love' provided an explanation for its being the completion of the Trinity.

From all the above, one would think that for the mediaevals love was clearly the Spirit's distinguishing note. However, the matter was not that simple. Love was something all three persons possessed, indeed were. How restrict it to the Spirit, then? Obviously, any answer required defining more closely the sort of love one was talking about. This was precisely what Bonaventure and Aquinas, to quote only the two leading thirteenth-century theologians, did.

Both distinguished between love as an aspect of the divine essence, and love as unique to the Spirit. For Bonaventure, the latter love was unique because it was the expression of the mutual love of Father and Son (*I Sent.*, d 10, a 2, q 1; see Congar 1983c:111). Only the Spirit can be *that* love. Aquinas, on the other hand, using his parallel between acts of knowledge and acts of love, saw the love proper to the Spirit as residing in the hypostasized *terminus* of an act of divine love (*Summa*, Ia, 37, 1). Just as the divine mind produces a Word, and just as that *Word* (but not the ability to know) is proper to the Son alone (indeed is the Son); so too the divine will produces a Love (Thomas does not use the word like that, confessing a lack of vocabulary at this point), which *Love* (and not the divine ability to love) is proper to the Spirit alone (indeed is the Spirit).

D. THE DOCTRINE OF APPROPRIATIONS

The issue as to whether love was distinctive to the Spirit was closely related to another one: the matter of appropriations. The former issue concerned the inner-divine life. The latter concerned the relationship between the divine persons and creation.

Augustine's saying that everything done by the divinity *ad extra* (i.e., that had an effect outside the Godhead) was done by all three persons led in mediaeval times to an extensive scholastic theology of 'appropriations'. As was mentioned before, an 'appropriation' is the attribution of a function or attribute to one divine person rather than another for reasons of fittingness, appropriateness, even though the function or attribute was performed or shared equally by all. Thus 'creation' may be appropriate to the Father because of his position as ultimate source. The basis of an appropriation is a similarity between what is appropriated and what is distinctive of the person to whom it is appropriated. Aquinas therefore held that the purpose of appropriations was to manifest each person's distinctive characteristics, to make them stand out in clearer relief (*Summa*, Ia, 39, 7).

The doctrine of appropriations represented the suppression of the older biblical tradition, preserved by the East, that each of the persons has a distinctive role to play in our lives. It therefore also suppressed the idea that every Christian had a distinct relationship to each of the divine persons. The descent of the Spirit at Pentecost, the Spirit's indwelling, gifts, and sanctifying activity — all were now regarded as simply appropriated to the Spirit, since all three persons were involved in each case. That all three were involved was of course true. But the fact that each person was active in a distinctive way was lost sight of.

E. THE SPIRIT'S WORK WITHIN BELIEVERS

The doctrine of appropriations did not mean that the mediaeval scholastics ceased to speak about the Spirit's activity in the lives of believers. Far from it, even if in theory all such activities were merely appropriated to the Spirit. The logical starting-point of theological reflection on this matter was the idea of a divine 'mission'. 'Mission' means 'a sending'. A divine 'mission' therefore referred to the sending of a divine person. The Father sends the Son, while both Father and Son send the

Spirit to us. The use of the word *missio* to describe the sending of Son and Spirit to us was a very old one, going back at least to Augustine's time. By the thirteenth century, the divine 'missions' became a theme on its own, in which theologians analysed what a divine mission was, how it took place, what the conditions for it to occur were, and so forth.

Two missions were distinguished. The first was the *visible* mission, which I suspect was the older meaning of the term (see Michel 1950:1839). It referred to visible manifestations of the persons such as the Son's incarnation or the Spirit's descent in visible form (dove, tongues of fire, e.g.). The second kind of mission was called an *invisible* one, and it referred to the sending of a person into a believer's soul, resulting in the divine person dwelling there. Of course, it was realized that all three persons dwelt in the souls of the just. However, of those three only two were said to be sent.

The reason Thomas gave for this is interesting (*Summa*, Ia, 43, 5, resp.): since the Son and Spirit are not without origin, their presence within us is a presence reflecting their respective origins. Therefore their presence is always a 'sent' presence in the sense that it is a presence reflecting a coming-forth from someone. For this reason not only the Spirit but also the Son can be said to be sent invisibly. What is interesting about Thomas's observation is that he is appealing to a very important principle here: a divine person's origins stamp the way that person is present. This in fact provided a way out of reducing the indwelling of the Spirit to mere appropriation. However, the opportunity was not grasped. Perhaps one reason was that not all agreed that a mission revealed the person's origins. Some believed, for example, that the Son could send himself or even be sent by the Spirit (see Aquinas, *Summa*, Ia, 43, 4, resp.).

At any rate, all agreed that the invisible mission of the Spirit was to dwell within the souls of the just and sanctify them. The technicalities of sanctification debated by the mediaevals need not concern us here. However, one technicality is worth noting, since it bears directly on the Spirit's character as love. The issue was the relationship between a believer's love and the presence of the Spirit (see Landgraf 1952:220–237).

Peter Lombard is usually credited with having launched this particular debate, though it was already in the air when he wrote his *Sentences* (Landgraf 1952:225). At any rate, he asserted that the Spirit was the love with which we loved God and neighbour. Many viewed the acts of faith, hope and love as flowing from created effects within our souls. Such effects came to be called the 'infused virtues' of faith, hope and love. They were conceived of as powers, principles of supernatural actions, enabling Christians to believe, hope, and love as Jesus wished them to do. Peter Lombard's point was that while the above was true of faith and hope, it was not true of love. What enabled Christians to love was not any created 'virtue' but the uncreated Spirit of God dwelling in their souls. It was the Spirit, and no such 'virtue', that was the immediate source of our ability to love. To justify his position he appealed to texts like Rom 5:5, which spoke of the love of God being poured into our hearts by the Holy Spirit who had been given us.

A lively debate ensued. However, despite its attractiveness, Peter Lombard's position did not find a very wide following. It was eventually abandoned by all. One major objection was that, if taken seriously, it led to the idea that there was no distinction between the Spirit and sanctifying grace (this latter is the transformation of the believer's soul that was seen as part of justification; what the Greeks called the soul's divinization). The distinction between grace and the Spirit was defended strongly by the followers of Gilbert of Poitiers, and won the day against the Lombard.

From a technical point of view, Peter Lombard may have been wrong. But the close bond he forged between the Spirit's presence and our own ability to love was important. One example of how fruitful the idea of such a bond can be is to be found in William of St Thierry. Like Peter, William was a twelfth-century theologian, but he lived earlier than Peter, and also belonged to quite a different school of theology, what has come to be called 'monastic theology'. This was a way of doing theology that laid great stress on spiritual experience, on the symbols for expressing it, and the divine realities involved in it. Within that perspective, what brought insight was not intellectual analysis but love. Love conformed the soul to the divine and as a result enabled it to understand the divine so much the better.

William placed tremendous emphasis on love's epistemological role as regards the divine. Love enabled one to know divine realities. Moreover, he linked that idea to the Spirit's presence within the believer in quite an original and thought-provoking way (see his *Letter to the Brethren*, I, xiv). For William, the believer's love is so transformed by the Spirit's presence that the two loves — that of the soul and that which is the Spirit — become virtually one love. The result is that the soul actually becomes one with the Spirit in uniting Father and Son to each other. Transformed by the Spirit, the soul's love *becomes part of the love uniting Father and Son*. A closer sharing in the divine life by the believer cannot be imagined (see also Malevez 1932:200–201). And the resultant insight into the things of God is appropriately greater.

William represented a tradition of theologizing closely linked to mystical experience. This contrasted sharply with scholasticism. A monastic theologian analysed experiential realities, a scholastic analysed concepts. The contrast was not always as sharp as that. The great scholastics were also mystics in their own right, and conceptual analysis was by no means foreign to some practitioners of a monastic type of theology (e.g., Hugh and Richard of St Victor). But the two ways of theologizing were of themselves very different. As it turned out, it was the academic, scholastic form of theology that became the norm. As a result mystical experience ceased to be part of theology and mystics tended to retreat into a rather anti-theological attitude. Theology came to be seen by mystics as a presumptuous and irrelevant rational analysis of divine realities. This break began to show from the fourteenth century onwards (see Vandenbroucke 1950). It was, in effect, the beginnings of a break between the Spirit and what came to be seen by many as an excessive institutionalization of the Spirit. Scholastic theology was institutionalized theology. But that is another story.

Let me turn now instead to the mediaeval development of a theology of the gifts of the Spirit. The gifts in question were not those listed in 1 Cor 12:8–10 (which do not seem to have evoked much interest at the time) but rather those drawn from Is 11:2. As translated by the old Latin Vulgate (which added to the original Hebrew list 'piety' as a one-word repetition of 'fear of the Lord'), there were seven of them: wisdom, understanding, counsel, fortitude, knowledge, fear of the Lord, piety. These were what not only the mediaevals but also the Latin and Greek Fathers usually had in mind when speaking of the Spirit's gifts to us (Bardy 1957:1579). The number seven, of course, took on immense symbolism, indicating fullness, perfection. Augustine therefore spoke of the Spirit's 'sevenfold work', Gregory the Great (d. 604) of the 'septiform Spirit' (Gardeil 1911:1763–1766). This 'septiform' idea was enshrined in the famous ninth-century hymn, *Veni Creator Spiritus* ('Come, Holy Ghost, Creator, come'). There the Spirit is addressed as 'thou who art sevenfold in thy grace'.

Systematic thinking on these gifts began only in mediaeval times. Indeed, relatively little is to be found about them in the western Fathers, and almost nothing in the eastern ones (Kenny 1967:319). The early scholastics (i.e., up to the thirteenth century) limited themselves for the most part to investigating the nature of the gifts and their relationship to the cardinal virtues of prudence, justice, fortitude and temperance (Gardeil 1911:1771). Were the gifts the same as the virtues or distinct from them? Prior to 1230 the common, though not unanimous, opinion was that the two were the same (Lottin 1949:455). However, a changed occurred in Paris at about 1235, when Philip the Chancellor began to argue for a distinction between the gifts and the virtues, and the superiority of the former over the latter. The matter was not purely academic: it was tied to a theology of the spiritual progress of the soul which distinguished three stages in the latter, the stages of virtues, gifts and beatitudes. Philip's viewpoint became the one accepted by all the great Paris masters of the thirteenth century, including therefore Albert, Bonaventure, and Thomas Aquinas. The gifts of the Spirit were superior in that they enabled the cardinal virtues to be exercised more easily (Lottin 1949:456).

Aquinas's own position was that the gifts of the Spirit were the infusion into the soul by God of permanent dispositions, enabling it to be more receptive to the Spirit. Even when viewed as supernatural gifts from God, the four cardinal virtues (prudence, justice, fortitude and temperance) do not have such a specific aim. Nor do the three 'theological' virtues of faith, hope and love. The gifts are distinct therefore from both. They are, moreover, superior to the cardinal virtues, which have earthly conduct in view, but inferior to the theological, which have the knowledge and love of God as their object and which form, as it were, the root of the gifts (Lottin 1954:669–670; see *Summa*, Ia IIae, 68).

This position was fairly influential for a period following Thomas's death, even though his followers quietly dropped the idea that the gifts were derived from the theological virtues (Vandenbroucke 1957:1595). For the next three centuries, however, his views on this as on other issues did not command widespread interest. The dominant scholastic school for that period was the Scotist one. Scotus himself denied any distinction between the gifts and the virtues, seeing the former as an unnecessary addition to the latter, which were quite sufficient to enable us to live Christian lives (Vandenbroucke 1957:1594). The dislike for unnecessary distinctions in this matter was endorsed, as can be imagined, by nominalists such as William of Ockham (d. 1347) and Gabriel Biel (d. 1495; Gardeil 1911:1777–1778).

As noted above, the doctrine of seven *distinct* infused gifts was introduced as part of a broader scheme, one touching on the progress of the soul towards God. Yet, strange to say, the doctrine of the gifts was never a major point of interest with the mystics, the 'spirituals' of the fourteenth to the sixteenth centuries. What little interest there was was understandably concentrated on the two gifts most closely associated with contemplation: wisdom and understanding (Vandenbroucke 1957:1596–1603). Indeed, the only period when any really intense interest was shown in the matter was the thirteenth century. The same lack of general interest continued right up to the nineteenth century, though the Thomist school did produce a major work on the topic by John of St Thomas (1589–1644). In 1897 Pope Leo XIII issued an encyclical on the Holy Spirit, *Divinum Illud Munus*, in which the

Thomist position on the gifts was set forth. A revival of interest in the gifts ensued, with the Thomist position dominating. The interest lasted almost down to our own day, when there has been a shift of attention to what was traditionally called the 'charisms'.

'Charisms' was the term used for the list of gifts taken from 1 Cor 12:8–10. There is very little evidence of interest in these after the influence of Montanism died out. People generally assumed they had been given to help set the Church on its feet and then withdrawn. Detailed research on the history of Christian ideas concerning these gifts is still lacking. However, indications are that they did not disappear entirely. Two obvious cases of their continuance were miracles (the mediaevals were fascinated by the miraculous) and prophecy (see Congar 1983a:121–122). Even glossolalia (the gift of tongues) was not unknown, but since such utterances were seen as a manifestation of diabolical possession it is not surprising one does not hear of many claimants to the gift (Kelsey 1981:46).

In the mediaeval period these gifts or 'charisms' were known by the scholastics as *gratiae gratis datae*, 'graces freely given' (see Mt 10:8). As such they were distinguished from graces given to sanctify a person (*gratiae gratum facientes*). There was a strong tendency to focus on the recipient of these *gratiae gratis datae* (which were also seen as embracing more than just the list of charisms in 1 Cor 12). However, Aquinas stressed the element of service to others in them: they are given to serve others, especially the sanctification of others, and above all to build up the Church, which is a particular concern of the Spirit (see *Summa*, IIa IIae, 177, 1, resp.). Thomas's treatment of this matter too became commonplace in nineteenth- and twentieth-century manuals of Catholic theology. However, while the idea of their being given as a service to others was maintained, the explicit link with the Church was forgotten (on this see Bovis 1967:754–756).

I would like to complete this section on the Spirit's work within the individual with a brief reference to the sacrament of confirmation. This sacrament is the only one whose direct purpose is described as being the imparting of the Spirit. The sacrament has a most interesting history (see Neunheuser 1982 and the brief summary in Küng 1974). Originally confirmation was not a separate sacrament from baptism. It developed as such in the West from the post-baptismal anointings and layings-on of hands that were part of the original undivided rite of initiation. It was associated with a prayer for imparting the Spirit as God's gift to the newly baptized. With the spread of Christianity in the West and the danger of infants dying unbaptized (a serious matter for those influenced by Augustine's doctrine of original sin), the practice arose of the priest baptizing the baby and leaving to the bishop on his rounds the ceremonies associated with imparting the Spirit. This delay, however, now caused a problem that did not exist when there was but one ceremony with two aspects (washing away sin/imparting the Spirit). Two clearly separated ceremonies raised the problem of the reason for imparting the Spirit to someone who had already been baptized. If the Spirit is given in baptism (as all believed was the case), what is the purpose of this second giving of the Spirit? Faustus of Riez (d. *c.* 490) is credited with providing the answer: the Spirit is given in the second ceremony *ad robur*, that is to say, to strengthen the Christian for battle against the forces of evil (which is where the idea of confirmation as making one a soldier of Christ comes from).

Peter Lombard reflected Faustus's view by remarking that whereas in baptism the Spirit is given for the remission of sins, in confirmation the Spirit comes to strengthen us, to enable us to perform power-filled deeds. Through the Lombard's work this idea entered into scholastic theology. Aquinas, for example, spoke of confirmation as enabling the recipient to conduct spiritual battles against the enemies of the faith (*Summa*, IIIa, 72, 5, resp.). This links up with the Pentecostal event, since those who are able to fight for the faith can witness to it as the apostles did after Pentecost. Thomas also added the idea that confirmation made one spiritually an adult, comparing baptism and confirmation to birth and growth into adulthood (*Summa*, IIIa, 72, 2, resp.). His theology of confirmation became the traditional one within Catholicism.

F. THE SPIRIT AND THE CHURCH

The Spirit and the Church covers so much that I must severely limit my treatment of the theme. I wish in fact to deal with one issue only: the institutionalization of the Spirit that occurred at this time, and the reaction it evoked.

The mediaevals inherited a tradition that linked Spirit and Church to each other in an unbreakable bond. On the one hand, the Church was a Spirit-filled reality. It was this Spirit that filled the Church's sacraments with divine life, and guided it into all truth, protecting it from mistaking error for God's truth. The Church was the *Spirit's* Church. On the other hand, the Spirit was the *Church's* Spirit. Individuals shared in the Spirit because they shared in the Church, not the reverse.

The contours of this tradition had been clearly delineated by Augustine in his fight with the Donatists. The latter linked the Spirit far too much to individuals, making the Church and its sacraments dependent on their holiness. Augustine insisted on the Church's holiness as a source, and not the result, of the holiness of its members, since the Spirit operated through the Church. There is already present here what one might call an 'institutionalizing' of the Spirit. However, the Church was seen primarily as community and the Spirit's work within it as fostering its saving unity.

The mediaevals inherited Augustine's ideas and accepted them fully. However, a subtle change occurred. It was a change in ecclesiology that resulted in a changed way of viewing the Spirit's activity. This was caused by basically two, connected, factors. The first was the battles that began to be fought (from the eleventh century onwards) between ecclesiastical and secular authorities over their respective powers. The second was the canonical studies that mushroomed as part of the systematized institutionalization of Church structures and defence of Church rights and powers. The result was an obscuring of the idea of the Church as a Spirit-filled *communio*, a community whose unity, sacraments and consensus in faith are guaranteed primarily by the Spirit. Instead, it was now conceived of in the first instance as a legal body (see Oakley 1979:163), a legal structure, a clearly defined society structured along legal lines.

This meant that the Church's unity, consensus in faith, and sacraments were no longer seen as resulting above all from the Spirit's work. Instead, legal structures were seen as the immediate source of such effects. The Church's unity was brought about by adherence to legal structures. The validity of the sacraments was ensured in the first instance by performing the essentials of the ritual. The legality of a council becomes all-important in ascertaining whether it can be recognized as valid and its consensus a true expression of the Church's faith. In all this the Spirit was not replaced by law, but continued to be seen as functioning in Church and sacraments and councils. However, the legal structures became the primary *guarantor* of the spiritual reality. The Spirit became almost a servant of the structures, being there to give them spiritual content. There is a slight hint of this already in Aquinas, who linked the Greeks' rejection of papal supremacy to their rejection of the *Filioque*. Since the Spirit proceeds from the Son, the Spirit is at the service of the *Son's* Church, which is the one under the papacy. As Congar comments, there is here an idea that to deny the *Filioque* is to deny the Spirit's total dependence on the Son and therefore to grant the Spirit a certain degree of independence of external structures (Congar 1968:374).

The picture I have described may be a trifle exaggerated. No one I know of actually spoke as if the Spirit were at the command of structures. But the general mentality moved undeniably in that direction. It was, moreover, a mentality that gave the Church and its structures divine sanction, an ability to transmit divine life, and an ability to appeal to divine prevention from error despite the widespread corruption and political wheeling and dealing of the higher clergy. Where, so it seemed to many, was the Spirit of God in that? And so counter-movements began, movements that played down the institutional and stressed the role of the Spirit within the individual. The movements took many forms, from a safe mysticism that simply let the corrupt ecclesiastical world go by, to a perilous challenging of the *status quo* by people passionate for reform but far too radical in their ideas. These people formed the group of mediaeval heretics who, despite their various differences, all rejected the growing institutionalization of Christianity. As a counterweight, they stressed the individual's personal relationship to God, right to private judgement, and lack of dependence on the sacraments (see Leff 1967:8). The inspiration of the Spirit was appealed to as the sole or ultimate authority, justifying ideas and practices contradicting the traditional institutionalized ones.

The most bizarre expression of this mentality was the 'Free Spirit' movement. Known as 'The Brethren of the Free Spirit', the phenomenon was more of a movement than a clearly defined sect. Its adherents were pantheists of a kind. Their basic standpoint was that by becoming one with God, one with the divine spirit, they were free of all restraint (see Leff 1967:308ff.). This included freedom from moral (especially sexual) laws and even from the need to be a follower of Christ. Here the break between the Spirit and Christ is complete. The 'spirit' they appealed to seems to have meant the divine spirit in the sense of divinity, rather than the Holy Spirit specifically. But they did represent the lunatic fringe of the trend that would give greater freedom to the Spirit, and some did identify the Free Spirit with the Holy Spirit (see Leff 1967:313, 328; Lécuyer 1957:1489–1490).

The Free Spirit group had a libertine element in it that contrasted with other movements whose asceticism bore witness to their sincere desire for holiness. However, it was one with the others in stressing the authority given to the individual through her or his possession of the Spirit, an authority that in one way or another was a threat to the institution's claim to possess the Spirit. For these movements, the real Church was a spiritual one. This did not necessarily imply the absence of visible form, but the form was secondary to the Spirit's inspiring and sanctifying activity. Such a Church was seen by many as a Church 'of the Holy Spirit, destined to succeed an outworn dispensation' (Knox 1950:110).

The reference to an 'outworn dispensation' reflects the ideas of Joachim of Fiore (d. 1202). Joachim divided history into three ages, each bearing the stamp of a different person of the Trinity. The first age lasted to the end of the Old Testament period and was the age of the Father. It was characterized by law, fear, and the marital state. The second age was the New Testament one, which for Joachim was still in existence at the time he wrote. It was the age of the Son and was characterized by grace, faith, obedience and (celibate) clergy. Joachim believed that this second age would cease in 1260 and be succeeded by the third and final age: that of the Holy Spirit. It would be characterized by love, obedience and contemplative monks. They would convert the world and usher in the Spiritual Church, one with sacraments and hierarchy but of a far more spiritualized, less institutionalized form (Congar 1983a:127).

Some years after his death, Joachim's writings became very influential. They reflect an attitude that breaks the close bond forged hitherto between the Spirit and Christ. Bonaventure criticized him for this, emphasizing that the time of the Spirit *was* the time of Christ. There could be no time of the former distinct from the latter (Congar 1983a:127).

Joachim's theory of three ages was also reflected in a trinitarian theory that amounted to tritheism: the three persons were three distinct, though utterly alike, substances (Fortman 1972:198–199). Of course, he did not really wish to be a tritheist — only to stress the distinction of persons. But it is interesting that his desire to defend the distinction is so strong that he was prepared to use tritheist language. Aquinas regarded him as a theological dolt (Congar 1983a:127). The Fourth Lateran Council condemned him. But his age of the Spirit and all it represented for those disenchanted with the Church's excessive institutionalization lived on in the dreams, hopes and idea of countless generations. Congar traces his influence down to Hegel and beyond (1983a:129–133).

From the twelfth century on, then, a new direction is visible, one that began increasingly to appeal to the Spirit *against* a highly institutionalized Church and its rather mechanically administered sacraments. The movement was, in effect, one that sought to allow freer rein to the Spirit, loosening the close links that had been forged between the Spirit and institutional structures. During mediaeval times the movement was persecuted and repressed in many of its forms. The Reformation, however, was to provide a soil within which it could grow and flourish and make its necessary contribution to a Christianity that had indeed become too enslaved to institutions and traditions.

QUESTIONS

Check questions

1 What was Boethius's famous definition of person?
2 What were its drawbacks?
3 How did Richard of St Victor improve on it?
4 In what form did the old problem of three distinct persons who were nevertheless fully divine, surface again?
5 What solution did Thomas Aquinas offer to this newly formulated problem?
6 When was the *Filioque* added to the creed by the Pope, and why?
7 Who raised the *Filioque* to a point of open controversy between East and West?
8 What were the arguments he levelled against it? What argument touched on the heart of the issue?
9 What were the West's counter-arguments? What was regarded by it as its clinching argument? Who in the West rejected that supposedly clinching argument?
10 What was Gregory Palamas's nuanced version of earlier Greek ideas on the role played by the Son as regards the Spirit's procession?
11 How did the Council of Florence resolve the *Filioque* issue?
12 How and why did the agreement fail?
13 What were the two major lines along which Augustine's idea of the Spirit as love developed?
14 How did the idea of the Spirit as love enable the West to offer a meaningful solution to the question as to why the Spirit was not a 'son'?
15 How did the idea of the Spirit as love provide an explanation for the Spirit being the *telos* or completion of the divine processions?
16 How was love regarded as proper to the Spirit alone?
17 What was the doctrine of appropriations that developed in mediaeval times? What was the basis for particular appropriations and what did Aquinas see as their purpose?
18 What distortions did the doctrine cause?
19 What was a divine 'mission' for the mediaevals and how many 'missions' did they distinguish?
20 What was regarded as the invisible mission of the Spirit?
21 What were the main points at issue in the debate about the relationship between a believer's love and the presence of the Spirit? Which view became the accepted one? What was valuable in the abandoned one?
22 What did the mediaevals understand by 'the gifts of the Spirit'?
23 What did Thomas Aquinas see as the purpose of those gifts?
24 What was the term used for gifts such as those mentioned by Paul in 1 Cor 12? What sort of 'graces' were they described as being? What was believed to be their purpose?
25 What are the origins in the West of the sacrament of confirmation? Where does the idea of the Spirit being given in it *ad robur* come from? What final touches did Aquinas give to this idea?
26 In what way was Augustine's close link between Spirit and Church reinforced by the mediaevals? Why can the result be called an 'institutionalization' of the Spirit?
27 What reaction did this 'institutionalization' of the Spirit evoke?
28 Describe the essentials of Joachim of Fiore's idea of three ages.

Discussion question

How can one reconcile the Spirit's freedom and lordship with the fact that the Spirit is linked to what must always have institutional structures?

RECOMMENDED READING

The only work I know of devoted to the doctrine of the Spirit in the Middle Ages is H. Watkin-Jones, *The Holy Spirit in the Mediaeval Church* (London: Epworth, 1922). Unfortunately, I have been unable to consult it myself, and so cannot comment on its contents. The relevant sections of Congar 1983a (pp. 85–137) and 1983c (pp 49–71; 79–127) can be consulted with profit. They cover in some depth the following: the *Filioque*, the Spirit as love, Joachim of Fiore's ideas.

On the Council of Florence, Gill 1982 remains essential reading for anyone who wants a reasonably thorough knowledge of it. He has, however, provided a good summary of his findings in his article 'Florence, Council of' in *The New Catholic Encyclopedia* (New York: McGraw-Hill, 1967, vol. V).

The interested reader can also consult Thomas Aquinas's treatment of the Spirit in any one of the many available translations of the *Summa theologiae*. His views on divine persons are in Ia, qq. 29, 39–43; on the Spirit as such, Ia, qq. 36–38; and on the gifts of the Spirit, Ia IIae, q. 68.

On confirmation see Küng 1974 and Neunheuser 1964.

On Joachim of Fiore, see M. Reeves, *The Influence of Prophecy in the Later Middle Ages* (London: Oxford University Press, 1969).

6

Luther to the present century

This, the final chapter of the historical section, covers the period extending from Luther to the present century. The emphasis here will be not only on the West, but on the Protestant West, as it is there that the most significant developments occurred.

A. MARTIN LUTHER (1483–1546)

Luther marks a definitive break with many of the beliefs that had by this time become traditional within the Church. However, we are only interested in his view of the Spirit, which was very traditional in many respects. The main break made with the past here concerns the traditional relationship between the Spirit and the Church — and even that break was by no means a novelty, if one remembers the movements mentioned towards the end of the preceding chapter.

As regards the person of the Spirit (for much of what follows see Lienhard 1965), Luther adds nothing to what has already been said and agreed upon in the western Church. Thus, he affirms that the Spirit is God, and yet a distinct person, the third in the Trinity (though some have claimed to have found traces of modalism in his writings). However, he does give his own twist to the traditional argument that the Spirit's role in salvation implies the Spirit's divinity. The traditional argument was that only the Spirit can *divinize* us. Luther, in line with his emphasis on the role of faith in our salvation and his rejection of any idea of an inner divine quality bestowed on us, argues that since scripture evidently demands we have faith and confidence in the Spirit, and since we can have faith and confidence only in God, the Spirit must be God too. Luther therefore also agrees with the now traditional practice of addressing prayers to the Holy Spirit. As regards the use of the term 'person' for the members of the Trinity, Luther uses it and, like the tradition preceding him, gives it a special meaning. He also seems to accept the mediaeval identification of person and divine relation (e.g., the relation of paternity is what makes the Father a person). Luther also accepts the traditional appropriation of power to the Father, wisdom to the Son, and goodness to the Spirit. True to his stress on justification by faith, he teaches that it is this divine power, wisdom and goodness that is our justification — not any inner quality that the mediaevals claimed was produced in the soul by the Spirit's presence. Luther also accepted the traditional doctrine that all divine activities *ad extra* were performed by all three persons. He accepted the western doctrine of the *Filioque* and subscribed to the argument that the Son's sending of the Spirit was but the sign of the immanent procession of the Spirit from the Son.

He does not add anything very new, therefore, to the older ideas concerning the person of the Spirit. However, he does try to make sure that whatever he says on the subject is firmly rooted in scripture. In his view, anything else is useless speculation regarding a mystery that transcends our powers of comprehension.

As regards the Spirit's work, here too there is much that is traditional in the roles he assigns to the Spirit. Thus, the Spirit is the one who gives us the gift of faith, who interprets the scriptures for us, who sanctifies us, and who maintains the unity of the Church. However, Luther saw himself as differing radically from traditional, especially mediaeval, ideas about faith, about the way in which scripture was interpreted by the Spirit, about sanctification, and about how the Church's unity was preserved. All these differences imply a break with the sort of relationship between the Spirit and the Church that I described earlier as an 'institutionalization' of the former. Luther wished to eradicate any idea that the Spirit could be made present simply by the decision of a council or a Pope (hence his rejection of the infallibility of councils or Popes, as well as of the idea that scripture *must* be interpreted by the agreed tradition of the Church), or by performing the correct sacramental ritual (hence his rejection of Catholicism's sacramental practice on the grounds of its being superstitious 'magic'). Nor was the Spirit, Luther insisted, a reality that God could be forced to give us in return for whatever good works we may have performed (Luther believed that such a distortion was Catholic teaching). Hence he insisted on justification by faith alone, and on the fact that good works were the *fruit*, and not the cause, of the Spirit's presence.

But hardly had he broken with this 'institutionalization' of the Spirit than he found himself plagued with the sort of situation that had contributed in the past to its development. A group of Christians appeared on the scene who claimed to be led directly by the Spirit. Luther had appealed to the sovereignty and freedom of the Spirit to justify his own rejection of the traditional position that Church and

Spirit cannot be separated. He had insisted that the Church could cease to be the true Church of Christ, in which case the Spirit would raise up a community of true believers. This community would then be the true Church, even if it were now visibly quite separate from the old one, the one that used to be the Church. For it was the Spirit that created the Church's presence — not the Church that created the Spirit's presence. The Church and the Spirit could not be separated. But it was the Spirit that showed us where the true Church was, not the Church that showed us where the Spirit was truly present.

Luther appealed, then, to the sovereign freedom of the Spirit. But his appeal led to an outbreak of Spirit-orientated movements of the kind that had been surfacing here and there ever since the days of Joachim of Fiore. These 'Enthusiasts', as they were called, thought Luther had not gone far enough in his reform, since he had retained certain institutional structures such as the ordained ministry and the sacraments. The Enthusiasts felt that these institutional structures were not really necessary. The Spirit guided people directly. That and the Bible were sufficient.

Luther's reaction was one of violent rejection of the Enthusiasts and their ideas. However, their appearance on the scene forced him to clarify his standpoint regarding the Spirit and the institutional side of the Church. The Spirit was, he agreed, never trapped in external things like scripture or the sacraments. In other words, the Spirit cannot be institutionalized in such a way that certain structures can *force* the Spirit to be present. However, *de facto* the Spirit always comes to us *through* institutional structures such as scripture and the sacraments. The Enthusiasts, Luther said, wanted to have the Spirit apart from these institutional realities. However (he writes) 'God acts towards us in a twofold way: exteriorly and interiorly. Exteriorly, he acts through the spoken Word of the Gospel and the corporeal signs of Baptism and the Sacrament. Interiorly, he acts within us by the Holy Spirit and by faith as well as by other gifts. But all this takes place in the following order: the external realities must precede the others; the internal realities follow and come through the external ones, because he has decided not to give anyone the internal realities without the external ones' (*Werke*, Weimar edition, 18, 136, 9ff.). The Enthusiasts, he says, inverted that order.

Luther's argument here is substantially the same as the age-old one of the Fathers: the Spirit and Christ, and therefore the Spirit and his Body, cannot be separated. The Spirit witnesses to Christ's message — and that message is contained in scripture. The Spirit builds up Christ's Body — and the signs of sharing in Christ's salvation and therefore of belonging to his Body are the sacraments. In fact Luther stresses not only that the Spirit must be sought through the mediation of these external realities, but also that the Spirit will certainly be there for those who have faith. His position here is very similar to the traditional Catholic one. He himself would distinguish it from the latter by insisting that the Spirit is present only to faith, a faith that the Spirit itself creates through the media of Word and Sacraments. Catholic doctrine, Luther would say, is that the Spirit is present in the sacraments *apart from* and *prior* to the recipient's faith. There is some truth in this description of Catholic belief. However, the whole point of such a belief was to stress something Luther wished to underscore: the fact that the Spirit's presence in the sacraments was not dependent on us, even on our faith.

B.   JOHN CALVIN (1509–64)

Calvin has justly been called a theologian of the Holy Spirit. Claims have been made that it was only with the Reformation that the true biblical doctrine of the Spirit was rediscovered (see Quistorp 1964:3, to whom I am also heavily indebted for this section). Such claims are extravagant. However, it remains true that with Calvin there is a rediscovery — in the West at any rate — of a biblical idea virtually forgotten since patristic times. It is the idea of the Spirit as God in action.

Calvin, too, accepts all the important traditional beliefs about the Spirit. Thus, he accepts that the Spirit is the third person of a divine Trinity. He defends this truth vehemently against Michael Servetus, who denied the doctrine of the Trinity. Like Augustine, Calvin is not too happy with the word 'person', because it was open to misunderstanding. He believes that 'hypostasis' is less open to misunderstanding. Like Basil, he understands by this a mode of being, a mode of existing. He also accepts the traditional western belief in the *Filioque*. In fact, the *Filioque* plays an important role in this theology of the Spirit. Finally, he also accepts the traditional western idea of the Spirit as the link between Father and Son, and the unity of all divine activities *ad extra*.

Calvin therefore stands firmly within the traditional western theology of the Spirit. However, he injects a long-forgotten life into that theology by his emphasis on the old biblical idea of the Spirit as God in action. His emphasis on this can be seen at once from the fact that for him *the* characteristic of the Spirit is energy and efficacy of action, and not simply 'goodness' or 'love'. The distinctive characteristics of each of the divine persons are for him as follows: the Father has the characteristic of a source, the source of all action, the Son has the characteristic of wisdom, arranging all action wisely; the Spirit has the characteristic of being the power, the source of the efficacy of action (*Institutes*, I, 13, 18). Moreover, the Spirit's action is totally at the service of Father and Son. The Spirit's role, in fact, is simply to be 'the hand of God' (*Institutes*, III, 1, 3). The special role of the Spirit is not to do something independent, then, but to be the means whereby the work of Father and Son is achieved. The Spirit is quite clearly for Calvin the Spirit of both Father and Son.

As the Father's, the Spirit is the means whereby the world was created. The Spirit's role in creation is important for Calvin. Quoting Ps 104:30, he sees the constant presence of the Spirit to the world as being absolutely necessary for its continued existence. Calvin, therefore, does not limit the Spirit's activity to Christians as Origen did. Rather, he attributes to the Spirit a cosmic activity: the creation and preservation of the cosmos. It is this same Spirit that will lead the cosmos to its final fulfilment, the new creation. It is not surprising that Calvin often uses 'Spirit' and 'God's providence' synonymously.

Humanity is the special work of the Spirit. Despite its fall we can see something of the gifts of the Spirit to it in its social, cultural and political achievements. These are 'blessings of the Spirit who, for the common good of humanity, dispenses them to whomsoever he pleases' (*Institutes*, II, 2, 16). Calvin seems to take very seriously indeed the Spirit's direct action in the world, so seriously that he regards the inequalities amongst people as deriving from the different gifts given them by the Spirit.

However, the whole point of the Spirit continuing to be present to creation is so that humanity and its world may benefit from salvation. The Spirit is also Christ's Spirit. As eternal Word, Christ created the world through the Spirit. Moreover, as eternal Word, Christ continues to preserve the world in existence. The incarnation is in no way an interruption of that work. The same Christ is both conserver and saviour. As such he sends out the Spirit not simply as the world's conserver, but also as the one who brings salvation to people. This the Spirit does by uniting people to Christ in the closest imaginable way, so closely that we are slowly but surely transformed into images of Christ. The conscious beginning of a person's unity with Christ is through faith, which is the Spirit's gift. The normal way in which faith comes to us is through hearing the scriptural word being preached. Calvin takes up an old patristic idea when he argues that the same Spirit that produced scripture enables us to understand and be convinced by it. The Spirit also leads a person to the conviction that he or she personally shares in salvation. This working of the Spirit within us, enlightening us as to the true message of the word of God, convincing us of its truth and of our sharing in the salvation witnessed to there — this inner working of the Spirit is Calvin's famous *testimonium Spiritus sancti internum* ('inner testimony of the Holy Spirit').

C.   THE FLOWERING OF SPIRIT-ORIENTATED MOVEMENTS

The twelfth century, as we saw (Chapter 5, F), witnessed the emergence of movements expressing an eagerness for a renewal of Christian life and for emancipating it from what was seen by many as an excess of institutionalization and formalism. Such movements blossomed in the seventeenth century. It was a century known for its interest in the 'interior life' (as many put it), for its focus on the piety, the spiritual progress of the individual. Literature on how to pray, how to meditate, how to progress in one's Christian life abounded. Accompanying this interest in the individual's union with God was a widespread stress on feeling, experiencing the Spirit's presence. This was the remote beginning of eighteenth-century English and American revivalism. The emotionalism associated with the stress on feeling expressed itself in a variety of ways, the most extreme being bodily convulsions, tremblings, foamings at the mouth and similar occurrences. Devotees saw all this as induced by the Spirit and as a characteristic accompaniment of what was called 'prophesying' (Knox 1950:356–388). One is reminded of the very old sense of 'prophesying' (see Chapter 1, B). It is not surprising then that the period is also one in which glossolalia — speaking in tongues — appears, though sporadically. Even the Jansenists laid claim to it (Kelsey 1981:52–55).

Within Catholicism the movements for a renewal of inner spirituality took various forms — from the acceptable piety of St Ignatius's *Spiritual Exercises* to the unacceptable views of the Jansenists and Quietists. Though opposed to each other on many issues (Knox 1950:237), both of the latter stressed the workings of the Spirit within the individual to the point where institutional factors faded in significance. Indeed, for the Quietists externals were depreciated as a distraction, an obstacle to the soul's becoming totally possessed by the Spirit. The sign of such total possession was the will's experience of powerlessness under the Spirit (Watkin-Jones 1929:183). There was no attempt to separate Church and Spirit in quite the same way as occurred in Protestant movements of the time, despite Jansenism's jaundiced view of papal authority. Any such separation would have found Catholic soil too inhospitable for extensive growth. As it was, the excessive claims associated with their doctrines of the individual's possession of the Spirit evoked a strong enough reaction, being one of the reasons for the eventual condemnation of Jansenism and Quietism.

Jansenism and Quietism did not survive. However, Quakerism and Pietism did, being influential to this day. Both were Protestant movements. And both were not only movements to reform the lives of Christians but also protests against an institutionalism and formalism that their own churches had sunk into, despite the Reformation. As such they were liberation movements. The freedom of the Spirit that they appealed to was also a cry for the freedom of the individual Christian from excessive enslavement to externals. Despite the widespread exaggerations associated with them and similar movements, they were nevertheless a cry for the restoration of the full dignity of the Christian. They were a demand that as a possessor of the Spirit, the Christian be allowed to participate fully in the Church — indeed, be allowed a certain independence of institutions and structures. By focusing on the individual's possession of the Spirit and the accompanying value of her or his Spirit-given insights into Christian living, the individual's dignity was restored. No longer were Christians simply disenfranchised laity, powerless before the clergy and clerically controlled ecclesiastical institutions. The Pietists therefore argued that Luther's doctrine of the priesthood of all believers had not been taken seriously enough (Brown 1978:57). The Quakers, too, rejected the distinction between clergy and laity. They insisted on the dignity of all who possessed the Spirit. However, since they believed that even non-Christians could possess the Spirit, could possess the 'inner light' brought by the Spirit, they stressed the dignity not simply of Christians but of all human beings. The Quakers therefore became the earliest of Christian fighters for human rights.

It is impossible here to do full justice to either Quakerism or Pietism: their various forms, mutual differences, richness of insights and exaggerations. All that can be done is to focus on an element they had in common, one that is of importance to our theme: the idea that what mattered was the individual's possession of and guidance by the Spirit, not ecclesiastical structures, authorities, or sacraments. The Spirit–Church link is weakened in all of them, in some cases disappearing altogether.

The Quakers or Society of Friends, as they are called, originated in mid-seventeenth-century England, their founding father being George Fox. Their nickname comes from the 'quaking', the bodily convulsions associated with their earlier meetings. Knox (1950:356) observes that they had only one positive point of doctrine: the 'inner light'. This was a light that guided every individual. It was the light of conscience. But it was also seen as a light coming from the presence of the Holy Spirit (of which they had no particular theology, apart from the Spirit as source of light — Congar 1983a:142–143). The light was not placed in opposition to scripture, but was seen as leading the individual beyond it. Interestingly enough, while Catholicism was appealing to the Spirit to justify the existence of *traditions* beyond scripture, the Quakers were appealing to the Spirit to justify *personal illuminations* that went beyond it. Scripture, in fact, was not an ultimate criterion of truth. That role (according to Barclay's 1676 defence of Quakerism) was played only by the Spirit's inspiration (see Lewis 1978:197). The Spirit, Barclay stressed, was given to all people to guide them into all truth. The 'all' includes non-Christians (see Watkin-Jones 1929:229) — as mentioned above. There is here rather a radical (for those times) theoretical break between Spirit and Church. But even on a practical level, little place was given to 'Church'. In their own meetings there was no organized external worship, no sacraments, no ministry. The Spirit alone was the source of worship, true baptism, and of the order by which believers should be guided (Congar 1983a:142).

'Pietism' is the name given to a variety of movements, German in origin, that concentrated on renewing the spiritual quality of Christian lives. Unlike the Quakers, there was no positive rejection of Church structures. Many remained happily obedient to them. This is especially true of the early Pietists (Bauch 1974:30, 48). However, the tendency in Pietism was to devalue their importance, and the later Pietists did become more antipathetic to Church structures (Brown 1978:62). What was important, once again, was the work of the Spirit in the hearts of individuals. The Church was increasingly seen as being basically invisible (Brown 1978:46). The visible Church was but the gathering together of Spirit-filled individuals. The Church therefore was the communal expression of what was primarily an individual reality, not the traditional sharing of the individual in a communal reality (Berkhof 1976:46).

Pietism was also far more biblically orientated than Quakerism (see Aland 1970). But it was the Spirit who revealed the Bible's meaning to the individual. Another difference between Pietism and Quakerism was that the former paid more attention to the Spirit's *sanctifying* role. In Pietism the guiding idea was not so much an 'inner light' (though that idea was there too) as the presence of the Spirit as *power*. The emphasis was on feeling, experiencing the Spirit, an experience that was seen as some sort of spiritual rebirth (see Weber 1985:1743). One of the most significant shifts of Pietist thinking away from its orthodox Protestant roots was its focus on regeneration, 'new birth', rather than the forensic idea of justification. *That* was the beginning of personal renewal, and later Pietists stressed the need to be able to date that experience, the experience of conversion (Brown 1978:118).

Though more traditional in its attitude to the Church, then, Pietism nevertheless conceived of the Spirit's role almost entirely in terms of what the Spirit did for the individual believer: convincing the believer of the truth of the biblical message and of his or her personal sharing in salvation, and guiding the believer throughout her or his Christian life. Pietism's strength lay precisely in being able to emphasize these elements and yet remain within the broad lines of a Christian tradition that believed in a Church, a ministry and sacraments. Remaining in that tradition enabled it to be a valuable antidote to the tendency to overemphasize Christianity's institutional elements. It was Pietism, rather than Quakerism, that led to Wesley and, through him, to the Holiness Movement, from which in turn sprang the Pentecostal and contemporary charismatic movements. It would therefore be natural at this point to study the rise of Pentecostalism. However, before doing so I would like to say a few words about Hegel's views on the Spirit.

D.   HEGEL

The late eighteenth and early nineteenth centuries saw the flowering in Germany of a philosophical movement known as 'idealism'. Its basic postulate was that all reality was simply the manifestation of the development of one universal spirit. 'Spirit' here means 'spiritual substance', not 'the Holy Spirit'. There are obvious similarities to the neo-Platonic idea of all reality being an emanation from one original substance. Neo-Platonism too is a form of 'idealism'. However, for neo-Platonism the emanations were conceived of simply as a release of ever-decreasing reflections of the primordial spirit. For German idealism, on the other hand, the emanations were the unfolding of all the potentialities of spirit. Neo-Platonism's emanations represented a progressive diminution of spirit, ending in nothingness. German idealism's 'emanations' resulted in the fulfilment of all the potentialities of spirit.

The most famous of the German idealists was Hegel (1770–1831). He distinguished three stages in the development of spirit's potentialities. The first stage he calls 'thesis'. The second stage is the achievement of a situation which is the exact opposite of the first one, and is therefore called '*anti*thesis'. Two opposed extremes have now come into being. However, they do not remain opposed but immediately seek reconciliation. This leads to the third stage, appropriately called '*syn*thesis'.

For Hegel, the Holy Spirit is the third stage of spirit's march to self-realization. The link with the traditional idea of the Spirit as the bond of unity is obvious. But there is also a link with two other ideas. The first is that of an 'era of the Spirit' as a final stage in history (see

Joachim of Fiore. Chapter 5. F). The second is that of the Spirit as the soul of the world — an idea that cropped up here and there in the Church's history.

Hegel connects each stage of spirit's self-unfolding with a specific member of the Trinity. The first stage is spirit's awareness of itself as a living substance with potentialities for self-realization. This stage is identified with the Father. To realize all its potentialities spirit must first go out of itself, so to speak, and produce its opposite. This it does by producing the limited world of nature. Nature is seen as part of spirit, but that part in which spirit produces what is most unlike itself in order to realize all its potentialities. This second stage, spirit's unity with nature, is the stage of the Son. Hegel uses here the traditional Christian idea of the incarnation. These two stages are only transitional ones. Spirit's total fulfilment demands a final stage. In this stage the clear contrast between nature and spirit disappears as a unity is achieved which represents the fulfilment of all the potentialities of spirit that have now been unfolded during the course of history. This final stage of spirit's existence is identified by Hegel with the Holy Spirit.

This approach to the Trinity caught the imagination of several nineteenth-century theologians. However, it is questionable whether Hegel's trinity bears any real relationship to the three persons Christians believe in. In Hegel we see idealist philosophy changing a traditional Christian belief so that it fits idealism's mould. This is in sharp contrast to the early Fathers' changing idealist philosophy so as to fit Christianity's mould. Nevertheless, Hegel's philosophical ideas about the inherent propensity of spirit to develop itself have been used by several theologians, one notable example being Karl Rahner's work.

E.   THE HOLINESS MOVEMENT AND THE RISE OF PENTECOSTALISM

The Holiness Movement is generally acknowledged to be the main inspiration behind the rise of Pentecostalism. Other origins do exist (see Menzies 1975). However, for our purposes it is sufficient to focus on Wesley and the Holiness Movement he inspired.

The father of Methodism, John Wesley (1703–91), preached a doctrine that marks a high point in the period's search for spiritual renewal. It was that perfect holiness was indeed possible and should be striven after. Lutheranism had stressed the *simul peccator* — that we remain sinners even after justification. Wesley took an opposite tack: perfect holiness is not only possible, but also necessary if one is to be a Christian in the fullest sense. There were, in his view, ordinary Christians and

Christians who had been 'sanctified'. This 'second blessing', as it was called, could be achieved in a single experience, or be progressively realized (Wesley himself never clearly opted for one view or the other).

The 'second blessing' was to be achieved by the power of the Spirit. Wesley preached a doctrine reminiscent of the now old idea of the Spirit's coming in confirmation *ad robur*: the need of a reception of the Spirit over and above justification and baptism by water, in order to strengthen the believer against sin and provide the strength needed for the attainment of holiness. True to the spirit of the times, he also stressed the importance of *feeling*, of experiencing the Spirit's work within one (see Knox 1950:538ff.).

Wesley himself was no charismatic in the modern sense of the term. He was indeed very open to the idea, being increasingly mooted in his day, that the Spirit's charisms had continued down the ages. But he was sceptical of many of the claims to them being made at the time, preferring to direct attention to the greater importance of the ordinary work of the Spirit within the believer, one that provided assurance and spiritual strength (see, for example, his sermon in Lewis 1978:212).

Wesley's idea of a 'second blessing' distinct from justification was transported to America. There its incorporation into revivalist circles launched what came to be known as the 'Holiness Movement'. This was composed of a variety of movements whose avowed aim was the attainment of the Christian perfection Wesley had preached.

The first significant steps towards transforming Wesley's second blessing into the 'baptism of the Spirit' characteristic of Pentecostalism appear to have been taken at Oberlin College, Ohio (see Dayton 1975:43ff.). Wesley himself did not speak of the second blessing as a 'baptism of the Spirit'. His few uses of the term refer it to initial conversion, i.e., justification (Dayton 1975:42). However, at Oberlin Wesley's second blessing/sanctification began to be called a 'baptism of the Spirit' and comparisons began to be drawn with the phenomena that occurred on Pentecost day.

The next important stage was a clear option for the idea that sanctification/baptism of the Spirit took place in a single, clearly felt experience (not as a gradual process). Very influential here was a Methodist laywoman, Phoebe Palmer. She in turn had been influenced by something she had experienced while on a visit to England. In 1856 an English Methodist, William Arthur, published a book called *Tongues of Fire*, in which the Spirit was invoked to renew Pentecost and baptize people with tongues of fire. The revival that followed its publication appears to have identified Wesley's second blessing with a datable experience of power, described as a 'baptism of the Holy Spirit' (Dayton 1975:46).

That this should have occurred in England is interesting, since two decades earlier a remarkable phenomenon had occurred in London. There a Presbyterian preacher, Edward Irving, had become convinced, contrary to his own doctrinal tradition, that two members of his flock had actually received the 'gift of tongues and prophecy' (see Christenson 1975:19). He began to allow such glossolalia and prophetical utterances to be practised during worship and promptly found himself at logger-heads with the trustees of his church. He nevertheless remained con-vinced that the Spirit had been poured out anew, and came to prize glossolalia as a 'standing sign' of the presence of the Spirit (see Lewis 1978:236ff.). Such an evaluation of tongues was to become central to Pentecostal belief. The Irvingites, as his followers were called, formed the relatively short-lived Catholic Apostolic Church (its last priest died in 1972). Its members were convinced that Christ's second coming was imminent and in view of it attempted to restore the Church to its 'pentecostal purity' (Congar 1983a:145). Their church therefore com-bined a strong hierarchical structure with the full exercise of the charisms of the Pauline churches. It was the first full-scale institutional-ized expression of belief in the *charismata* of the Spirit since Montanism.

As noted above, it was interesting that this church existed in London at the very time Phoebe Palmer was experiencing the aftermath of William Arthur's *Tongues of Fire*. Yet Christenson (1975:23) is con-vinced there is no causal connection between Irvingism and the rise of Pentecostalism. Christenson sees both as expressions of an increasingly widespread experience of transhistorical reality (1975:25). It seems to me that both could have been mutually independent expressions of ideas and trends 'in the air' at the time. Be that as it may, Phoebe Palmer returned to America, filled with zeal for what she had experienced. She proclaimed the importance of dramatically experiencing the Spirit's action ('baptism') in imparting the Wesleyan second blessing or sanc-tification (Dieter 1975:62).

This emphasis on a definite, indeed crisis, experience of the second blessing raised an important issue — that of its verification (Dieter 1975:62ff.). What criteria were there to show that the experience was truly the Spirit's baptism? The birth of classic Pentecostalism will be associated with a particular answer to that question: the gift of tongues.

But to return to Mrs Palmer (and Mr, who also played a significant role). The Palmers' London experience also imprinted a Pentecostal way of speaking on their minds. As a result they began to popularize such language. A notable shift from the Holiness Movement's older stance now occurs: there is talk of a new Pentecost *age*, of a dispensation of the Spirit. Wesley himself had kept the traditional close links between the Spirit and Christ, despite the loosening of those links that occurred already in his day. Such a loosening now takes place within the Holiness Movement with talk of a 'dispensation of the Spirit'. The Movement's millennialist associations are also worth noting; they form a further link between it and Joachim and Montanus.

However, it was once again an Oberlin theologian (Asa Mahan) who turned a flame into a fire (see Dayton 1975:46ff.). He gathered together the aforementioned ideas in a book entitled *Baptism of the Holy Ghost*, which became an instant success. The soil was ready for the flowering of Pentecostalism.

In 1900, an evangelist of the Holiness Movement, Charles Parham, suggested that his students study Acts 2 with the specific aim of discovering the criteria enabling one to judge whether or not an individual had received baptism of the Spirit. The students concluded that the evidence of such baptism was the activity of speaking in tongues (Dayton 1975:52). Not long after (1906), W. J. Seymour, one of Parham's students, preached this (very divisive) doctrine at revival meetings in Azusa Street, Los Angeles. Pentecostalism was born.

With Pentecostalism, the growth of Spirit-orientated movements found its climax. Entire churches were now organized with the Spirit as their focus. However, it was the Spirit's *activities* rather than the Spirit's being and nature that formed the centre of interest. Most Pentecostal groups officially accepted the traditional western faith that the Spirit was the third person of the Trinity, proceeding from Father and Son. But if Hollenweger (1975:311) is to be believed, they did not pay much attention to this doctrine. Curiously enough, there exists a unitarian Pentecostal church, regarded as an outcast by the trinitarian ones (see Reed 1975). The origin of their unitarianism was the 'revelation' (at a prayer meeting) that since in the scriptures baptism was always done in the name of Jesus, Jesus was the 'dispensational name' for God. The one divine person became incarnate in Jesus. Father, Son and Spirit are but three aspects, manifestations, offices of one and the same person. This is modalism all over again. Their belief in the incarnation (of the one and only divine person, God) distinguishes their unitarianism from the more rationalistic one that arose in sixteenth-century Europe (the Socinians) and spread to the United States in the eighteenth century.

As it spread, Pentecostalism developed its own divisions and differences of opinion regarding its central focus: baptism of the Spirit. Most identified Wesley's second blessing with baptism in the Spirit, opting therefore for two events in the Christian's life: conversion and sanctification/baptism of the Spirit. Others (the older group in fact) distinguished between sanctification and baptism of the Spirit, thus opting for three key events: conversion, sanctification, baptism of the Spirit. However, these details need not concern us here.

One final comment. In the very early stages the phrase 'baptism *of* the Spirit' was used. The implication was that it was the Spirit who baptized. However, in response to accusations that this broke the link between Christ and the Spirit, Pentecostals came to prefer the phrase 'baptism *in* the Spirit'. The reason for the change was to indicate that *Christ* did the baptizing, but baptized in the Spirit. Christ was the baptizer, the Spirit the 'water'. This concern for maintaining the unity between the Spirit and Christ puts a serious question-mark behind Hollenweger's assertion (1975:311) that the Pentecostals did not really understand what the traditional trinitarian formulae meant. More important, however, is the fact that a Spirit-orientated movement took pains to arrest the process of divorcing the Spirit from Christ. This move to unite the two was to find its fullest expression in the charismatic movement, where in addition the Spirit and the Church are reunited within the context of a Spirit-orientated movement.

F.   THE SPIRIT IN CATHOLICISM

In post-Reformation times, Catholic interest in the Spirit concentrated on the Spirit's link with the Church. While others were weakening the link, Catholicism was strengthening it. Thus, in response to the Reformation's rejection of the authority ascribed by Catholicism to tradition and the Church's teaching office (*magisterium*), Catholic theologians stressed the Spirit's role in guiding the Church and protecting it from error. However, this was not simply a reaffirmation of traditional views. It also represented a tendency to 'give an absolute value to the Church as an institution by endowing its magisterium with an almost unconditional guarantee of guidance by the Holy Spirit' (Congar 1983a:152). An extreme example of this is Pius IX's reported statement: '*I* am tradition'. Certainly, at the turn of the century tradition came to be identified solely with the teaching of the magisterium, with little room left for any yardstick whereby such teaching could itself be evaluated (see Mackey 1962:20–41).

The Spirit became to all intents and purposes, then, the guarantor of the magisterium's decisions. The Spirit as guide of the entire people of God, whose beliefs therefore played an important role in evaluating what was or was not part of the Church's deposit of faith — such a view had all but died. Newman's *On Consulting the Faithful in Matters of Doctrine* was, in effect, a repudiation of that idea. For his troubles, he paid the penalty of ostracism by Church authorities. In their view he had presumed, as one prelate put it, that the sheep should do more than simply be led. The general view of Roman theology was that the

Spirit's role within the individual was pretty much limited to being a sanctifier.

Sanctifier of individual believers, inspirer and guarantor of official teaching and the Church's sacraments — these were the main roles ascribed to the Spirit. They were well outlined in an encyclical on the Holy Spirit published by Leo XIII in 1897, *Divinum Illud Munus*. The same encyclical also strengthened the connection between Spirit and Church by describing the former as being 'the soul' of the Church: 'just as Christ is the Church's head, so too is the Spirit its soul' (§6). The idea, of course, is Augustinian. However, as Congar (1983a:154) points out, whereas Augustine was comparing the *functions* of the Spirit to the animating functions of the soul, Leo spoke of the Spirit as *being* the Church's soul. In the atmosphere of the times this only too easily made the Spirit appear as the Spirit of the Church, rather than the Church as the Church of the Spirit. The difference in emphasis is important. The former way of relating Spirit and Church tends to blur the fact that the Church is under the lordship of Christ's Spirit; it tends to see the Spirit as a component of the Church.

Of course, no one really thought of the Spirit in that way. However, there was the very real danger of thinking of the Spirit as being united to the Church in a way analogous to the hypostatic union (the union between the Word and its humanity). J. A. Möhler had already spoken earlier in the century about the Church, Christ's Body, as a sort of continuation of the incarnation. It was an idea rich in meaning, but open to serious misunderstanding. Now the danger arose of a similar misunderstanding of the soul–body image. The soul was conceived of by the revived scholastic theology as forming one living thing with the body. It was believed to be the 'form' of the body. It was therefore only too easy to conceive of the Spirit and the Church in the same way, leading to what Congar called 'ecclesiological monophysitism' (1983a:154). This would be a situation where Spirit and Church were conceived of as forming a sort of human–divine substance, where human actions and structures become but the external manifestations of a divine reality. The danger in this misunderstanding was obviously a very real one, since theologians found it necessary to emphasize that the body–soul image could not be pressed that far (see, e.g., Schmaus 1958:373).

However, even if such extremes were avoided, others were not. Two can be mentioned. First of all, the image was taken sufficiently literally to launch a debate about whether or not the Church had two souls: the uncreated one of the Spirit, and the created one of grace. One body, two souls! Secondly, the combination of this image with the virtual identification of the Church with the hierarchy and other institutional structures pushed the acts of that hierarchy beyond the bounds of even reasonable criticism. The 'creeping infallibility' syndrome, as the tendency to regard every utterance of the papacy as divinely protected from error has been called, was in part the effect of too literal an identification of the Spirit with a soul. Of course, on the positive side was the fact that the unity of Spirit and Church and the life-giving function of the former within the latter was highlighted. But it was not by chance that the Council that identified the Church first and foremost with the people, and that abandoned the idea that in the Catholic Church alone is Christ's Church to be found, deliberately reverted to Augustine's way of comparing the Spirit to a soul. For whereas in an early draft of Vatican II's *Constitution on the Church* the Spirit was said to *be* the soul of the Church, in the final version (§7) the Spirit's life-giving activity was *compared to* that of a soul (see Alberigo and Magistretti 1975:31).

Leo's encyclical may have had its drawbacks. However, it did focus attention on the Spirit within Catholicism. This, combined with a movement to restore to 'church' its full meaning of a people and to people their rightful role within the Church, laid the early foundations for Catholicism's own experience of a 'new Pentecost' in recent years (see O'Connor 1975).

The renewal in ecclesiology began with Möhler's book *Die Einheit in der Kirche* ('Unity in the Church'). In it the Church is presented not simply as an institution but as a living organism, a community of love enlivened by the Spirit. As regards the people's role within the Church, Newman's *On Consulting the Faithful* drew attention to it. But a strong movement to restore to laity a fuller role in the life of the Church only got under way in the present century. Not surprisingly, this movement went hand in hand with an increasing interest in the gifts of the Spirit.

Leo's encyclical conceived of such gifts exclusively in terms of the seven drawn from the mistranslated text of Isaiah. These gifts were directed more to the individual's holiness than to service of the Church. However, as the twentieth century and the movement for lay involvement progressed, so too did interest in the *gratiae gratis datae*, the charisms. To be sure, 'charisms' included more than the gifts listed by Paul. The term was taken to refer to whatever talents the Spirit may give an individual for the service of the community. But the crucial point was that theologians were increasingly recognizing the importance of the charismatic element in the life of the Church.

While all the above was taking place, the doctrine of appropriation was undergoing review. Already in the nineteenth century Scheeben had questioned it. He believed that it did not do justice to the *distinct* role that the Spirit played within our lives, a role clearly attested to in Scripture. He argued that the Spirit was united to us in a way that the other two were not. As the means whereby we are united to Father and Son, the Spirit must be in some sense closer to us than they. To drive his point home he compared the Spirit's special union with believers to the hypostatic union in Christ and (worse still) spoke of the Church as a sort of 'incarnation of the Spirit' (see Congar 1983b:88). But his rejection of an unnuanced doctrine of appropriation led to a long debate on the issue in Catholic theology. It resulted in the recognition of distinct roles for all three persons. One of the more interesting points made in the debate was Rahner's observation that the Spirit's work within us was not in the full sense a work *ad extra*, 'outside' the divinity. It could not be, since the whole point of this work of the Spirit was to enable us to share in God's own inner life (Rahner 1970:34ff.).

The assault on the doctrine of appropriation highlighted the *distinctive* character of the Spirit's work. Yet another significant development of the period was a debate about the possibility of *experiencing* the Spirit's presence within one. Was a *cognitio experimentalis*, an experiential knowledge of grace, of the Spirit's presence, possible? For centuries now, these supernatural realities had been viewed as being beyond the reach of experience. But a growing body of opinion began to hold (as the mediaevals had done) that if God's Spirit was at work within us, then we must be able to experience that fact in some way or other. This particular development meant that within Catholicism the experiential side of the Spirit-orientated movements was beginning to be taken seriously.

The above developments (and others — see O'Connor 1975) prepared the soil for the entry of Pentecostal ideas and experiences into Catholicism.

In 1960 a new phenomenon appeared on the Pentecostal scene: experiences of 'baptism in the Spirit' and tongue-speaking within a traditional, hierarchically structured church: an Episcopalian church in California. Seven years later two Catholics, students at Duquesne University, attended a Protestant Pentecostal prayer meeting. They were prayed over, had hands laid on them and experienced baptism in the Spirit and glossolalia (Sullivan 1984:1040). They subsequently shared their experience with others and soon a Catholic Pentecostal or charismatic group came into being, with its main centre at Notre Dame University. The 'Charismatic movement' (as the growth of Pentecostal experiences and ideas within the older churches is called) grew rapidly throughout the world. It has also — especially in Catholic circles — come to be known as the charismatic *renewal*, a word that recalls Pope

John XXIII's prayer for a 'new' Pentecost to renew the life of the Church.

Catholic charismatics have had to rethink the theology of baptism in the Spirit and the role of glossolalia in a way that would harmonize with and not obscure their other Catholic beliefs.

For example, lest water-baptism and the sacrament of confirmation be devalued, many charismatics began to speak of baptism in the Spirit as a 'release' of the Spirit, a release of powers of the Spirit already present within the believer, already given to the believer in the sacraments of initiation. Some charismatics have even classified this experience, using Thomas Aquinas's categories, as a special invisible mission of the Spirit for an 'increase of grace' (Sullivan 1984:1045; see Aquinas, *Summa*, Ia, 43, 6).

Another example concerns glossolalia. An excessive stress on tongues as essential to baptism in the Spirit was experienced by many as divisive, as creating an elitist group within the Church, basing its elitism on a gift that Paul himself clearly did not expect everyone to have. Hence many Catholic charismatics began to speak of glossolalia as a welcome but by no means essential sign of baptism in the Spirit.

But it was not only Catholic charismatics who had to do some rethinking. The experience by Catholics of baptism in the Spirit posed interesting questions for traditional Pentecostals, because of their opposition to Catholicism. Would this experience by Catholics mean that they would be led to abandon the (for Pentecostals) falsehoods of their church? Or would the Catholic church reform itself by eliminating its errors? As things turned out, the charismatic movement within Catholicism came to display increasingly a return to conservative Catholic values, especially devotion to Mary. This is not only curious, in view of the strong ecumenical bonds created between Catholic and other charismatics, including Pentecostals. It is also a remarkable testimony to the basic compatibility of charismatic and institutional elements. Catholics came to realize that there was no reason why they should not be as fully charismatic as they were Catholic, and vice versa.

The Catholic charismatic movement spread to all levels of the church, capturing the adherence of many outstanding theologians (e.g., H. Mühlen, R. Laurentin and F. A. Sullivan) and prelates (e.g., Cardinal Suenens). As a result it has made a major contribution to the theological investigation of Pentecostal ideas and the rethinking of Pentecostal categories (see Chapter 16, A (iv)). Moreover, the movement has enriched not only the lives of countless Catholics but also our common theological heritage. At long last Catholicism has opened itself wholeheartedly to a Spirit-orientated movement, and has been blessed as a result.

QUESTIONS

Check questions

1 In which areas did Luther (a) repeat, (b) break with traditional western beliefs concerning the Spirit?

2 How did Luther's views on the relationship between the Spirit and the Church develop? What role was played by the Enthusiasts in this regard?

3 Which biblical idea of the Spirit did Calvin revive?

4 What did Calvin see as being the Spirit's distinctive role? How did he conceive that role being exercised in (a) creation and (b) salvation?

5 What did Calvin mean by the 'inner testimony of the Holy Spirit'?

6 Give some examples of the seventeenth century's interest in the 'interior life'?

7 In what way did each of the following reflect the growing Spirit-orientated mood of the seventeenth century: (a) Jansenism; (b) Quietism; (c) Quakerism; (d) Pietism?

8 In what sense can the Spirit-orientated movements of the seventeenth and eighteenth centuries be seen as 'liberation movements'?

9 What effect did these movements have on the relationship between the Spirit and the Church?

10 How did Hegel use — and distort — traditional ideas of the Spirit?

11 What connects: (a) John Wesley to the Holiness Movement; (b) the Holiness Movement to Pentecostalism; (c) Pentecostalism to the charismatic movement?

12 Where and when can the Pentecostal movement be said to have been born?

13 What aspects of the Spirit did post-Reformation Catholicism focus on? What distortions arose as a result?

14 How did Leo XIII's use of the soul–body analogy of the Spirit's relationship to the Church differ from Augustine's? What were the dangers in Leo's version?

15 What factors contributed to Catholicism's eventual ability to incorporate within it a Spirit-orientated movement such as the charismatic movement?

16 Give examples of how Catholics had to rethink certain charismatic ideas in order to avoid obscuring traditional Catholic beliefs.

17 Did the Catholic charismatic movement develop along increasingly anti-institutional lines or not? Give reasons for your answer.

Discussion question

How is it possible that a purely spiritual reality like the Spirit can be experienced by spatio-temporal beings? Can one single out in a specific experience certain elements that come from the Spirit, enabling one to assert that what was experienced was indeed the Spirit?

RECOMMENDED READING

Watkin-Jones 1929 is a useful survey of the period between Arminius and Wesley. The relevant sections of Congar 1983a are also worth reading. As regards the Spirit-orientated movements of the seventeenth and eighteenth centuries, Knox 1950 shows its prejudices, but remains a mine of information. On Pietism specifically, Brown 1978 provides a very readable introduction — see especially chs 1 and 5. On Pentecostalism, the massive Hollenweger 1972 is still worth reading. On more detailed aspects of Pentecostalism's origins, see Synan 1975. For a rather potted history of the charismatic experience see Kelsey 1981. On the Catholic charismatic movement see O'Connor 1971 and, for a collection of essays on several aspects of it, McDonnell 1975. For an example of an attempt at writing a Catholic charismatic theology see Mühlen 1978. Finally, Lewis 1978 yet again provides a useful selection of historical texts.

Part Two

A systematic theology of the Holy Spirit

Those who have studied the historical developments outlined in Part One should be in a position to write their own systematic exposition of the doctrine of the Holy Spirit. In fact, it would be a very useful exercise for the reader to pause at this point and attempt to write an outline exposition, jotting down the main points belonging to such an exposition and their mutual relationships. At any rate, what follows is my own personal way of writing a systematic theology of the Holy Spirit. It too is but an outline, albeit a somewhat detailed one. Nothing could be explored in very great depth. Since the Spirit is involved in every aspect of the Christian life, writing an adequate book on the Spirit would involve a detailed examination of every aspect of the faith. Obviously I have not even attempted such a thing here. Instead, I have concentrated more on trying to show how the traditional western idea of the Spirit as love is able both to illuminate and to unify the main ideas associated with the Spirit. The thread running throughout my exposition is one I ascribed, rightly or wrongly, to Augustine: love unites, and by uniting transforms all that it unites.

If the Spirit is truly love, then such an approach requires no justification. However, I need to acknowledge two things.

First of all, the thread of my exposition is unambiguously western in its approach. As such, Orthodox readers may well find themselves in disagreement with the very thread I am using to tie the various elements of my theology together. All I can do is hope that they may find something in what follows to enrich their own tradition, just as I have found much in their writings to enrich mine. What follows is a theological exposition of a faith I believe we hold in common.

Secondly, I realize that my ideas about how love unites and transforms are drawn not simply from revelation but also (indeed especially) from my own experience of love and the wider experiences of humanity. This approach will be criticized by many who feel that it allows human ideas to intrude too much on God's revelation. I cannot respond to this objection here, except to say that no theologian can ever think about revelation other than through the medium of human ideas. If revelation itself leads me to associate the Spirit above all with love, then I am entitled to probe my understanding of the Spirit by means of love as known and experienced by human beings.

7

Who or what is the Holy Spirit?

A.   TWO WAYS OF VIEWING THE SPIRIT

It is perfectly clear from scripture and tradition that the Spirit is divine, 'of one substance' with the Father and the Son. The doubts expressed about the Spirit's divinity in the early Church (see Chapter 3, G) were but a relatively brief aberration in an otherwise clear and consistent tradition.

However, the same clarity and consistency is lacking when one enquires more precisely about the sort of divine reality the Spirit must be said to be. Is the Spirit a person, just as Father and Son are? Or is the Spirit not more accurately described as a force, the means whereby God and the risen Christ are present to us? In short, is the Spirit a 'who' or a 'what'?

Here scripture and tradition seem to part ways. In the scriptures (see Chapters 1 and 2) all the stress is on the Spirit as a 'what'. This way of putting it is perhaps misleading, since the Spirit is not usually viewed in the Bible as a purely impersonal reality. On the contrary, the Spirit is seen as the way in which transcendent personal realities are experienced. To say that the Spirit is the way in which God and the risen Christ are present to us, is to say that the Spirit can never be experienced as an impersonal force. Anyone who experiences the Spirit experiences a person. However, the persons experienced are God and Christ. This is so much the case that even the few passages — such as the famous Paraclete ones in John's gospel and the trinitarian (e.g., baptismal) formulae — are not as clear proof that the New Testament conceived of the Spirit as a person as used to be thought. Within the terms of our distinction between a 'who' and a 'what', therefore, we must say that the stress in the scriptures is on the Spirit as a 'what'.

However, when we turn to tradition — at least from the fourth century onwards — the position is reversed. Now the Spirit is seen as a third person or *hupostasis* within a divine trinity of persons or *hupo-*

staseis. The 'power' or 'force' element is still associated with the Spirit, but this is increasingly seen in western Christendom as a sort of figure of speech, an 'appropriation' (see Chapter 5, D) to the Spirit of something that belongs equally to all three persons of the Trinity.

The origins of this development need not be repeated here (see Chapters 2, G; 3, E). They do indeed go back to the New Testament. But the contrast between the two ways of viewing the Spirit is marked. Indeed, they seem to be mutually exclusive. To regard the Spirit as the way in which Father and Son are present to us, seems to deny the Spirit a distinct personality. The Spirit is simply a divine activity, a divine instrument used by Father and Son. On the other hand, to regard the Spirit as a distinct person is to think of that Spirit not so much as the way in which God and Christ become present to us, but as either a person who comes to us *with* God and Christ (the typically western view), or as a mediator *between* God, Christ and us, a sort of 'go-between God', as Taylor 1972 put it.

However, these two ways of viewing the Spirit are by no means contradictory. The Spirit is both a person and the means whereby the Father and Christ are present to us. Indeed, the Spirit's very identity as a person is constituted by the fact of being the means whereby Father and Son are present to each other. To show how this is so is the main burden of this chapter. The explanation will take us through some difficult ground — the sense in which the Spirit is a person — but the end result will, I trust, be both illuminating and enriching.

B.   IN WHAT SENSE IS THE SPIRIT A PERSON?

(i)   The word 'person' and the Spirit

One of the problems about conceiving the Spirit as a 'person' is that for us a person is a being that has not only its own distinct identity, but also its own separate existence. A person is a being with its own mind, will, freedom — and that for us means a mind, will and freedom separate from all others. If we apply such a notion to the Spirit, then the Spirit becomes a separate God from Father and Son. Indeed, applying it to the Trinity would turn the latter into a doctrine of three separate gods.

However, when applied to the three that make up the divine trinity, the term 'person' never meant a being with its own separate mind, will and freedom. Christianity's belief in *one* God necessarily meant that Father, Son and Spirit shared one and the same mind, one and the same will, and therefore one and the same actions flowing from these faculties. What precisely the term *did* mean was not all that clear when it was first used. Nevertheless, it had the basic meaning of a unique form of existence (see Chapter 4, A).

The traditional Greek term for 'person' as applied to the Trinity was *hupostasis*, and it had this basic meaning: the *concrete, particular way* in which something existed. A hypostasis was therefore something unique, something that cannot be shared. What can be shared is the 'stuff', that is to say the substance of which the hypostasis is a particular, concrete manifestation. But there was a further and most important idea entailed by the term, and that is that a nature was now complete. It was finished off, so to speak, as a full stop finishes off a sentence. Without this completion you do not have a hypostasis. All you have is an indeterminate substance — an unfinished blob.

The Latin word for 'person' was *persona*, and this came to be regarded as the western equivalent of *hupostasis*. Whereas the Greeks spoke of three *hupostaseis* in one *ousia*, the Latins spoke of three *personae* in one *natura*. But the literal Latin translation of *hupostasis* was *subsistentia*. A hypostasis was a *subsistentia* — a 'subsistence'. In mediaeval times, the term 'subsist' came to mean the sort of existence possessed by a hypostasis, a person (Michel 1922:391–407). For the Latins, therefore, the word 'subsistence' was used to convey this idea of a complete and, as a result, unique, existence. They talked of 'persons' as 'subsisting'.

When applied to Father, Son and Spirit by early writers such as the Cappadocians, 'persons' (i.e., hypostases) had, then, this basic meaning: three ways in which the one undivided divinity existed. Each of these ways was a necessary full stop to a particular aspect of God's existence. Father, Son and Spirit were three ways in which the divine substance was said to 'subsist'.

The idea of completeness is an extremely important element in the concept of a hypostasis. Without it, one falls into modalism. Unless Father, Son and Spirit are seen as three complete hypostases, they will be regarded simply as three ways in which *one already complete hypostasis, i.e., one and the same person,* is manifested. This latter was the typical modalist position (see Chapter 3, E).

It was in order to bring out clearly the distinction between an undetermined substance and an already complete existent manifesting itself, that the Greeks preferred the word *hupostasis* to the word *prosōpon* for referring to the divine three. *Prosōpon* is, in fact, the Greek equivalent of the Latin *persona*. However, *prosōpon* had as part of its meaning the very idea that the Greeks wished to exclude, namely the way in which an *already complete* existent manifested itself. *Prosōpon* originally referred to the mask through which actors spoke on stage. It was the

way in which the actor manifested the personality portrayed. To call
Father, Son and Spirit three *prosōpa* ran the obvious risk of interpretation as three masks of one and the same person. By contrast, the word
persona was much more acceptable to the Latins than *prosōpon* was to the
Greeks. *Persona*, too, originally meant a mask. However, it soon came
to mean a human being and could therefore more easily be used of
Father, Son and Spirit without fear of modalism. Furthermore, as
mentioned above, *persona* eventually came to mean the same as *hupostasis*.

To sum up what has been said thus far, the Greeks used *hupostasis* in
order to convey the idea that Father, Son and Spirit represented three
ways in which the divine nature existed and achieved its completion.
Each divine 'person', to use the West's term, shared fully in one and the
same divine nature. However, each divine 'person' represented a
particular way in which the divine nature 'subsisted'. As traditionally
formulated in the West, the Father is the divinity subsisting as unbegotten, the origin of all else; the Son is the divinity subsisting as the
begotten expression of all that the Father is; the Spirit is the divinity
subsisting as the bond or result of love between Father and Son.

One can appreciate why, from as early as Augustine (see Chapter 4,
C), reservations were expressed about the suitability of the term
'person' for the members of the Trinity. In our own times, the
limitations of the term have been pointed out by several theologians,
including the two giants of the century, the Catholic Karl Rahner
(1970:103ff.) and the Reformed theologian Karl Barth (1936:412). The
latter has suggested (1936:413) that we take up once again the old term
'mode of being', as more appropriate, something that Rahner does not
find too problematic providing one steers clear of modalism. As we
saw, 'hypostasis' meant a particular way in which the divine nature
subsisted.

However, for all its defects the term 'person' remains, to my mind,
the most appropriate one, because the unique ways in which the divine
nature subsists, the unique modes of being proper to it, are not simply
things, but three conscious awarenesses of existing in a unique way.
And beings consciously aware of themselves as unique ways of existing
are called 'persons'.

(ii)   Person as a conscious, relative, unique reality

Bringing the element of consciousness into the notion of person
requires some further comment. It has been pointed out that the three
divine persons share one and the same divine nature and therefore one

and the same mind and will. Consciousness is an activity of the mind. Hence one cannot assert that each divine person has its own distinct source of consciousness, unshared by the others.

The fact that all three share a single mind and will has been stressed *ad nauseam* in western thought. Warnings have been issued again and again that one must not identify a trinitarian person and self-consciousness, as this leads to tritheism. Even that most personalist of contemporary Catholic theologians on the Spirit, Heribert Mühlen, repeats the warning (1967:45). But one is left wondering what possible use the term 'person' could continue to have were the idea of consciousness of its own unique character removed from its content.

There is of course some truth in the warnings, and it is that if we view each person as having a consciousness of itself that is separate from that of the others, then tritheism is the inevitable outcome. However, western theology has overlooked for too long the implications of the Greek idea of *hupostasis*. To say that each person is a unique way in which the divine nature exists and achieves its completion is to say that each person is a unique way in which *all* that God is — knowledge, freedom, power, love, etc. — exists and achieves its completion. In other words, *all* that God is exists, is completed, in three different ways: as originating source, as begotten, as the result of the union of the former two.

Hence, one can and must say that the mind and accompanying consciousness that form part of the divine nature subsist in three different ways. And this in turn means that each divine person is a unique *conscious* way in which the divinity subsists. Using once again traditional western ideas, one can express these ways as follows: the Father is the divinity conscious of itself as the source of all else; the Son is the divinity conscious of itself as the begotten reflection of the Father; the Spirit is the divinity conscious of itself as the love binding Father and Son to each other, or (as others would put it) the result of such love.

Viewing the divine persons in this way not only restores to them the self-consciousness necessary for all persons, but also gives body to our conception of them. To preserve God's unity, traditional western theology stressed the lack of any real differentiating factors between the persons. What differentiated them was stressed as being 'only' their relationship to each other. It was purely the relatedness of Father to Son and of both to the Spirit that was seen as unique. As Rahner (1970:103) once wryly observed, this made relationships within the divinity the most unreal of entities, whereas they are the most real of all. One can only appreciate Rahner's remark if one recalls that the persons are distinct ways in which the entire divine nature exists and achieves its completion.

This leads to another point, viz., the essential link between 'person' and relatedness, at least as regards the persons making up the Trinity. This relatedness does not come out in Boethius's famous definition of a person as 'an individual substance of a rational nature' (see Chapter 5, A). In that definition a person is defined simply as a rational individual. However, what constitutes the divine persons as persons is their relationship to each other. One can also argue that relatedness as constitutive of personal identity is not simply a divine oddity but essential to the structure of person. This has been emphasized in contemporary personalist philosophies, which argue that there can be no 'I' without a 'thou'.

The Spirit, then, is a person in this sense of the word: a unique way in which the divine nature *has a related character* and therefore exists and achieves its completion.

Finally, there is a need to stress the 'uniqueness' of persons. Their uniqueness is to be found not simply in the natures they share. A human person is not unique because human nature is a unique form of existence. What makes a person unique is above all its inability to be shared. You can be a human being, like me, but you can never be me. This was not clear in Boethius's definition of 'person', and so Richard of St Victor suggested that, at any rate as applied to the Trinity, the term should be defined as an *incommunicable* way of existing. As was seen (Chapter 5, A), subsequent authors took Richard's point and observed that each person's incommunicability made it impossible to provide a universal essence of 'person', one that could be shared in by various individuals in their own different ways. To assert uniqueness as essential to the structure of a person is to assert that no two persons are persons in exactly the same way.

This is worth remembering when reflecting on the Spirit as a person. As Lonergan and more recently the Lutheran theologian Jürgen Moltmann have pointed out, 'the Holy Spirit is not a person in the same, identical sense as the Son; and neither of them is a person in the same identical sense as the Father' (Moltmann 1981:189; see also Bourassa 1970:121). Hence, it is wrong to expect that, as a 'person', the Spirit has the clear personality found in those designated 'Father' and 'Son'. As we shall see, the Spirit's personality could very well be constituted precisely by its lack of any clear face of its own.

To summarize, the Spirit is a person *not* in the sense of possessing a separate mind, will and freedom but rather in the sense of a unique way in which the divine nature exists and finds its completion as a shared reality. The relationship existing between each of these three ways of subsisting constitutes the persons in their uniqueness, a uniqueness that further implies that the three persons are not all persons in exactly the same way.

C. THE PROCESSION OF THE SPIRIT

Having stressed that the Spirit is a unique way in which the divine nature subsists, the question must now be tackled: what is unique about it? But to do that it is necessary to study first the Spirit's 'procession', that is to say the way in which the divinity arrives at the unique way of subsisting we call the Spirit.

(i) The Spirit proceeds from the Father of the Son

All Christians agree that the Father is at the origin of those movements whereby the Godhead is structured as a trinity of 'persons'. All agree, therefore, that the Spirit 'proceeds' or 'comes forth' (language is inadequate here) from the Father. However, as was seen in the historical section (Chapter 5, B), a division arose between East and West as to whether or not the Son too could be regarded as a source of the Spirit.

To recall some of the points outlined earlier, the typical western position is the assertion that the Spirit proceeds from the Father and Son, a belief known as the *Filioque* ('and from the Son'). The basic reason for this is that the scriptures see the Spirit as being also the Son's Spirit, as coming from the Son to us. However, on the principle that the economic Trinity reveals the immanent one, the Son's role in sending the Spirit to us must reflect a role he has as regards the 'production' of the Spirit within the Godhead. The West's complaint to the East was that the latter did not take seriously enough the fact that the Spirit was the Spirit not only of the Father but also of the Son.

The East, in its turn, acknowledged that the Son had some role to play in the Spirit's existence within the Trinity. But this was not a causal one. The Son was not a source of the Spirit. Instead, the Son's role (as I understand the matter) is a more negative one: by being 'already' there, the presence of the Son ensures that the movement whereby the Father produces the Spirit is not a 'generation' (i.e., the production of a Son), but simply a 'spiration' or 'breathing-forth'. The Father gives the Spirit existence. The Son's presence ensures that the Spirit's 'character' is not that of a Son. The Son therefore does not produce the Spirit but his presence 'manifests', that is to say reveals the character of, the latter (see Orphanos 1981:25ff.; Garrigues 1981:157–161). It is this and not any causal role within the divinity that is the reason for the Son's sending forth of the Spirit into our lives. The Father and the Father alone is the source of divine processions: the generating of the Son and the spirating or breathing-forth of the Spirit.

The East concentrates on the belief that the Father is the source of everything in the Godhead. This property of being a source is distinctive to the Father. It distinguishes him from the Son and the Spirit. Hence 'being a source' is non-transferable. Just as the Son cannot be the Father, so too can he not be a source of a divine person. Moreover, the East argued, to see the Son as being a source of the Spirit would be to split the divinity. To have two sources implies that one must contribute something the other lacks. The Father's character as 'source' would therefore be compromised. The East believed that the unity of the Godhead could only be maintained by affirming the Father to be the sole source of the other persons.

The West's reply to this was that they regarded Father and Son as forming a single source of the Spirit, thereby strengthening the unity between Father and Son. However, this did not convince the East. Father and Son remain distinct hypostases, and therefore the Spirit's origin must be attributed to two sources and not one. The only alternative would be to regard Father and Son as a single hypostasis, which of course would be nonsensical.

Towards the end of the nineteenth century, a Russian Church historian by the name of Bolotov made a remarkable attempt to get out of the above impasse with his 'Theses on the *Filioque*' (for bibliographical details see Bobrinskoy 1981:135). Two things in that essay were especially noteworthy.

The first was the distinction Bolotov made between *dogmas*, which all must believe in; the *theologoumena*, which have a high degree of authority, but to which the Church has not yet committed itself once and for all; and *theological opinions*, which lack authority since they are the private opinions of the theologians. He then applied these distinctions as follows: that the Spirit proceeds from the *Father* is a dogma; from the Father *alone* is a theologoumenon; from the Father *and the Son*, a private opinion.

The second point to note is his observation that the Father, from whom the Spirit proceeds, *is only Father in relation to the Son*. The Son is therefore a presupposition for the procession of the Spirit. 'The begetting of the Son-Word is a condition proper to God . . . for the *unconditioned* procession of the Holy Spirit, the motive and the basis (and therefore the logical "prius") for the procession of the Holy Spirit from the Father' (Bolotov, as quoted in Garrigues 1981:151–152). This gave rise to the illuminating expression, used by Moltmann: 'the Spirit proceeds from the Father *of* the Son' (Moltmann 1981a:182; 1981b:167)

The French patristic scholar Fr Jean-Miguel Garrigues has built on Bolotov's work and provided what I believe to be the most promising way of resolving the division caused by the *Filioque*. He does this by distinguishing between the dogma inherent in the *Filioque* and what belongs to the realm of theologoumena. As regards the former — the dogma — this can only be that the Spirit proceeds from the Father *precisely as Father* (i.e., as begetting and therefore in relation to the Son). 'On the basis of the Scriptures and the symphony of the Fathers of the Church, the only strictly dogmatic content of the *filioque* which can claim any rightful place in the Church's confession of faith, is that the Holy Spirit goes forth . . . from the Father, *as Father, i.e., as begetter of the unique Son.* Understood in this way the *filioque* simply spells out the dogma of the Third Person, whom the Niceno-Constantinopolitan Creed presents to us as proceeding from the Father who begets the unique Son' (Garrigues 1981:152).

The non-dogmatic elements, or theologoumena, in the *Filioque* are the attempts to state and then explain more precisely *how* the Son is involved in the procession of the third person. The traditional western view that the Son contributes positively (as a source) to the Spirit's position would fall under this category (Garrigues 1981:157), as would the more detailed explanation that the reciprocal relationship of Father and Son constitutes one single source (Garrigues 1981:161).

East and West, Garrigues argues, can agree on the dogma, while differing on the theologoumena outlined above.

(ii)   The Spirit proceeds from the Father and the Son

Let us now move on to those theologoumena and examine more closely the role played by the Son in the Spirit's procession.

The options open here are enriching, but too varied to discuss in any detail. The basic division, of course, is between granting the Son a negative or passive role (the typically eastern view) and granting him a positive or active one (the typically western view). I personally continue to adhere to the western view, not only because of the authority (even if not final) it has for me, but also because I believe it makes more sense of all the factors involved.

The first and most crucial such factor is the dogma that the Spirit proceeds from the Father *of the Son.* If the Father is only Father in relation to the Son, then 'the Father' is a relational reality. This in turn means that a relational reality is the source of the Spirit. And this — as I see it — means that the relationship must somehow or other be the very source of the Spirit's procession. Unlike a human parent, God the Father has no personal identity whatsoever apart from the Son. Now the relationship of Father to Son is one in which the Father is the source of all that the Son is. The Father therefore is source of that relationship. As such he is the source of whatever flows from it — i.e., the Spirit.

However, since the Spirit flows from the relationship of Father to Son, the Son too can be spoken of as a source of the Spirit. In traditional western jargon, the Father is the principal, the Son a derived or secondary source. As a constitutive element of the relationship, the Son too must be regarded as producing the Spirit. The relationship itself is not a hypostasis, a person, for that would imply that two *hupostaseis* or persons coalesced to form a third person — which contradicts the very notion of person. Hence, what flows from it is attributed not to the relationship itself but to the persons thus related. However, as the source of the relationship, the Father is the source of the Spirit in a way the Son can never be. Hence there is a sense in which the Father alone is the source of the Spirit.

So far I have spoken of the relationship of the Father *to* the Son. This is normally distinguished from the relationship of the Son to the Father. The former is that of paternity, the latter of filiation. However, the ground of these relationships is clearly a single procession. One can therefore talk of a single personal relationship with two aspects: that of paternity and that of filiation. It is this single relationship, this link between Father and Son that is the source of the Spirit. This relationship is unique to *them, shared* by them, though by each in his own way. Therefore we have here a case of something that is common to Father and Son, but not to the Spirit. Understood in this way, the *Filioque* does not (as the East claims) contradict the trinitarian principle that what two persons have in common is shared by the third too. Indeed, the fact that Father and Son share a relationship unique to them demonstrates the need to rephrase that famous principle in a more nuanced way. Moreover, by ascribing the source of the Spirit to a single reality shared by two persons, one is able to say without contradiction that there is but one activity, one 'spiration' giving rise to the Spirit, even though two 'spirators', Father and Son, do so.

(iii)   The Spirit proceeds as the love of Father and Son

In this final section I would like to probe still further, and ask *in what way* the link between Father and Son gives rise to the Spirit.

Augustine's answer was that it did so by giving rise to love (Chapter 4, C). Father and Son seal their relationship to each other by means of an act of love. This idea was taken up by subsequent theologians and became so much a part of the West's theology that it can be regarded as the unanimous view of Catholic theologians even today.

Love proceeds from the will. It is a volitional act. Therefore, the Spirit proceeds from the divine will, but as shared by Father and Son.

Recall that each person possesses the divine nature in a particular way. Just as both Father and Son are God but are distinguished by the way they possess the Godhead, so too both share the divine faculty of volition and the acts (of love) flowing from it, but each in his own way. As their common property, the divine will is the single source of an act of love. But this love is shaped by the relationship existing between Father and Son. As possessed by the Father, it is a love that is without origin, and moves in the direction, so to speak, of the Son whose existence makes it a *fatherly* love (just as it is the Son's existence that makes the Father *Father*). As possessed by the Son it is a received love, which moves in the direction of the Father, whose existence makes it a *filial* love (just as it is the Father's existence that makes the Son *Son*). In short, it is the love of the Father for the Son, and by that very token the love of the Son for the Father.

The Spirit proceeds then by way of an act of love whereby the Father shares the divine nature with the Son *in a second way*. Note the stress on the Father's role in this. It reminds us yet again that the Father is the source of the Spirit in a way the Son can never be. Note also the phrase 'in a second way'. The first way in which the Father shared the divine nature with the Son was one whereby the Father was *distinguished* from the Son, one in which the Son mirrored the Father. This way of sharing, the procession of the Son from the Father, gives rise therefore to two distinct ways in which the divine nature subsists, two distinct *hupostaseis* or persons. The second way in which the Father shares the divine nature with the Son is a process in which the *unity* in their distinction, a unity of love, is brought to its perfection, 'hypostasized'. Hence, it is a process in which only one further hypostasis results, and not two. This hypostasis (according to one group of theologians) is the bond or (according to another group) is the fruit of the bond uniting Father and Son to each other.

One last point. The eastern approach has always found it difficult to give a meaningful explanation of why the Spirit's procession is not, like that of the Son, a generation. The traditional western approach has the added value of being able to do that (see Chapter 5, D). The explanation is based on the distinction between the divine faculties from which each procession flows. The first faculty is that of the intellect. The purpose of intellection is to produce understanding, to produce a mental 'word' that reflects as accurately as possible the object to be understood. The very purpose of the Son's procession therefore is to produce a likeness of God, to be the perfect expression of what God is like. He is referred to as the Father's 'Son' and as having been 'generated' precisely because a 'son' is a being that comes forth from another by means of a process ('generation') designed to produce a likeness of the parent being. The

Spirit's procession, however, flows from another faculty, the will. The Spirit's procession has quite a different purpose from that of the Son. Certainly the Spirit too is fully divine and therefore a perfect likeness of God. But the point is that the whole purpose of the Spirit's procession is not to be a *likeness* of God, but rather the means whereby Father and Son are present and united to each other in love.

This brings us back to the question raised at the beginning of this entire section: what is unique about the Spirit? What is characteristic of the Spirit's personality? The western answer was the one we have just seen: love. This answer has had such an influence on western theology (it even found an echo in eastern thought) that it deserves a section to itself.

D.   THE SPIRIT AS LOVE

(i)   Objections to the idea

The idea of the Holy Spirit as love became classic within western theology (see Chapter 5, C) and continues to be subscribed to in modern times by Catholics and Protestants alike. However, curiously enough the biblical support for it is not immediately evident. Von Balthasar (1967:107) felt the lack of evidence to constitute a *prima facie* case against the entire trinitarian theology built on it.

Nevertheless, the evidence is indeed there, even if it needs to be made explicit. The scriptures repeatedly see the Spirit as the way in which God and the risen Christ are present to us. Hence one is justified in seeing 'presence' as the biblical clue to the Spirit's distinguishing characteristic. On the principle that the economic Trinity reveals the immanent one, it can be said that the Spirit is the way in which Father and Son are present to each other within the Godhead and therefore the way in which they are present to us.

Now 'presence' and 'love' are closely connected ideas. The Father's presence to the Son and the Son's presence to the Father are but the expression of their love for each other. Their presence to us is but the expression of their love for us. It is not by accident that Jesus speaks of the Spirit in the context of unity and love (Jn 14:15–31), and that Paul ascribes the pouring of God's love into our hearts to the Spirit (Rom 5:5), while listing love as a fruit of the Spirit's presence (Gal 5:22). Indeed, the New Testament regularly ascribes to the Spirit the realization within us of the fruits of the Father and Son's love for us — our justification and sanctification. In short, it is clear from the New Testament that the Spirit's especial role is to unite us to Father and Son, a unity that is clearly that of love. Hence to describe the distinctive characteristic of the Spirit as love or, more specifically, presence-in-love, unity-in-love, is far from lacking biblical support.

Nevertheless, an objection can and has been raised to the above idea from another, more speculative quarter of western theology. Love is part of, indeed is, God's very nature. As 1 Jn 4:8 put it, 'God is love'. How can one propose as distinctive of the Spirit something that is common to all three divine persons, since all three share one and the same divine nature?

A response to this objection demands explaining more clearly the precise sense in which love is specific to the Spirit. Historically there have been basically two divergent views on the matter. They can be summed up as follows: the Spirit is the *fruit* of the Father and the Son's love; the Spirit *is* that very love itself. The latter is the classic Augustinian view, and experiences the full force of the objection just raised. The former has its roots in Anselm's adaptation of Augustine's psychological model of the Trinity, and by identifying the Spirit more specifically with a *fruit* of love is able to evade the objection. Both views need to be examined in more detail. Hence the sections that follow.

(ii)   The Spirit is the fruit of love

Let us begin with the view inspired by Anselm. As was seen earlier (Chapter 5, C), the love Anselm connected with the Spirit was not so much the mutual love of Father and Son for each other, but the love both had for the divine goodness and therefore for what they were. In this perspective the love that produces the Spirit is distinguishable from the Spirit, just as the intellectual activity that produces the Son is distinguishable from the Son. It is a short step from this to seeing the Spirit as the term or fruit of an act of divine love, just as a word or idea is the term or fruit of an act of intellection.

The Spirit's procession parallels that of the Son, therefore. The only difference is that the latter is the term of an act of divine self-knowledge, while the former is the term of an act of divine self-love. Of course, there is the obvious difficulty that within our experience intellection does indeed terminate in an inner word or concept, whereas love does not. However, an appeal can be made to the divine infinity to argue the possibility of infinite love having some sort of term.

As can be seen, within this viewpoint love *strictly speaking* is no more specific to the Spirit than knowledge is to the Son. The act of loving is an act of the divine essence and as such common to all three. What is specific to the Spirit is being the term or fruit of such love and for that reason love is *appropriated* to the third person.

In recent years, Herbert Mühlen has developed the idea of the Spirit as the fruit of love by using the personalist categories of 'I', 'thou', 'we'. For Mühlen the Spirit can be described as the inner-trinitarian 'we', the fruit of the 'I–thou' relationship of Father to Son.

As noted above, an act of love lacks any term that could serve as a clear counterpart to the term of an act of understanding. By superimposing personalist categories onto the traditional psychological ones (of mind and will) Mühlen believes he can provide suitable analogies for all three persons, including therefore the Spirit.

Basic to his position is the argument that there are two, and only two, irreducibly different types of personal relationships: 'I–thou' and 'we'. 'I–you (plural)' is but a variant of 'I–thou'. In an 'I–thou' relationship the persons concerned face each other, stressing their distinction, even while seeking unity (Mühlen 1967:61ff.). By contrast, in a 'we' relationship the persons stand side by side, so to speak, acting together. Here the stress is not on their distinction but on their unity (Mühlen 1967:74ff.). A further characteristic of an 'I–thou' relationship is that one can distinguish between an initiator who seeks a reply, and the one to whom the call is made.

Applying this to the Godhead, the Father as the source of all else can be regarded as the 'I', while the Son who turns in answering love to the Father can be spoken of as the 'thou'. The Father is the 'I' within the Trinity, the Son is the answering 'thou'. What about the Spirit? The Spirit is the expression of quite a different relationship, that of 'we'. The Spirit is not, for Mühlen, the mutual love of Father and Son, but the term of that love. This term is the subsistent existence of that love as turned away from each other to a third. Mühlen appeals, as others have done, to the example of the production by parents of offspring, and especially to Richard of St Victor's idea of the Spirit as the *condilectus* of Father and Son. For Richard, the Father loves the Son, but for love to be complete there must be a third loved by both of them, a *condilectus*. For Mühlen, the Spirit is that love as (to use the terminology outlined earlier) a third completion of the divine nature: the divine nature as possessed by two united in love and turned towards the sharing of that unity with a third.

The term or fruit of the love binding Father and Son is therefore the sort of unity that is most aptly described as 'we'. It is a unity in which they no longer face each other but rather stand side by side to bring about the existence of a reality distinct from either of them: viz., the Spirit. The act of Father and Son uniting themselves in a 'we' formation results in that very formation. The *unifying activity* giving rise to a 'we' formation is Mühlen's equivalent of the traditional 'active spiration', that is to say the activity of breathing forth the Spirit (Mühlen 1967:157). The *result* of that unifying activity is the 'we' formation itself. The 'we' formation is, as said above, the divine nature subsisting in a third, completed form. It is therefore what is called a 'person'.

In short, for Mühlen the three ways in which the divine nature subsists can best be described in personalist categories. It subsists as 'I' (the Father), as the responding 'thou' (the Son), and as the sort of unity — 'we' — that looks to the production of a reality distinct from them (the Spirit).

It needs to be stressed — as Mühlen himself repeatedly does — that even these personalist categories are but analogies. They give us some insight into the mystery of the Trinity, but remain quite inadequate as an explanation. Hence, like any other analogy, Mühlen's must break down at some point. One example of such a breakdown is its inability to describe the Spirit's own relationship to Father and Son. One can hardly call it a 'we–you' or 'we–us' relationship. It can really only be described as an 'I' (Spirit)–'you' (plural: Father and Son) one. Clearly, to think of a subsistent 'we' as being also an 'I' is difficult. However, one must remember that 'I', 'thou', 'we' here describe particular ways in which the divine nature subsists, particular ways in which it finds its completion. Each is moreover a conscious way of subsisting. Hence it can be called a 'person' and act as an 'I'. In other words, within the Trinity, a second 'I' (the Son) is characterized by the fact of being a responding 'I', a 'thou'; while a third 'I' (the Spirit) is characterized by being the very unity of Father and Son, the sort of unity described as a 'we' one.

Mühlen's theology of the Spirit belongs to the group that sees the Spirit as the 'fruit' or 'term' of love. But by stressing that that term is the very unity of Father and Son, he arrives at a position very close to the other, classic Augustinian view. The traditional exposition of the Spirit as the term or fruit of an act of love was that the Spirit represented the termination of an act of divine volition that paralleled the termination of an act of divine intellection. The fact that two persons were the subject of that volition seemed somewhat incidental to its nature, being of real value only for the upholding of the principle that the Spirit proceeded from both Father and Son as from one principle. In Mühlen's (as in Augustine's) view, the difference between the Spirit's procession and that of the Son is accentuated by seeing the unity between Father and Son as not incidental but central to the Spirit's very 'personality'. Mühlen comes very close then to the other stream of thought. The difference, expressed in his own terminology, would I think be as follows: whereas for him the Spirit is a subsistent 'we' unity, one that exists *in addition to* 'I–thou', for the classic Augustinian stream the Spirit is a *subsistent* 'I–thou' unity. This difference may seem so slight as to be negligible. However, a 'we' unity is rather different from an 'I–thou' one and has different implications for the way the Spirit's specific 'personality' is viewed.

(iii)   The Spirit is love itself

The second viewpoint is that the Spirit is not any fruit or term of love, but love itself. An immediate implication of this is that the Spirit is not the *object* of Father and Son's love (Bourassa 1970:80, 126, 132), not a *condilectus*, one upon whom love is poured out. Of course, since Father and Son can be said to love the love that binds them, the Spirit can be said to be loved by them, as Augustine observed (*The Trinity*, VIII, 8, 10; see also Bourassa 1970:163 and Chapter 5, C). However, the Spirit is not the expression of a third reality loved, but is the very love binding Father and Son to each other.

As it has developed, this viewpoint does not see love simply as something appropriated but rather as specific to the Spirit. The Spirit and the Spirit alone is subsistent love, the divine nature existing as a love-bond.

But if that is the case, the objection raised earlier recurs here with all its force: if the Spirit's specific (i.e., differentiating) characteristic is to be subsistent love, then surely one must deny that Father and Son possess the characteristic of love? If they did possess love, then there would be nothing to distinguish the Spirit from them.

In response to this objection, it needs to be noted first of all that the very love constitutive of the Spirit is the love of *Father* and *Son* for each other. Hence, far from implying that Father and Son cannot possess love, the Spirit's very personality presupposes that they have it. But this observation does not resolve the basic problem of distinguishing the love that is the Spirit from the love that Father and Son exercise.

To pinpoint the distinctive character of the love that is the Spirit, one needs to recall yet again that while all three persons share all that the divinity comprises — love, knowledge, power, and so forth — each does so in a specific way. Each person possesses the divine nature and therefore knowledge and love in a specific way. Indeed, as we saw, each person *is* the divine nature, *is* divine knowledge, *is* divine love subsisting in a specific way. Bearing this in mind, I would reply as follows to the objection raised (see also Bourassa 1970:169).

The Father loves, indeed *is* love, but love subsisting as the origin of all else. Such love is specific to him. The originating character of the Father is what defines the specific character of his love and not vice versa. Hence being an unoriginated origin is seen as the specific characteristic of the Father, and not love. As regards the Son's love, indeed, as regards the love that the Son *is*, this is love subsisting as the reflection of all that the Father is. As such it is specific to the Son. Here too, the particular character of the Son as reflection of the Father is what characterizes the Son's love. Hence, being an 'image' of the Father, rather than love, is seen as specifying the Son's 'personality'. As regards the love specific to the Spirit, it is love *subsisting as the bond* between Father and Son. Here the specific character of this love is not defined by something other than love itself. Rather, it is defined by love's property: its bonding character, its uniting of persons. Hence the Spirit's specifying characteristic is not something other than love, but love itself, as the bond uniting Father and Son to each other. That bond is distinct from those bound by it, and hence is a third, distinct person.

To be sure, further objections can be raised to the above response. However, I believe they are the sort of objections that can be raised to the classic solution of the broader issue of how the divine persons can all possess fully one and the same divine nature, and yet be distinct. To respond to those objections would demand going into trinitarian theology to a degree that is not possible here. For our purpose it is sufficient to take the classic solution — viz., that what distinguishes the divine persons is the way in which each possesses the divine nature — and show its applicability to the case of the Spirit conceived of as subsistent mutual love.

I believe that this second theory corresponds better to the revealed role of the Spirit than the previous one does. If the Spirit is above all the way in which God and the risen Christ are present to *us*, then it can be inferred that the Spirit is above all the way in which Father and Son are for all eternity present to each other. The Spirit is revealed to us as a way of being present, a way of acting and not as the object of the attentions or affection of Father and Son.

I also think that by identifying the Spirit with love and not just the fruit thereof, this second theory is able to give us a better insight into three other traditional characteristics of the Spirit.

The first is the Spirit's 'facelessness'. The Spirit's 'personality' has always lacked clear contours — in contrast to the personalities of Father and Son. Aquinas would see the reason for this in the fact that (as he believed) the created world knows only one way in which natures are communicated from one being to another, the way of generation (*Summa*, Ia, 27, 5 ad 3). In other words, the problem for him would arise out of the lack of an adequate analogy in the created world.

Connected to this is the problem, experienced by the first theory, of providing a suitable creaturely comparison for the fruit of an act of love.

Mühlen, as we saw, overcomes this difficulty to a great extent by providing the analogy of the 'we' structure. Having done that, he is able to see the Spirit's anonymity as arising out of being the expression of the unity of two persons. The Spirit's very personality is constituted by that unity. Hence the Spirit's only 'face' is that unity. The Spirit is, as Mühlen loves to stress, '*one* person in *two* persons' (Mühlen 1967:164). Mühlen not only provides the sought-for analogy. He also highlights the real reason for the Spirit's anonymity: the fact that the Spirit's 'face' is that of being the bond between Father and Son. This, of course, is not a new idea. Barth, for example, used it when he spoke of the Spirit's 'neutrality' as expressive of being the 'common factor between the mode of existence of God the Father and that of God the Son' (1936:537).

The Spirit's 'facelessness' is therefore due not so much to a lack of suitable analogies, as to the very nature of the Spirit's personality. This comes out even more clearly if one adopts the view that the Spirit is the mutual love of Father and Son for each other. Love is 'faceless'. The only face it seeks and therefore has is the face of the beloved. It seeks to unite lover and beloved so closely, so perfectly, that it has no identity of its own, other than that unity. The reason for the Spirit's anonymity is made crystal clear: the Spirit is love, and love is faceless. This is also the reason why the Spirit is experienced as the presence of Father and Son, and not as a person with a clear and distinct identity.

The second characteristic illuminated by the theory outlined in this section, is that of the Spirit's being a 'gift'. The idea of the Spirit as 'gift' is a very old one, having its roots in texts such as Acts 8:20 and Lk 11:13. In the scriptures the Spirit is conceived of as God's gift to his *creatures*. This is also the way the Greek Fathers saw the matter (Bourassa 1970:193, 210). However, one can apply the principle that the economic Trinity reveals the immanent one, and conclude that the gift-character of the Spirit to us is a reflection of an eternal, inner-trinitarian reality, even though Augustine, who gives the lead, did not actually draw this conclusion.

To be a gift within the Trinity, the Spirit must either be a reality given by only the Father to the Son, or by the Son to the Father, or by both to each other. If the first is accepted, then one must reject the western tradition of granting the Son a positive role in the Spirit's procession. If the second option is accepted, then this would contradict the idea that the Spirit is above all God the Father's gift to us. The third option is the only viable one: viz., that the Spirit is the mutual gift of Father and Son to each other.

The mutuality of this gift is best explained if the Spirit is seen as the mutual love of Father and Son, and not simply the result of such love. Were the latter to be the case — even in Mühlen's version of expressing a 'we' structure — the inner-trinitarian gift would either lack a recipient, or not be characteristic of the Spirit's personality. To be characteristic of that personality, 'gift' must be something constitutive of the Spirit, and not simply an added quality to an already constituted reality. To assert that the Spirit is the *fruit* of love, a fruit that Father and Son then exchange with each other, is to conceive the *fruit* as constitutive of the Spirit's personality with the gift character tacked on. However, if one identifies the Spirit with the mutual love of Father and Son for each other, then the 'gift' is not only mutual but also constitutive of the Spirit's personality. That mutual love is the mutual gift. It is the way Father and Son give *themselves* to each other. The gift too therefore has the facelessness of love. It is their love, a love that completes the divine nature in a third and final way.

Mention of a 'final' way of completing the divine nature brings us to the third characteristic of the Spirit: that of being the *telos* or final completion of the divine nature. This too is a very old idea (see again Chapter 5, C, towards the end). The Spirit is seen as the terminus or final point of a movement within the Godhead whereby the divine substance is experienced and shared in three different ways. For Richard of St Victor, as we saw, the movement is completed by the presence of a *condilectus*, a third person loved in order that love may be complete. For Mühlen, completion requires moving from an 'I–thou' to a 'we' structure. Neither of these requirements for completion seems very convincing to me. What I do find convincing is the idea that unity between two persons is only complete when the bond uniting them goes beyond merely sharing a substance or nature, when it goes beyond that to become one of love. The mutual love of Father and Son for each other is in itself the terminus, the *telos*, the completion of the divine life. Conceiving of the Spirit as that mutual love therefore makes greater sense of this traditional characteristic of the Spirit too.

Finally, it can be pointed out that if one adopts the view that the Spirit is subsistent mutual love, then the three characteristics illuminated by such a view can be seen to be simply aspects of love. They are not really distinguishable from love. All they do is to point out love's facelessness, its gift-character, and the completion it brings to life.

E.   THE SPIRIT IS A PERSON WHOSE IDENTITY IS TO BE THE MEANS WHEREBY GOD AND CHRIST ARE PRESENT TO EACH OTHER AND TO US

The present chapter began by contrasting two conceptions of the Spirit: the means whereby Father and Son are present to us; a divine person. It was pointed out that although these two views seemed mutually exclusive, they in fact were not. From all that has gone before, it should be clear that the Spirit can be both. Indeed, the Spirit's very personality can be said to be *constituted* by the fact of being the means whereby Father and Son are present to each other. Let me recall the main steps in the argument.

I began by examining the meaning of the word 'person' as applied to the Trinity. A 'person' was found to be a unique way in which the divine nature subsisted. Moreover, it was pointed out that therefore each was a 'person' in a different way. The three ways in which the divine nature found its completion — as source, as knowledge, as love — differ: a source is not knowledge, and neither of these is love. Yet each of these is a completion of the divine nature and as such gives rise to the existence of a unique 'person'. There is therefore no contradiction between being love and being a 'person' in the sense explained.

The love in question was, I argued, the mutual love of Father and Son for each other. This is the way in which Father and Son are present to each other. Hence, there is no contradiction between the Spirit being a person and the way in which Father and Son are present to each other — and, of course, to us.

I believe it is therefore incorrect to say that the Spirit is a person and *also* the means whereby Father and Son are present to us. We should rather say that the Spirit is that person whose whole identity is constituted by the fact of being the means of their presence.

From the above it follows that the Spirit is not a person we relate to in the same way as we relate to Father and Son. Father and Son can be objects of our attention. We can focus on the Son without seeing him simply as the reflection of the Father (though perhaps the real reason for this is the Son's appearance in flesh in Jesus Christ). We can focus on the Father without seeing him simply as the source of the other two persons. With the Spirit, however, it is different. It would be somewhat of a distortion to make the Spirit an object of our attention in a similar way. I do not mean that one cannot pray to the Spirit — though it is significant that in the earliest Christian traditions prayers to the Spirit were not customary, and the liturgical norm remains of asking *Father and Son* to pour out their Spirit upon us. But any prayer to the Spirit should always be a prayer for the Spirit to fulfil the role of bringing us closer to Father, Son and each other. It has often been said that the Father is our father, the Son our brother, and the Spirit our lover. That is not quite accurate because it gives the Spirit an identity parallel to that of Father and Son, enabling us to relate to the Spirit as a lover, to the Father as a father, and the Son as a brother. The truth of the matter is that it is the Spirit's identity to be the way in which we experience the presence of our real lovers: Father and Son.

The point being made here is not simply a quibble about minutiae. On the contrary, it is of immense importance. It is the failure to observe and learn from it that has led to the many movements that appeal to the Spirit as if the Spirit were a source of revelation apart from Father and Son. I will return to this theme again in Chapter 12, A. For the moment it is sufficient to point out that just as (and precisely because!) the Spirit has no face other than to be the presence of Father and Son to each other, so too does the Spirit have no revelatory role other than to bring *their* truth to us, to unite us to them in *their* truth.

QUESTIONS

Check questions

1   What are the two answers that have been given to the question: what sort of reality is the Holy Spirit?
2   What is meant by 'person' as applied to the members of the Trinity?
3   In what sense is self-consciousness part, and in what sense can it not be part, of the notion of a trinitarian person?
4   What is meant by the Spirit's 'procession'?
5   As regards the *Filioque* belief, what should be regarded as (a) dogma; (b) authoritative tradition that has not yet achieved the status of dogma; (c) private theological opinions within that tradition?
6   What are the two diverging streams of thought concerning the more precise sense in which the Spirit's specifying characteristic is love?
7   Why is it not a contradiction to say that the Spirit is at one and the same time a person and the way in which Father and Son are present to each other?

Discussion questions

1   Discuss the arguments that have been given for and against the *Filioque*.
2   Discuss the pros and cons of each of the two theories on the more precise sense in which the Spirit's specific character is that of love.
3   St Augustine and the monastic theologians of the twelfth century insisted that it is essential for us to love if we wish to understand God, if we wish to understand the meaning of the ideas we use in theology. What connections are there between that idea and the theology of the Spirit outlined in this chapter?

RECOMMENDED READING

On the concept 'person', see the following articles in the *New Catholic Encyclopedia* (New York: McGraw-Hill, 1967): 'Person (in theology)' (vol. XI); 'Subsistence' (vol. XIII); 'Hypostasis' (vol. VII). A useful potted history of the term and a discussion of its value as well as of related concepts can be found in Barth 1936:408–421. Well worth reading is Rahner 1970:103–115, for an analysis of the drawbacks of the term as well as for its suggestion of alternatives.

On the *Filioque* controversy, the entire volume Vischer 1981 is valuable. More specifically, I would recommend the ecumenical statement in part I, and the essays by Orphanos, Garrigues and Moltmann. Moltmann's contribution can also be found in Moltmann 1981a.

On the theme of the Spirit as the mutual love of Father and Son, Congar 1983a, ch. 3, gives a summary account of the views of Anselm, William of St Thierry, Richard of St Victor, Bonaventure and Aquinas. It is not easy reading, but useful as a jumping-off point for further research.

Mühler's concept of the Spirit as person: short account in English by Mühlen in McDonnell 1975:11–33.

8

The Spirit's mission

The word 'mission' comes from the Latin word *missio*, meaning 'a sending'. To carry out one's 'mission', therefore, is to carry out the purpose for which one is sent. In this chapter, then, I want to discuss the reason for the Spirit's coming. Of course, the rest of the book can be viewed as an answer to that question. However, in this chapter I want to discuss the basic ideas concerned with the Spirit's mission, ideas which are the foundation of all that follows.

A. THE SPIRIT'S MISSION IS TO BE THE LOVE THAT UNITES AND, BY UNITING, TRANSFORMS ALL IT UNITES

Traditionally two missions have been distinguished: the visible and the invisible (see Chapter 5, E). The former was seen as the visible sign of the latter, which was said to be the Spirit's indwelling for the purpose of sanctifying the recipient.

All this, of course, is true. However, I think we need to take more seriously Thomas Aquinas's assertion that divine missions reflect divine origins (see Chapter 5, E). If that is so then the character — and the purpose — of the sending of a divine person must reflect the character and purpose of that person's inner-trinitarian origins. If the procession of the Spirit has as its purpose the uniting of Father and Son together in an unbreakable bond of love, if its purpose is to be the loving way in which Father and Son are eternally present to each other, then the basic reason for the Spirit's mission must be the same: to be the love that unites Father and Son to us, to be the way (i.e., in love) that they are present to us.

Let me expand on this a bit. What we call 'God' is, of course, a community. This statement may sound rather odd to some, but if we take seriously the belief that in the one God there are three 'persons', then what we call 'God' is a community of three. Divine life is in no way an isolated life. The one motive the Father could not have had for creating us was to assuage his loneliness! In fact, loneliness is so terrible precisely because it is so ungodlike. What we call the divinity then is not a static substance but a single, infinite life shared by three 'persons', a never-ending life of loving and being loved.

God, we read in Genesis, made human beings in the divine image and likeness (Gen 1:26–27). People are God's image in various ways. The point the *Bible* stresses is that human beings, like God, have (thanks to God's gift) mastery over creation (see Gen 1:26; Ps 8:5–6). In *Christian history* our abilities to know and love have been stressed as the way in which we are God's image. However, these and other ways in which people are said to be God's image view God and us simply as individuals. Christianity has revealed to us another point of comparison between God and humanity, namely that just as God is a community, so too is the humanity created by God. We were not created as a group of isolated individuals but as a community. Gen 2:18 tells us that it is not good for human beings to be alone, and the reason no doubt is because it is not good for God to be alone.

Now it was never God's intention that the two communities should exist separately. The divine motto was not 'apartheid' but 'unity'. The two communities were meant to become one. But how?

Christians believe that this was brought about by God becoming part of our world. The one who, within the Trinity, is the divine image of the Father became his human image. What within God reflects what the Father is like became the human reflection, the human revelation of the Father. The Word, as John put it, took on flesh (Jn 1:14). Moreover, the Spirit uniting them within the Trinity continues to unite them. In this way the Spirit too becomes part of this world. The Spirit of love continues to flow from the Word, uniting Father and Son.

However, it is now from a *Word made flesh* that the Spirit proceeds. This rather important observation has received far too little attention from theologians. David Coffey has, it is true, made the idea central to his thinking on the Spirit (see Coffey 1979, 1984, 1986). But there are, I suspect, enormous as yet untapped implications for theology in it. For example, does it not imply that the very divine processions — Son from Father, Spirit from both — have become part of humanity's world? That of itself is a rather staggering thought.

Now, I believe that the divine plan to become one with humanity was not the result of a divine decision taken after humanity had sinned. On the contrary, to form one community with humanity was God's original purpose in creating us. Sin's contribution was to threaten the unity planned by God. Sin's very nature is to cause division. It separates people from God (Gen 3:8–10) and from each other (Gen 3:12 and 4:8).

It divides people inwardly (Gen 3:7). It even separates humanity from its environment (Gen 3:17). The result of all this separation and division is suffering. The most dramatic sign of it is death.

Sin did not send God back to the drawing-board, so to speak. It did not bring about a divine change of plan. But it did mean that both God and humanity would suffer in the process of realizing the desired unity between the two. Sin made suffering a built-in feature of the world. What we call 'salvation', then, is simply the achieving of God's plan *despite* sin. We are saved from the divisive effects of sin by the fact that God was determined to be one with us, even at the cost of suffering the consequences. Salvation is a creating of community. It is the achievement of unity between God and humanity and, as a result, between people, within individuals, and between people and their environment.

The Spirit's mission therefore is to unite God and us (and by 'us' I include Jesus Christ), and thereby transform us and our world. Spelled out in a bit more detail, the Spirit's mission is (a) to unite God and Christ and give us a sharing in that unity, (b) to create community by uniting Christ and us to each other, (c) to transform each of us so that all our energies are united in the service of love, and (d) transform our world so that it is a world at the service of love and no longer of selfishness.

All this, of course, does not deny the traditional ideas about the Spirit's mission — that the Spirit was sent to achieve a divine indwelling and bring about our sanctification. It simply provides a more basic setting for those ideas.

The divine indwelling can best be viewed as our sharing in what is called the divine *perichōrēsis* or *circumincession*. This is the belief that within the Trinity each of the persons are 'in' the other. It can be viewed statically (as the West tended to do with its static term 'circuminsessio' — 'residing in one another'). Or it can be viewed dynamically (as the East does) as a ceaseless movement ('circumincessio') whereby one person flows into the other. Either way, the basic point is that sharing as they do one nature, the persons can be said to dwell in one another.

As the bond of their love, the Spirit plays a role in the *perichōrēsis* that goes beyond that played by the divine nature. Certainly, sharing one nature means that all the persons dwell in one another. However, what makes their mutual indwelling one of love (and not simply the dwelling of a source in what flows from it and vice versa) is the Spirit. Moreover, the Spirit, and the Spirit alone, is constituted a person by being simultaneously in Father and Son (see Mühlen 1966:164). In other words, the Spirit's very personality is constituted by dwelling in two persons simultaneously. Hence the Spirit's very nature is to transform 'physical' indwelling, for want of a better word, into one of love.

The divine indwelling is no less than our sharing in the inner-trinitarian *perichōrēsis*, our sharing in the communal life of Father, Son and Spirit. Therefore, to say that the Spirit has been 'sent' for the sake of the divine indwelling in us is to say that the Spirit enables us to participate in the eternal indwelling or *perichōrēsis* that occurs within the divinity.

As regards our sanctification, this is but the transformation that must take place within anyone who is brought into a new relationship with God. But more specifically, it is the transformation that love always achieves. To be one as Father and Son are (Jn 17:21) demands a transformation so total that even the limitations of space and time as we experience them must be broken to achieve it. Such a transformation has already occurred: it is the risen life present in Jesus, Mary and — according to some theologians — all those who have died in Christ. But that is another matter. The only point I wish to make here is that our sanctification is our 'divinization', our transformation. And as such it is the work of love. Love unites and by uniting transforms all it unites. This, I believe, is the key to understanding the Spirit's mission. For that mission is simply to be the love that unites and by so doing transforms us and (since we are bodily creatures) our world.

B.   THE SPIRIT'S MISSION AND THE MISSION OF THE CHURCH

From the above it is clear that the primary purpose of the Spirit's mission is to unite God, Christ and us, and thereby to transform us and our world. I therefore differ from those who see the main reason for the Spirit's coming in more pragmatic terms: for example Green (1975:58) writes that 'there can be no doubt from a candid examination of the New Testament accounts that the prime purpose of the coming of the Spirit of God upon the disciples was to equip them for mission'. However, I do indeed doubt that this is, even in the New Testament's perspectives, the *prime* purpose of the Spirit's coming. Certainly the Church's mission is of the utmost importance and it is clear that the Spirit did equip the disciples for mission. But that that was the prime purpose of the Spirit's coming I seriously doubt. Rather, the Spirit appears primarily as the eschatological gift, that is to say, the gift of the end times, the gift whereby the Father is present to his people through the presence of his Son. In other words, the Spirit appears primarily as the means whereby God and Christ are present to us. This is especially clear from Paul's writings. For him the stress is not on the Spirit and mission but on the Spirit and the unity the Spirit creates between God, Christ and us.

Nevertheless, to deny that the prime reason for the Spirit's coming is to equip the disciples for their mission is not to deny that the prime reason for the Spirit's coming is for *the achievement of the Church's mission*. The mission of the Church is to be the visible sign and instrument, the visible embodiment of the unity in Christ to which God has called all people (see Vatican II, *Constitution on the Church*, §1). The Church's mission, therefore, is to be the visible embodiment of unity in the Spirit, unity in love. Its mission is to be the visible sign and instrument of the Spirit's mission. The two missions — that of the Church and that of the Spirit — are really one. This is why Pentecost has rightly been regarded as the day on which the Church was born.

The same thing can be seen if one remembers that the Spirit is the way in which Christ continues to be actively present in the world. The Spirit's mission is the way in which Christ brings to fulfilment his own mission of enabling others to share in his unity with the Father. The Church and the Spirit are sent for the same reason. The former is the visible sign, embodiment and instrument of the latter's mission.

Subsequent chapters will deal with the details of the Spirit's work. However, all these details, whether they be the transformation of the world, the inspiring of scripture, the sanctification of the individual, or the equipping of the missionary, are but aspects of the one basic mission of the Spirit: to bring about that unity between God and humanity that has always been the Father's plan for us.

C.   THE SPIRIT'S MISSION IS DISTINCTIVE TO THE SPIRIT ALONE

Basic to our trinitarian faith is the revelation that Jesus' Father is our Father, that Jesus is our brother, and the Spirit the way in which they are present, united to us in love. Our relationship to each of the persons is distinct. Only the Father is our Father. Only the Son is our brother. Only the Spirit is the way in which we are united to them and each other. Indeed, the Trinity was revealed precisely in the distinct relationships the early Christians saw themselves as having to the Father and the Son, and the distinctive role played by the Spirit in their experience of the presence of Father and Son.

Nevertheless, a tradition developed (see Chapter 5, D) that reduced to a mere 'appropriation' the distinct relationship Christians have to each of the persons. The logical — and ludicrous — conclusion was one that even Aquinas was forced to reach: viz., that all the divine persons adopt us as children, all are really our Father. Since all three persons both created and redeemed us, it is only by appropriation that we can view the first person of the Trinity as our Father (*Summa*, IIIa, 23, 2).

Small wonder that Christians became trinitarians only in theory, being in their actual Christian lives to all intents and purposes sheer unitarians, unaware of their distinct relationship to each of the divine persons.

The reason for this deviation was Augustine's principle that all divine activities *ad extra* (that is to say, beyond the 'borders' of God) were common to all three persons. All shared a single nature, which was the instrument producing all *ad extra* effects. Therefore all such effects were produced by all three persons. It is, of course, perfectly true that all activities *ad extra* must be common to all three persons. All three must be involved. However, in applying this principle two things were forgotten, or at any rate their implications for the principle were not seen.

The first is that each divine person shares the divine nature in a distinct way. If that is so, then each of the persons will indeed be involved in every *ad extra* activity, *but always in accordance with the way in which that person possesses the divine nature*. The Father, and he alone, is always the unbegotten source of all things. It is as such that we relate to him and he alone therefore is our divine parent. The Son is always the expression, the manifestation of the Father. 'To have seen me is to have seen the Father' (Jn 14:9). As such, the Son alone is the revelation of the Father. Moreover, as the begotten expression of the Father, the Son is the Father's offspring. Therefore the Son and the Son alone is our divine sibling. Therefore, too, the Son and the Son alone could meaningfully become incarnate, the *human* expression, the *human* revelation of the Father. Finally, the Spirit is always the way in which Father and Son are present in love. Hence the Spirit and the Spirit alone will always be the way in which Father and Son are present to us in love, creating, redeeming, transforming us and our world. In short, as the ancient formula put it so well, all *ad extra* activities reflect the inner life of God in that all proceed from the Father (as ultimate source), through the Son (as the expression of all the Father is and does), in the unity of the Holy Spirit (as the love uniting them, the way in which they are present to each other).

The second point overlooked by those who stressed the common character of all divine activities *ad extra* was the fact that our salvation was not simply a work *ad extra* (Rahner 1970:34ff.). To be sure, we do not become divine. The borderline between God and us remains. Whatever God does to us is an activity terminating 'beyond' the divinity. However, the whole point of God's creating and saving us is to enable us to share in the inner divine life, the life of the Trinity. The whole *point* is that the Father becomes *our* Father, the Son *our* brother and the Spirit *our* bond uniting us to them and to each other. Hence divine *ad extra* activities towards us are rather different from such activities directed at the preservation in being of mere physical objects such as mountains, plants, stars, etc. In such a case, each of the divine persons acts indeed according to the way in which the divine nature is possessed and therefore distinctly. But no distinct personal relationship is created between the mountains or the stars and a particular divine person.

QUESTIONS

Check questions

1 What is the Spirit's mission?
2 How does your answer relate to the idea that the Spirit's mission is (a) to achieve a divine indwelling; (b) to bring about our sanctification?
3 In what sense has the Spirit, like Christ, become part of our world?
4 What is the relationship between the Spirit's mission and that of the Church?
5 'All divine activities *ad extra* are common to all three persons.' How would you do justice to that principle and yet argue that the Spirit's mission belongs to the Spirit alone?

Discussion questions

1 Is it possible to do justice to the Pentecost story and yet assert that the *prime* purpose of the Spirit's coming was not to equip the disciples for mission?
2 What insights do you think can be gained by highlighting the fact that the Spirit proceeds from a Word that is now incarnate?
3 Reflect on and discuss the extent to which your Christian life has been in fact, and not just in theory, trinitarian.

RECOMMENDED READING

See the article 'Missions, Divine' in the *New Catholic Encyclopedia* (New York: McGraw-Hill, 1967), vol. IX, which also gives a further bibliography, of which note especially M. J. Scheeben, *The Mysteries of Christianity* (St Louis and London: Herder, 1947), pp. 149–180. Well worth reading, though not easy, is Rahner 1970:21–46, 76–77. Also worth reading is Coffey 1984.

9

The Spirit unites God and humanity in Christ

The preceding chapter argued that the Spirit's mission was to unite, to be the way in which Father and Son were present to us — and us to them. The present chapter is devoted to examining some basic aspects of that unity.

The unity between God and humanity achieved by Christ rests on two foundations. The first is Christ's unity with God. The second is his unity with us. It is necessary to examine the Spirit's role in each of these relationships. This will be done in sections A and B. The Spirit's role in Christ's unity with God and with humanity will enable us to understand the Spirit's role in the saving events of Christ's life: his incarnation, life, death and resurrection. This will be discussed in section C. The final section (D) will look briefly at the fact that God's unity with humanity is something that reaches out *from Christ* to embrace others. The treatment will be brief because the matter will be discussed in more detail in subsequent chapters.

Needless to say, what follows is an attempt at studying a unified reality — the work of the Spirit — by looking at its different aspects. All these aspects are so intimately connected with each other that it is impossible to treat any one without at least mentioning the others. Hence there will be an unavoidable repetition and overlapping of material from this point onwards.

A. THE SPIRIT'S ROLE IN JESUS' UNITY WITH GOD

To understand the Spirit's role in Jesus' unity with God, I must point out that the word 'God' here means 'God *the Father*'. Christians certainly believe that Jesus is God. But this means that he is God's *Word*, that within God which reflects, reveals what God is like. Jesus did not speak about his unity with the Word. Nor can we speak about his unity with the Word. For Jesus *is* the Word. You cannot be united to yourself.

You *are* yourself. However, Jesus did talk about his unity with the *Father*. When he spoke about 'God' he meant 'the Father'. The early Christians, too, usually meant 'the Father' when they spoke about God. A good deal of confusion would be avoided if people remembered this.

So when I talk about 'God's' unity with humanity and Jesus' unity with 'God' as one of its foundations, I am talking about the *Father's* unity with humanity and Jesus' unity with the *Father* as one of its foundations. This means that the concern of this section is to understand Jesus's unity *with the Father* as the foundation of the Father's unity with us. What, then, is the Spirit's role as regards his unity with the Father?

At first sight it may seem that there is very little of a role for the Spirit to play, since the Word shares one nature with the Father. The Word that became flesh in Jesus Christ is 'of one substance with the Father'. Therefore the unbreakable link between the two would seem to be their common divinity. And since their common divinity is the source of the Spirit and not vice versa, the Spirit seems to have no real role to play in Jesus' unity with the Father.

However, while it is true that their common divinity is an unbreakable link between the Father and the Son, it is not their common divinity that unites them *as persons*. It is the Spirit of their love that does that (see Aquinas, *I Sentences*, d 10, q 1, a 3, c; as cited in Bourassa 1970:74). Their common divinity is, if you like, a merely 'physical' unity. True unity between persons only exists where there is love. We too have a 'physical' unbreakable link with God: our very existence is something that has to be sustained by God's creative activity every instant of our lives. God is therefore always present to us, sustaining us in being. However, there is only a *personal unity* between God and us when we love each other. Love, and only love, can create true unity between persons.

The fact then that the man Jesus shared substantially in the divinity did not of itself mean that there was truly a personal unity between him and God (= God the Father). Similarly, we can surmise that the mere fact that within the Trinity the Word is of one substance with the Father is not in itself sufficient for there to be a true unity between them. True unity, i.e., personal unity, is created by love. Therefore, what is further required is their *unity in the Spirit*.

Jesus' unity with his Father was therefore not merely a physical thing: sharing the divine nature. Rather, his personal unity with the Father was created by the fact that he and the Father were present to each other in the love that is the Holy Spirit. Jesus could, theoretically, have sinned. He was not a machine, but had freedom just as we do. He was tempted, just as we are (Heb 4:15; 2:18). He had to obey God, just as we must (Phil 2:8–9; Heb 5:8). He needed to pray, just as we do. Moreover, he needed to pray, not only to praise and thank his Father (Mt 11:25, Jn 11:41), but also to ask him for his help (Heb 5:7; Mt 26:39). Jesus' ability to be tempted, his need to pray, and particularly his need to obey, demonstrate his freedom. If he had freedom, then theoretically he could sin. And such sin would, of course, have been the one thing that could have broken the unity existing between him and God (= the Father). It is an old tradition that Jesus was incapable of sinning. The reason given was that he was divine. I agree that Jesus was *in fact* incapable of sinning. However, I disagree that the reason was the mere fact that he shared God's divine nature. For if that were the reason, then we would have to conclude that the divine nature was a sort of machine forcing Jesus always to be good. Rather, we must look for the reason why Jesus could not sin in his love. He could not sin because he *loved* so much. And he loved as much as he did because he was so perfectly united with his Father *in the Spirit*, that Spirit that now proceeded from the incarnate Word (see Chapter 8, A). It is only love that can make us incapable of sinning while yet leaving us with the freedom to do so. So then, just as it was not the mere fact that he shared God's nature that united him to the Father, so too it was not the mere fact that he shared God's nature that made Jesus sinless. What truly made him one with the Father and what truly made him incapable of sinning against the Father was the Love that bound him to the Father.

In Jesus we also see how God's Spirit can totally transform a human life. For it was the unbreakable love-bond between him and the Father, brought about by the Spirit, a love-bond stretching back into eternity, that enabled him to have the unique insight into the things of God that he had. It is important to remember that the Word made flesh had a human, not a divine, mind. To confess that the Word became flesh is to confess that the Word became a limited human being. Jesus' mind was a human mind, subject to the limitations that inevitably affect every human mind. He had to learn and grow in knowledge (Lk 2:52). He did not know absolutely everything (see Mk 5:30–33 — he did not know who touched his garments; Mt 24:36 — he did not know when the end of the world would be; Mt 8:10 — he was surprised at the officer's faith and therefore could not read his heart). The belief that Jesus is divine must not be allowed to obscure the equally important belief that he is human. I stress this because people usually think of Jesus as having a human head with God's own divine, infinite mind inside it. Were that the case, he would not have been human. Therefore, Jesus' knowledge of God is a *human* knowledge and like all human knowledge it had to be *received* from somewhere. It could have been the result of the Father revealing many things to him. But I think that the uniquely close relationship Jesus had with the Father, a relationship forged by the Spirit, would have given him much of his insight into the things of God. In fact, one could surmise that even his awareness of his own divinity was experienced precisely as a relationship to God so close that his life and God's life were felt to be one (Jn 10:30). This experience of unity with God, of God's presence, was for Jesus an experience of the Spirit of the Father, an experience of the Father's Love.

In short, the Spirit's role was to make God and Jesus truly one, to unite them in the way persons, not things, are united.

B.   THE SPIRIT'S ROLE IN JESUS' UNITY WITH HUMANITY

The second of the two foundations on which God's (= the Father's) unity with us rests is Jesus' unity with us. The previous section showed how Jesus' unity with God itself rested on two foundations: the fact that he was 'of one substance' with God and the fact that he was united in love to God. Something similar can be said about Jesus' unity with us.

First of all, Jesus is 'of one substance' with humanity. In other words, he is a human being. This is very important. For it is already a tremendous advance on the kind of unity God had with humanity prior to Jesus' birth. With that birth someone who was 'of one substance' with God was also 'of one substance' with us. However, the fact that Jesus had a human nature created of itself only a 'physical' bond between him and humanity. For a personal bond to exist, there had to be a free decision on his part to love his fellow human beings. True, this love had to be reciprocated before there was a *mutual* bond of love between him and any particular individual. But the willingness of any human being to love even those who do not love in return already establishes a bond between them that goes beyond the merely physical. For already love is reaching out and enveloping others, even if there is as yet no response. From the point of view of the lover there is already an identification with the person loved. There is already a willingness to share that person's lot.

Jesus' link with us then was not a merely physical one. He *loved* people, all people. For all were God's children. He himself said that he came to serve, to give even his life as a ransom (Mk 10:45; Mt 20:28). He therefore accepted the human community as *his* community, us as his Father's other children, his sisters and brothers.

The Spirit's role in this link between Jesus and humanity is obvious. It was the Spirit that enabled him to love others so selflessly. It was the Spirit's power that enabled him to demonstrate that love tangibly in healings and exorcisms. But above all, it was the Spirit's power that so transformed him on Easter day that, by means of that same Spirit, he can now be as close to humanity as God is.

The Spirit, therefore, turns Jesus' physical identity with us into an unbreakable bond of love. Fortunately, nothing humanity can do can make Jesus withdraw that love. This basically is why our world is a saved world, which leads me on to the next section.

C.   THE SPIRIT'S ROLE IN JESUS' INCARNATION, LIFE, DEATH AND RESURRECTION AS SAVING EVENTS

The idea is still widespread among Christians that the only event in the life of Jesus that contributed anything to our salvation was his death. However, if one reads the New Testament it is clear that not only his death but also his incarnation (in the incarnate Lord eternal life has already been made a reality on this earth — Jn 6:57), his life of love and obedience (Phil 2:8–9, Heb 10:10), and his resurrection (Rom 4:25) have contributed to our salvation. If one were to ask the scriptures and early Christian tradition how we are saved, one would receive this answer: we are saved by the incarnation, life, death and resurrection of Jesus. Salvation is the bringing about of unity (Chapter 9, A). Therefore, the incarnation, life, death and resurrection of Jesus have all contributed in one way or another to the unity that exists between Jesus and God and between Jesus and us. The word 'unity' of course alerts one to the Spirit's role.

First of all, as regards the *incarnation*, it is the beginning of God's unity with us in Jesus. However, as I have already pointed out, the mere fact that the Word became flesh is not of itself sufficient to create a unity between God and us. What is needed for such unity is God's presence in love to the incarnate Word. In other words, what is needed is that in addition to becoming flesh the Word retains the love-bond with the Father in the Spirit, that love-bond that the Word enjoyed within the Godhead from all eternity. The epistle to the Hebrews makes it clear that Jesus' incarnation only has saving significance because, from the beginning, it was a sign of Jesus' love for and obedience to the Father. Hebrews does so by attributing to Jesus at the moment of his incarnation the words of Ps 40:6–8 (see Heb 10:5–7). Of course, Jesus entered the world like any other human being, i.e., as a new-born babe. He would therefore have had no clear human consciousness of God as his Father. But just as a mother's love envelops a baby and even evokes a response from it, so too the Father was present in his Spirit to the infant Jesus, and, we can surmise, that same Spirit was already evoking from him an infantile response that would mature into a conscious and determined love of his Father in adulthood. The unity between God (= the Father) and Jesus resulting from the incarnation was not forged simply by the Word becoming flesh, but also by the loving presence of God in the Spirit to that now incarnate Word. In fact, the very becoming flesh of the Word is the work of the Love that binds that Word to the Father. The incarnation is from the beginning the work of the Spirit, the work of a Love that binds Father and Son (see Mt 1:20).

As such the Spirit plays a *unique* role in the incarnation, as Malmberg pointed out years ago (see Coffey 1986:240). If our being brought into the inner-trinitarian life is not strictly an *ad extra* activity, but rather one in which the Spirit plays a unique role, then so too is the unity of the man Jesus with his Father not an activity beyond the borders of the divinity. Indeed, if I understand him correctly, Coffey (1984; 1986:242) sees the incarnation as being in a sense the result of an incarnation of the inner-trinitarian love-bond. The Spirit establishes a unity between a human nature and the Father that expresses perfectly the Son's unity with the Father. It is this that makes that human nature the Son's nature, the human expression of the Son's relationship to the Father. Having come across this idea in the final drafting stages of this book, I cannot give it the deep thought it deserves. I do have an initial misgiving — it does not reflect the inner-trinitarian order of things, where the Spirit is in no way the cause of the Son's existence. But the idea is a fascinating one and worth pursuing.

In the above I have concentrated on Christ's unity with his Father. But, of course, the Love that was active in Jesus was also there to enable him to reach out in love to all people.

Let me move on now to the contribution made by Jesus' *life*. By Jesus' 'life' I mean the sort of life he lived, not just the fact that he was there.

This contribution can be described very briefly as follows: by his love and obedience he lived out the unity between God and humanity that began with his incarnation. As regards his unity with God, Jesus loved and obeyed his Father's will in absolutely everything (Phil 2:8, Jn 4:34). As regards his unity with humanity, Jesus' life was one of love for and service to others (Lk 22:27). His love for God showed itself in his love for others and for us. Jesus never allowed sin to enter his life and so to separate him from God and from us. He refused to submit to the separating power of sin.

What enabled Jesus to do this was the Spirit that bound him to the Father in love, a love that reached out to others too.

The importance of Jesus' *death* for our salvation is obvious from the attention that the scriptures as well as Christian tradition pay to it. This is also the reason for the length of my own comments on it.

In the Bible itself, his death is pictured as saving us by releasing us from captivity in the way a ransom does (Mk 10:45; Mt 20:28; Acts 20:28); by atoning for our sins through the purifying shedding of blood (blood was believed by the Jews to be able to purify people from their sins), especially that blood shed in an atonement sacrifice (Heb 9:11 – 10:18); by uniting God and us in a new covenant sealed, as the old one was, in blood (Lk 22:20); and by conquering the powers of evil (Jn 12:23, 31).

Christian tradition added the following ideas to those found in the Bible. First of all, there is the idea that Christ's death saved us because it merited our salvation, that is to say earned it as a reward for his love and obedience. Then there is the idea that Christ's suffering and death saved us because he thereby endured the punishments God laid down for sin. This is called the doctrine of vicarious punishment, which is the one favoured by Protestants. Finally there is the idea that Christ's death saved us because it made satisfaction for the dishonour shown to God by sin. This is known as the doctrine of vicarious satisfaction, which is the explanation favoured by Catholics.

However, I do not wish to discuss here any of these explanations of the role of Christ's death, explanations that I think need to be looked at again so as to see to what extent they are the product of the cultural ideas of their times and to what extent they embody certain fundamental truths about our salvation. Instead, what I wish to do is to point out that Jesus' death was the culmination of a life of love and obedience. His death was the supreme expression of his love and obedience (Heb 10:10; read 10:5–10).

People usually think that Jesus' death was an expression of love and obedience in the sense that his Father demanded his death and he in turn submitted to his Father's will. This is the way Mt 26:39, 42 is interpreted. However, even if God did not expressly command Jesus to 'go to earth and die' (and many would doubt whether God did give him such a command) the sort of love Jesus preached was bound to get him into the kind of trouble that led to his death. His mission was to preach God's unlimited love for us, to show that love in his own life, and to make clear that we were expected to show a similar love to each other. He taught that God's love reached out to and encompassed one and all — including those whom religious society regarded as cursed by God, such as the poor. He practised such a love and called on others to do the same. All of this was very threatening to people, especially to those in positions of power and status such as the Pharisees. However, people like the Pharisees were not only threatened by what he said (and also by his explicit criticisms of them — e.g., Mt 23:27–28). They were also *shocked* by his words as well as his deeds. They were shocked to hear the words 'blessed are the poor', for poverty was seen as God's curse. They were shocked to hear him say that tax-collectors and prostitutes would get into the kingdom before they did (Mt 21:31). They saw this as meaning that sinners would be rewarded while the virtuous (those, like themselves, who observed the Law) would be punished. And this was contrary to all that the scriptures taught (Deut 30:15–18, Ps 1, Job 4:7). The Jewish leaders were shocked also by Jesus' actions, by his claim to be a prophet while mixing with sinners (Lk 7:39), even to the extent of eating with them, a sign that they were acceptable to him and therefore to God (see Mt 11:19, Lk 7:39 and 15:1–2). The Jewish leaders were shocked when Jesus preached that people were more important even than God's laws, because God made his laws for the sake of people and not vice versa (Mk 2:27). The shock was even greater because this man Jesus was being hailed as God's holy Messiah and worse still, he distinctly claimed a unique relationship with God, calling him his 'Abba' (Jn 10:33). This, in their eyes, was blasphemous. Jesus was blaspheming because he was, according to their ideas, an ungodly man who nevertheless pretended to be God's prophet, God's holy Messiah, God's Son. He therefore deserved to be condemned.

Now the point of this rather extensive explanation of the reason why the Jewish leaders condemned Jesus is this: Jesus could only avoid death by changing his message and altering his ways. He could only avoid the clash he was heading for with the Jewish authorities by agreeing with their view of things. He could only avoid death by withdrawing his message that God loved as much as Jesus said he did, and that we must therefore love people in a similar way. Jesus could only avoid death by siding with the Pharisees, preferring their religious views to what he believed to be his Father's views. He could only avoid death by withdrawing his own love for sinners, by not eating with them, and by not telling them that the Kingdom was theirs.

But this would have meant abandoning his Father and his all-embracing love for sinners. Jesus died, therefore, rather than break his unity in love with the Father and with humanity, a unity that began with his incarnation and which he lived out and intensified in his life on earth. Jesus' death saved us because it was a refusal to break his unity in the Spirit with the Father and with sinful humanity. Because of the love created between him and the Father by the Spirit, he died rather than be untrue to that love. He died trusting God (Lk 23:46), despite the fact that God seemed to have let him and the poor he preached to down. There was no Kingdom to be seen; only a failure on a cross. He died forgiving all who rejected him (Lk 23:34), determined not to withdraw the love that he had preached and practised so generously. A love so great was the work of the Spirit in him. His unique possession of the

Spirit enabled him to love God and humanity uniquely.

The result was spectacular: Jesus' *resurrection*. So great was his transformation by the Spirit of love that Jesus and the unity he died for are preserved forever. Had the attempt to eliminate him from our midst by killing him been successful, that would have been the end of any possible unity between God and humanity in Jesus. However, God's Love, God's Spirit, triumphed even over death. For even death could not banish God's Love from the human race it had become a part of. What saved humanity then was Love's refusal to abandon the beloved. Our salvation was therefore very much the work of the Spirit too. It was the work of divine Love transforming human love to the point where the latter became the perfect human expression of the former, the expression of all that the Spirit was.

The resurrection's contribution to our salvation is so enormous that a whole book could be written on that topic alone. However, I would like to point out two things. The first is that Jesus' transformation has made him and his unity part of our world forever. It is important to remember that by rising from the dead Jesus did not cease to be a human being. He did not become a ghost (Lk 24:39). Nor did he go back to being 'just God' again, as some seem to think. The risen Lord remains part of humanity. The unity between God and humanity has not been broken. However, the risen Lord is a gloriously transformed part of our world. In him the eternally planned process of the transformation of humanity and its world has begun. This leads me to the second point I wish to make.

With the resurrection the fullness of salvation planned by God for us has begun to exist. With it there has begun to exist a world in which God's Spirit has united God to a human being to such an extent that the human being has been totally transformed. A human being now sees God 'face to face' (1 Cor 13:12; Heb 9:24). A human being can now be present in the Spirit to others in the way God is. This is the state that everyone who is united to God in the Spirit will one day enjoy. For then we will all resemble Christ Jesus as he is now.

D.   THE SPIRIT GIVES OTHERS A SHARING IN JESUS' UNITY WITH GOD

The early Christians experienced their unity with God as a sharing in *Jesus'* unity with the Father. Hence they experienced the Spirit as *Jesus'* Spirit. Of course, the early Church's experience of the Spirit was also an experience of the presence of the Father. But it was an experience of the Father's presence *through* Jesus. It was an experience of Jesus sharing with them his Father's Spirit, that is to say sharing with them the way he and the Father were one. Needless to say, as the Word made flesh, Jesus is unique. He is 'of one substance' with the Father. We can never be that. Moreover, the Spirit proceeds from the Father to him as Word, and from him as Word to the Father. We cannot be a source of the Spirit in that way. However, we can share in the love-bond forged by the Spirit between them.

The Spirit, then, is always at one and the same time the Spirit of the Father and the Spirit of the Son. The unity created by the Spirit between God and us is a sharing in the divine *perichōrēsis*, a sharing in the eternal love-bond between Father and Son.

From all eternity, the Son experiences the Spirit as the Father's presence. This experience became incarnate with the Word. In other words, what the Word experienced from all eternity was now experienced by a man — Jesus. The fact that Jesus was uniquely endowed with the Spirit (Chapter 2, C (i)) was but the continuation on this earth of a relationship with the Father that the Word possessed from all eternity. In other words, just as the Word was, from the beginning, united with God (Jn 1:1) in the Spirit, so too the Word made flesh continued to be united to that God (whom the Word now addressed as Father) in the Spirit. As noted before, the Spirit now proceeds to and from an incarnate Word, though of course not from that Word's human nature. Hence, Jesus' experience of the Spirit was an experience of the abiding presence of God, his Father, something that comes out clearly in the accounts of Jesus' baptism (e.g., Mt 3:16–17).

To experience the Spirit, then, is to experience the Father's presence, because the Spirit is the Spirit of the Father. This is true of the Word's experience of the Spirit within the Trinity as well as of the Word's experience of God as Father on becoming a human being.

But the Spirit is also the Spirit of the Son. From all eternity, the Father must have experienced the Spirit as the Son's presence and therefore as the Son's Spirit. Of course, the Father could not experience the Spirit as the Son's Spirit in the same way we do. We can experience the Spirit purely as a gift from the Son. The Father would experience the Spirit as his gift *to* the Son. He would be experiencing his own Spirit achieving its purpose.

Furthermore, the Spirit-filled actions of the historical Jesus can, with the hindsight afforded by the resurrection, be seen as reflecting the eternal relationship of the Word to the Spirit. For during his lifetime people experienced in Jesus a man who not only claimed a unique relationship with God but also displayed a unique right to 'use' (for want of a better word) that Spirit for the benefit of others. In Jesus' lifetime we already see him laying the foundations of the community that was to become the Church. In other words, we see Jesus already enabling others to experience and share something of his relationship with God. Jesus was able to do this through the power of the Spirit, i.e., through the power of the Love that he shared with God.

Even during his earthly life, then, the Spirit was also the Son's Spirit, the Spirit whereby the Son reached out in love to others. However, the historical Jesus could not be experienced in the Spirit in the way the Father was, simply because he (Jesus) was subject to the limitations of space and time. His presence to others could only be expressed and experienced in spatio–temporal categories. During his historical life he could only relate to others and be related to by others in the same limited way that all human beings relate to each other in this life on earth.

After his resurrection, things were different. The Spirit of love had brought about a transformation so total that his desire to share with one and all his own unity with the Father in the Spirit could then be realized. In other words, the Son could now be present in the love of the Spirit to all people of all times and all places. He could now share the Spirit with all people of all times and all places. He could now share his unity with the Father with all peoples of all times and all places. The Spirit of the Son — that is to say, the way in which the Son is united to the Father — could now be available to all.

The early Christians, therefore, experienced the Spirit as the Spirit of Jesus, the Spirit of the Son (Chapter 2, C (iii) and (iv)). The Spirit unites us to the Son so closely that the Son is said to live in us (Gal 2:20; Eph 3:17; 2 Cor 13:5; Jn 14:23, 17:23). We become like Christ (Rom 8:29; Gal 4:19), sharing in all that he is and has, just as Christ himself shares in all that the Father is and has.

Therefore, we share in Christ's relationship to God. Christ's Father is also our Father. Christ gives us the Spirit of his Father which enables us to cry out, with him, *abba* (Mk 14:36; Rom 8:15; Gal 4:6). We share too in Christ's relationship with all the other members of his Body. The Spirit enables us to share not only in all that Christ is, but also in all that his Body, the Church, is. We share in Christ's ability to love others as he himself did (Jn 13:34). We share in Christ's freedom from slavery to sin.

We also share in Christ's God-likeness. Christ's unity with God in the Spirit is so close that we must confess that he is 'of one substance' with God. Sharing in Christ's Spirit of unity with God, we also share in his God-likeness. Obviously we will never become God. That is impossible. But it is clear that we will become as much like God as is possible (1 Jn 3:2; 2 Pet 1:4). The Greeks expressed this idea by saying that the Spirit 'divinized' us. The Cappadocians, as was seen (Chapter 4, A), used this divinizing role of the Spirit as an argument for the Spirit's divinity.

We share, furthermore, in Christ's knowledge of the things of God (1 Cor 2:10–11). Christ's Spirit enables us to understand all that Christ has taught us. The Spirit leads us into all truth (Jn 14:26, 16:13). The culmination of this will be to see God as God really is (1 Jn 3:2; 1 Cor 13:12), just as Christ does.

Therefore, we too will one day be as totally transformed as he was on the day of his resurrection (Phil 3:21; Col 3:4; 1 Cor 15:25–44). When that happens, then we also can be perfectly united to our Father, to Christ, and to each other in the Spirit. We too will no longer be prevented by space and time, or by the decay that is an inevitable part of our present life, from being in instantaneous and perfect unity with all the other members of Christ's Body. Then God's plan will be realized. A human community will have been established that is completely part of God's own trinitarian life. Then Jesus' prayer will be fulfilled 'that they may be one as we are one. With me in them and you in me' (Jn 17:22–23). Jesus' Spirit will have become completely our Spirit too.

Already in his lifetime a group of disciples gathered around Jesus. These formed the nucleus of the future Church. However, it was only after his resurrection that Jesus was able to be present to all of humanity in the Spirit. It was only then that we see his unity with the Father spreading rapidly to others, 'beginning at Jerusalem' and going out to embrace all nations (Lk 24:47). The chapters that follow will discuss this sharing of others, and indeed of the whole cosmos, in Jesus' unity with the Father.

QUESTIONS

Check questions

1 What is the Spirit's role in Jesus' unity with the Father, if Jesus is 'of one substance' with the Father?
2 What is the connection between the Spirit's work and Jesus' sinlessness?
3 What is the connection between the Spirit's work and Jesus' unique insight into the things of God?
4 What is the Spirit's role in Jesus' unity with us, if he is already a human being?
5 What is the Spirit's role in (a) Jesus' incarnation; (b) his life; (c) his death; and (d) his resurrection as saving events?
6 What was the relationship between the early Christians' experience of the Spirit as the Spirit of the Father and their experience of the Spirit as the Spirit of the Son?
7 What was the relationship between Jesus' and the eternal Word's experience of the Spirit?
8 How does the Father's experience of the Spirit as the Spirit of the Son differ from ours?

9   Why could the historical Jesus not be experienced in the Spirit the way the risen Lord is?

10   Give some examples of the way in which the Spirit makes us like Jesus.

Discussion questions

1   What does it mean to be moulded into Christ's likeness? How is this compatible with love, if love respects the individual's individuality?

2   If we become like Christ in all things, if Christ lives in us, then we too are sources of the Spirit. In what way can we be such? What are the similarities and dissimilarities between us and Christ in this respect?

RECOMMENDED READING

I cannot think of anything specifically on the themes dealt with here except for Dunn 1975, which shows how Jesus' experience of the constant presence of God to him as an *abba* was, psychologically, an experience of the presence of his Father's Spirit.

10

The Spirit creates the community that is the Church: introducing the theme

A.   SOME INTRODUCTORY REMARKS

The Church's remote origins go back to before Pentecost. In a sense they go back to Old Testament times, to God's calling of the people of Israel. However, as a specifically Christian reality, the Church's story begins only with Christ's coming. As a Christian reality, its remotest origins can be traced to the moment when Christ was conceived and became part of this world. When Mary accepted in faith what the angel said to her (Lk 1:26–28) and the Word became flesh in her womb, the Church began to exist in embryo. For from that moment Jesus and another human being — his mother — were united in the Love that is the Spirit. Mary was the first to form one body with Jesus, a bodily unity that can be taken as the sacramental expression of the embryonic beginnings of Christ's Body. Mary remains forever as the expression of all that unity with Christ, all that the Church is meant to be.

This embryonic Church began to take on some recognizable shape when Christ gathered a group of disciples — especially the Twelve — around him. However, the Church was not fully born until the day when the infant community experienced the outpouring of Christ's Spirit. For it was only from that moment that they saw themselves as a community united to the Father and to Christ in a Spirit whose presence was the sign that the last days, the days of salvation had arrived (Chapter 2, A). It was only then that the disciples were impelled actually to go forth and preach their message and spread their communal life, to be a real sign of a community open to all. For it was only then that the Spirit turned the small group of disciples into the sign and instrument of the unity that is the Spirit's specific mission (Chapter 8, A). The Church is the Spirit's own creation (Chapter 2, D).

Justifiably, therefore, Pentecost has from ancient times been regarded as the birthday of the Church.

My aim in this and the next three chapters is to show how dependent every single aspect of the Church is on Christ's Spirit. Of course, it is impossible to deal with everything. Many sections in the chapters that follow could be expanded to fill several books. However, I hope that these chapters will succeed in giving some indication of how the Spirit fills every part of the Church, giving real life to what otherwise would be only an illusion thereof.

The present chapter will introduce the theme of the Spirit and the Church. Subsequent chapters will deal with various aspects of this general theme.

B.   WHAT IS THE CHURCH?

The word 'church' is associated with many things in the average person's mind. Two meanings in particular predominate there. One is the building in which Christians worship. The other meaning is that of the institution, represented by the clergy and a set of rules, regulations, and doctrines. The second meaning of 'church' is possibly the most widespread one. It is perfectly illustrated in the English custom of saying that a man who is ordained to the ministry thereby 'enters the Church', despite the fact that only those who already do belong to the Church can be ordained!

In the New Testament the first thing that strikes one about the word 'church' is that it means a people, a community. It means 'the people of God'. This description of the Church stresses the fact that the Church is the true continuation of the Old Testament community, one that gloried in the title 'God's people'.

However, there is an obvious difference between the new people of God (the Church) and the old (Israel). The difference is that the new people of God are united to each other not only by their faith in God but also by the life of the risen Christ. What is new is that the New Testament people of God form 'the Body of Christ'.

'The Body of Christ' is a description of the Church given to us by Paul. Read 1 Cor 12:12–27, 6:15, 10:16 and also Col 1:18 and Eph 1:23. Exactly what Paul meant by this phrase is not easy to say in a few words. Paul himself seems to have had no one clearly fixed meaning for it. However, one meaning that Paul does give to it and which became enshrined in the doctrine of the 'Mystical Body of Christ' is that we form with Christ one body because we share the life that brought into being and fills Christ's risen body. My hand is part of my body because it lives with the life that fills my whole body. My watch, however, is not part of my body, because it does not have my body's life flowing through it. For the same reason, a plastic heart valve is not part of my body, but a transplanted heart does become such. Whatever lives with the life of a body is part of it. It is for that reason that we can be said to be parts of Christ's risen body. I am sure if Paul had lived in an age of organ transplants he would have said that we have been 'transplanted' into Christ's body. Christ himself, of course, got the same idea across with his image of the vine and the branches.

What exactly is this 'life' that fills Christ's risen body and which we too share in? It is the Love, the Spirit, binding Christ and us to the Father. This Love, this Spirit binds Christ to us so that we, like him, may call God our Father. We share in his relationship to the Father, not the other way around (him sharing in a supposed prior relationship of humanity to the Father). Hence the community united by the Spirit is one in which the Son's relationship to God is shared by many, one in which the many live with a Love that is specifically one that binds the *Son* to the Father, and not a love that belongs equally to Christ and the rest of us. Therefore that community is rightly said to live with *Christ*'s life, to be *Christ*'s Body.

But why the image of a 'body'? Why not simply talk of 'sharing Christ's Spirit', of being 'Christ's sisters and brothers', etc.? The original reason for the 'body' image was, as far as I know, simply its usefulness as an image of unity in difference. Thus Paul in 1 Cor 12 stressed the need to respect different functions within the one Church, just as with a body. However, the body image soon revealed far greater depths. It was useful not only as an analogy for the Church's difference-in-unity. It was also useful as an image of our unity with the risen Christ. More specifically, it was useful as an image of our unity with Christ's risen body. There is a clear tradition in the New Testament that sees Christ and his followers as being one to the point of virtual identification. The persons remain distinct, but in all other respects they become one. Jesus identifies himself with the least of his sisters and brothers (Mt 25:40, 45). This was a lesson that Paul learnt dramatically when he was struck down on the road to Damascus, and heard the voice saying 'Saul, Saul, why are you persecuting *me*?' (Acts 9:4). It was a lesson he never forgot.

John 17:21 gives the reason for this extraordinarily close unity: that we may be as close to both the Father and the Son as they are to each other. By becoming one 'body' with the Son, therefore, we share in the Son's unity with the Father.

The Spirit's role in all this is obvious. The Spirit is the love that unites and, by uniting, transforms all it unites. But as the love uniting *Christ to the Father*, the Spirit unites us to the Father only by enabling us to share Christ's relationship to the Father. Hence, the community created by the Spirit pivots around Christ. It forms with Christ a unity so close as to be able to be called Christ's 'body'. It is the *Father*'s people, the people of God. But it is such precisely because it is his *Son*'s Body.

The Church can therefore be described as the community in which we see God's planned unity with humanity taking shape. The essential characteristic of this unity is that through the Spirit humanity shares in the Son's relationship with the Father. We see that unity taking visible shape in the Church, because in the Church we see a community of people who profess God as their Father, Christ as their brother, and the Spirit as the means whereby all of them are united to each other. It is in the Church and only in the Church therefore that we *see* the sort of community planned by God from all eternity growing and spreading throughout the world. In the now famous words of Vatican II's document on the Church (*Lumen Gentium*): 'The Church is a kind of sacrament or sign of intimate union with God, and of the unity of all mankind. She is also an instrument for the achievement of such union and unity' (§1; translation in Abbott 1966).

Another way of describing the Church, therefore, is to say that it is where we see the community created by the Spirit taking shape. The Church is the visible result of the Spirit's activity in the world. The Church's mission is to be the visible sign and instrument of the Spirit's mission.

C. THE SPIRIT AND OUR FORMING 'ONE MYSTICAL PERSON' WITH CHRIST

There is a tradition that speaks of Christ and us forming not simply one mystical *body* but indeed one mystical *person*. The idea of us forming one 'person' has its roots in the sort of identification between Jesus and us that was manifested dramatically in the risen Lord's demand to Paul: 'why are you persecuting *me*?' And then there is Paul's remark in Gal 2:20 that he no longer lives of himself, but Christ lives in him. Augustine spoke explicitly in terms of Jesus and us forming one person 'in a sense' (*una quaedam persona* — see references in Mühlen 1968:28–29), Thomas of us forming one 'mystical' person (*Summa*, IIIa, 19, 4, resp.). The formula is repeated by Pius XII in his encyclical *The Mystical Body of Jesus Christ* (1943; no. 67).

This image of 'one person' stresses in the heaviest way possible the closeness brought about by the Spirit between Christ and us. However, it has obvious drawbacks. The one distinction that must always remain between Christ and us is our identities as persons. Otherwise the community, 'people' aspect is dissolved into a unity lacking any differentiation at all.

I suspect that the phrase may well have more disadvantages than advantages. Its chief value resides in a sphere where its explanatory power is no longer as vital as used to be the case: viz., in the matter of our sharing in Christ's merits. If we form one 'person' with him, then his merits become ours. However, the phrase remains part of our tradition and Heribert Mühlen makes it central to his conception of the way in which the Spirit forms the Church.

In a profound and wide-ranging study entitled *Una Mystica Persona* (Mühlen 1968), he applies to the Church his idea of the Spirit as a subsistent 'we' formation in the Trinity. The Spirit's very identity is to be one person in two persons (Chapter 7, D (ii)). In the Church the Spirit becomes one person in not just two but many persons.

Seeing the Spirit as the 'we' dimension in the Church has advantages and disadvantages similar to those involved in the seeing the Spirit as the 'we' dimension in God. However, linking the idea to that of 'one mystical person' adds a new factor that brings its own problems. The major one is that the 'we' formation here is that of our unity with Christ, since that is what the formula refers to. Mühlen's theology logically demands that our unity with *the entire Trinity* should form *una mystica persona*. The Spirit as 'we' in the Trinity is, in his theology, *una persona*. The Spirit giving us a share in the inner-trinitarian life is the same *una persona*, the only difference being that it is now a case of one person in *many* (and not just two) persons. If there is to be any 'mystical' person formed by our involvement in the unity between Christ and his Father, it must logically be formed around not Christ but the Spirit. We should say something like 'the Spirit and we form one mystical person'. Such an idea has already been suggested by the Lutheran theologian Klemroth (see Congar 1983b:19, 23). And, of course, there is some precedent for it in the tradition that sees us becoming so identified with the Spirit as to share in the Spirit's role of uniting Christ and the Father (Chapter 5, E). A related idea is the one Scheeben made famous, viz., that the Church is a sort of 'incarnation' of the Spirit, since the Spirit and the Church formed one living reality. The close association of the Spirit with the human Church (recall that the Spirit was seen as the 'soul' of the Church — see Chapter 5, F) justified the analogy of the incarnation, though the idea was fraught with many dangers. One danger was that of seeing the Church as the 'body' of the Spirit. This moves in a direction similar to the logic of Mühlen's linking of *una mystica persona* to the Spirit as 'we': the Spirit, rather than Christ, becomes the head of the Church, the one on whom the Church is modelled. Perhaps this was why Mühlen felt it necessary to disavow any misinterpretation of his position that would see it as affirming the Church to be the Spirit's 'body' (Mühlen 1968:583).

But such a conception — viz., forming one mystical person with the Spirit — has its own dangers, for which it is best avoided. The chief danger, and source of all others, is that it makes the Spirit the centre of attention. This is always dangerous, since the Spirit's role is to direct the attention of lover to beloved and vice versa. The idea of forming one mystical person with the Spirit (which, of course, is not what Mühlen is actually saying, though my contention is that his position implies it) would therefore leave Christ's role out of perspective. It would blur the fact that our unity with the Father is a sharing in *Christ's* unity with him. In short, it would be a falling into the age-old trap of breaking the link between the Spirit and Christ.

To view the problem from another angle, Mühlen's approach forces us to drive too sharp a distinction between the community formed by Christ and us, and the larger one formed by it and the Father. Certainly, there is a distinction between our unity with Christ and our unity with the Father. Christ is our sibling, the Father our parent. The relationship in each case is quite different. Hence we are identified with Christ in a way in which we are not identified with the Father. We share, once again, in Christ's relationship to the Father, and not in the Father's relationship to Christ. All this is the truth in the image of Christ's 'body' and of forming 'one mystical person' with him. But the *community* formed by the Spirit in uniting us to Christ is but one community, the community formed by the Father and his offspring, begotten and adopted, in the love that is the Spirit. Needless to say, Mühlen would not deny that there is but one community formed by the Spirit. However, the logic of his position seems to me to move in a different direction. By linking *una mystica persona* to the idea of the Spirit as 'we', as one person in many persons, Mühlen makes our unity with Christ, rather than unity with the Father, the created expression of the Spirit's trinitarian role. There is a difference. If unity with the Father is *the* expression of the Spirit as 'we', of being one person in many persons, then for a logical transition from Mühlen's inner to his economic Trinity he would need to see *una mystica persona* as referring to our unity with the Father albeit in and through Christ. If however unity with the Son is seen as the expression of that 'we' formation, then there is the logical break of the 'we' no longer being Father and Son, but Son and us. One then has to posit a third 'we': (Son and us) + (the Father). It seems to me more logical to see the expanded 'we' as from the beginning having the Father on the one side and offspring on the other. But, as I say, any 'mystical person' identified with this 'we' character of the Spirit should logically be the mystical extension of the person of the Spirit, not of Christ.

In Chapter 7 (D (ii)) I pointed out that Mühlen's theology of the Spirit belonged to the category of those who saw the Spirit as the fruit of love, rather than the love-bond itself. I also pointed out what I considered to be the drawbacks of such a position. A similar conception is operating in Mühlen's application to the Church of his ideas on the Spirit. The mystical person formed by Christ and us thanks to the Spirit is itself the fruit of love. It is the 'Great-I' (*Gross-Ich*) formed by Christ and us. The Spirit's nature as 'we' is identified with this fruit of love, just as the Spirit's character as 'we' within the Trinity is identified with the fruit of the Father and Son's love for each other. But this leaves the (from a logical point of view) untidiness of having to accommodate a further fruit of love: the unity of all with the Father.

I believe that the idea of the Spirit as love itself, the bond of love, is less problematic. For then one does not need to identify the Spirit with any mystical union resulting from love, but simply with the love that does the uniting. By sharing his Spirit, his Love with us, Christ shares with us his unity with the Father.

D.   THE RELATIONSHIP BETWEEN THE INSTITUTIONAL AND CHARISMATIC ELEMENTS IN THE CHURCH

The central role played by the Spirit in the Church finds historical expression in a variety of ways. These range from the formation of certain structures that become a permanent part of Church life (e.g., the threefold ministry of bishop, priest and deacon; the formation of the canon of scripture) to passing contributions (insights, prophetic statements, healings, etc., that serve a passing need). They express what can be called the 'charismatic element' in the Church. The 'charismatic element' is therefore broader than simply the 'charisms' or gifts of the Spirit so much at the centre of attention today. It includes *everything* that is an expression of free initiative in the Church and which can legitimately be seen as a result of the Spirit's presence in it.

As such, the charismatic element is distinguished from the 'institutional' one. The latter represents permanent structures with structured, defined ways of operating. These are, like the charismatic element, essential to the Church. Spatio-temporally conditioned as it is, the Christian community could not exist without them.

As was seen in the historical section, the two elements have been opposed down the ages. Again and again the Spirit was appealed to against the institution, or the institution invoked to deny the legitimacy of a claim to the Spirit's guidance. Already in apostolic times Paul had to remind those who in the name of the Spirit were cursing the earthly Jesus (i.e. Jesus before his death and resurrection) that it is to that very limited, historical figure that the Spirit is linked and bears witness. Then there was the conflict between the second-century Church and the Montanists. The former insisted on the link between the Spirit and the Church, while the latter insisted on the lordship of the Spirit. The problem reappears every time the Spirit is appealed to as the justification for rejecting or altering in a basic way those structures that have up to then been regarded as essential to the Church. Therefore, the problem reappeared at the time of the Reformation. Catholicism felt that the Reformers had broken the link between the Spirit and the Church's basic institutions. The Reformers, on the other hand, felt that Catholicism had simply institutionalized the Spirit and thereby made it impossible for the Spirit to break through and reform structures that were stifling the Gospel. The Enthusiasts felt that the Reformers had not sufficiently freed the Spirit from being shackled to the institutional. The Reformers, on the other hand, were of the opinion that the Enthusiasts had broken the essential links between the Spirit and the Church.

However, the opposition so often placed between charismatic and institutional elements is, at root, a false one. For it is the same Lord, the same Christ operating through his Spirit, that is the source of both. It is wrong therefore to conceive of the institutional aspect as coming ready-made from Christ, with the Spirit and the charismatic element being a different item added to it, present only to give life to the preordained structures (see Congar 1983b:9). The charismatic was part of the Church's very structure (paradoxical though that may sound) from the very beginning and remains *essential* to it (Congar 1983b:9; Rahner 1974:94). The Church is, as Rahner (1974:88–89) described it, an 'open' and not a 'closed' system. In a closed system, all initiatives are ultimately directed from a point within the system itself. In an open system, however, the ultimate source of initiative is outside it. In the case of the Church this ultimate source is the Spirit — or more accurately Christ operating through the Spirit.

It is also necessary to realize that the majority of the institutional factors Catholics are familiar with today derive from the charismatic element. The development of the papacy and the threefold ministry of bishop, priest and deacon cannot, in their present form, be traced back to the historical Jesus. They are the result of the operation of the charismatic element in the Church. Five of Catholicism's sacraments are explicitly regarded by mediaevals such as Bonaventure to be the result of the charismatic element, of the Spirit at work in the post-apostolic Church (Congar 1983b:9). The development of doctrine, of canon law, the calling, proceedings and decisions of councils, the founding of religious orders — these and many more well-known institutional factors are the result of the charismatic element in the Church.

Many of these represent basic structural elements — e.g., ministry, sacraments, order (as opposed to chaos) — that will always be part of the Church's being. However, their presence does not make them impervious to reform. Once established they do not 'imprison' the Spirit but stand as abiding signs of the Spirit's activity. Even those institutional elements that can be traced back to Jesus himself such as the role of baptism, the Eucharist, the Twelve, Peter's position amongst them, do not 'imprison' the Spirit. They take on various forms down the ages, forms that are an expression of the charismatic element in the Church and which therefore can always in principle be re-formed. Ministry can be structured and exercised in one way in one era and in a different way in another. The sacraments can be performed in a particular way in one era, differently in another. The same applies to the way in which the Church's teaching is formulated. When abuses creep in and reform is needed, what has happened is not that ministry itself or the sacraments themselves or the Word that the Church must preach has become obsolete and must be abandoned. What rather has happened is that the way in which these structures exist and are exercised needs reforming. And the Spirit is always free to break through the concrete manifestations of the Church's essential structures and reform them. The Church will always need reform — but total abolition will never be necessary. For the Church itself is essentially something visible. As such, it is the abiding sign of Christ's presence in the world. For Christ to abolish it would be to abolish the visible aspect of his own presence in the world. It would be to abolish the Body he himself created and promised to be with to the end of time. But to say that Christ will not abolish his own Body does not mean he cannot reform it. He remains Lord of his own Body.

I have wandered somewhat from my theme, which was that both institutional and charismatic elements derive from the same source. This cannot be emphasized enough, since it means they cannot be seen as irreconcilable opposites, but rather as complementary to each other. It is necessary, therefore, to eliminate the false opposition that has often been placed between institution and charism. Once that is done, then one can identify where and why real clashes occur, and see them as necessary and valuable for the Church's growth.

The false opposition sees it as necessary to choose ultimately either for the Spirit or for the institution. It is an approach that sees the issue as one of ultimate power or authority. In such a perspective, the problem of relating the institutional and Spirit-guided elements in the Church becomes acute. If one chooses the institution, then one stifles the Spirit, reducing the Spirit to a servant at the beck and call of the institution. Radical reform of the institution's structures, should it be necessary, is well-nigh impossible.

What is wrong with this 'either–or' approach is that logically it breaks the link between Christ and the Spirit. In the last resort such an approach is saying: who is the ultimate authority — Christ, or the Spirit? For the historical Jesus in all his historical limitations is the very core of the institutional aspect of the Church. The man Jesus and what he said and did are a permanent part of human history. A question as to what may be the ultimate authority in the event of a clash between what the Spirit is saying and Jesus' legacy is a question about a situation that, for a Christian, is impossible. There can be no clash between Jesus and the Spirit.

Institutional and charismatic elements are not to be viewed as competing authorities, then. Both are essential to the Church. Both derive from the same Lord working through the same Spirit.

However, in practice tension between the institutional and charismatic elements is inevitable. The reason for the tension is that both find historical expression through the activities of believers. The Spirit does not bypass the members of the community in building it up, for it can only be built up by their love, a love transformed by the Spirit's presence. Believers are historically limited. The structures they both form and inherit are limited. Even what they inherit from the historical Jesus has its inherent limitations. Their charismatic insights too are culturally conditioned and limited.

It is of the very nature of their historically conditioned lives and structures that progress takes place through the assimilation of new elements, new insights, and the discarding of outmoded ones; that progress takes places through a never-ending process of distinguishing between kernels and husks, babies and bath water, essentials and non-essentials. It is a never-ending process of growth, of continuity in change and change in continuity. The stable elements reflect the institutional, the changes the charismatic elements.

Clashes arise because believers protective of institutional elements close themselves off to a greater or lesser degree to believers who are convinced of the need for change, and vice versa. Hence it is not surprising that we see such clashes occurring from the earliest days of the Church. What was often lacking in such clashes was love. Love, tolerance, respect for the other, allows the interplay of institution and charism to take place to the benefit of all. The result may be different from what the partisans of either factor wanted. But it will be an expression of the Church's growth in the Spirit of Love.

The ability of love to overcome even the most intractable difficulties is evident to anyone who has taken part over a prolonged period in serious ecumenical dialogue. In a group whose members remain the same through the period, trust builds up, participants open themselves out to each other and thereby begin to understand and truly appreciate each other and the values in each other's positions. As a result agreements are reached which often enough are baffling, sometimes a scandal, to those not involved in the process. In a similar way, if those protective of institutional factors, as well as those pushing for greater openness or change as regards certain issues, were to treat each other as sisters and brothers in Christ rather than as representing opposed interests, then the clashes would become fruitful rather than divisive.

One needs to remember that it is Christ's *love*, the Spirit of *love* that is the source of both the institutional and the charismatic elements in the Church. Therefore the inevitable tension they will cause in the community can only be resolved by love. There is no rule, no legal or institutional formula for resolving the issue (Rahner 1974:95). Were there such, then the institutional would indeed have to have the final say, crushing effectively the charismatic element. However, only love can have the final say. What love dictates in practice cannot be determined in advance. But it will at least require that the protectors of institutional elements be open to the charismatic factor, and the claimants to the charismatic factor be willing to have their claims examined, tested, and evaluated by the institutional element.

E.   THE SPIRIT AND THE CHURCH'S BORDERS

The relationship between the Spirit and the Church is so close that the issue of the Spirit's action beyond the Church's borders (*extra ecclesiam*) became quite a problem from early on in the Church's history. The history of this specific issue cannot be gone into here — it is the history of the belief that outside the Church there is no salvation. Suffice it to say that even where the Spirit's action was conceived of as occurring beyond the borders of the Church it was nevertheless always seen as bringing people into some sort of relation to the Church.

To most people's surprise, Catholicism does *not* believe that there is no salvation outside the Church, if by that one means that people who are not Catholics or even Christians cannot be saved. Vatican II makes it clear that even atheists are not necessarily excluded from salvation (*The Church*, §16). The theological reasons for this cannot be gone into here. At bottom they are the conviction that if God wants everybody to be saved (1 Tim 2:4), then no one can be lost who has not culpably rejected God. If one believes that, then one must believe that the Spirit acts beyond the visible borders of Christianity (unless one wishes to hold the outrageous view that all non-Christians are subjectively guilty of rejecting God). One must see the Spirit's work of enabling people (albeit without them realizing it) to share in Christ's unity with the Father as something that extends as far as humanity itself.

Yet Catholicism insists that in another sense there is indeed no salvation outside the Church. This implies that wherever the Spirit is at work, there too in some way or other is the Church. It implies that any share an atheist may have in Christ's unity with the Father is also a sharing in the life of the Church. Such an atheist is in some way or other part of the Church.

How can someone be part of the Church who to all intents and purposes is totally outside of it? This apparent contradiction can only be resolved if one believes that 'church' is a reality that can find visible expression in varying degrees. To believe that the Church is the sacrament of a unity that stretches beyond its borders is to believe that the Church is the visible, structured embodiment of a larger reality. This larger reality is the unity, in Love, of a wide variety of people. Such a unity can manifest itself in a variety of ways, from genuine human love, through belief in God, to the structured sacrament of unity in Christ that is the Church in the strict sense of the word. However, since the Church in that strict sense of the word is the sacramental embodiment of a larger reality, that larger reality can also be given the name 'Church', but in a wide sense.

Karl Rahner was one of the pioneers of this line of thinking (see e.g., Rahner 1963, esp. p. 86) and its basic ideas are enshrined in Vatican II's *Constitution on the Church* and *Decree on Ecumenism*. A detailed examination of this approach belongs to a book on the Church. But its implications for a theology of the Spirit's activity need to be mentioned here.

Its basic implication is that wherever Church is manifested in a broad way, there we have a sign of the Spirit's presence. It means that we can and should look for signs of the Spirit's saving activity beyond the strict borders of the Church. The theology of the Church being considered here sees 'Church' as manifesting itself in a variety of ways. These reflect, according to differing degrees of clarity, its nature (see Vatican II, *The Church*, §§14–16; *Ecumenism*, §§3–4). The Church's sacramentality (its character as a sign) contains many elements: belief in God, in Christ, in the importance of love of God and neighbour, etc. Some of these elements are specific to Catholics (e.g., belief in the Petrine ministry as a sign of service to the unity of the universal Church). Others are common to Catholics and other Christians (belief in Jesus, in salvation through Jesus, etc.); others common to Catholics and Jews and Muslims (the Judaeo-Christian tradition); others common to all who believe in God. And there are others that are common to all humanity (e.g., belief in the value of love). Where all the elements essential to the Church's character as a sign are found, there one has the sacrament and therefore 'Church' in all its fullness. Where some elements are found (e.g., belief in Christ), but not others (e.g., no ministry), then (Catholicism believes) there are communities that reflect 'Church' only imperfectly. In short, the unity in Christ that God has called us to can have degrees of visibility according to whether or not all the essential elements of the sacrament 'Church' are present. All such reflections of the Church's nature, whether found beyond the Church's borders or not, can be signs of the Spirit's presence. They can be seen as a visible link between the Spirit's action beyond and within the Church's borders (see also Vatican II, *The Church*, §16).

The fact that Vatican II endorsed the essential ideas of the above approach has revolutionized Catholicism's way of relating itself to other churches (see on this Mühlen 1968:494ff.), other religions, and indeed the world at large. The contribution of the Quakers — that the Spirit can be at work in and give dignity to every human being (Chapter 6, C) — has been absorbed into it.

QUESTIONS

Check questions

1 What is the Church?

2 What do the titles 'people of God' and 'body of Christ' teach us about the Church?

3 What is it about the Church that enables us to see taking shape the sort of unity God has called all people to?

4 What are the advantages and the disadvantages in describing the Church as forming with Christ 'one mystical person'?

5 (a) How does Mühlen link this idea to his conception of the Spirit?
   (b) What criticisms can be made of this procedure?

6 What is meant by the 'institutional' and the 'charismatic' elements in the Church?

7 Give an example of how these two elements can be falsely opposed to each other.

8 What factors link the two elements to each other?

9 Why are clashes between them inevitable in practice? What value do such clashes have?
10 What is essential to the fruitful resolution of such clashes? Would it be a good idea to have a fixed, legalized formula for resolving them (give reasons for your answer)?
11 In what sense is there salvation outside the Church, and in what sense is there not?
12 What implications does a broader view of 'Church' have for a theology of the Spirit's activities?

Discussion questions

1 What are the valid and valuable elements in Mühlen's extension of the Spirit's 'we' character to the Spirit's role in the Church?
2 How should the Church be structured so as to allow for an optimal balance between institutional and charismatic structures?

RECOMMENDED READING

On the notion of the Church see Vatican II's *Constitution on the Church, Decree on Ecumenism* (see Abbott 1966), and commentaries on these documents (e.g. Vorgrimler 1967 and 1968). On the charismatic and institutional elements, see Rahner 1974. Congar 1983b:7–12 has some useful material on the Spirit as 'co-instituting Principle of the Church'. For a Protestant (Reformed) perspective on the relation between the two elements see Berkhof 1976:51–65. On the issue of salvation outside the Church and the wider concept of Church, see Rahner 1963.

11

The Spirit creates the Church's unity

Having dealt in a general way with the Spirit and the Church it is necessary now to examine some more specific issues concerning the Spirit's activity within the Church. This chapter deals with the most fundamental of all those actions: the unity created by the Spirit.

There is no need to labour the point that the Spirit is the bond of unity between Father, Son and us. All I wish to do here is to discuss briefly the main characteristics of this unity.

A.   A UNITY IN LOVE

The unity created by the Spirit is before all else a unity *in love*. It is the sort of unity that exists between persons. It is therefore the sort of unity that respects legitimate differences between people (see Rom 14:1–6). It does not allow differences to become divisive. In that sense there is in Christ 'no more distinction between Jew and Greek, slave and free, male and female' (Gal 3:28).

In other words, we are now all brothers and sisters of Christ. It is Christ's love, the Spirit, poured into our hearts that is the foundation of our unity with each other, not our national identity or our cultural heritage. However, precisely because our unity is based on Christ's love and *not* on national identity or cultural heritage, these latter can be respected and maintained without having any divisive effect. In short, the unity created by love is not uniformity, and must not be confused with it.

It is wrong, therefore, to seek the Church's unity *primarily* in uniform structures and practices. In the past, the Catholic Church possessed an extraordinary degree of uniformity throughout the world. This was a powerful unifying force, and because of the good it did it can be regarded as an expression of the charismatic element in the Church, responding to the need of the times. But it also had the unquestionably negative effect of causing people to see the unity of the Church as residing mainly in uniform structures and practices. Such a view is false, since the Church's unity resides primarily in the fact that one Spirit, one Love animates all. It is a unity in love. Uniformity may be a useful sign of such unity. But it can also obscure it. It can lead to a denial of the legitimate differences, freedom and responsibilities of individuals and individual communities. Uniformity within the Church can very easily become a form of tyranny masked as unity, an ecclesiastical version of the man who demands, as a sign of her love, that his wife accedes to all his wishes, accepts his opinions, does things the way he thinks they should be done. Overemphasis on the institutional aspect of the Church can easily lead to excessive uniformity, stifling the charismatic element. Balance is restored by stressing the fact that Christ's presence in our midst through his Spirit is the real source of our unity.

However, the unity created by the Spirit must be expressed visibly. And this is where visible structures of unity — including a certain degree of uniformity — have a role to play. It is as erroneous to seek unity *exclusively* in the presence of the Spirit in our midst as it is to seek it mainly in uniformity of structures and practices. For people are visible creatures. Their unity must be expressed visibly. Such visible expressions of unity, moreover, contribute to the very unity they express. In other words, common visible ties will strengthen the very unity that created them. The Enthusiasts can perhaps be cited as a group that wished to go too far in the direction of abandoning all uniformity.

A certain amount of uniformity is necessary, then, in order that the Church's unity may have structural expression. The three main structural expressions of the unity of the Church are its confession of faith, its ministry, its sacraments.

The Spirit, therefore, not only creates a common faith, but leads the Church to express it in commonly accepted formulae. The Spirit not only creates ministries as the need for them arises, but also brings about the establishment of certain ministries that have to some extent been uniformly structured (the ordained ministries) and that fulfil an important role as regards the visible unity of the Church. The Spirit not only unites us to Christ but does so through ceremonies (the sacraments) that visibly express an individual's unity with Christ and his Body. All these basic visible structures, and the many others that are created and abandoned as time goes by, are important for the visible expression of the Church's unity. They cannot be dismissed as being rather unimportant on the grounds that it is the unity created by the Spirit that matters. Nevertheless they are there to serve the Spirit of love by giving visible expression to love's unity. The Spirit of love is not there to serve institutionalized structures.

B.   A HOLY UNITY

The unity created by the Spirit is a *holy* unity. This is so because it is a unity with God, a unity brought about by the *Holy* Spirit, *holy* love, God's love.

Holiness and unity are very closely related. They are not identical, since there can be unholy alliances, unholy unities. However, there can be no holiness without unity, since unity with God is part of the very concept of holiness. The word 'holy' originally meant 'separated from the world'. God was a 'holy' God because of the gulf that separated God from the world. God was, in modern terms, the 'totally other', totally unlike the world, unworldly — i.e., holy.

The term 'holy' came to be applied to any person, place or thing that was, so to speak, set apart from the world and given to God (e.g., God's people in 1 Pet 2:9). The very concept 'holiness' therefore implies unity, unity with God, while the reverse is equally true: unity with God implies holiness.

But what happens when one can no longer see the world and God as separate, when one can no longer talk meaningfully of passing from the one to the other? What happens if God becomes part of the world? The conclusion is inescapable: the world now is 'holy'. It is united to God. As a sacrament of the unity God has called all people to, as a sign of God's unity with the world, the Church is also a sign of the world's basic holiness. When it proclaims that its unity is a holy unity, a unity forged by the Spirit of love, then it is also proclaiming the holiness of the world as something united to God forever. The Spirit of love active in the Church is not a Spirit of pride, a Spirit that lords it over others for not being holy. Such pride, such triumphalism is one of the many sins the Church needs to confess. True, it has its roots in the culturally bound world of the New Testament where believers, dividing the world into areas of light and darkness, identified themselves with light and all others with its opposite. However, the pride so deeply rooted in all of us has only too often turned mere error into a sinful lording it over others. Love — and therefore the Spirit — was absent in such pride. If the Church's unity is a unity in love, God's love, and (as Vatican II has proclaimed loudly and clearly — see Chapter 10, E) if that unity, that Love exists beyond the visible borders of the Catholic and any other Christian church, then the Church's holiness extends there too.

As a sign of the world's holiness, the Church is committed to respecting the world and all its peoples. This was realized by the bishops at Vatican II. It is enshrined in the conciliar document *The Church in the Modern World*.

Of course, to say the world is 'holy' is not to say that everything found in it or all the possibilities it opens to us are of equal value. A very real distinction remains between 'worldly' and 'unworldly'. However, the distinction must now be drawn between what in the world fosters unity in love and what opposes it. The unity in love in question is at one and the same time a unity between people and between them and God. It is therefore a unity in Love, a unity in the Spirit. As Rahner has argued so eloquently, love of God and love of neighbour are identical. They are aspects of one and the same act (Rahner 1969a).

Moreover, to acknowledge the world's basic holiness is not to say that there is no longer any distinction, from the point of view of holiness, between the Church and the world. There is indeed a sense in which the Church is holy and the world not. As *the* sign of the world's holiness, of the holy unity that already exists between God and the world, the Church obviously has a unique, though not exclusive, role to play in fostering it. As a sign of holy unity, the Church has a visible closeness to God that the world lacks. As such the Church has a holiness the world lacks, a visible holiness in the sense of a visible belonging to God. The Church is the sacrament of holiness and as such also contributes to sanctifying creation in a way the world cannot do.

But this is to move too much into the field of ecclesiology. Let me recall the main points made so far. The Church's unity is a holy unity because it is a unity with God, a unity created by God's love. As such it is not exclusive to the Church, but present wherever the Spirit is at work uniting people to each other and to God, even if they do not recognize God as God. However, the Church remains distinctive as the sacrament of holiness, the sacrament of holy unity.

So far I have concentrated on holiness in the sense of 'consecration', of belonging to God. There is, however, a further and most important sense in which the Church's unity is a holy unity: it is such because those so united lead holy lives. The Love that unites us also transforms us, enabling us to love in return. Such love is holy and makes us holy in a moral sense.

The early Christians were very much aware of the fact that their unity was a holy one, that it made them holy. This is why they referred to themselves (and not just to those who gave heroic examples of Christian living) as 'saints' (e.g., Acts 9:13; Rom 1:7). To this day we talk in the creed about the 'communion of saints', a phrase that has come to mean both sharing the unity of holy people, and sharing in holy things such as the sacraments and the value of the prayers, sufferings, holy lives of all. However, the 'thing' shared by all and that which makes all else holy is Love, God's love, the Spirit.

Finally, it needs to be recalled that the Love at work here is *Jesus'* love, *Jesus'* unity with the Father. Jesus is *the* 'saint', *the* 'holy one' of

God (Lk 4:34). Our holiness is a sharing in his — which is another way of saying our unity with God is a sharing in his unity with the Father.

C.   A CATHOLIC UNITY

The unity created by the Spirit is a *catholic* unity. The word 'catholic' is used here in its etymological meaning of 'universal', 'all-embracing'. To say that the unity created by the Spirit is a 'catholic' unity is therefore to say that it is open to all people (see Mt 28:19).

Christ's Spirit, as was seen, creates a unity based on God's love — not on national, cultural, or any other human identity. It is a unity open, therefore, to one and all. It is a unity that need threaten no one's individual identity. Christ's mission and therefore the mission of his Spirit is to unite God and the whole of humanity.

This means that those who are responsible for spreading the Gospel and building up the Church must make sure that the Church is not identified with any particular culture, class or nation. The Gospel must be preached in such a way that the unity offered by the Spirit is not a threatening but rather a fulfilling one. (This has obvious and very serious implications for the way the role of canonical and liturgical law is conceived.) The Spirit's unity should appear threatening only to those who wish to make their own identities divisive, by refusing to be truly united in love to those who are outside their group identity.

The catholicity of the Spirit's unity is of course a reflection of Christ's catholicity. For Jesus himself, especially after his resurrection, was open to all and brought God's love to all. While on this earth he indeed limited his preaching to the Jewish people (Mt 10:6, 15:24). He did not try to start a new religion but saw his task rather as the fulfilment of the Jewish faith (Mt 5:17). 'The Twelve' he chose (Mk 3:13–19) were symbolic of the beginning of a new, purified Israel that people had looked forward to for centuries. Yet this did not mean that others would be excluded. Even in Old Testament times there was the hope that all nations would share in Israel's blessing (Is 2:3). After his resurrection, when he was able to be truly one in the Spirit with all people of all places and all times, Jesus was able to distribute those blessings beyond the borders of Israel.

However, even after the resurrection and the experience of Pentecost it was still not immediately clear to the disciples that non-Jews could share in the blessings of salvation without first becoming Jews. Initially, they evidently thought that non-Jews could share in the blessings of the last days only if they became Jews and observed the Law of Moses, part of which forbade mixing between Jews and Gentiles.

One of the first lessons the Church therefore had to learn about itself was its catholicity. It had to learn that it was open to all without posing a threat to anyone's identity or compelling anyone to take on Jewish nationality, Jewish culture, Jewish (Mosaic) Law, Jewish exclusivism. The way the Church learnt this lesson is one of the earliest examples of the operation of the charismatic element in the Church. Acts 10 tells the story of how God taught Peter the lesson that Gentiles must no longer be looked upon as unclean, and therefore as people with whom Jews may not mix. Peter had to learn that 'God treats everyone on the same basis . . . no matter what race he belongs to' (Acts 10:34–35). The lesson that Peter was taught in a vision was dramatically driven home by the descent of the Spirit on his Gentile hearers (Acts 10:44). In this event, sometimes called the Pentecost of the Gentiles, Christ made clear that his Spirit was for all people. Moreover, the unity offered by that Spirit to everybody need not threaten individual identity. The Spirit was a Spirit of love. This led to the famous decision taken at what is called the Council of Jerusalem (Acts 15:2–29; most scholars believe that this is really a conflated version of two meetings that took place). The decision was that Gentiles did not have to become Jews and observe the Mosaic Law. However, this same event also provides us with a good example of how the visible expression of unity *can* demand a certain amount of uniformity at certain times and in certain places. True love can demand putting aside legitimate liberties. Therefore, while the decision was made not to impose the Mosaic Law on Gentile converts to Christianity, nevertheless those Gentiles who lived in areas where many Jews were living too (e.g., Antioch, Syria and Cilicia — see Acts 15:23) were asked to have some consideration for the feelings of their Jewish Christian brethren by abstaining from doing certain things that would offend them greatly (Acts 15:20).

This decision was one of the most important ever made in the life of the Church. It made it perfectly clear that the unity Christ had created between God and humanity was open to all people of all races and all nations without posing a threat to their identities. It is open to all in this way because what unites everybody is Christ's Spirit of love, not national or cultural identities, or even a religious reality such as the Law of Moses.

Precisely because it is open to all, the Church's unity is — or should be — such that the contribution of each member is valued. The Love that binds us values each one of us. Hence the 'catholic' character of unity implies not only openness to diversity but also a love for wholeness, a positive recognition of the superiority of the whole to the part. This aspect of 'wholeness' was part of the meaning of catholicity from very early on in the Church's history.

D.   AN APOSTOLIC UNITY

Finally, the Church's unity is an *apostolic* unity. This means that it is a unity that goes back to the days of the apostles and finds in the Church of that time its essential visible characteristics. The unity between the Church of today and that of preceding ages right back to the time of the apostles is before all else a unity in love, a unity in Christ. Its bedrock is not any visible structure, but rather the Spirit of Christ's abiding presence in his Church.

This is why *excessive* concern with physical continuity is a lack of faith in the unity created by the Spirit. An illustration will clarify what I have in mind. The 'apostolic succession' is the name given to the fact that the Church of one generation receives and continues the faith, sacraments and ministry of the Church of previous generations. However, because of the very important part played by ministry in preserving unity, not only within the Church of one generation but also between that generation and the preceding and succeeding ones, 'apostolic succession' came to mean almost exclusively the fact that the ordained ministry was handed down from one generation to the next through the rite of ordination. 'Apostolic succession' came to mean an unbroken line of bishops stretching back to the time of the apostles. All the emphasis came to be placed on the word *unbroken*. It was understood to mean that there was a *physical* continuity with apostolic times, a physical continuity that was *essential* for the apostolicity of the Church. This physical continuity consisted in the fact that any true bishop must be able, in principle, to establish that the man who laid hands on him, as the sign of his ordination to the office of bishop, himself had hands laid on him by someone who in turn had had hands laid on him by someone who etc., etc., stretching right back to apostolic times.

It goes without saying that this sort of visible continuity is very important. It is part of the visible expression of the Church's unity down the ages. However, it is placing excessive emphasis on it to think that a fault in the 'pipeline' (as it has been called) invalidates all who can trace their episcopal ancestry to that fault. For example, let us suppose that someone who by accident was never baptized (and no one is aware of this) is one day ordained a bishop. Only baptized people can be ordained to a ministry. Therefore his episcopal ordination is invalid. During his episcopal life he ordains many bishops. It is unthinkable that all those bishops and the bishops *they* ordain and the bishops these in turn ordain, etc., etc., are not really bishops at all. They *are* bishops because the real origin of the ministry and the real bond of unity between the Church of apostolic times and the Church today is the

Holy Spirit — that is to say, Christ's active presence in our midst.

There is a well-known maxim in canon law: *ecclesia supplet* ('the Church supplies'). This maxim was really an attempt to cast in legal form the point being made here. Of course, the Spirit does not 'supply' for deficiencies in the sense that it is only when such a need arises that the Spirit becomes involved. But the Spirit does 'supply' in the sense of always being present, always building up the Church despite all deficiencies. The importance of this principle for a theology of apostolic succession was recalled by Congar some years ago: 'its reality and its exercise are, in our opinion, absolutely *indispensable* if one wishes to avoid the conclusion that a great number of sacramental acts have been invalid down the centuries . . . . Dozens of facts and texts exist' (Congar 1971:799).

But, once again, all this does not mean that the visible signs of apostolicity are unimportant. On the contrary, the visible expression of this unity is an essential part of it. The three main structural expressions of this unity are the same three I have mentioned already: the confession of faith, the ministry, and the sacraments.

The fact that the Spirit is the bedrock of the Church's apostolic unity means that that unity does not depend on slavish adherence to all that developed in the past or even to everything that occurred during apostolic times. Apostolic unity, too, must not be confused with uniformity. Certainly there are essential visible expressions of the Church's apostolic unity, just as there are of its inner unity in any particular age. But this unity must not be confused with uniformity.

The Church of the next generation need not, therefore, feel threatened by its past. It should always feel free to change, to express its unity in ways that are meaningful to it, observing always the essentials. Of course, a fair amount of uniformity will usually mark one age's unity with that immediately preceding it. Otherwise it is very difficult for the Church of a later generation really to experience its unity with that of the previous one. But the point is that the Church is, in principle, free to structure itself in ways that are meaningful to it. Of course this freedom is one that needs to be open to the impulses of the Spirit. This in turn means, once again, valuing the contributions of all.

It is this freedom that enables the Church to reform itself — or rather, to be reformed by the Spirit of freedom in its midst. The Spirit must continually be allowed to set the Church free from unhealthy and stifling servitude to the past, so that its unity with the past may be the living unity of love and not the degrading unity of an enforced system. The past is important and tradition is the Church's memory. No individual, no community can survive without a memory. But it is true that our traditions, our memories, can enslave us. The fact that it is the

Spirit and not a system, culture, era or tradition that is at the heart of our unity enables us to break loose from such an enslavement.

E.   UNITY: A GIFT AND A TASK

Our unity with each other, our sharing in Christ's unity with the Father, is Christ's *gift* to us. It is the Spirit of love dwelling in our hearts, enabling us to reach out in love to Christ, the Father, and each other.

As has been pointed out repeatedly in recent years, this gift is also a *task* laid on us. Our task is to make that unity a living reality, one that shines forth in the way we live and structure our lives. Henced the many exhortations to unity in Paul's letters (e.g., Eph 4:3). In section A I pointed out that the Church's unity needed visible expression. In that section I had in mind mainly institutional structures. However, such unity needs other forms of visible expression, forms that reflect more directly the Love that is its source. Christians must express their unity therefore above all in the way they relate to each other and in the social structures they create. These latter must moreover be expressive not of the oppressive domination of Christian doctrinal or even moral ideas over others of different persuasions, but of love, of the Love that is the deepest nature of the God Christians worship.

All this can be very demanding indeed. It is easy for rich and poor, black and white, 'upper' and 'lower' classes to kneel together at Mass and celebrate impersonally their unity in Christ. It is very threatening, however, for those enjoying a more privileged status in society to make that unity real in their lives. It is easy to practise the demands of Christian morals and profess Christian beliefs when Christians have sufficient power to structure society in such a way as to make *their* outlook on life the norm. It is very demanding to give others a freedom that in fact removes much of the legal support of one's Christianity so that the genuineness of one's personal commitment to Christian values is severely tested. It is only when one takes this task of unity seriously that one can begin to understand why the Jewish leaders reacted to Jesus' teaching the way they did (see Chapter 9, C, above). In my own country, South Africa, the madness that is apartheid has struck at the heart of Christianity by erecting structures that make any meaningful large-scale experience of unity in Christ extremely difficult. It has also struck at the heart of humanity, by being in fact a denial of genuine love for the other.

Not only unity, but also holiness, the holy aspect of unity, requires visible expression. The Church is indeed an expression, a sacrament or sign of that holiness (see B above), but it needs to be reflected in the way

Christians relate to each other and to the world at large. The holiness of our unity must be manifest in the holiness of our lives. Do Christians treat each other as holy? Do they treat the world around them as holy? The theology of ecology is a theology not only of love for people, but also of love for the world, respect for its inherent holiness as something of which God is irrevocably a part.

Similarly, the catholic character of the Church's unity is the Spirit's gift to it. But it lays upon us the task of being truly open to all. It lays upon the Church the task of creating a unity in love that truly respects legitimate differences, the task of not allowing itself to be identified with any particular culture, race or nation. An extreme example of the error that identifies the Church with a particular culture can be found in my country, where the divisiveness of apartheid spawned Reformed churches that were for whites only. To this day one of these churches has a 'for whites only' clause in its constitution. Such a constitution is a radical denial of the basic meaning of the Church, of the catholicity of our unity. The church in question certainly believes that other races can have their own Christian churches. But the denial of visible oneness contradicts not only that unity but also its catholic character.

Finally, the apostolic character of our unity is, once again, a gift to us as well as a task. The unity between the Church of today and the Church of apostolic times is God's gift to it. But it is up to us to make that apostolicity shine out both in our fidelity to the Church's essentials and in our recognition of the need to change when the non-essentials become a real stumbling-block in the way of being able to appreciate in our present age the unity Christ offers us in the Spirit.

QUESTIONS

Check questions

1   What is the most basic characteristic of the Church's unity?
2   What implications does your answer have for seeking unity in uniformity?
3   Why is visible unity important if what unites us is the Spirit?
4   What are the three main structural expressions of the Church's unity?
5   How are holiness and unity related?
6   Why is the world 'holy'?
7   What is the relationship between the Church's holiness and that of the world?
8   In what way does the Church have a holiness the world lacks?
9   What connection is there between belonging to God and leading holy lives?
10 What is meant by saying that the unity created by the Spirit is a 'catholic' unity?
11 What is the connection between the Spirit's character and 'catholicity'?

12   What conclusions follow for the life of the Church from the fact that its unity is a 'catholic' one?
13   What is the connection between unity and apostolicity?
14   What is the connection between the Spirit's character and 'apostolicity'?
15   What conclusions follow for the life of the Church from the fact that its unity is an 'apostolic' one?
16   Give examples of how unity and its characteristics of holiness, catholicity and apostolicity are both gifts and tasks.

Discussion question

Reflect on your experience of church life and relate it to the ideas expounded in this chapter. Critically examine both the ideas in relation to the realities of church life and church life in the light of the ideals expressed in the ideas.

RECOMMENDED READING

Congar 1983b, chs 2–5 has extensive material on the themes dealt with in this chapter.

12

The Spirit consecrates the Church in truth

In John's Gospel we read that during the Last Supper Jesus prayed that his disciples should be 'consecrated in the truth' (Jn 17:17). In other words, he prayed that they should be made holy *in the truth*. As was seen, 'holiness' is the quality attributed to persons or things that belong to God, and to actions that are the fruit of a person's union with God. Therefore, Jesus was praying that his disciples might be united to God and bear the appropriate fruits of that unity by means of the truth he had revealed to them.

The truth, then, enables the Church to be what it is: a community visibly centred on Christ. It is the truth that enables the Church to be free of the slavery of ignorance and selfishness that results from being cut off from God (Jn 8:32). The Church's possession of the truth is crucial to its existence, an essential part of its structure.

A. THE SPIRIT AND THE TRUTH

Jesus described the Spirit as the *Spirit of truth* (Jn 14:17, 16:13). But remember that Jesus himself is the Truth (Jn 14:6). Therefore, to say that the Spirit is the Spirit *of truth*, is really only another way of saying that the Spirit is the Spirit *of Jesus*. The Spirit is the way in which Jesus is present to us. Therefore, the Spirit is the way in which the Truth is present to us.

The Spirit is, then, not the *source* of the truth that is essential to the Church. Jesus is that. The Spirit does not reveal to us a truth that is not already contained, somehow or other, in the truth revealed by Jesus. As Jesus put it, the Spirit 'will not be speaking as from himself but only what he has learnt' (Jn 16:13).

As we have seen, the Spirit's guidance cannot be appealed to to justify a doctrine that goes against or has no connection with what Jesus has taught. It is, therefore, most misleading to talk of the Spirit as a 'revealer' of truth. Obviously there is a sense in which this is true. The Spirit is a 'revealer' of truth in the sense of enabling people to believe in and understand Christ's truth. However, such talk is misleading, for it can give the impression that the Spirit reveals new things to us, whereas what is being given us is an insight into the truth revealed to us by Christ almost two thousand years ago. In late mediaeval times talk of the 'revelation' of the Spirit was widespread, and led to the practice of justifying many questionable traditions on the grounds that they were 'revealed' by the Spirit to the Church.

Strictly speaking, then, the Spirit does not *reveal* the truth to the Church but rather enables it to believe, understand, live by and preserve the truth revealed to us by Jesus. Jesus is faithful to the revelation he gave us. His visible presence ceased when his revelatory work was complete. Now he leads us to a knowledge and the practice of that truth through his Spirit.

B.   THE SPIRIT ENABLES THE CHURCH TO REMAIN IN THE TRUTH

The truth revealed to us by Christ is not a long list of statements that must carefully be preserved. Christ did not issue a document entitled 'truths to be believed in'. Had he done so, to remain in his truth would have been easy. Copies of the statement could simply have been made and distributed.

But Christ's truth is not like that. It is a truth that is too vast to be expressed exhaustively in any list of statements, no matter how long that list may be. It is a truth that has to live and grow in human minds and hearts — not lie dormant in documents.

One does not remain in the truth, therefore, by slavishly repeating the exact words Christ may have said. A cursory examination of the New Testament is sufficient to see how the Church of apostolic times usually gave the meaning of what Christ taught rather than his exact words (see for example the different versions of the account of the institution of the Eucharist). Slavishly repeating a formula prevents God's Word from coming alive within *us* and being truly part of *us*. On the other hand, one cannot be sure of remaining in the truth if one cuts oneself adrift from the memory of the form in which that truth was originally learnt.

The Church's 'remaining in the truth' therefore involves two things. First of all, it involves understanding that truth within the context in which the Church lives, and developing all its implications in the Church's teaching and way of life. Secondly, it involves preserving the memory of the truth in the form in which the Church originally learnt it. The form in which the Church learnt the truth will always have to be the source to which it must return again and again in its attempt to live, understand and apply that truth.

The first of these two things gives rise to what is called 'tradition', the second to the scriptures. In discussing how the Spirit enables the Church to remain in the truth, therefore, it is necessary to discuss the Spirit's role as regards the creation of the Church's tradition and the Church's scriptures.

C.   THE SPIRIT AND THE CHURCH'S TRADITION

(i)   The concept and the importance of tradition

The word 'tradition' normally refers to a custom or belief that is handed down from one generation to the next. It is also used to refer to the actual process of handing down customs and beliefs. Tradition is an important part of the life of any community. No community can live without it, as it is the link between the past, the present and the future of every community. It is the handing-down of the community's life from past to present, and the handing on of it into the future.

Tradition is also an indispensable part of the Church's life. We can see this clearly in the life not only of the Church as a whole, but also of every particular Christian church. For the Catholic Church has its tradition, the Lutheran Church its Lutheran tradition, the Baptist Church its Baptist tradition, the Orthodox Church its Orthodox tradition, and so on. It has been pointed out that even the churches most violently opposed to the idea of a Christian tradition display a tradition of being anti-tradition (see, e.g., Outler 1961:46)!

(ii)   How tradition originates

The Church's tradition originates and grows as a result of its attempts to understand, apply and develop the implications of the truth it has received from Christ. In the course of this process we see the human mind with all its limitations, in the context of its own cultural setting, receiving the Word of God as it sees and understands it, and passing on this knowledge to others.

This process also gives rise to what is known as 'the development of doctrine'. This is the growth of the Church's understanding of the Word down the ages, a growth that is expressed in the form of doctrines. The Trinity is an example of such a development.

This growth in understanding, this doctrinal development is an *inevitable* part of the Church's life. The reason is that our minds are made in such a way that they must *grow* in their understanding of anything. Full understanding does not come all at once.

Because such development is an inevitable part of the Church's life, it started the moment the disciples went forth on Pentecost day with their message. A close study of the New Testament will reveal how even in apostolic times the Church grew in its understanding of Christ's truth. For example, Paul's doctrine that we are 'the Body of Christ' represents a growth in his understanding of Christ's truth.

(iii)   The Spirit's action and tradition

The process of understanding, applying and developing the implications of Christ's truth is not carried on in isolation from God. On the contrary, it is a process that takes place in the unity of the Spirit (see Acts 15:28, 1 Cor 7:40: here decisions are made under the influence of the Spirit). It is a process in which the Spirit is at work fulfilling the mission of leading the Church to complete truth (Jn 16:13), of declaring to the Church 'the things to come' (Jn 16:13). Christ's statement that the Spirit will declare to the disciples the things to come has puzzled many commentators, but R. Brown believes that it is simply another way of affirming the Spirit's mission to lead the disciples to all truth. It is saying that the Spirit will interpret 'in relation to each coming generation the contemporary significance of what Jesus has said and done' (Brown 1966:716).

Precisely how the Spirit works within us so that we may understand, apply and grow in our knowledge of the truth is unknown to us. The Spirit is divine, and we do not know the how of divine activities. However, we do get some insight into the Spirit's action by considering two things. The first makes clear to us what the Spirit does *not* do. The second gives us a clue as to how the Spirit may actually operate here.

The *first* consideration is the fact that the Spirit's guidance does not result in a situation where everything the Church says, believes or does is necessarily the truth. This is an obvious fact, admitted by all Christians. Error not only can but does infiltrate into the Church's understanding and practice of the truth. This is why tradition must constantly be purified. It can obscure as well as reveal the riches of the truth. Now if this is so, then it means that the Spirit does not guide us *by pouring knowledge into human minds*. Apart from the fact that such an action bypasses normal human processes (something which God does not normally do), it would also result in all having the right ideas in their heads. To form a wrong opinion would be impossible.

The *second* consideration is that the Spirit's character is one of love, a presence-in-love. This gives an indication of the way in which the Spirit *does* act. There is a stream of Christian thought going right back to Augustine that stresses the role love plays in enabling us to know and understand, especially to know and understand the things of God (see Gaybba 1985). The logic of this position, especially as worked out by monastic theologians such as William of St Thierry, is that since God is love, love conforms us to God, thereby enabling us to know God better. Rahner summed this tradition up beautifully when he wrote that love was the lamp of knowledge (Rahner 1969b:100). There is a very deep truth here. Even in our ordinary experience love opens our eyes to aspects of things and persons that we would otherwise be blind to.

Applying this to the Spirit's actions, we can surmise that the Spirit enables us to understand the truth *by enabling us to love Christ and his truth*. Loving the truth enables us to understand it. The more we love it, the more we grow in our knowledge of it. The fact that we have human limitations implies that we will always in this life have a limited and therefore misleading and prone-to-error understanding of the truth. But it is our lack of love that, I suspect, allows error to enter into the Church's life on a large scale. Since the Spirit enables us to understand by enabling us to love, the guidance of the Spirit will be effective to the extent that we open our hearts to the love the Spirit wishes to generate within us. 'Harden not your hearts', we read in Ps 95:8. We can harden our hearts. We can close them to a greater or lesser extent to the Spirit's guidance.

Of course, the Spirit's action and the effects of our response are far, far more complex than I have indicated here. Nevertheless, I believe an awareness of the Spirit's character as love is illuminating here too. It is interesting that Protestantism has always insisted on humanity's sinfulness as the reason for rejecting infallibility, the idea that the Church's understanding of the truth can in certain circumstances be said to be necessarily a true reflection of Truth. Catholicism would want to point out that there is no reason why God cannot protect sinners from doctrinal error. However, the Protestant position is a reminder to us of the crucial role love, graced love, plays in the development of the Church's understanding of its faith.

(iv)   The value (i.e. authority) to be ascribed to tradition

The discussion on how the Spirit works leads to the next point: if the

Spirit guides the Church's tradition, what value does that tradition have? In other words, what value does it have as an expression of the truth? Is it a trustworthy expression? If so, how trustworthy? This is the question traditionally known as the 'authority' of tradition.

The virtually unanimous view up to the time of the Reformation was that the Church's tradition *was* a trustworthy expression of the truth because of the Spirit's guidance. The degree of trustworthiness ascribed to it varied, however. 'Tradition' is not a homogeneous entity that is either all good or all bad, all perfectly trustworthy or all totally untrustworthy. It is made up of a multiplicity of beliefs and practices which vary in value. Even if one were to accept the principle, therefore, that the Church's tradition taken as a whole is of value because of the Spirit's guidance, this does not mean that everything contained in tradition is of equal value. Thus, those things that were part of Church belief and practice for a long time would be regarded as having greater value than things which had only recently become part of the Church's tradition. The greatest value, and therefore the greatest trustworthiness and authority, was given to those teachings that were *unanimously* agreed upon as being *the faith to which the Church was irrevocably committed.*

From the earliest days unanimity was seen as a sure sign of the effective guidance of the Spirit. It is interesting that Augustine saw such unanimity as a form of love, and therefore a sure sign of the presence of the Spirit of love (Chapter 4, C). Of course, unanimity is very difficult to gauge. Its best expression can be found in decisions made by councils. This is why certain doctrinal decisions of ecumenical councils were seen as having the highest authority, i.e. as being the most trustworthy of all. In fact, such decisions came to be regarded as *completely* trustworthy expressions of the truth. In other words, they came to be regarded as infallible. A similar reasoning was applied, in the West, to doctrinal decisions made by Popes. The doctrine of infallibility became more nuanced as time went on, but that is a topic belonging to a study of the Church.

Tradition, therefore, came to have a very great value in both the eastern and the western Church. Because of this value it came to be regarded as an essential key for the correct understanding of scripture. The ancient argument was that as their author the Spirit alone can enable us to understand the scriptures. We are able to discover the Spirit's guidance in the tradition of the Church.

By the sixteenth century, however, the value and authority of tradition was being appealed to far too glibly in the West in order to justify a host of questionable practices and beliefs. Anyone who studies this period will be left with no doubt as to the Church's crucial need for reform — not only in respect of its life-style, but also as regards the ideas that most people had about the faith. Ignorance and superstition were rampant, even amongst the clergy. The theology of the time was sterile, abstract and irrelevant to daily life. If the Church is compared to a barque (it was called 'the barque of Peter'), then it was a barque covered with the barnacles of 1,500 years of sailing. Those barnacles were the traditions that had accumulated during that extremely long period. Radical reform was needed but so often tradition stood in the way.

It is not surprising, then, that in those circumstances the Reformers took a very different view of tradition from the (by then) traditional one. The Reformers themselves, aware of the Spirit's action within the Church, did not deny that tradition had some use. They recognized the importance of the Fathers and the Councils of the ancient Church. But they rejected the degree of authority that tradition had been granted in the past. For them, tradition only had authority to the extent that it clearly reflected the biblical message. Developments of doctrine that were not clearly demanded by scripture, even if they were not incompatible with it, could not be regarded as a necessary part of the Christian faith.

The Reformers, therefore, also rejected the idea that tradition provided us with an indispensable key for understanding the scriptures. *Scriptura sola* (scripture alone) became their slogan.

As time went by, the rejection of tradition virtually became a Protestant battle-cry. Tradition came to be viewed as having no real value at all. On the contrary, it was seen simply as a perverter of the Gospel. In reaction to this, Catholics developed a doctrine of tradition that made the scriptures all but superfluous. Spirit and institution were so closely linked that the institution became virtually self-sufficient. Fortunately, in the present century an increasing degree of understanding between Protestants and Catholics on this issue is noticeable. Today Catholics are not only emphasizing the unique authority of scripture, but also the dangers of tradition and the constant need for reform. On the other hand, many Protestant theologians are beginning to emphasize the role played by the Spirit in the Church's understanding of the truth as well as the resulting authority possessed by tradition. At the doctrinal heart of tradition there is, wrote Max Thurian, a Reformed theologian, 'a universal and ecumenical reading of Scripture by the Church in the light of the Holy Spirit. Only that ecclesial reading will introduce us to the plenitude of the Word of God' (Thurian 1961:11).

D.   THE SPIRIT AND THE CHURCH'S SCRIPTURES

The extent to which traditions can obscure rather than mediate the Gospel shows the necessity of the second of the two things involved in the Church's remaining in the truth: namely, preserving the memory of the form in which the Church originally came to learn the truth.

(i)   Scripture as the inspired record of the way in which the Church learnt the truth

The way in which the Church originally learnt the truth was through the testimony of the apostles. By 'apostles' I mean those who had been personally chosen by Christ as witnesses to all that he revealed through his life, death and resurrection. Moreover, I am referring particularly to the Twelve who were not only eye-witnesses to the resurrection of Christ (in the sense that they had seen the risen Lord), but (unlike Paul) also witnesses of all he said and did during his lifetime (see Acts 1:21–22). Their testimony was absolutely crucial to the process of founding the Church (Eph 2:20; see also Rev 21:14).

From the earliest times the Church believed that the apostles' testimony was inspired by the Spirit. If the Spirit had inspired the prophetic words of those whose testimony was only pointing in a veiled way to the Christ still to come (see Lk 24:44, 1 Pet 1:10, Mk 12:36 and Chapter 1, C above), it seemed obvious to the Church that the same Spirit must be the inspiration behind the testimony of those whose God-given task it was to be the eye-witnesses to Christ after his coming.

Moreover, the Spirit was believed to be the inspiration behind the records of their testimony that were written while the testimony was still being given or at least still fresh in the minds of their hearers. The belief that the Spirit inspired people not only to speak (give verbal testimony) but also to write (give written testimony) goes back to Old Testament times. The Spirit-inspired writings of those times were called 'scriptures' (literally, 'writings'; see 2 Tim 3:16). Because of inspiration, 'scripture says' was regarded as an unanswerable argument, equivalent to 'God says' (see, e.g., Mt 4:4, Jn 7:38, Mt 11:10, Mt 26:24).

Christians believed, then, that the Spirit inspired not only writings originating during the period preparing the way for Christ, but also those of the period during which the eye-witnesses' testimony to Christ's actual arrival and achievements was either being given or still fresh in the minds of their hearers. The earliest record we have of belief in the inspiration of such writings is 2 Pet 3:16, which is itself one of the writings belonging to this period. Paul's letters are spoken of there as 'scripture', that is to say, as inspired by the Spirit.

The scriptures are, therefore, the Spirit's gift to the Church, enabling it to preserve the form in which it originally learnt the truth. The Church believes that they are documents written under the inspiration of the Spirit because their purpose is to be part of the Spirit-inspired testimony that is one of the essential cornerstones of the Church. For, in order to remain in the truth, the Church must preserve that truth in the form in which it received it. The Spirit, as the one who creates the Church and gives it its essential structures, is therefore the one who gives the Church a record of the form in which it originally learnt the truth.

In the above paragraphs, my aim was to make clear why the Spirit inspired the scriptures and what grounds the Church has for believing that documents (which look like all other documents) dating from the period of its foundation have been 'inspired by the Spirit'. The reason is the same in both cases: the Spirit, in creating the Church, creates its essential structures, including therefore the testimony on which it is founded and the written record of that testimony.

I would now like to go on and examine very briefly what exactly is meant by 'inspiration' and in what sense the Bible can, as a result, be regarded as free from error. For belief that scripture is inspired goes hand in hand with believing it to be an absolutely reliable record of God's revelation to us.

(ii)   What does it mean to say that the scriptures are 'inspired'?

What does it mean to say that the scriptures are 'inspired'? Nowadays, Christians are no longer agreed as to what it means, as I will explain in a moment. However, what it used to mean for everybody can be stated quite simply. It is that the Spirit moved various people to write the different books of the Bible. In other words, it meant that God inspired the authors of the biblical books. God's Spirit was pictured as the chief author, and the human author was regarded merely as an instrument.

Conceiving God's Spirit as the chief author of the scriptures gives rise to the question: how do we conceive of the Spirit's inspiring activity? In simple terms, what exactly does the Spirit do?

I do not think we can answer that question. God has not given us the answer, and there is no way in which we can find it out for ourselves. We cannot put the Spirit's activity under a microscope and say: 'there it is — that's what it looks like'! This applies to all the Spirit's activities — not only the activity we call 'inspiration'. I think that to see the Spirit as the one who enables people to love the truth and because of this love want to record it can be a help, but it does not really give us a clear insight into the nature of inspiration. My opinion is that we simply have to say that the scriptures are so much the result of the Spirit's work that we must regard them as endowed with God's own authority — and leave the matter at that.

However, in point of fact, Christians have tried to conceive of the way in which God has acted through the Spirit. It is impossible to discuss the matter here in any detail, but one view must be mentioned because of its powerful influence. It is the viewpoint known as 'verbal inspiration'. Verbal inspiration pictures God as virtually dictating to the person writing the book exactly what that person was meant to write. This theory never pictured God as actually whispering into the writer's ear, or dictating as someone may do to a secretary. But it did see the result of God's inspiring activity as the welling-up in the mind of the author of the precise words God wanted to use. The logical conclusion of this way of conceiving inspiration is that the contents of scripture must be absolutely perfect. Such a viewpoint must conclude that there is no erroneous statement whatsoever in the Bible. If the Bible says, for example, that Noah was 600 years old when the flood came on the earth (Gen 7:6), then that must be true (unless it can be proved that this number was intended to be symbolic).

The doctrine of verbal inspiration took a severe beating with the advent of critical–historical studies of the biblical text. They revealed just how very human the Bible actually was. They revealed the long and involved history behind the composition of the biblical books, the different styles of writing, different cultural backgrounds, different ideas about one and the same religion present in them. This in itself was difficult to reconcile with the idea that God virtually dictated the message to be written. For, if so, why the different styles? Why the rewriting and correcting of older documents? Furthermore, the Bible was shown to contain factual errors (e.g. Gen 1:6–7 which talks about a dome in the sky, a dome that we know is not there) and even what seem clearly to be contradictions (cf. Lk 24:13–33 and Mt 28:7–10).

The result of these studies was that most Christians abandoned the doctrine of verbal inspiration. There are some who still subscribe to it, but they do so by ignoring or rejecting the conclusions of the studies I have alluded to. Other Christians do take some cognizance of them and as a result subscribe to a refined version of the doctrine of verbal inspiration (e.g., by picturing God as adapting to the culture of the time in which the particular biblical book was written, thus inspiring the author to work within the framework of that culture). However, most Christians, as I said, have completely abandoned the doctrine of verbal inspiration.

Nevertheless, very many — probably most — have retained the basic meaning of inspiration, namely that God's Spirit acts in such a way that the scriptures are the direct result of that action, and for that reason possess a unique and sacred authority, for which reason they must be called 'God's Word'. However, many theologians (I do not know of any Catholics among them) have abandoned completely the original meaning of inspiration (i.e. that the Spirit inspired the *authors* of the Bible). Instead, they interpret inspiration as meaning that the Spirit inspires the *readers* of the Bible. To say that the Bible is 'inspired' means for them that the Spirit uses the Bible in order to have an effect on the minds and hearts of its readers, so that they may respond in faith to the truth contained therein.

Of course, everybody agrees that the Spirit uses the scriptures to 'inspire' us (i.e. to arouse in us a knowledge of and a response to the truth). But it needs to be pointed out that this divine activity differs completely from what was traditionally regarded as the 'inspiring' of the Bible.

I believe that the original idea of inspiration has played too important a role in our faith to be totally abandoned. We must retain its central idea that the Bible is the *result* of God's action. But when trying to conceive this action we should see it as an aspect of the general presence of Father and Son to us through their Spirit, and not in the way the notion of verbal inspiration conceived it.

This still does not explain precisely what God does. But it has the enormous advantage of making us see the scriptures as the written record of the faith of a *community*. As such, they will bear the traces of the chequered history of that community. For the one thing made crystal clear by critical–historical studies is that the scriptures reflect the faith of a community — or at any rate the saga of that community's struggle to express, formulate and understand the implications of its faith. Of course, the actual writing, copying and editing were carried out by individuals. But they worked as part of a community, and the divine influence on them came to them as *part and parcel of God's presence to the community through the Spirit*. As was seen earlier, the primary mission of the Spirit is to create a community.

In conceiving the Spirit's action it is also necessary to stop picturing it simply as an intervention *from outside the world*. Of course, there is some truth in picturing it that way. God is not the world. The world is not God. But the world is shot through with God's presence, God's Love. It is that Love that moved people to record in writing one or other aspect of their historically conditioned belief in God. They did so within all the limitations that their historical situation imposed on them. Love respects the identity of the beloved. Hence God's Spirit respects the freedom and historical situation of the individuals inspired. What is produced under inspiration looks no different from any other document. There is no contradiction here. Just as there is no contradiction between Jesus being thoroughly human and yet God's Word, so too can the Bible be thoroughly human and yet inspired by God.

I said right at the beginning that the scriptures are a record of the form in which the Church first learnt the truth. They are a record of the form in which God's revelation came to the Church. They are an *inspired* record, that is to say, they are the direct result of God's presence to people in the Spirit. The scriptures therefore are a permanent — and the only such — example of the way God acted in history during Old and New Testament times. Abraham, Moses, the prophets, the apostles are all dead. Jesus is no longer visible to us. However, one example of the immediate result of the Spirit's activity during those days does remain: the scriptures.

(iii)   In what sense are the scriptures free from error?

In common with most theologians I reject the idea that the scriptures are free from error in the sense that they contain no erroneous statements and are free from any contradictions and other human shortcomings (see Gaybba 1983). But in what sense, then, are they free from error? My personal view is that the scriptures are free from error in the sense that they have truly preserved God's revelation for us in the form in which it came to us. With all its human limitations the Bible, taken as a whole, shows both *the way* in which God's revelation has come to us (through the history of the Jewish people, and through the human life, death, and resurrection of Jesus Christ) and *what* has been revealed to us. The fact that God's message (*what* has been revealed to us) comes to us in the very human and therefore very inadequate wrappings of the culture of a particular person at a particular time does not falsify that message. The Bible, very human as it is, is as true an image of God's revelation as the very human Jesus was an image of what God is like. Just as to see the very human Jesus with his limitations was to see the Father (Jn 14:9), so too to see the very human scriptures is to see God's message in the form in which it came to us.

It is worth remembering that what the scriptures record is the way in which people experienced, understood and drew conclusions from *their unity with God*, from their experience therefore of God's Spirit. The scriptures are free from error in the sense that they reflect accurately the warts-and-all historical character of the way in which the Spirit's

presence affected the believing community's understanding of God and
God's designs.

QUESTIONS

Check questions

1 Why is the Church's possession of revealed truth crucial to its existence?
2 What is the relationship between the Spirit and the truth?
3 What are the two basic requirements for the Church to remain in the truth? How are
   these two requirements fulfilled in the Church's life?
4 What ideas need to be excluded from the vision of the way the Spirit operates in
   tradition?
5 What insights do we have into the way the Spirit does act?
6 What values should and should not be ascribed to tradition if the Spirit is believed to
   be involved in its formation?
7 What divisions occurred between Protestantism and Catholicism over the issue of
   tradition and what signs are there of these divisions being overcome?
8 What does it mean to say that the scriptures are inspired?
9 How far back does belief in the inspiration of the scriptures go?
10 What is the connection between inspiration and the fact that the Church is the
    creation of the Spirit?
11 In what sense can the scriptures be said to be 'free from error' and in what sense must
    they be acknowledged to contain error?

Discussion question

In the light of this chapter, probe once again the relationship between love and insight into
the things of God. Try to work out the various ways in which love brings about insight.
Pay particular attention to the communal insight that a community of love can arrive at.

RECOMMENDED READING

On tradition, Congar 1966 is well worth reading. The section specifically devoted to the
Holy Spirit is to be found in the second part of the book, ch. 3, C: 'The Holy Spirit, the
transcendent subject of Tradition'. As regards inspiration, there are several works
available. The most accessible general surveys would be those found in *A New Catholic
Commentary on Holy Scripture* (London: Nelson, 1969; see the article 'The inspiration of
Scripture' by L. Swain on pp. 53–60) and in *The Jerome Biblical Commentary* (Englewood
Cliffs: Prentice-Hall, 1968/London and Dublin; Geoffrey Chapman, 1969; see R.F.
Smith's article 'Inspiration and inerrancy' in vol. II, pp. 499–514). Also worth reading is
Rahner's well-known *Inspiration in the Bible* (Quaestiones Disputatae series; Freiburg/
Edinburgh and London: Herder/Nelson; in K. Rahner, *Studies in Modern Theology*,
Freiburg/London: Herder/Burns & Oates, 1965).

13

The Spirit enlivens the Church's sacraments and empowers its ministries

The final chapter on the Spirit and the Church concerns the role played by the Spirit in the Church's sacraments and ministries.

A.   THE SPIRIT ENLIVENS THE SACRAMENTS

The sacraments are ceremonies in which people visibly participate in what the Church is: a community of people sharing Jesus' relationship to the Father, and sharing in God's own communal life. In these ceremonies, therefore, people share in the unity the Spirit has created between God and humanity. For example, the sacrament of baptism enables people to share visibly in that unity for the first time, while in the eucharist they celebrate that unity and the sacrifice that made it possible.

What distinguishes a sacrament from other ceremonies is that the express purpose of the former is to symbolize the real sharing *here and now* of an individual or a community in what the Church is. A sacrament is not just a *sign* of sharing in what the Church is, not a *mere* symbol, an 'empty' symbol as people often say. Rather, it is filled with the reality it symbolizes. A sacrament is not only a sign of sharing in what the Church is, but actually *is* such a sharing for those who, through their faith, open themselves to receive the life that is being offered them at that moment.

That life is the love-bond created by the Spirit between Father and Son and the rest of the community. Love is the ultimate way of living, being God's way. Love transforms all it unites, giving new life to those united by it. Hence love is truly described as 'life', and the Spirit as the 'Lord and giver of life', as we say in the Nicene Creed.

It is the Spirit, then, that turns symbols of life into real life, symbols of sharing in a love-bond into a real sharing. Put another way, it is the presence of Father and Son through their Spirit, the presence of Father and Son through their Love, that makes the sacraments a true sharing in that Love and therefore in the community or Church built up by it. As symbols of sharing in what the Church is, the sacraments are also symbols of sharing in love. It is a sharing in the Love that is the Spirit uniting Christ to the Father. But it is also a sharing in the human love transformed by the Spirit, the love that gives visible shape to Love.

Baptism symbolizes (and makes real for the one baptized) the beginning of such a sharing, the washing-away of all obstacles to unity with God. Confirmation symbolizes (and makes real) the fact that as a result the baptized person now shares fully in the Love that transforms, enabling people to witness to Christ as the apostles did on Pentecost day. The eucharist celebrates and deepens our unity in Love, the fact that we are Christ's Body, sharing in his relationship to the Father, and the sacrifice that made such unity possible. What is more, the change of bread and wine from being mere food to being the embodiment of Christ present in our midst can be seen as an anticipation of the future transformation of all material reality by the Spirit so that space and time no longer limit our ability to be present to each other in love (see on this theme *inter alia* Martelet 1972:195–196; for a critique of it see Wainwright 1971:104ff.).

Penance symbolizes and makes real for the believer the fact that the Love shared in is never withdrawn, always forgiving, even when sinned against. It also reminds the individual of the need for personal penance to overcome all the inner effects of sin, the obstacles to love that remain even after forgiveness has been experienced. The sacrament of the sick symbolizes and makes real for a sick person the fact that the Love uniting us is one that will triumph even over sickness and death, transforming us to the point where we will be as close to each other as Father and Son are. Marriage symbolizes and makes real for Christian couples the fact that human love is a sacrament of divine love, that their love for each other is a sign and medium of the presence of the Spirit in their midst. Finally, the sacrament of Orders symbolizes and makes real for its recipients (as well as for the larger community) that the Love that unites, transforms and leads us is a service, a ministry, Christ's ministry, the continuation of his ministry in his Church.

Of course, much more could be said as regards the way in which each sacrament is a symbol of the Spirit of love, of the presence of Father and Son to us in love. But the above is sufficient to indicate the inner connection between the Spirit and the sacraments. As with the Church, so too with the sacraments, the Spirit is not given simply to 'supernaturalize' or vivify a preordained structure, whose meaning is not directly related to the Spirit's nature. On the contrary, the sacraments express a sharing in the Spirit's very nature — viz., a sharing in love, in the bond uniting Father and Son, in the communal life that the Spirit forges within the divinity and therefore within the broader community centred on it. Once again, William of St Thierry's comments on our sharing in the Spirit's role of uniting Father and Son (see Chapter 5, E) have profound depths yet to be explored in theology.

An awareness of the role of the Spirit in the sacraments has been part of the Church's faith from very early on in its history. Prayers, for example, abound in which the Spirit is asked to fill the waters of baptism or the bread and wine of the eucharist. This is especially true of the East, which has stressed heavily the Spirit's role in the eucharist. Indeed, a controversy broke out in the fourteenth century between West and East on whether the words of institution or the invocation of the Spirit (known as the epiclesis) changed the bread and wine into Christ's body and blood (see Congar 1983c:228ff.). The West argued that it was the words of institution that did it (their position was typical of the institutionalizing of the Spirit that occurred at the time). The East, however, insisted on linking the change to the prayer to the Spirit to transform the gifts. The two positions are far from irreconcilable and the entire controversy yet another sad chapter in the history of misunderstandings, squabblings and refusals to listen amongst Christians.

The crucial role played by the Spirit is the reason why the Church has always insisted that it is not the faith or the holiness of the minister that makes a sacrament effective. It is also the reason why we must say that it is not even the faith of the recipient that makes the sacrament what it is. As Augustine put it, it is Christ who baptizes (recall that the Spirit is the way in which Christ is present). Of course, the sacrament would be ineffective were it not received in faith. But just as it is not the recipient's faith that creates the Church's unity, so too it is not the recipient's faith that creates the sure offer of a sharing in that unity (and it is such a sure offer that is a distinguishing characteristics of a sacrament). What makes a sacrament a *sure sign* of unity with Christ's Body is Christ's fidelity to his promise always to be with us through his Spirit. The Church offers what it does offer out of faith in the permanent life-giving presence of Christ within it through the Spirit. The sacraments, therefore, are ceremonies in which we see the Church's as well as the recipient's faith in action. It is a faith in a reality that precedes it, that moreover creates as its gift the faith that is the response to it.

In late mediaeval times a sacrament was seen as something almost magical. If the words were said correctly and the actions properly done, then something mysterious and marvellous suddenly happened (a position one could hardly blame the Greeks for not understanding). The necessity of faith, while affirmed, was allowed to fall into the background as all the emphasis was placed on what was seen as the sacrament's 'power' to work, a 'power' that came into operation once the ritual was correctly performed. This mechanical view of the sacraments was rightly rejected by the Reformers, who stressed the relationship between the sacraments and faith. For them the sacraments were meant to be ceremonies that strengthened the faith of the recipient because in the sacrament one saw God's Word in action, so to speak. One did not just hear a sermon on forgiveness, but actually experienced God's forgiveness ceremonially.

It is unfortunate that in post-Reformation times Catholics and Protestants found themselves arguing about what made a sacrament 'work'. The Protestant viewpoint seemed to Catholics to downgrade the sacraments to nothing more than dramatic actions designed to stir up faith, which faith brought about the desired effect. On the other hand, the Catholic viewpoint seemed to Protestants to smack of magic since it had the appearance of guaranteeing the goods even if faith were not present. Happily it is possible today to overcome a good deal of this division. Catholics are stressing the fact that faith is the prerequisite for a sacrament to be fruitful. Protestants can agree that because it is the Spirit that makes the sacraments effective, they are more than mere symbols.

In short, then, just as it is the Spirit that turns a community of ordinary people into the Body of Christ, so too is it the Spirit that turns symbols of sharing in that community into a real participation in its unity with Christ and through Christ with the Father.

B.   THE SPIRIT EMPOWERS THE CHURCH'S MINISTRIES

The word 'ministry' comes from the Latin *ministerium*, which means 'service'. A ministry, therefore, is a service performed by and for Christ and his Church.

'Ministry' and 'minister' are words that many Christians associate only with clergy. However, it is important to remember that 'ministry' is a service to Christ and his Church that can be exercised by a wide variety of people in a wide variety of ways. For example, in apostolic times not only the apostles, the *episkopoi* (overseers), *presbuteroi* (presbyters) and *diakonoi* (deacons), but also prophets, teachers and healers (1

Cor 12:28) were true 'ministers'. These latter persons performed the 'ministries' of prophesying, teaching and healing. Moreover, the gifts of the Spirit listed by Paul could, with perhaps the exception of the gift of tongues, be regarded as 'ministries', that is to say services rendered to the community.

However, even in apostolic times there seems to have been a distinction between what can be called the 'special' ministries and the others. The distinguishing characteristic of the former is that they seem to have been part of the leadership structure of the Church (e.g., apostles, teachers, prophets, but especially *episkopoi, presbuteroi* and perhaps *diakonoi*), while the others were not. In later history the distinction between the special ministries and the rest came to be known as the distinction between the 'ordained' and the 'non-ordained' ministries.

But it is not my task to enter here into a discussion of the forms of ministry or to explain the nature and function of each. All I wish to do is draw attention to the relationship between the Spirit and all ministry — whether ordained or non-ordained.

To understand the relationship between the two, it is necessary to recall that Christ is *the* minister in the Church. Christ himself said that he had come to serve, not to be served (Mt 20:28). He is God's Servant (Is 42:1; Acts 3:13), that is to say, God's minister. His mission is his ministry. By sending others as the Father had sent him (Jn 20:21; Mt 28:19), he was empowering others to share in his own continuing ministry. All ministry, therefore, is a sharing in the ministry that Christ continues to perform within his Church. All ministry is meant to be the sign of Christ's continuing love for and service to his Church.

Thus, the ministry of being an overseer or *episkopos* (the word 'bishop' comes from here via the Old English word *biscop*) is obviously a sign of Christ's continuing leadership of his community. So too is the ministry of *presbuteroi*. Both are called 'shepherds' of Christ's flock (1 Pet 5:2), for their ministry is the sign of that of the Good Shepherd himself (Jn 10:11). However, the 'non-ordained' or 'non-structural' ministries are also signs of Christ's continuing ministry within his Church. Thus, the gift of prophecy is a sign of Christ's ministry of bringing to us a message from God, giving us an insight into God's wishes for us. The gift of healing reflects Christ's healing of sickness. The gift of faith, of confidence in God, is the reflection of Christ's own faith, Christ's own confidence in God. It, too, is a service to the Church, building up its confidence. As such, it is a sign of the presence of Christ's Spirit of confidence in our midst.

All ministry is then a sign of Christ's continuing service to his Church. However, such service is an expression of love. Hence all ministry is an expression of Christ's love, which is to say it is an expression of Christ's Spirit at work in the Church.

As with the sacraments (and the conferring of the ministry of bishops, priests and deacons is seen as part of the sacraments) so too with ministry, the symbol of love serving is of itself useless unless the reality symbolized — Christ's Love, the Spirit — is present. It is the presence of Christ in the Spirit that enables ministry to be an *effective* service to the community. It is the power of love, the Spirit, that makes ministry a power within the Church. It is an old idea that the minister acts 'in the person of Christ'. A person can only do that if also acting in the Spirit of Christ.

The purpose of all ministry is, of course, to build up the Body of Christ (Eph 4:13), to create the unity that is the whole point of the Church's existence. Such unity is the specific role of the Spirit. Hence ministry is able to achieve its purpose only if the Spirit is at work through it, only if the Love it symbolizes is indeed present and active. Of course, this is not meant to suppose that there need be any doubt about the Spirit's presence. The only point is that the building-up of Christ's Body is ultimately the Spirit's gift to it.

The Spirit, then, empowers ministry. But more than that, the Spirit creates ministry (see Chapter 10, D). The ministry of the apostles has its roots in Christ's calling of the Twelve during his lifetime, and his sending them forth after his resurrection. But other ministries — a wide variety of them (ordained and others) — developed within the apostolic (and post-apostolic) Church. The Spirit is credited with being the creator of these ministries. 'There is a variety of gifts but always the same Spirit; there are all sorts of service to be done but always to the same Lord; working in all sorts of different ways in different people, it is the same God who is working in each of them' (1 Cor 12:4–6). Paul is here stressing the unity that binds together the diversity of gifts and ministries (the distinction between the two is by no means perfect — many gifts are also ministries).

How does the Spirit create ministries? The Spirit must not be imagined as planning a special programme ('I need ten prophets here, three apostles there, etc.'). I suspect that the Spirit creates ministries by creating the love that prompts people to see and respond to needs. This is why the form that ministries take have reflected and always will reflect the cultural conditions of the times, just as the form God's revelation took reflected the cultural conditions of the times. Of course, one cannot exclude the idea that the Spirit may specifically inspire somebody to think up a new and special ministry. But I believe that even in such a case the Spirit, as the love-bond between Christ and us, always works through love.

From the above it should be clear that, as expressions of the Spirit's work, the unity between the ordained and non-ordained ministries is greater than their distinction. To stress their distinction and value the one far above the other is to devalue the Spirit's gifts to the Church. Unfortunately, over the centuries the ordained ministries have, because of their undoubted importance, given rise to a situation in which the Church is divided into two groups: 'clergy' and 'laity'. The former are 'reverend', the latter are not! What sins against the unity of the Spirit are being committed here — and enshrined in Church law! The division is not a particularly Catholic sin, since it is found in most churches, though in varying degrees. It is to my mind a testimony to a defect of love in the Church, to an apartheid that has been in the heart of Christendom long before the South African Nationalist government applied it on a wider and more horrific scale. It is worth remembering that the same Spirit gives different gifts and different ministries to each person. All ministries are for the service of the Body and all are needed and to be valued. Somehow or other we must find structures to express their unity rather than their division, to express the fact that they reflect the Spirit of love rather than the pride of division.

Through the Spirit, then, Christ continues to enable Christians to share in his mission, his ministry, by being the visible executors of his love for and service to the Church. Ministry is really love made visible: the Love that binds the members of the Church to each other. Or rather that is what ministry is meant to be. Ministry, too, is not only a gift but also a task. This means that a minister must make sure that the actions he or she performs in the execution of his or her ministry are performed out of love for and in service to the community. However, even where such love and service may be found lacking in the minister, it is still possible for ministry to be effective, since it is the Spirit that is the real agent at work in all effective ministry.

QUESTIONS

Check questions

1　Show how each of the sacraments is a sign of sharing in unity and therefore in Love.
2　What value did the Greeks wish to stress in linking the consecration of the bread and wine to the epiclesis?
3　What does the Spirit's role in the sacraments imply as regards the relationship between the recipient's disposition and the ability of the sacrament to be a true sharing in the community's life?

4 What is the connection between the Spirit's power to transform bread and wine into Christ's body and blood, and the risen life we are all destined for?
5 What is 'ministry'?
6 What distinguishes the 'ordained' from the 'non-ordained' ministries?
7 What unites all ministry?
8 What is the connection between Christ, the Spirit, and ministry?
9 In what sense is ministry a sign of the Spirit's specific character and therefore of the Spirit's presence?
10 Why is it correct to talk of the Spirit 'empowering' ministry?
11 How does the Spirit create ministry?
12 What implications does the Spirit's role in ministry have for our traditional clergy/laity distinction?

Discussion question

Discuss critically any of the main points made in this section. State what you agree with, what you disagree with, and why.

RECOMMENDED READING

I am not familiar with any English work specifically on the themes dealt with here. Congar 1983c:228ff. has some material on the theme of the Spirit and the sacraments, but most of it concerns the issue of the epiclesis. As regards the epiclesis itself, McKenna 1975 covers the matter pretty thoroughly, half of it being devoted to the history of the problem.

14

The Spirit enables individuals to share in what the Church is and has

A. SOME INTRODUCTORY REMARKS

After dealing with the Spirit and the Church, it is now time to focus attention on the individual Church member. This too, is a lengthy theme. I have therefore devoted three chapters (14 to 16) to the topic.

It is necessary to distinguish between the Church and the individual and study first the one and then the other. However, it is worth remembering that the individual is part of the Church and the Church is made up of individuals. The Spirit's action within an individual has as its sole purpose the enabling of that individual to share fully in the unity enjoyed by the Church. The Spirit's action within the Church, on the other hand, has as its sole purpose the uniting of individuals to each other — the creation of a community and of its essential visible structures. The Church and all the individuals comprising it therefore cannot be separated from each other. Nevertheless, one can clearly distinguish between the Church as a community and any *particular* individual or group of individuals belonging to it. It is because of this distinction that one is able to (and indeed must) deal separately with the Church and with individuals within it.

However, dealing with these issues separately immediately poses the problem of order. In which order should they be dealt with? This is not an unimportant question, for the choice of order can reflect and may encourage either an individualistic or a social view of salvation.

An *individualistic* view of salvation sees it primarily as the saving of individual human beings. It sees salvation primarily as uniting individuals to Christ and through him to God. It stresses greatly what is often referred to as the 'vertical' dimension of salvation. In this view the

Church is seen either as mainly the result of individuals associating together (see Berkhof 1976:46), or as an institution founded by Christ for the sole purpose of enabling individuals to obtain and grow in their personal union with him. This latter was the view that was typical of Catholicism until recently.

A *social* view of salvation, however, sees it primarily as the creating of community. According to this view the community is of prime importance because God existed as a community prior to the human individuals who are invited to share in that communal life. Such a sharing began historically with Jesus' birth and extended from him to all who believed in him. In this view, then, the Church is seen as the visible expression of a community that precedes the individual and in whose life the individual shares. If salvation is the creation of community, then the individual's sharing in salvation is a sharing in a community.

The two views of salvation mentioned above (individualistic and social) have still further ramifications. The former, for example, tends to stress the distinction between 'religion' and 'politics' (i.e. between Christianity and the socio-political order) while the latter inclines more towards stressing that socio-political structures should reflect the values on which the Christian community, the community that is salvation, is based. However, this is an issue that cannot be discussed here, though in Chapter 17 I will touch briefly on the theme of Christianity and the social order. It is sufficient for the moment to be aware of the importance of the order in which Church and individual are dealt with. As the Reformed theologian H. Berkhof has noted, 'the answer to this question has a far-reaching influence, as history shows. It is not a mere theological answer; it decides the shape of the Christian faith' (1976:42).

Why I have chosen the order I have should be clear. I believe firmly that salvation is the creating of community. Our destiny is a unity in love with God *and neighbour*. Individuals are saved by having their isolation from this communal life washed away. They are saved by sharing in it, that is to say by sharing in what the Church is and has. Hence the title of this chapter.

To become part of the community that is salvation, one must have faith. The individual must share in that basic attitude of openness to God that we call faith. This faith is, like every other life-giving reality in the Church, the result of the Spirit's action. The Spirit as the giver of faith will therefore be the first topic I will deal with (B). The actual becoming part of the community is called 'justification'. The Spirit and justification will therefore be the next topic (C). The unity that the individual now enjoys with the other members of the community is a

unity that from the moment of justification slowly but surely transforms him or her, a transformation that will one day blossom into his or
her personal resurrection. This transformation is called 'sanctification'.
Section D will therefore be about the Spirit and the individual's
sanctification. This leads on to the next topic: the Spirit and grace (E).
Finally I will say something about how the Spirit enables the believer to
contribute to the life of the community (F).

Once again it is necessary to note that the topics to be discussed here
— faith, justification, sanctification — can only be dealt with in a very
general way. The focus all the time will be on the Spirit's action. A full
treatment of these topics belongs elsewhere.

B.   THE SPIRIT ENABLES THE INDIVIDUAL TO BELIEVE

Faith is a response to a person (see the superb booklet by Coventry
1968). It is a response of trusting, believing, relying on that person.
Faith is absolutely necessary for any sort of unity in love, for unity is
built on mutual trust. Living faith (and not just a cold intellectual assent
to doctrines) is a form of love. It is a way of showing love for someone.

Of course, the person Christians respond to is Christ. They believe in
Christ in the same way as they believe in God. Jesus himself, we read in
John's gospel, said to his followers: 'Believe in God and believe also in
me' (Jn 14:1). However, these are not two acts of faith: one in God,
another in Jesus, since the Christian makes but one act of faith. It is an
act demonstrating a belief in God *by believing in Jesus*. To believe Jesus
is, for the Christian, the same as believing in God, since Jesus is the
Word of God, the Image of God. As Jesus himself says in John's gospel:
'Whoever believes in me, believes not in me, but in the one who sent
me, and whoever sees me, sees the one who sent me' (Jn 12:44–45).

As a response to Christ and God, faith, if it is a living faith, is also
repentance, conversion. Repentance and conversion are simply different aspects of a single response to a love that forgives.

Since faith is a response of trusting, believing a person, it also
includes accepting what that person teaches us. Accepting Christ
includes accepting Christ's message. Christians, therefore, not only
believe God and Christ. They also believe *that* Christ saved us, *that*
Christ is Lord, *that* Christ gives his flesh to eat and his blood to drink in
the Eucharist, and so on. These statements ('Christ has saved us',
'Christ is Lord', etc.) are doctrines. Faith, therefore, also involves
believing in the truths expressed in doctrines. This is why in the New
Testament 'faith' very often means believing the *message* preached by
the apostles, believing the Good News. John's gospel, we are told, was

written so that we may believe the message 'that Jesus is the Christ, the Son of God' (Jn 20:31).

Now the scriptures make it quite clear that faith in Jesus Christ is God's gift to people. 'No one can come to me unless he is drawn by the Father who sent me' (Jn 6:44). Jesus was talking there about people believing in him while he was still on this earth. After his resurrection the same is true — viz., that faith is God's gift to us. But now the 'drawing' of people to Jesus is attributed to the Spirit. 'No one can say, "Jesus is Lord" unless he is under the influence of the Holy Spirit' (1 Cor 12:3). This makes sense. For as the one who unites us in love to Christ and each other, the Spirit is the one who enables us to make the initial response of faith in Christ.

Everything about the act of faith is God's gift to us. There is no special area where our minds or our wills can say to God: 'Thanks, Lord, for getting me started, but I can take over from here now'!

Thus, Christ's invitation to us to believe, is his gift to us. This invitation comes to us through the preaching, teaching, proclaiming of the Word (Rom 10:17). This proclamation of the Word is his gift to us, a service performed in his name for us by his followers, moved by the love and faith that the Spirit has already created within them. The first move comes, then, from the side of God, from the Love of Father and Son at work in our world. Dramatic accounts of the Spirit's initiative can be read in Acts 8:29 and 10:19. However, *all* testimony to the Gospel — whether it be in the form of preaching, teaching, etc., or in the written form of the scriptures — is the Spirit's gift to us (what was said in Chapter 12, C (iii) also applies here).

However, the Spirit's role does not cease once the invitation is issued. With the invitation comes a further gift. It is the gift of being able to recognize the invitation for what it is: an invitation from God to believe in Christ. In other words, the Spirit enables us to be convinced that the Christian message is indeed God's message, that Christ is indeed Lord. This is part of the *testimonium Spiritus Sancti internum* which plays such an important part in Calvin's theology (see Chapter 6, B). This gift of the Spirit is *essential* if we are to believe. Without it we would be completely at the mercy of the blindness and slavery to ourselves that is the legacy of our sinfulness.

But this raises a problem. If we need the Spirit in order to be convinced of the truth of the Christian message, then surely faith is something irrational, something that has nothing to do with the normal processes whereby a human mind becomes convinced of something? And, indeed, repeated emphasis on the gift character of faith has led people to conclude that the normal processes whereby the mind becomes convinced of something, the processes that make our convictions reasonable, play no part in faith: 'you just believe, and that is all there is to it'. However, as an act performed by a being to whom God has granted the gift of reason, faith must engage that reason. Faith must be reasonable. This is why Christians have always given *reasons* for their faith. We cannot go into these reasons here, but they were all things that happened historically: Jesus' preaching, his way of life, his miracles (see Jn 10:38, where Jesus appeals to his works), his being seen again after his death, etc.

But if there are these reasons, why is the Spirit's enlightening presence *essential*? Why cannot our unaided reason see the convincing character of the reasons advanced by Christians for believing?

The answer, or an essential part of it, is as follows.

First of all, faith is not simply an intellectual assent to abstract truths. Such faith is what James calls a 'dead' faith, one that even the devils have (James 2:17, 19). Faith is an abandonment of oneself to God. It is — if it be true living faith — an act that already contains the beginnings of obedience and love (recall what was said a few paragraphs earlier). Our selfishness, left to its own devices, would dump us firmly in the category of the 'none so blind as those who will not see'. In other words, God's Spirit has to change our hearts so that our minds may see. Those who have never seen America have no difficulty in believing in its existence, for this is not something vital to them; it is not something that affects their moral life. But when it comes to believing in something that is going to make demands on them, then the matter is different. How difficult it is to convince many an affluent person that the poor are not 'content with their lot', to convince them that the situation of the poor is an agonizing one! The reason is that such a conviction would lead to obvious demands on such a person's generosity. Similarly, our selfishness would make us wary of seeing a message that will make demands on us as the revelation of God.

However, by no means everyone who does not believe in Christ is avoiding such a belief on account of selfishness. The second reason must therefore also be kept in mind. It is this: human sinfulness has created a world in which we are all blind to the things of God, even if we were willing to respond to God. To recognize God's presence requires being 'tuned in' to God's 'wavelength' so that we can 'pick up' God's message, to use radio language. It is the Spirit who enables us to do this (1 Cor 2:11).

What the Spirit does, then, is to enable us to see that the reasons for believing really are reasons for believing. The Spirit does not *turn* them into reasons for believing, but rather enables us to see them for what they *already* are: true signs of God's presence. In other words, the *reasonableness* of the reasons for believing is not the Spirit's gift. What is the Spirit's gift is the illumination of our minds (through love) enabling us to see that reasonableness.

I believe that here, too, it is the Spirit's character of love that enables the believer to see that the Father is revealing himself to us in Jesus. God's 'wavelength' is love. God is love and therefore those who love are attuned to God (recall the epistemological role of love referred to in Chapter 12, C (iii)). By enabling us to love, the Spirit enables us to recognize God's presence in Jesus. Love, as Rahner put it, is the lamp of knowledge.

Finally, the Spirit not only issues the invitation to believe, enables us to recognize it as God's invitation, but also enables us to respond to that invitation with the act of faith. Even our actual response of faith is the Spirit's gift. Love enables us to take even the first steps towards love, the step of trusting, believing, abandoning ourselves in faith to Christ. Without this action of the Spirit within us we would simply be the slaves of our selfishness. Faith is totally and completely God's gift to us. With this response there also comes assurance, the assurance that we do indeed share in salvation, the assurance that we are recipients of God's mercy, sharers in the new life Christ has brought us (2 Cor 1:21–22). This assurance, too, is part of the *testimonium Spiritus Sancti internum*.

C. THE SPIRIT JUSTIFIES THE BELIEVER

When a person becomes part of Christ and his Body, he or she is said to be 'justified' (e.g. Rom 5:1). 'Justification', therefore, is the transition from a state of alienation from God to the state of being God's child. It is the passage from a state of not belonging to God's community to the state of belonging (Eph 2:12–13). This transition is described in various ways in the scriptures. For example, it is described as being taken out of the power of darkness and into Christ's kingdom (Col 1:13), as passing from death to life (1 Jn 3:14), as dying and rising with Christ (Rom 6:3–4) and as rebirth (Jn 3:5). However, the essential point is that a person passes from the state of alienation to one of unity with God. Such a person is now in a 'just', i.e. a correct, a right relationship with God.

It is obvious from all I have said that it is the Spirit who 'justifies' an individual (see also Jn 3:5). For to say that it is the Spirit who justifies an individual is the same as saying that it is the Spirit who unites an individual to God, to Christ and to the rest of the community.

The unity with God and others that the Spirit brings to a believer is, as has repeatedly been said, a sharing in *Christ*'s unity with others. To repeat briefly what has already been said elsewhere, Christ's Spirit enables the believer to call Christ's Father his or her Father (Gal 4:6; Rom 8:15). Christ's Spirit stamps Christ's image on the believer (Rom 8:29). Christ's Spirit unites the believer to Christ so closely that Christ lives in her or him (Gal 2:20; Eph 3:17; 2 Cor 13:5; Jn 14:23). Therefore the Father too, who from all eternity lives within the Son (Jn 14:23; 17:21–23), will henceforth live in the believer. Christ's Spirit therefore makes the believer God's temple (1 Cor 3:16). Since it is the Spirit that is the way in which God and Christ are present to the believer, the believer can also be described as the temple of the Spirit (1 Cor 6:19). All this has been mentioned several times already and so there is no need for me to labour the point here.

The basic difference between Protestant and Catholic theology is usually seen as residing in the issue of justification 'by faith alone' (Protestant position) versus justification 'by faith and works' (Catholic position). It is both impossible and unnecessary to go into a matter here that perhaps owes more to misunderstandings than to irreconcilable doctrinal differences, serious though these differences may be. However, it is worth pointing out that Catholics and Protestants do have in common the conviction that it is the Spirit who justifies us. Moreover, we agree that this work of the Spirit precedes any merit on our part. As was seen, even the first step — faith — is God's gift prior to any action on our part. Protestantism's basic concern was and is to maintain that our justification is totally unmerited. Catholics can and must agree. Our justification is the work of a Spirit of love that reaches out to us prior to any merit on our part. It is traditional Catholic teaching that one cannot merit one's transition from alienation from God to unity with God, from a state of 'mortal' sin to a state of grace. We rely for our share in salvation, therefore, not on any good in us, but on God's goodness, on God's love.

D. THE SPIRIT SANCTIFIES THE BELIEVER

'Sanctification' is a word used to describe something that happens when a person is justified. The word comes from two Latin words — *sanctum facere* — meaning 'to make holy'. 'Sanctification', therefore, is the word used for describing the fact that those who are justified are made holy.

As was seen earlier, the unity created by the Spirit is a *holy unity*, for whatever is united to God is holy. By uniting us to Christ, therefore, the Spirit enables us to share not only in Christ's unity with God, but also in the holiness that was his because of it. Or to say the same thing in another way, in sharing in the community's unity a person shares also in its holiness. This holiness is a state that influences us more and more as time goes by. The change in our lives brought about by unity in love does not take place all at once. Rather is it, like life itself, something that grows. It therefore can and in this life does co-exist with all the effects of our sinfulness other than our actual separation from God and the divine–human community centred on God. This is the basic reason for the famous Reformation slogan (and the sense in which Catholics can also accept it): *simul justus et peccator* — 'a justified and sinful person at the same time'. However, it is a true inner transformation and not simply (as Catholics wrongly believed all Protestants to teach) a mere legal fiction whereby God regards us *as if* we were new creatures. Love truly changes us in the depths of our being.

This new situation in which we are placed by the Spirit is meant to influence every part of our existence, eliminating more and more of the effects of sin in our lives. Having been reborn, we now live with a new life, Jesus' life (Jn 5:26; 15:1–7; Gal 3:27), one that must grow within us. This growth is basically a growth in love, the fruit of the presence of God's own Love in our hearts. Slowly but surely the Love that is now present to the believer must be allowed to overcome the effects of sin within him or her.

This growth is directed towards the realization of that inner harmony that would have been ours had it not been for sin. For sin not only separates a person from God and neighbour. It also divides the individual inwardly. Because of sin, all our different desires and needs become a bundle of chaotically competing demands that we have to struggle to control. Instead of being united in the service of love, as they were meant to be, they are divided in the service of their own individual satisfactions. The terrible divisions caused by sin are graphically described by Paul in Rom 7:14–25.

Our minds and wills are particularly affected by sin. The mind is so darkened that we are unable to see that the world is a sign of God's constant love for us (hence the possibility that a human being can become an atheist or an agnostic). We have difficulty in distinguishing clearly between what is right and what is wrong. Our wills are the slaves of their own selfishness. Once we have chosen ourselves rather than God, we find that again and again we end up by choosing ourselves. We become the slaves of our own desires.

The Spirit enables the believer gradually to conquer these chaotic effects of sin. The Spirit's power enables human beings to make sure that sin no longer 'rules' in their 'mortal bodies' (Rom 6:12). As the Love that unites, the Spirit enables the believer to unite all her or his desires and faculties in the service of love. Minds are enabled to perceive God's love and understand God's truth. Hearts are enabled to respond to that love. The result is a life that bears fruit (Jn 15:5). In Gal 5:22–23

Paul lists the fruits of the Spirit's presence: love, joy, peace, patience, kindness, goodness, faithfulness, humility, self-control. Of course, the list is not meant to be exhaustive. It is simply an indication of what does result from the Spirit's ability to heal our inner disharmony, thereby enabling us to unify all our faculties and desires so that they serve one purpose only: love.

Our sanctification implies that the fruits of love produced by us have a value. By transforming us the Spirit of love makes our own love valuable and worth loving in return. Our sharing in Christ's unity with the Father implies our participating in a love relationship. That in turn implies that our love becomes, like Christ's, worth loving in return by the Father. Our transformed love, total gift though it be from God, evokes from God the response of further love, thus deepening our relationship with Jesus, the Father, and all others united to them.

The value given to our love by the Spirit is the basis of the traditional Catholic doctrine of 'merit'. In the past the doctrine was presented too much in categories that allowed people to take a certain pride in their good works and see God's rewarding of them as a matter of justice. This was certainly the way Protestants viewed Catholicism's beliefs concerning merit and formed a major part of their objection to it. Protestantism emphasized the sinfulness of human nature even after justification, with the result that we could never glory in whatever fruits of sanctification may be produced in it. Such fruits remain God's pure gift to us. Protestants stressed the sheer graciousness of God's rewarding of our good works. Catholics on the other hand spoke of sheer graciousness only in connection with justification. Sanctification was seen by them as a process in which good works evoked a reward as a matter of justice (albeit because of God's promises).

Much of the dispute can, I think, be resolved if one abandons the 'justice' and 'reward' categories and returns to personal ones. Good works are, all can agree, the expression of love. The fruits of Love's presence are but expressions of love in various ways. Such love, if true love, always implies a love for God as well as neighbour. As a fruit of the Spirit's presence it is a *true* act of love and as such *evokes* a loving response from God, resulting in a deeper relationship with God. God's responding act of love and the accompanying deeper relationship it brings can be called a 'reward'. It is moreover possible to speak of the believer's love as 'meriting' such a 'reward'. But such words are really out of place when talking about personal relationships, love relationships. They belong to legal categories that ill suit our relationship with our Father, to Jesus and to each other.

It is also worth remembering that what is 'rewarded' is the love the *Spirit produces within us* by transforming us. Father and Son are really 'rewarding' their own gift to us, as Augustine once remarked (*Sermon* 298, 5). The Spirit of Love remains the unmerited source of the entire love relationship set up between God and us. In that sense we can all agree that even the fruits of justification are the product of God's graciousness to us.

The transformation brought about within the believer by the Spirit is not something different from eternal life. It does not 'earn' eternal life as though this were a sort of lollipop given to people for being good. On the contrary, our transformation is *already* a sharing in eternal life (1 Jn 5:11). Eternal life, the risen life, is but the full flowering of a life that already exists within us. 'If the Spirit of him who raised Jesus from the dead is living in you, then he who raised Jesus from the dead will give life to your own mortal bodies through his Spirit living in you' (Rom 8:11).

The growth that takes place on this earth therefore reaches its goal when the believer rises from the dead as gloriously transformed as Christ is. The point of this transformation, as I see it, is not simply that the believer will never die again. Rather is its purpose to overcome every conceivable obstacle to the most perfect unity in love imaginable. The believer's resurrection is a sharing in Christ's resurrection (2 Cor 4:14). And just as Christ's resurrection enables him to be immediately present to all people of all times and all places, so too will our resurrection enable us to be similarly present to each other. When that happens, then the unifying, transforming power of the Spirit, the power of God's Love, will have achieved its goal. For then we will truly be one with God and each other in the same way as God and Christ are one in the Spirit (Jn 17:22–23).

The Spirit is indeed aptly called the 'pledge' that one day·we will share fully in the risen life (Eph 1:14; 2 Cor 5:5; see also 2 Cor 1:22) and the 'first fruits' (Rom 8:23) of a greater harvest yet to come.

All the detailed aspects of the Spirit's work are simply the effects of love. As Love, the Spirit unites the individual with God, with Christ and the Body of Christ. This love-bond transforms the individual, a transformation that begins in this life and achieves its perfection with the individual's resurrection. In this way the Spirit enables a person to share in all the aspects of salvation: the restoration of unity between God and humanity, between people, within the individual and, as will be seen in Chapter 17, between human beings and their environment.

E.   THE SPIRIT AND GRACE

The term 'grace' translates the Greek *charis*, which has several connected meanings. As used in Christianity it originally referred to God's attitude of kindness to us. However, it rapidly came to refer also to the result of that kindness: our actual sharing in salvation, the effects of that kindness within us.

In scholasticism the theology of grace became a nightmare for students. The different aspects of our sharing in salvation came to be presented as different types of grace, whose unity was far from clear. The theological student had to cope with antecedent and consequent grace, actual and habitual grace, created and uncreated grace, efficacious and sufficient grace, and several other kinds of grace. Moreover, grace came to be viewed almost as a 'thing'. It was conceived of as a sort of physical modification of our souls, a supernatural reality 'infused' into us. This warped perspective spawned a furious debate about how material realities (such as the sacraments) could convey this supernatural reality.

The truth of the matter, of course, is that grace is fundamentally a relationship and all that that does for us. It is a unified reality with many aspects. It is God's presence to us in love, and the transformation effected within us as a result. Grace is but Love's unitive activity and the transformation that is thereby brought about.

Any consideration of grace must start with what was called 'uncreated grace'. This is the Spirit within us as the way in which Father and Son are present to us. It was called *uncreated* grace because it is the presence of the uncreated Spirit, and uncreated *grace* because it is totally unmerited, the result purely of God's graciousness to us.

Love's presence to us does not leave us unaffected. The result may be that an unbeliever is able to take the first halting steps towards faith and love, or that a believer responds in faith and love to particular situations. Such effects were traditionally called 'actual graces'. 'Habitual' or 'sanctifying' grace was the term used for the lasting effect of the Spirit's presence: the inner transformation that made of the believer a new creature, living habitually with a new life.

Catholic theology used to speak of the necessity of (sanctifying) grace for salvation as though grace and salvation were quite distinct things. Constantly referred to as a necessary means for salvation, it came to be pictured by many as though it were a 'ticket' to heaven. However, such grace is not something distinct from salvation. It *is* salvation. Salvation is simply sharing Christ's unity with the Father, sharing the Love that is the Spirit. And that is precisely what sanctifying grace is.

Of course, there is another sense in which grace is necessary. We could not respond to God without first being transformed by God's Love. The power of the Spirit of Love is also necessary for us to counteract the power of sin in our lives and remain faithful to God to our dying day. But the point is that grace and salvation are identical realities viewed from different aspects. Calling salvation 'grace' draws attention to its gift character and also to its effects within us. Calling grace 'salvation' draws attention to the effects of sin from which we have, thanks to God's Love, been saved.

The fact that grace is but our sharing in the Love that is the Spirit also explains the traditional Catholic belief that grace differs in people. The difference tended to be viewed as quantitative. Grace was pictured as being given in increased or decreased measure to believers according to their individual merits (as well as, of course, according to God's good pleasure). However, if grace is sharing in a love relationship, then what is 'more' or 'less' is not a thing given us but the depth of the relationship and the consequent effects such a depth has on us. Moreover the depth of the relationship depends not simply on God's love but on our response.

It hardly needs pointing out that justification and sanctification are themselves grace. If grace is our sharing in Christ's unity with God and therefore God's presence and its effects within us, then justification as our unification with God and sanctification as our progressive transformation are just other words for grace.

In all this the Spirit's role is evident. Moreover, that role is exclusive to the Spirit. As was seen, the Spirit and only the Spirit is the bond of love uniting us to Father and Son. Only the Spirit, therefore, is the Love that mediates their presence and transforms us. However, it is *their* love (i.e., Father and Son's love) that is at work within us. Hence our justification and sanctification is their work too. One must not go to the opposite extreme and make the Spirit the sole agent of grace. All three persons are involved in our salvation, but each has a distinctive and exclusive role to play therein.

F.   THE SPIRIT ENABLES THE BELIEVER TO CONTRIBUTE TO THE LIFE OF THE COMMUNITY

The Spirit enables the individual not only to benefit from the community's life, but also to contribute to it (see Eph 4:12). Without such a contribution, not only the community but also the individual is the poorer. For love can only be an enriching experience if it is returned. The receiver must become the giver and the giver the receiver for love to achieve its purpose.

There are countless ways in which the believer can contribute to the life of the community (for a few examples see Rom 12:6–8). One must not list under 'contributions to the life of the community' only the more obvious or spectacular ones such as exercising one of the structural ministries or having outstanding gifts such as those mentioned in 1 Cor 12:10. Every fruit produced by the Spirit in the believer's life is a contribution to the life of the community. Every act of love, no matter how small, is such a contribution — and a valuable one too. Indeed, if love is the community's life-blood, then acts of love are the most valuable contribution of all.

The believer's contribution will therefore often look very ordinary. It will often look simply as though the person is exercising ordinary, very natural talents. However, nothing can be of any value whatsoever for the life of the community if the Spirit does not use it to deepen the faith and love of the community. In the opinion of several authors, it is quite likely that even extraordinary phenomena like glossolalia or miracles of healing have their origin in natural human powers (see e.g., Samarin 1972:227ff.) which scientific research does not yet understand sufficiently. Were that the case, it would not prevent such phenomena being in addition gifts of the Spirit. For their appearance in the believer could be used by the Spirit as a means of contributing to the life of the community. One could even argue that to talk of the Spirit as 'using' an otherwise natural talent is misleading. It can give the impression that a talent in a believer is purely natural until the Spirit decides to use it. However, it is arguable that *all* the talents of one who is justified and sanctified by the Spirit are permanently filled and used by the Spirit. The reason is that such talents are now rooted in a being whose life is transformed by the Spirit's presence. They are rooted in a life that is itself rooted in the Spirit (Hasenhüttl 1969:116). They are rooted in a love transformed by Love. The Spirit is therefore at the source of *all* that is good and valuable in the life of a believer. Whatever is good and valuable in the life of a believer is a gift of the Spirit and a contribution to the life of the community. The Spirit is given to all believers. Therefore all have something to contribute (1 Cor 7:7).

Perhaps the view outlined here makes the contribution of the Spirit too difficult to distinguish from the individual's natural talents. The Jesuit F. A. Sullivan, for example, stresses that the Spirit's contribution is to add something over and above the natural talent (Sullivan 1982:13). This could range from an attitude of willingness to use the talent for the service of others, to the power needed for healing. Certainly it is clear that for any contribution to be regarded as a charism or gift of the Spirit there must be a contribution of the Spirit that goes beyond the purely natural. However, this does not necessarily mean that it is possible to distinguish in a particular case between the contribution of nature and that which comes from the Spirit. As Rahner has pointed out, 'pure nature' is a theoretical entity, something that never existed and of which we have no experience. All we can experience is a world called to unity with God. To distinguish in a particular case God's contribution from that of nature it would be necessary to have a prior, clear experience of nature without God. It seems to me that the nearest we can get to that is in the experience we have of the absence of love, the experience of hatred, oppression, meaninglessness. Hence (it seems to me) the nearest we can get to pin-pointing God's contribution is to look for signs of love or of its transforming power. But even there one cannot actually separate the experience of God's Love from spatio-temporal experiences.

Of course, it is possible for the Spirit to use the natural talents of the individual as well as whatever outstanding gifts the Spirit may create within the individual, even if the individual in question lacked love. This is clearly implied in 1 Cor 13:1–2. However, in such a case the individual does not contribute as a person to the life of the community. He or she would be nothing more than a dead instrument of the Spirit, giving nothing of him or herself to the community. It is only when one's life and talents are allowed to be filled with the love that the Spirit creates within the heart that one is able to be a true contributor to the life of the community. It is only then that one can contribute to the essence of the community's life: the love that unites the members to each other. This is why Paul wrote those famous words: 'If I have all the eloquence of men or of angels, but speak without love, I am simply a gong booming or a cymbal clashing. If I have the gift of prophecy, under-standing all the mysteries there are, and knowing everything, and if I have faith in all its fulness, to move mountains, but without love, then I am nothing at all' (1 Cor 13:1–2).

The believer's contributions form part of the charismatic element in the Church's life (Chapter 10, D). Such contributions can indeed occur without love. However, actions expressive of love are the most valu-able. They raise the level of love in the community. They can evoke further responses of love from community members towards each other and from God towards the community. This is the basis of the ancient tradition that the sufferings, prayers, penances and saintly lives of Christians can benefit each other. This in turn is at the heart of the doctrine of indulgences, for at bottom the doctrine is the belief that we can help each other overcome the debilitating effects of sin (sin's 'temporal punishments') in our lives. All this is possible only because what binds us to each other is love, a love whose source is the Spirit of love. By uniting and transforming all it unites, love becomes a power that can reach far beyond the immediate circumstances of those doing the loving. This is known even on a purely human level. One can therefore only imagine the power of such love when it is shot through with the presence of the Spirit of Love.

QUESTIONS

Check questions

1 What importance can the order in which one treats of the Church and the individual have?
2 What is faith? How is it related to love?
3 Show how each stage of faith is the Spirit's gift.
4 Why is the Spirit's operation essential to faith?
5 How does one reconcile such a necessity with the fact that in rational creatures faith cannot be irrational?
6 What role does the Spirit's character as love play in the believer's recognition of God's revelation as God's revelation?
7 What is 'justification'?
8 Why is justification obviously the work of the *Spirit*?
9 What can Protestant and Catholics agree on as regards justification and the Spirit's role in it?
10 What is 'sanctification'?
11 How does the Spirit 'sanctify' us?
12 What implication does the Spirit's sanctifying work have for the value of our own love? How does this illuminate the traditional doctrine of 'merits'?
13 What is 'grace'?
14 What is the relationship between grace and the Spirit's character as love?
15 Are grace and salvation different entities? Justify your answer.
16 What is the relationship between justification, sanctification and grace?
17 In what ways can the individual contribute to the community's life under the power of the Spirit?
18 What is the most important contribution that can be made?
19 What is the relationship between the believer's natural talents and the presence of the Spirit within her or him?
20 What is the connection between the Spirit's character as love and the doctrine of indulgences?

Discussion question

'There is not much evidence of a Spirit of love transforming people. Look at all the evil there is in the world!' How would you respond to such a comment?

RECOMMENDED READING

Congar 1983b, Part 2 has thought-provoking material on the theme of the Spirit's work within the life of the believer. A book-length treatment by a Catholic and well worth studying is one already referred to: Coffey 1979. Pope John Paul II's Encyclical *The Holy Spirit (Dominum et Vivificantem)* §§55–60 deals with some aspects of the Spirit's work in individuals. For some other perspectives see Green 1975:76–99 (Anglican); Palmer 1958:63–99 (traditional Calvinist perspective) and Berkhof 1976 (a more modern Calvinist approach).

15

The gifts of the Spirit

A believer's justification, sanctification, the fruits produced in her or his life by the Spirit's presence, the contribution that that presence enables the believer to make to the life of the community, in fact everything received from the Spirit is a gift of the Spirit. Everything so received is grace. Hence, whatever list of gifts Christians may use, it must never be forgotten that no list is exhaustive. It is impossible to exhaust the list of all that the Spirit does for us.

However, Christians customarily reserve the term 'gifts' of the Spirit for certain specific gifts mentioned in scripture. Even so, different Christian groups have traditionally used the term to refer to different lists of gifts in the scriptures. Catholics and many Anglicans tradition-ally meant by 'the gifts of the Holy Spirit' the qualities mentioned in Is 11:2 (see Chapter 5, E). Others, however, used the term for the gifts mentioned in 1 Cor 12:8–10. I think it quite likely that the influence of the charismatic movement has resulted in the list in Corinthians being what most people have in mind today when mention is made of the gifts of the Spirit.

Those who meant by 'gifts' the list in Is 11:2 preferred to call the gifts listed in 1 Corinthians 'charisms' (from the Greek word *charismata*, meaning 'gifts'). They expressed the distinction between the 'gifts' (Is 11:2) and the 'charisms' (1 Cor 12:8–10), as follows: the former were given for the sanctification of the recipient, and every believer received them (*gratiae gratum facientes*); the latter were given so that people other than the recipient may be helped, and only some would have these special gifts (*gratiae gratis datae*; see Chapter 5, E).

This chapter, therefore, falls naturally into two parts. The first part (A) will discuss the list drawn from Is 11:2. The second part (B) will examine in some detail the list taken from 1 Cor 12:8–10.

A. THE LIST OF GIFTS TAKEN FROM ISAIAH 11:2

The list of gifts taken from Is 11:2 is as follows: wisdom, understanding, counsel, fortitude, knowledge, piety, fear of the Lord (see Chapter 5, E). The belief (which, though widespread, was never regarded as a dogma) that Christians receive these gifts originated in the idea that the Spirit of Christ enables us to share in everything that Christ himself is and has. As the Messiah, Christ had the messianic gifts mentioned in Is 11:2. Since we become part of Christ's Body, we too, share in them.

The gifts form two groups: those affecting a person's intellect (wisdom, understanding, counsel, knowledge) and those affecting the will (fortitude, piety, fear of the Lord). The gifts, therefore, have been seen as an expression of the way in which the Spirit overcomes the effects sin has on our minds and wills. The gifts affecting the mind 'give insight into the mystery of salvation, they orientate the Christian in the world towards the horizon of God, they sharpen his hearing for the will of God . . .' (Schmaus 1969:60). The gifts affecting the will 'enable man to love and adore the Father almighty and to combine with other men to build up a brotherly fellowship. With the help of these gifts, he is steadfast in hardships, trials, and dangers . . .' (Schmaus 1969:60). As you can see, Isaiah's list has really provided Christian tradition with a convenient enumeration of the ways in which the Spirit overcomes the effects sin has on our minds and wills. We need not go here into an analysis of each gift for, unlike Paul's list, the one from Isaiah does not represent particular gifts that were actually being exercised in the community, but rather an enumeration of general qualities whose immediate meaning is fairly clear, but the detailed contents of which can obviously be discussed and debated at length.

Since these gifts represent ways in which the Spirit overcomes the effects of sin within us, they are gifts that have always been regarded as given to every believer at the moment of justification. What this really meant, of course, was *not* that from that moment a person actually was completely wise or strong in will, but rather that such a person was now disposed to the Spirit's operations enabling him or her to be wise, strong, etc. (see again Chapter 5, E)

As I said above, these gifts were regarded as intended for the benefit of the recipient, for the recipient's sanctification, in contrast to those mentioned in 1 Cor 12:8–10. However, it is worth remembering that every gift of the Spirit — even the individual's sanctification — is also intended to be of value to the community as a whole. In fact, as was seen, the individual's sanctification is the most important part of her or his contribution to the life of the community. It is interesting that Isaiah himself thought of these qualities as gifts to enable an individual to rule justly and thus bring about the paradisal world longed for by all. In other words, these gifts were gifts that would contribute decisively to the salvation of God's people. In a similar way, a believer who has such qualities contributes enormously to the life of the Church.

However, the gifts that are normally associated with service to the community are those from 1 Cor 12:8–10, which is the subject of the next section.

B.   THE LIST OF GIFTS TAKEN FROM I CORINTHIANS 12:8–10

(i)   General comments

In 1 Cor 12:8–10 Paul lists nine gifts: a word of wisdom, a word of knowledge, faith, healings, miracles, prophecy, discernment of spirits, tongues, interpretation of tongues. These gifts can be divided into three groups of three. M. Green (1975:161ff.) arranges them as follows: gifts of utterance (tongues, interpretation, prophecy), gifts of action (healing, miracles, faith), gifts of knowledge (knowledge, wisdom, discernment).

The gifts may or may not manifest themselves in a spectacular way. But whether they seem ordinary or not, whether or not their exercise could be explained simply as the manifestation of a natural talent or a psychological force — if they build up the community, then all of them are the manifestation of the presence of the Spirit (see Chapter 14, E).

Attention has often been drawn to the similarity between these gifts and certain phenomena occurring outside the Church (see e.g., Behm 1964:722ff., Bunn 1973; see also Williams 1981, ch. 1 for an interesting comparison of tongues and Hebrew prophecy). In fact, the idea of ecstasies, miracles, prophesying, the muttering of strange sounds akin to the gift of tongues, was familiar to the Greeks. It was part of their cultural background. However, the gifts mentioned by Paul differ radically from those that the pagans were familiar with in this important respect: the gifts Paul talked about were services rendered to Christ and his community. They therefore lacked the chaotic, individualistic and irrational character of the phenomena familiar to the pagans. One can picture Paul seeing with satisfaction how all things — including phenomena such as unintelligible speech, gifted insights, apparently miraculous occurrences — are transformed by the Spirit so that they serve the building-up of the Body of Christ (see also Behm 1964:724). In the Church these gifts are not chaotic, but are given order by the unity the Spirit brings, so that they serve the building-up of Christ's

Body (1 Cor 14:26, 33, 40; 1 Cor 12:25). Like everything else within the believer, they are now rooted in and therefore shot through with a new life, the life that is God's Love, God's Spirit (Chapter 14, F). But believers must *allow* that new life to press them into the community's service, just as that new life must be allowed to sanctify the believer.

In fact, we owe Paul's treatment of the gifts in 1 Cor 12 – 14 to the fact that the subject of spiritual gifts led at the time to intense differences of opinion and chaos at Corinth. Individuals were clearly taking excessive pride in their gifts. Moreover, the spectacular gifts were seen as being of the greatest value. Paul points out to them (a) that the gifts are there for the building-up, not the destruction, of the community, (b) that everyone has something to contribute, a contribution that the others need, and (c) that the least spectacular of the Spirit's gifts is the greatest: the ability to love.

In the Church these gifts are therefore not for the individual's benefit but rather for the benefit of others (see also Eph 4:12). As D. J. Bennett (1975:16) notes, 'the gifts are not received by those who administer them, but by those who are helped by them'. The real recipient of the gifts is the one who is helped — not the helper!

Finally, in the Church these phenomena are not exercised in an irrational or frenzied state, but rather are under the conscious control of the believer, who must allow the Spirit of love to be the ultimate controller (1 Cor 14:32 — read verses 26–33 which presuppose control; Gal 5:25). The Greeks valued particularly those phenomena that were uncontrollable. They spoke of a divine madness induced into people so that they might prophesy a divine word. The irrational was also prized as a sign of the Spirit's presence in Old Testament times (Chapter 1, B). Paul, however, clearly believes that since the Spirit is a Spirit of order (1 Cor 14:33), a true gift of the Spirit is controllable. I would like to add once again that as love the Spirit respects the individual's freedom.

One of the things Paul points out to the overambitious Corinthians is that while everyone has a gift, not everyone has the same gift. There-fore, the nine gifts listed by Paul are not gifts that everyone must have (1 Cor 12:29–30). In Rom 12:6–8 Paul gives a completely different list of gifts (showing yet again that no one list is exhaustive). Sullivan (1982:28) suggests that the list in Romans is of the sort of gifts Paul would have expected to find in any church. Paul had not yet been to Rome and so did not know the Church there as he did the one in Corinth. If Sullivan's suggestion is correct (and it makes sense) then the list in Romans is further evidence that Paul did not expect to find the gifts mentioned in 1 Cor 12 in every church.

All this is worth keeping in mind, for it puts a serious question mark behind the view widespread amongst Pentecostals and

Neo-Pentecostals that a gift such as tongues is something everyone can and should expect to have. Paul does talk about being ambitious for 'higher gifts', but these are precisely those that contribute more greatly to the building-up of the community through mutual service. That gift is higher which is a greater expression of love. This is why Paul moves on immediately to recommend love as the greatest gift of all. He does not call it a 'gift' there. And it is obviously not a gift in the same sense as the others were gifts — love was something all without exception were meant to have. But it is also clear that Paul wanted his Corinthians to seek it above all the gifts. Gift seekers should look to love as the greatest gift of all, the one thing all should seek and be proud to have. It is surely not by accident that only after stressing the importance of love does Paul tell the Corinthians that they can indeed desire the spiritual gifts (1 Cor 14:1). Of course, this still does not imply that everyone *must* have them. Paul is simply pointing out that there is nothing wrong with hoping to receive spiritual gifts. However, *it is only love that will enable a person to want spiritual gifts for the right reason: to serve others*. It is interesting to note that in Rom 12:6–10 too an exhortation to love follows on a passage dealing with the Spirit's gifts.

Let me now examine briefly each of the gifts.

(ii) 'A word of wisdom' and 'a word of knowledge'

I group these two together because it is questionable whether there is a difference between them. Many, perhaps most (Hasenhüttl 1969:143) commentators see no difference. Paul could simply be splitting, for the sake of effect, two words that form a pair and which, as a pair, share a common meaning: 'wisdom and knowledge'.

Whether or not Paul intended there to be a real difference between the two is something I am not competent to judge with any semblance of authority. However, the fact that he does clearly distinguish the one gift as being given to one, and the other to another seems to me to be a fair indication that Paul did regard them as not absolutely identical, even if — as all concede — they are very closely related to each other.

Hasenhüttl (1969:143) in fact believes their unity to be so close that the question about their distinction is irrelevant. What is relevant is the fact that both have to do with the understanding and application of God's Word revealed to us in Jesus Christ. Certainly both are obviously gifts that enable someone to enrich the community's members with a deeper understanding of the faith and how to live it. The circumstances in which this may happen can, of course, vary enormously. It may be a word that enables a problem to be resolved. An example given by

Montague is Paul's own resolution of the problem caused by the faction
at Corinth. The word Paul gives is that of the Church as the temple of
God (1 Cor 3:16–17) and as the Body of Christ (1 Cor 12:27). Montague
(1976:150, 152) is of the opinion that Paul's letters give many such
examples. Or it may be a flash of insight that gives someone the ability
to make a profound and singularly enlightening comment about a
particular Christian belief. It may be a gift that someone has permanently — for example, the gift of discovering and imparting the deeper
knowledge of the faith that is alluded to on various occasions in the
epistles (cf. 1 Cor 2:6; Ph 3:15; Heb 5:11–14, 6:1). Or it may be a passing
gift that a person receives for a particular occasion. No rules can be laid
down about the way in which these gifts manifest themselves. But this
rule can be laid down about the purpose of the gifts: to build up the
community by providing a word that enables people to have a deeper
understanding of the Word and how to apply it to their lives.

The connection between these gifts and the Word becomes clearer if
one recalls the cultural background of the Corinthians. They were
Greeks and were, therefore, familiar with and influenced by the popular
philosophico-religious movement called Gnosticism. Gnostic systems
varied considerably, but they all stressed the importance of knowledge
(*gnōsis* is the Greek word for 'knowledge'). For them it was knowledge
that saved and made a person perfect. Actions were irrelevant — except
to the extent that an ascetic life could perhaps increase one's ability to
receive knowledge. The knowledge in question concerned theories
about the basic structure and origin of all reality. Possession of this
knowledge was a matter of great pride, a pride that made it difficult to
preach the Gospel to them, for they scrutinized and judged it as another
piece of 'knowledge'. This same pride also infected those Christians
who displayed signs of the gifts of wisdom and knowledge. Paul fought
hard against the influence of Gnosticism. He mocked the wisdom of the
Gnostics (1 Cor 1:22) as being sheer foolishness (1 Cor 1:20) — a good
riposte to their judgement of the Christian message as 'madness'. What
they regarded as madness was the wisdom of God (1 Cor 1:22–24).
True wisdom, true knowledge is the wisdom and knowledge found in
the Gospel message (1 Cor 2:6–9; Eph 1:17). It is a wisdom and a
knowledge that is not merely speculative but which also influences
one's life profoundly. The Spirit that grants the gift of wisdom and
knowledge is a Spirit whose presence shows itself in right living, in the
fruits Paul mentions in Galatians. The gifts of wisdom and knowledge
brought by the Spirit are not, therefore, gifts that turn Christians into
profound but irrelevant philosophers. Rather are they gifts that enable
the community to grow in its understanding of Christ, the source of all
the hidden treasures of wisdom and knowledge (Col 2:3). Of course,

philosophy can play a great role in this growth in understanding. But it will always be the servant, not the master, of our attempts to understand God's Word.

Having stressed their unity, let me now return to the question of the distinction between these two gifts. As I have said, I find Paul's separate mention of them in that context a fair indication that he thought of them as somewhat distinct, even though very close to each other. What could this distinction be?

Opinions differ — a sign of how difficult it is to distinguish between them. I will simply mention a few opinions to illustrate this.

One opinion regards both as gifts of teaching. They would therefore both be the sort of gift that Paul referred to in Rom 12:7 (see also 1 Cor 12:28). However, they differ in that 'wisdom' is the gift of expounding the deepest Christian truths, while 'knowledge' is the gift of expounding the elementary Christian truths (see the notes on 1 Cor 12:8 in the Jerusalem Bible). The distinction between these two kinds of truths is based on Heb 6:1.

Another opinion links wisdom with practical advice ('a special insight . . . on how to live the Christian life' — Montague 1976:150). This opinion is based on the practical character of wisdom in the Old Testament. Knowledge on the other hand is linked with either the inspired knowledge of the sort of fact that can lead to someone's conversion (e.g. Jn 4:18), or 'an inspired insight into the Christian mystery granted especially for the purpose of teaching' (Montague 1976:151).

Green seems to regard 'knowledge' as being the gift of being able to know a fact that would normally not be known to the recipient (he quotes Acts 5:3–4 as an example), while 'wisdom', he suspects, is probably 'a settled disposition of mind, illuminated by the Lord, the Spirit, which has a broad understanding of the purposes of God, the Scriptures, and supremely of Jesus himself and his cross' (Green 1975:188).

Finally, A. Bittlinger explains 'wisdom' as follows: 'In a difficult or dangerous situation a word of wisdom may be given which resolves the difficulty or silences the opponent' (1967:28). He gives several examples, inter alia Lk 20:20–26 and Acts 6:10. As regards knowledge, he writes 'the word of knowledge consists of the old message spoken in the new situation in such a way that it still remains the old message' (1967:30). He quotes as an example the way in which the gospel of John presents the message so as to 'meet the situation of the readers in the hellenistic world of the end of the first century'.

Well, there they are. I think trying to choose between them depends as much on personal preference as on anything else.

(iii)   Faith

The gift of faith is much easier to define. Paul himself describes it in 1 Cor 13:2 as the faith that moves mountains. It is therefore (and all agree) not the faith necessary for becoming a Christian, the faith necessary for salvation (obviously not — Paul is talking about a gift given to people who already have this faith), but rather the gift of having confidence in God despite all odds. It too, can manifest itself in various ways. It can be a specific gift for a specific need — e.g. Elijah's faith on Mount Carmel that expected a miracle (1 Kgs 18:33–35), Peter's faith in telling the cripple to rise (Acts 3:1–10). Or it can be a more lasting ability of trusting God for years on end, even though the need one is praying for seems unlikely to be satisfied.

(iv)   Healing

This gift is closely related to the previous one since, as Green (1975:181) put it, 'you cannot heal in the name of the Lord without having faith that the great Healer himself will act'. The healing envisaged here is not that which results from the applications of medical expertise (Montague 1976:152–153) but rather from a trust in the Spirit's ability to overcome all sickness. Certainly Paul would have had in mind what we would call miraculous healings. Today there are people who feel that many 'miraculous' healings have a psychosomatic explanation. That may be the case, but this does not exclude the possibility that such healings may well be gifts of the Spirit. Recall what was said in Chapter 14, F.

Miraculous healing plays an important role in the scriptures, not simply as a wonder (in fact scripture is not very interested in the wonder aspect) but rather as a sign, a sign of God's power to overcome the effects of sin in humanity's world. In the Old Testament God is revealed as the one who heals us (Ex 15:26). In the New Testament, this divine work of healing is performed by Jesus the image of God, united to God by the Spirit. Sickness was seen as one of the effects of sin (see Jn 9:2; Mk 2:8–12; see also Chapter 2, C (i)). Left unchecked, sickness ends in death, the sign of sin's victory (Rom 5:12; 6:23; 1 Cor 15:55). Healing was therefore a sign of God's forgiveness but especially of God's ability and will to transform our world. This is why Jesus' miracles were seen as a *sign* (a favourite word in John's gospel for these miracles) that the time for the Kingdom had come, the time when humanity's world will begin to be transformed by God's presence (Mt 11:3–5, 12:28).

The gift of healing is therefore a sign that the transforming power at work in Jesus (i.e., the Spirit) continues to work in the community. The community is advised to look to that power in prayer (James 5:13–15). Healings are a way of saying: be reminded that the Spirit that we share will one day transform these mortal bodies of ours so that neither sickness nor death may ever again touch them. The gift of healing is a striking reminder of the power of the risen life within the Church. Again, of course, it needs to be pointed out that healings performed outside the Church do not contradict the statement that *within* the Church they are the sign of the power of the risen life. Just as the Church is where God's plan for mankind takes on visible shape, so too the Church is where the power of the risen life takes visible shape. Within the Church healings are done with faith in the Spirit's power to overcome sickness and death. Such healings therefore take on the character of a sign of the presence of such a power in our midst. It is also important to remember that even if healings are psychosomatic or even the product of the power of the mind of the healer over the matter of the person healed, within the Church such healings occur through powers that are rooted in the Spirit (again see Chapter 14, F).

Healings have, of course, been the one gift that has remained prominent down the ages. In our own day Lourdes has become famous the world over for its healings. No one who has been there and has seen the crutches left on the walls by cured cripples can go away unmoved. Sudden, inexplicable healings have a power to make us aware of God's presence that few other events do. No doubt one of the reasons is not simply the wonder element but the love element within it. Healing is a loving act, a caring act. Healing is therefore a particularly good sign of the presence of the Spirit of love, of God's Love at work in our midst.

So important is the value of reminding the sick that they share in a Love that will triumph even over sickness and death that such a reminder has entered into our sacramental structure. The sacrament of the sick is widely viewed as a sacramental expression of the gift of healing. Whether it is meant to be that or rather the sacramental celebration of God's power to triumph over sickness and death can perhaps be debated. To see physical healing as its primary purpose is arguably a distortion of the sacrament. However, it is clear that where healings follow they are a valuable part of the sign value of the ceremony. Moreover, the text from James 5, on which the sacrament's structure is based, clearly has in mind the achievement of physical healing from sickness. Healing is certainly at least a secondary purpose of the sacrament. Unfortunately, the true meaning of the sacrament became obscured in mediaeval times when it was seen as the last anointing, the sacrament that prepared the recipient for death. Today, however, the sacrament's true significance has been restored to it. Its purpose is to remind people of the fact that the Love that binds us to God and each other will triumph over sickness and death. Physical healings that may result serve to reinforce the message, giving people a tangible experience of its veracity.

However, the gift of healing should not be restricted to physical healings. Mental, spiritual healing is equally if not more important (see Congar 1983b:179). It may not have the striking sign value for observers that physical healings possess. But for the person cured of a psychical or spiritual affliction it can be as great a reminder of the presence of the healing power of Love in our midst as the most striking of physical healings.

It should go without saying that the gift of healing is not meant to be a substitute for consulting a doctor and receiving scientific medical care. The gift is not meant to wipe out sickness in this life. The present life is one in which sickness and death will always exist. It is only in the risen life that they will cease to be. This is why it is important to see and appreciate the sign value of healings. They are *signs* of the presence in our redeemed world of the power that will one day totally eliminate illness.

It is misleading, therefore, to talk as though healing was God's answer in this life to the problem of sickness. There is a stream of Pentecostal and charismatic thought that confuses the present and future situations. They correctly note the incompatibility between illness and the fullness (i.e., including the risen life) of salvation. But they incorrectly argue that our present experience of salvation should, if we are truly saved, include the experience of being healed from our illnesses. They argue that if Jesus bore our infirmities (Mt 8:17) and if we are healed by his stripes (Is 53:5; 1 Pet 2:24), then we are not expected to bear our illnesses ourselves but to be rid of them through our faith (Culpepper 1977:119).

This standpoint is contradicted by the simple fact that we all die. Death is the sickness that destroys us all. Death results from uncured sickness. Moreover, there are several examples of uncured illnesses in the apostolic Church. Paul had to leave Trophimus ill at Miletus (2 Tim 4:20). He also advised Timothy to take a little medicinal wine for his stomach complaint. He did not advise him to seek a supernatural healing (1 Tim 5:23).

The point would not be worth labouring were it not for the psychological damage often done to people who are not healed and made to feel that the fault is theirs. If healing is made to be an infallible accompaniment of conversion, faith, salvation, then its absence understandably leaves the victim riddled with guilt or with the feeling of having been rejected by God. Once again, it is of the utmost importance that healings be seen for what they were even in Jesus' hands: signs of a power already at work in the world, but one that will totally transform it only in the *next* life.

(v)   Miracles

Next there is the gift of 'miracles' as it is usually called. Literally, it is the gift of 'operations of works of power'. Sullivan (1982:33) believes that 'each miracle or manifestation of divine power is a distinct charism'. Whether that is so or not, how does this differ from healings? Does it simply have a wider range than healings or is it something quite distinct from healings? Both Montague and Green seem to see it as the latter. Montague (1976:152) says it refers to outstanding examples of power such as Peter's raising of Dorcas or Paul's raising of Eutychus to life (Acts 9:40; 20:10). Healings by contrast are less spectacular. Green (1975:179), however, arguing from variant manuscript readings of 1 Cor 12:10, thinks Paul is probably referring to the powerful impact that the words and deeds of some Christians can have, thereby furthering God's work. At any rate the gift is clearly one in which the *power* of God's Spirit is amply demonstrated.

(vi)   Prophecy

The next gift mentioned by Paul is that of prophecy. 'Prophecy', 'prophetic' and 'prophet' are words used in so many different (though connected) ways that it is worth making clear at the outset what does *not* seem to be meant by prophecy here.

First of all, it does not seem to refer to the calling, the vocation to be a prophet. While every prophet must have the gift of prophecy, not everyone who has been given that gift is called to be a prophet (see Sullivan 1982:91). A person may be given the gift for a specific occasion, without having a vocation to the prophetic life such as Jeremiah or Isaiah had. Paul himself seems to have made a distinction between Christians called to be prophets in the community and the gift of prophecy that all can aspire to. He lists prophets with apostles, teachers, pastors in a way that suggests they are vocational positions, positions to which only some are called (Eph 4:11; 1 Cor 12:28–29). Acts 13:1–2 and 11:27–28 also speak of 'prophets' as though this was a description of a particular leadership role to be found in the Church. On the other hand, the esteem in which 'prophets' were held suggests that

Paul's injunction to the Thessalonians not to despise 'prophecies' referred to utterances of members of the community not belonging to that select band. A similar comment can be made about Paul's comments on the correct headgear for prophesying during worship (1 Cor 11:4–5). As Sullivan (1982:97) observes, one gets the impression that Paul expected others besides 'prophets' to prophesy. Furthermore, Paul's exhortation to the Corinthians to desire the higher gifts such as that of prophesying suggests that he did not consider it to be as limited as the office of prophet was. This is also strongly implied in Paul's comment that during worship 'all' should prophesy 'in turn' (1 Cor 14:31). Finally, the early Christians' claim that Joel's prophecy had been fulfilled (Acts 2:16ff.) only makes sense if prophesying became a widespread activity in the community rather than something limited to prophets (Sullivan 1982:95–96). None of these arguments is conclusive, but they do strongly suggest that in the early Church the gift of prophecy was something more widespread than the circle formed by 'prophets'. At any rate charismatics have good grounds for the distinction they generally make between the two (Culpepper 1977:110).

Secondly, the gift of prophecy does not refer to the ecstatic gabblings with which prophecy was identified in early Old Testament times (Chapter 1, B). Rather it is an intelligible message, delivered under the full control of the individual (1 Cor 14:32) and which can be regarded as a revelation from God (1 Cor 14:30).

Thirdly, it does not refer to the sharing in Christ's prophetic office that is the privilege of every Christian. Obviously, it is connected with such a sharing. But whereas every Christian shares in Christ's prophetic office, not every Christian receives the gift of prophecy being talked about here (Sullivan 1982:91–92).

Fourthly, 'prophecy' does not necessarily mean a prediction of the future. This is true whether prophecy is thought of as a passing gift of the Spirit or as a function performed in the exercise of a prophetic vocation. In fact, prophecy's proper function is to address a word to the community concerning its present life, its present needs (1 Cor 14:3). The predictions for the future that were linked to prophecies were connected with the word being spoken about present needs.

Fifthly, prophecy is not the same as preaching or teaching (see Green 1975:171; Sullivan 1982:100–101). The two are mentioned in Acts 13:1 and 1 Cor 12:29 as though they were distinct gifts. The distinction between them would seem to be as follows. In the case of teaching one consciously and with deliberation prepares what one is to say, even though one looks to the Spirit for guidance. Preaching and teaching are talents one has in such fashion that one can exercise them at will. In the case of prophecy, however, one has the experience of being taken over in some way or other by the message one feels impelled to proclaim. There is an element of inspiration here, one that cannot be called up at will.

How then describe this gift positively? Prophecy would seem to be that gift whereby a Christian who is not necessarily a prophet by vocation is moved to deliver to the community an inspired message relevant to its present situation.

As for the message itself, obviously its contents would differ according to the situation. However, its basic character must be such as to 'build up', give 'consolation' or 'encouragement' to the community (1 Cor 14:3; Acts 15:32). Hence the prophetic word could be the marking-out of an individual for a particular office (1 Tim 4:14; see Acts 13:2; Sullivan 1982:102). Or it could be a prediction about the future that calls forth mutual support (Acts 11:28–29). Or it could be something from which the community could learn more about itself and its faith — a form of inspired teaching (1 Cor 14:31). Or it could be a word of consolation (Rev 2:8ff.). Or it could even be a severe criticism of the community (Rev 3:1–6). Whatever its specific content, its purpose is the building-up, the strengthening, the instructing of the community.

It is for that reason that it was so highly prized, and that Paul stressed its superiority to the gift of tongues, a gift the Corinthians misguidedly prized above all others (1 Cor 14:1ff.). It continued to be prized in the early post-apostolic Church, judging from the fact that the earliest references to the Spirit's activities focused on the Spirit as the inspirer of prophetic activities (see Chapter 3, A). However, the increasing problem of bogus prophets (see *ibid.*) followed by the Montanist challenge to the Church led to an incipient institutionalization of the Spirit (Chapter 3, C) that apparently created a soil somewhat hostile to prophesying. The movement seems to have been towards combining the offices of prophet and bishop and with it the marginalization of *ad hoc* prophesying. Indeed, the entire movement towards greater institutionalization of the Church and its liturgy, together with its accompanying clergy–laity distinction, must also have played a significant role in the demise of the exercise of the gift of prophecy in its old form. The exercise of the gift clearly presupposes gatherings that are relatively small and not highly institutionalized. This in turn would have led to a situation where even genuine prophecy in the sense outlined above would no longer be called such. The charismatic element has never been absent from the Church and wherever it expressed itself in someone being inspired to say something that contributed to the building-up of the Church there surely the gift of prophecy was in fact being exercised.

The last remark is particularly important. It not only implies that prophecy is not necessarily something unusual or the revelation of stunning secrets. It also means that prophecy is something that need not be exercised during a prayer meeting. The inspiration an individual may receive may need clothing in a text or a talk or even a film in order to reach the community and build it up. It was pointed out earlier that prophecy and teaching differ in that the latter is the controlled exercise of natural talents while the former has the hallmarks of inspiration about it. This is true. But this does not, as far as I can see, prevent genuine prophetic inspiration from communicating itself through the talents of the individual.

A good example of this, perhaps, is *The Kairos Document* addressed to the churches of South Africa in 1985. It has serious deficiencies as a theological document (if by 'theology' one means a well-based, well-researched, well-argued exposition of the faith and its demands). It can be accused of superficiality. It can even be accused of hurling accusations at others that can with some justification be hurled back at it. However, for all its deficiencies it has made its mark as a prophetic statement. It has without question been a word to the churches that has made them re-examine themselves. It has put before people vital issues that can be longer be ignored. It has forced many people to look at the Church's role in South Africa in a new way. To those suffering under the yoke of apartheid, it has been a beacon of hope. To those supportive of the system it has been a searing indictment of their Christianity. To those who previously had lived with a naive outlook on the relationship between Church and social reality it has shattered comfortable illusions. It has evoked more reaction — positive and negative — than any other Church document in the history of the country. It was, I believe, clearly an inspired word, born of the situation of suffering in Soweto. Yet it was equally clearly one that would never have reached the Church had it not been put together in the planned way it was, drawing on the talents of a team of drafters.

The gift of prophecy, then, must not be limited simply to inspired utterances during prayer meetings. It is to be found in many forms.

(vii)   Discernment of spirits

Next there is the gift of discernment of spirits. This is the gift of being able to distinguish whether something comes from God or not. It is 'the ability to distinguish between divine, human and demonic powers' (Bittlinger 1967:45). Following as it does on Paul's reference to prophecy, one is entitled to see its especial field as the distinguishing of true from false prophetic inspirations (Sullivan 1982:33–34).

The discernment of spirits is an important function because, as will be seen in the final chapter, many of the signs of the Spirit's presence are ambiguous. Thus, what the girl in Acts 16:17 said was perfectly correct, but Paul discerned in her a demonic spirit, not God's Holy Spirit. To give another example, people could show signs of being under the influence of the Spirit and yet be cursing Jesus (1 Cor 12:3).

As with the other gifts we have seen, discernment, too, is one that works through the mind of the person exercising the gift. It does not need to be a sudden flash of insight clearly dropping out of heaven. On the contrary, precisely because it reflects the result of the Spirit's transforming presence, a presence that works through our natural .faculties, there are conscious criteria that can be applied in exercising this gift. The gift is really the ability to apply these criteria.

The New Testament mentions several things to look for in a person to test whether what is being manifested through that person is from God's Spirit or not: the fruits of such a person's life (Mt 7:15–23; Gal 5:22); whether or not Jesus is confessed as Lord (1 Cor 12:3); whether or not Jesus is acknowledged as having come in the flesh (1 Jn 4:2–3). Of course these last two criteria were *ad hoc* ones. In other words, they were criteria for distinguishing whether or not *the message being taught about Jesus* was from God. Any message that conflicts with the testimony of apostolic times could not be from God. Therefore, the criteria of confessing Jesus as Lord and as having come in the flesh do not exclude the possibility that God's Spirit can move a sincere non-Christian to say something of very great relevance to Christians — and that Christians can discern God's Spirit at work there. An excellent example of a case where I believe God's Spirit was saying something to the Christian community through a non-Christian was Gandhi's reproach that Christians do not live as Christ taught them to.

Other criteria, mentioned in early post-biblical documents such as the *Didache* and the *Shepherd of Hermas*, apply the yardstick of holy living to specific situations. Thus, if a 'prophet' stays longer than is necessary he has abused hospitality for selfish reasons and so is not a prophet. Also, a 'prophet' who orders a meal or asks for money for himself (it is fine if he advises you to give money to the poor) claiming to do so 'in the Spirit' is a false prophet. Another and important criterion is, to my mind, a willingness to submit to the judgement of the broader community, including institutionally structured authorities (see Chapter 10, D).

(viii)   Tongues

Next there is the gift of tongues, literally 'kinds of tongues'. This is also called glossolalia, from the Greek word *glōssa*, 'tongue'. This phenomenon was a form of speech that was unintelligible to bystanders and indeed to the person uttering it (unless someone with the gift of interpreting was present — see the next subsection). Many exegetes think the gift manifested itself in incoherent shoutings, being a Christian parallel to the emotional excitement and religious enthusiasm of pagan cults like that of Dionysus or Bacchus. This interpretation finds support in Paul's comment in 1 Cor 14:23. However, others would simply describe this gift as a controllable form of speech, a sort of babbling, that need not involve emotion-filled shouting. Paul's instructions to the Corinthians to control their exercise of this gift (1 Cor 14:27–28) supports this latter view, which is the one I subscribe to. It is indeed possible that pagan excesses of enthusiasm did occur. But Paul's point would in such a case have been that a true gift of the Spirit is one that can be exercised in an orderly manner. The Spirit is a Spirit of order (1 Cor 14:33).

The most striking characteristic of tongues is its unintelligibility. It was unintelligible not only to bystanders but also to the speaker, as is clear from 1 Cor 14:13–14. But this raises the issue of its purpose. What purpose can unintelligible speech have?

Judging from Paul's remarks, its primary purpose was clearly to enable the individual to communicate with God, not other people (1 Cor 14:2). Moreover, it enabled people to communicate with God on a deep level, on a level where words were not only unnecessary but a positive distraction. At times words cannot express what we want to say to God (Rom 8:26). In such a case, the gift of tongues can help people express their feelings and thoughts in a way that only God (or those with the gift of interpretation) will understand. It is a way of praising and thanking God, a sort of private love-language between the individual and God.

Secondly, the gift of tongues is meant to deepen the devotion of the person who has it (1 Cor 14:4).

A third purpose seems to be mentioned in 1 Cor 14:22, viz. to be 'a sign for unbelievers'. However, the meaning of this passage is disputed, the dispute turning on the sense in which tongues are said to be such a 'sign'.

Kugelman (1968:272) believes Paul is saying that tongues are a sign to convince unbelievers of the Spirit's presence in the community (though he adds immediately that the disorderly way in which the Corinthians are exercising it is more likely to put unbelievers off).

However, other scholars believe Paul is not speaking here of the positive sign value tongues can have. Instead, he is pointing out that amongst the Corinthians tongues are taking on a more negative significance. If, as seems likely, many tongues-speakers were seeing in their gift a sign of authority and status within the community (see Sweet 1966:241), Paul's point would be that tongues are no such thing. On the contrary they are a sign of something that is to the speakers' and the community's discredit.

Thus for J. J. O'Rourke Paul is saying that tongues are a sign to unbelievers that the Corinthians are mad (1969:1157). A nuance to this approach is that the impression of madness created by the uncontrolled exercise of tongues will be a sign to unbelievers that they are right not to believe. It will confirm them in their unbelief (Sweet 1966:244). Yet a further nuance sees the tongues exercised by the Corinthians as a sign of God's judgement on them for alienating unbelievers in that way (Allo is one who subscribes to this — see Sweet 1966:242). By allowing themselves to be dominated by the unintelligible speech of tongues, they were allowing what was a sign of God's judgement to be their hallmark. Unintelligible speech was a sign of God's judgement in Is 28:11–12, a text to which Paul refers in 1 Cor 14:21 (see also Green 1975:165–166).

The value that the gift of tongues has is for the individual (1 Cor 14:4). Its value to the community is only incidental, e.g. if there is an interpreter around or, I suppose, if someone is edified by a person using the gift in a controllable way. Because the gift was mainly of value to the individual, Paul considerably plays down its importance. He has no wish that it should disappear (1 Cor 14:2, 5, 39). But it is clear that, whereas the Corinthians esteemed it highly and no doubt individuals with the gift took great pride in what for them was most likely *the* sign of the Spirit's presence, Paul regards it as of far less importance than other gifts (1 Cor 14:5–12, 18–19, 27–28).

So far I have avoided a question that must now be tackled. Is the unintelligible speech a real language that is or was spoken somewhere but which the speaker does not know? Or is it a type of speech that is not really a spoken language at all, but simply a way of communicating with God? The former (a real language unknown to the speaker) is called xenoglossia or xenolalia to distinguish it from ordinary glosso-lalia, which would be the latter.

As regards Paul himself, it seems quite likely that he did not think of the gift of tongues as being the use of a real language unknown to the speaker. In Rom 8:26 he refers to a person speaking in tongues as talking in the Spirit about matters that cannot be put into words. This seems to imply that Paul had in mind a mysterious language created by the Spirit for conveying inexpressibly deep thoughts (for a brief rehearsal of the arguments for and against this, see Sullivan 1982:127–128). And all agree that tongues certainly does involve this sort of speech, even today.

However, if many present-day testimonies are to be believed, it seems that today at any rate the gift of tongues at times takes the form of a real language unknown to the speaker but possibly known to a bystander. There are innumerable stories about a speaker in tongues saying something in either a modern or an ancient language which is understood by someone present who knows that language (i.e., *not* someone who has the gift of interpretation) and who is frequently converted as a result. Clearly one must not be gullible about all the stories one hears. On the other hand, it is very difficult simply to write off all such accounts (see, e.g., the account in Bennett 1975:22). Moreover, one cannot discount the possibility that God may work such miracles for the spiritual benefit of people.

Nevertheless, all the indications of scientific research — and much has been done to date — are that xenoglossia does not exist. Indeed, Samarin (1972:128) concludes 'that no glossa, no matter how well constructed, is a specimen of human language, because it is neither internally organized nor systematically related to the world man perceives'. Certainly there are, he agrees, similarities to language (1972:118ff.). However, all the instances of glossolalia he studied lack the characteristics of a genuine language. He also points out true language is so systematic that it will always be decodable (1972:119). Hence, any example of xenoglossia would be decodable. This makes it difficult for anyone to try and argue that taped recordings of purported xenoglossia represent languages unknown to people today. As Kildahl (1975:137–138) has pointed out, if xenoglossia did exist, there would by now be some scientific evidence of it, considering the multitude of tape recordings that must have been made. Still, there is the multitude of testimonies, and I am not sure that they can all be explained away as always being 'third-hand' reports, as Kildahl does.

(ix)   Interpretation of tongues

I would define this as the gift of extracting a word for the community out of a particular instance of speaking in tongues. Those who believe that xenoglossia exists may regard the interpretation as approximating a translation. However, if one follows the more common opinion that the tongues spoken are not xenoglossia but simply a form of utterance lifting the mind and heart to God, then clearly any interpretation cannot be a translation.

If it is not a translation, then what is there in the tongues to be interpreted? Is there any specific meaning embedded in an outburst of tongues, a meaning that someone with the gift can detect? Kildahl tells of how he played tape recordings of speaking in tongues to several interpreters successively. Each gave quite a different interpretation (see Culpepper 1977:106). Such evidence suggests that the tongues do not objectively contain a message that can be decoded by someone. How then is one to understand 'interpretation'? I suspect that what happens is no more than that a particular speech in tongues triggers off in the mind of an 'interpreter' some message of value to the community. The fact that this could have a purely natural explanation is irrelevant. The Spirit works through us and our natural endowments. Hence, the entire process whereby one person feels urged to speak in tongues and another to interpret it could be just as much the work of grace, the work of the Spirit, as the work of well-known psychological factors.

What is important is that the community be served, be built up. Hence Paul's injunction that tongues should not be spoken in public unless an interpreter is present (1 Cor 14:28). This, of course, is not an absolute ban. One needs to remember the circumstances Paul was addressing. Hence, the widespread practice during charismatic prayer meetings of several people praising God in tongues does not go against the point Paul wished to make. However, such meetings need to remember that point — viz., that service to the community should be the paramount consideration.

Sullivan (1982:149–150) makes the pertinent observation that the sort of communal praying in tongues just referred to is not the sort that would call for interpretation. Interpretation would be called for in the case where the community is silent and the silence is broken by someone speaking in tongues. Such an event creates an atmosphere of expectancy, one that could well be inspired by the Spirit in order to open the minds and hearts of the community to the words that will be spoken as 'interpretation'. The two together form, says, Sullivan, a type of 'prophecy', a point made also by Green (1975:167). The tongues and interpretation form, as it were, two moments of a particular instance of prophecy. Paul implies in 1 Cor 14:5 that 'while speaking tongues by itself is inferior to prophecy, when combined with interpretation it is equal to prophecy, and performs the same function' (Sullivan 1982:149).

Clearly, like prophecy itself, this is an area in which the gift of discernment will need to be exercised. It may be that someone possesses the gift of interpretation in a more or less habitual way and has proved his or her reliability in this matter (Green 1975:167). In such a case discernment would normally be less problematic than in the case of someone offering an interpretation who had not done so before.

QUESTIONS

Check questions

1   Why can one not draw up a definitive list of the gifts of the Spirit?
2   What is the list of gifts drawn from Is 11?
3   What reason was given for the belief that every Christian received those gifts?
4   What purpose are those gifts meant to serve in the Christian's life?
5   What is the list of gifts drawn from 1 Cor 12:8–10?
6   What purpose are they meant to serve in the Christian's life?
7   Why does a natural explanation of the gifts not militate against their being gifts of the Spirit?
8   In what sense is love the greatest 'gift' and why does Paul first stress love's importance before conceding the rectitude of desiring to have spiritual gifts?
9   Explain the various suggestions as regards the nature of 'a word of wisdom' and 'a word of knowledge'?
10 What is meant by the gift of 'faith'?
11 What 'healing' is envisaged in the gift of healing?
12 What does healing symbolize?
13 To what extent does the sacrament of the sick's purpose coincide with that of the gift of healing?
14 Should healing be seen as a sign of whether or not an individual truly shares in salvation? Give reasons for your answer.
15 What is the gift of 'miracles' and how may it differ from healings?
16 What is meant by the gift of 'prophecy'? What is its basic purpose?
17 What is *not* meant by the gift of prophecy?
18 What is the gift of 'discernment of spirits'?
19 What sort of criteria should operate in exercising it?
20 What is the gift of 'tongues'?
21 What is its purpose?
22 Should everyone have it? Give reasons for your answer.
23 Why did Paul downplay its importance?
24 What is xenoglossia or xenolalia? What reasons can be advanced for and against its existence?
25 What is the gift of 'interpretation'?
26 What is being 'interpreted' when this gift is being exercised?

Discussion questions

1   Discuss the specific ways in which each of the gifts drawn from Is 11 could contribute to a Christian's life.
2   How would you explain the many sincere personal testimonies to the existence of xenoglossia?
3   What examples can be given of the exercise of the gift of 'prophecy' in your area?
4   If the gifts can be explained as being due to natural causes, what is there in them that would make believers see in them signs of the Spirit's presence?

RECOMMENDED READING

As regards the list of gifts drawn from Is 11, the seventeenth-century classic by John of St
Thomas is the obvious work to turn to. It has been translated into English: *The Gifts of the
Holy Ghost* (London: Sheed & Ward, 1951). A more modern and popularized account can
be found in Part Two of Riaud 1979. As regards the gifts drawn from 1 Cor 12:8–10, there
has been an explosion of literature in recent years. All I can do is mention a few books I
found useful. They are (in alphabetical order) Culpepper 1977, chs 4 and 5, where the
major gifts are outlined and a critical appraisal made of them; Congar 1983b:173–188;
Green 1975, ch. 10; Sullivan 1982 (of the works mentioned here, perhaps the best general
treatment of the issue of spiritual gifts). Specifically on the issue of tongues, Kelsey 1981 is
a book-length theological study of the issue, while Samarin 1972 is a fascinating scientific
study of it. As regards discernment of spirits, Guillet 1970 is a translation of the excellent
articles in *Dictionnaire de Spiritualité* on the topic, giving the entire history of the matter.
Finally, I can mention two other books that I have not used myself but which seem worth
including here. The first is G.T. Montague's brief booklet *The Spirit and His Gifts* (New
York: Paulist Press, 1974). The second is a classic Pentecostalist account of the gifts drawn
from 1 Cor: H. Horton, *The Gifts of the Spirit* (Springfield: Gospel Publishing House,
1934).

16

Receiving and experiencing the Spirit

The final chapter on the Spirit and the individual member of the Church is a brief one. In it I simply wish to consider two questions.

The first concerns the way or ways in which the Spirit is received. Catholics believe the Spirit to be received at baptism, but also in a special way at confirmation (not to mention the Spirit's role in the other sacraments). Then there are those who believe that the Spirit is received in a special way in the event or experience known as 'Spirit-baptism'. Indeed, I believe that amongst Pentecostal laity the view is still widespread that the Spirit is received for the *first time* in this 'Spirit-baptism'. The first section of this chapter will therefore consider the following issues: when is the Spirit received for the first time? what is the relationship between that and Spirit-baptism? what is the relationship between the initial reception of the Spirit and the sacrament of confirmation?

The issue of 'Spirit-baptism' also raises the whole question of the way in which the Spirit's presence is experienced. Can it be experienced at all? If so, how? This will be the theme of the second section of the chapter.

A. RECEIVING THE SPIRIT

(i) When does a person receive the Spirit?

When does a person receive the Spirit for the first time? The obvious answer is: when she or he is part of the Christian community. For it is the Spirit that makes a person part of the community. It is impossible to be a living member of the community without receiving the Spirit. I say 'living' member, for an adult can undergo baptism, the ceremony of initiation, and yet have an unrepentant heart. In such a case many would regard him or her as a 'dead' member of the community, which is really another way of saying that the person in question is only imperfectly part of the community. 'Dead' members are part of the visible community but lack the bond of love necessary for them to be members in the full sense of the word.

In New Testament times baptism undoubtedly was the way in which someone became a member of the community (see e.g. Acts 2:38; Rom 6:3ff.). And by baptism I mean 'baptism of water' (Acts 8:36). Baptism, therefore, is normally the time when a believer receives the Spirit. This is why the waters of baptism and the action of the Spirit are linked (1 Cor 6:11; Tit 3:5; Jn 3:5). Of course, there are exceptions (e.g. Acts 10:44–47). The Spirit is free. But normally baptism and reception of the Spirit go hand in hand.

It is unacceptable, then, to hold that following on baptism by water there must be another event in which the Spirit is received *for the first time*. In actual fact this is not a position officially subscribed to by any church I know of. But it is a widespread misunderstanding of the established Pentecostalist position both inside (by Pentecostalist laity) and outside the group. (I say that it is a misunderstanding of *established* positions since in Pentecostalism's formative period the idea was indeed subscribed to by some of its leaders.)

(ii)   Spirit-baptism: general comments

The misunderstanding has to do with the role of 'Spirit-baptism'. 'Spirit-baptism' has become a convenient phrase for designating the general phenomenon that has been referred to as 'baptism *in* the Spirit' or 'baptism *of* the Spirit' or 'baptism *by* the Spirit' or 'baptism *with* the Spirit'.

In the New Testament there are only seven places where there is reference to such a baptism. Six of them contrast the baptism administered by Jesus to that of John. In contrast to John, Jesus will baptize with the Spirit (Mt 3:11; Mk 1:8; Lk 3:16; Jn 1:33; Acts 1:5, 11:16). The main point is that Jesus and he alone will be the source of the Spirit, but there is also present the idea that a baptism in the Spirit is one filled with the power of the Spirit. The seventh reference is 1 Cor 12:13 where the point is that we all form one body because we all receive the same Spirit.

In the Pentecostal and charismatic movements 'Spirit-baptism' has become a central theme. Broadly speaking, it refers to the experience of the Spirit's power in a person's life. Dunn points out that experiencing the Spirit's power in one's life is also part of the meaning of references in the New Testament to having been baptized by (or 'in') the Spirit. The

Spirit 'was a *fact of experience* in the lives of the earliest Christians' (Dunn 1970:225). However, within this broad category of experiencing the Spirit at work within one's life there are considerable differences as regards what precisely is meant by Spirit-baptism. Differing views also exist as regards its relationship to the moment when one receives the Spirit for the first time.

(iii)   The traditional Pentecostal view of Spirit-baptism

First of all, there is what can be called *the traditional Pentecostal view* (for the historical background see Chapter 6, E). This sees Spirit-baptism as a datable event, a powerful experience of the Spirit's action within a believer's life. Its sign is the ability to speak in tongues. It is *not* the moment when the Spirit is received for the first time, but is a reception of the Spirit following on one's conversion. It is a second or (for the older though smaller Pentecostal group) third stage in one's Christian life. The Christian life is made up of two (conversion and sanctification/ Spirit-baptism) or three (conversion, sanctification, Spirit-baptism) clearly discernible stages.

The biblical basis for even a two-stage position (in the above sense) is weak. Several arguments are used but only two are strong enough to be worth mentioning here.

The first — and weaker — of the two is the argument from Acts 19:1–7. There, so the argument goes, we have a case of believers who have not yet received the Spirit (verse 2). Granted they were not yet baptized, but even when they were baptized the Spirit was poured out in a subsequent event — Paul's laying hands on them (verse 6).

The weakness of the text as a support for a two-stage theory is the strong evidence that, as many scholars point out, the Ephesians in question were not yet Christians (see, e.g., Dunn 1970:83–89). Clearly they believed the basic message being preached about Christ. But they did not display any of the familiar signs of the Spirit's presence such as tongues and prophecy. Paul was therefore puzzled and asked them whether they had received the Spirit. This is no proof of a conviction on Paul's part that one could be a Christian and then have to wait for a second-stage experience of the Spirit. It could simply be an indication of Paul's puzzlement. Paul probes further, and the question is interesting: what baptism did you receive? The reply: John's baptism! Hence they had clearly not yet received Christian initiation — baptism (by water) in the name of Jesus. As Dunn points out (1970:87), Paul's question clearly indicates that he associated the Spirit with *baptism* and not with any other event. Only after baptism did the Spirit descend upon them. The 'laying-on of hands' is clearly part of the single process of initiation (see Dunn 1970:87), not a second stage distinct from the first. In fact, what we have here is the sort of single rite of initiation that only later came to be split into the two rites of baptism and confirmation.

Acts 19 therefore is no evidence for a two-stage theory if by that one means that only those who have the sort of experience meant by 'Spirit-baptism' have received the fullness of the outpouring of the Spirit. On the contrary it points to the conviction that the Spirit was received in all fullness at a person's initiation.

The second text — Acts 8:14–17 — is much stronger evidence. Here there is undoubtedly a case of people who had been baptized in Jesus' name but who had not received the Spirit. In fact, the implication is that they had not received the Spirit *at all*. There is no hint that they had simply-not received the Spirit in a new way (as, e.g., in the sacrament of confirmation *ad robur*). Only one thing seems to be fairly clear about this text and to command widespread agreement amongst scholars: the text is problematic precisely because it appears to contrast so starkly with the otherwise unanimous New Testament viewpoint that those who believe and are baptized receive the Spirit as the pledge of their new life. In other words, the text's very problematic character testifies to the fact that the normal situation is one in which baptism goes hand in hand with the experience of the Spirit's power in one's life. Water baptism and Spirit-baptism coincide.

But how then explain the text? Explanations vary considerably. To my mind, the two most promising are the following.

One, the basic contours of which were proposed by Lampe (see Dunn 1970:62ff.), is that Luke wishes to underscore the link between the Jerusalem church and Samaria. Samaria was traditionally at odds with Jerusalem. Therefore if ever there was a need for unity with Jerusalem to be stressed it was there. Luke's vision is that of the early Church spreading out from Jerusalem to the whole world (see Chapter 2, A). In this text he uses the incident of the disciples at Samaria — who may well have been baptized and yet, unlike other newly baptized people, showed none of the signs of the reception of the Spirit normal in apostolic times — to stress his point. By sending Peter and John to lay hands on the Samaritans, the Jerusalem church ratifies what Philip did and makes it clear that this new community now shares fully in the Spirit-filled life of the Church. The incident also becomes yet a further example of the Spirit overcoming divisions between people.

A second promising explanation is that offered by Dunn (1970:63ff., esp. 66–67). Dunn sees the incident as a warning that baptism without genuine belief is ineffective, and that the test of genuine baptism is receiving (and experiencing) the Spirit. The Samaritans misread

Philip's message — something hinted at by the phrase that they 'believed *Philip*' (verse 12). Superstitious, they were still too much caught up in signs and wonders. The story shows how Simon persisted in that attitude (verse 18) while the rest came to true belief, as evidenced by their reception of the Spirit (verse 17). Dunn's view has the advantage of making the incident perfectly consistent with the norm of associating the Spirit with becoming a Christian. The difference here is that mere baptism does not make a Christian. It must be accompanied by genuine faith.

Both explanations have their difficulties (see, e.g., the critique of Lampe in Dunn 1970:62–63 and of Lampe and Dunn in Green 1975:137–138). I incline towards Lampe's position. Dunn's explanation strikes me as rather artificial. The salient point, however, is that the text's very problematic character only serves to highlight the norm: reception of the Spirit, even as a powerful experience, goes hand in hand with Christian initiation. Spirit-baptism is not a second stage.

(iv) Spirit-baptism in the charismatic movement

Secondly, there are the views to be found amongst those involved in the charismatic movement (as the spread of Pentecostal experiences and ideas to the older churches is called). Here there is considerable diversity, caused to no small extent by the need to rethink Spirit-baptism in the context of more traditional ideas. In his *Treasures Old and New. Interpretations of 'Spirit-baptism' in the Charismatic Renewal Movement* (for more details see below, *Recommended Reading*), H. I. Lederle has provided a detailed survey of the various viewpoints. What follows is heavily indebted to his work.

The two-stage Pentecostal idea was taken over by most charismatics in the early stages of the movement and is still widespread among them. Its supporters cover a wide spectrum, including Catholics (Lederle quotes Stephen Clark and Peter Hocken as examples). Once again, this idea asserts that the Christian's life has a two-stage structure. The first stage is conversion/regeneration (whether one associates this with the sacrament of baptism or simply with submitting oneself to Christ is a secondary matter). The second stage is the experience of the Spirit's presence and (for many though not all charismatics subscribing to this position) is testified to by the gift of tongues.

Apart from its questionable biblical support (see above), this position has an innate tendency to elitism that needs constantly to be fought against. The tendency is to view only those who have experienced the second stage as truly spiritual Christians.

A different approach is taken by what Lederle calls the *sacramental interpretation* of Spirit-baptism. Although subscribed to by several theologians of other churches (e.g., Lutheran, Anglican, Orthodox and Presbyterian), the sacramental approach was pioneered by Catholic charismatics (Lederle — a Reformed theologian — credits them with being the general pioneers of an in-depth theological interpretation of Pentecostal thought categories and experiences).

The sacramental interpretation holds that Spirit-baptism is simply the release of a grace or presence already within the believer thanks to the sacraments of initiation. These are baptism and confirmation, though it is the former that is normally focused on. Devotees of this approach prefer, for obvious reasons, to speak of a 'release' rather than 'baptism' of the Spirit.

Lederle describes this interpretation as coming close to being the 'official' Catholic position. This is rather an overstatement if by 'official' is meant a position embraced by the hierarchy or the Vatican. However, the interpretation has commanded wide support in the Catholic church and is the one embraced by the influential Malines Documents (see McDonnell 1980:39–40).

In 1974 Cardinal Suenens organized an international meeting in Malines, Belgium, of theologians and lay leaders in the Catholic charismatic movement. The purpose was to discuss and provide Catholics with guidelines on the renewal. With regard to Spirit-baptism, Kilian McDonnell's idea of distinguishing between the theological and experiential senses of Spirit-baptism was adopted. *Theologically*, Spirit-baptism is the reception of the Spirit in baptism (and confirmation). *Experientially*, however, it is the conscious awareness, the emergence into conscious experience of the power of the Spirit already present within one. This can be a sudden, powerful event in one's life. On the other hand it can be simply the experience of growth in Christian living.

The attractiveness of this position to traditional Catholic ideas is obvious. The 'two-stage' theory is effectively eliminated together with the need for evidence, such as tongues, of the second stage. On the other hand, the sacramental interpretation still provides a meaningful account of what charismatics were experiencing.

However, it is precisely this latter item that raises questions. To what extent does the sacramental interpretation fit in with the actual experience of charismatics? The criticism has been made, and with some justification, that simply to speak of the release of a hitherto dormant reality does not really conform to the experience people have of a new reality breaking into their lives. The experience, in other words, is not so much of a release as of a *coming*, a powerful event that has an unquestionable newness about it.

Sullivan (1982:69–72) is one who has made the above criticism. He has also offered an alternative view on Spirit-baptism. He draws on Thomas Aquinas's idea that there can be new 'missions' or 'sendings' of the Spirit to a believer over and above the Spirit's initial coming. However, such 'comings' of the Spirit are not to be conceived of as though the Spirit came from 'outside' the person. On the contrary, the Spirit already dwells within the believer. Hence what in fact is happening is that the Spirit's presence takes on a new aspect, one that results in the believer experiencing something new in his or her life. It is, in short, the charismatic element at work again, in the individual.

Sullivan's approach returns to Spirit-baptism a theological dimension lost in the sacramental interpretation. Spirit-baptism is (more accurately: can be) not merely experientially but also theologically a distinct reality from the reception of the Spirit in the sacraments of initiation. Moreover, there is not as much opposition between his and the previous approach as either he or Lederle seems to see. The link between the two approaches is in the idea that the Spirit is already present in the believer. The new mission is not a new presence but a new aspect of the abiding presence.

Shorn of its Thomist thought-categories, Sullivan's viewpoint is shared in various ways by a variety of theologians of widely different traditions. Lederle (1986:65) describes this approach as an *integrative* one. 'Here the charismatic experience is fully integrated into regular Christianity — it is seen as a fresh coming of the Spirit, a growth experience, the fullness of the Spirit or a spiritual breakthrough without any event-centredness or elitist ultimacy being associated with this charismatic dimension of life.'

Clearly, this third, integrative approach sees Spirit-baptism as a name applicable to a variety of events in the life of a Christian. For example, it applies to any spiritual turning-point such as is experienced by almost any Christian who takes the Christian life seriously. It also applies to spiritual growth, even if discernible only over a long period. Moreover, it is repeatable. A person can have several turning-points in her or his life. Sullivan therefore pleads that people should speak of and pray for 'new outpourings' of the Spirit or for 'a' (not 'the') baptism of the Spirit, or that the Spirit should baptize someone 'anew' (1982:75).

The flexibility and breadth of vision of this approach is its strength. It really does integrate experiences of the Spirit into the general Christian life. But therein, to my mind, also lies its weakness as an explanation of Spirit-baptism. By identifying Spirit-baptism with a wide variety of experiences of renewal the term is being emptied of the specific focus it had. Maybe such an emptying is necessary. However, I suspect it would be better to see Spirit-baptism as a *particular kind of* renewal by the Spirit, one distinguished by certain characteristics which would need to be sketched out. For example, glossolalia can be listed as a common, though by no means necessary, characteristic of this particular renewal experience.

Those then are the three approaches to Spirit-baptism found amongst Catholics and other charismatics: neo-Pentecostal, sacramental, integrative. Each approach provides an element that needs to be taken into consideration, providing a check against absolutizing any element specific to one of the other approaches. Thus, there are no normative 'two stages' to a Christian's life. However, there are some experiences of the Spirit that stand out above others, shared by many, and are of a character that deserve a special name, even if 'Spirit-baptism' is an unhappy one. The sacramental approach stresses the role of the sacraments and therefore the ecclesial dimension of one's reception and experience of the Spirit. It is a valuable reminder that Church and Spirit cannot be dissociated from each other. Moreover, any future experience of the Spirit needs to be related to that initial reception. The sacramental interpretation also reminds us that the Spirit is received fully at Christian initiation. There are no first- and second-stage (= class!) Christians. However, the other approaches, especially the integrative one, provide a reminder of the need to acknowledge the newness not only of later *experiences* of the Spirit but also of all the Spirit's work and the ordinary way in which the Spirit is active in the believer's life.

(v)   The sacrament of confirmation

In Catholicism the sacrament specifically associated with the Spirit is that of confirmation. Of course, it is recognized that the Spirit is given in baptism. But confirmation symbolizes in a distinctive way the gift of the Spirit. In this section all I want to do is concentrate on the relationship between confirmation and a Christian's initiation, a Christian's baptism. A proper exposition of the sacrament belongs elsewhere.

As was seen in the historical section, the precise purpose of the sacrament of confirmation only became problematic when it emerged as a clearly distinct and separable sacrament from baptism (see Chapter 5, E). I believe that from the beginning its basic meaning was simply to symbolize the gift of the Spirit that went hand in hand with becoming a Christian. In the single ceremony of initiation, the washing with water symbolized the washing-away of the old life and the birth to a new one, while the anointing and laying-on of hands symbolized the gift of the Spirit as the source and permanent accompaniment of that new life.

The subsequent split of the single rite of initiation into two ceremonies led to focusing on the specific character of the giving of the Spirit in the second ceremony. What purpose could it have? The answer that developed was the following: to strengthen the Christian for the purpose of being a fearless witness to Christ. Confirmation came to be seen as spiritual 'adulthood'. Catholicism developed its own 'two-stage' view of the Christian life. The only difference was that the second 'stage' was from the beginning meant to be the completion of Christian *initiation* and not something occurring after it.

Catholic doctrine has always held fast to the idea that confirmation was the completion of Christian initiation, that it completed the process begun in baptism. The two sacraments — baptism and confirmation — were always linked to each other. Theoretically they had to precede all other sacraments. The order of the first three sacraments was always: baptism, confirmation, eucharist. The order was important, since, theologically, a person was supposed to partake of the eucharist only once his or her Christian initiation was completed. The neophyte had to undergo sacramental rebirth and sharing in the community's Spirit before celebrating eucharistically this newly acquired unity and the sacrifice that made it possible.

Unfortunately, practice has come to contradict doctrine increasingly in this matter. The separation of the two sacraments goes indeed a long way back into history but it was only in the nineteenth century that the order of the sacraments was inverted and children came to be admitted to the eucharist ('first communion') before being confirmed (Küng 1974:87). The normal practice now became: baptism (at infancy), eucharist (at about seven), confirmation (at about nine or ten).

With the rise of the catechetical movement in the last few decades, the search for meaningful pastoral practices led leaders in the movement to link confirmation to physical adulthood. Already a long tradition had linked it to the age when a child began to be able to discriminate between right and wrong, the so-called 'age of reason'. This in turn was connected to Aquinas's idea of the sacrament as conferring 'spiritual adulthood'. Quite sensibly it was argued that the age of discretion or reason was hardly adulthood. Even the age of puberty could hardly be seen as such. Hence a movement arose of linking confirmation to the emergence, in late teenage years, of a more genuine adulthood. This also had the advantage of eradicating the idea that catechetical instruction could stop at the early age of nine or ten (when confirmation was given). This idea was particularly widespread amongst parents of children not at Catholic schools.

On the surface, therefore, the move seemed a sound one. However, it entrenched the distorted practice of conferring confirmation after eucharist.

The next stage of development was even more questionable. It was the confusion of confirmation with the personal ratification, customary in Protestant circles, of one's baptism as an infant. How widespread this was, I do not know, but it certainly existed in many places (see, e.g., Congar 1983c:223). Here the idea of spiritual adulthood, witnessing to Christ, was confused with personally ratifying what was done for one as a child. Confirmation became a sacrament expressive of commitment to Christ, thereby taking over the meaning of baptism. Baptism is the sacrament of commitment to Christ, for it is in baptism that one is marked out forever as belonging to Christ and his Body. In an effort to make confirmation meaningful in its separation from baptism the final stage is reached by transferring a central part of baptism's meaning to confirmation.

Of course, the idea of getting people on the verge of adulthood to ratify personally what was done for them in infancy is an excellent one. But there is no need for Catholics to distort confirmation for such a purpose. There already exists a ceremony specifically designed for the ratification of one's baptism — the renewal of baptismal vows during the Easter Vigil liturgy. This could easily be adapted so as to provide a forum for teenagers to ratify personally their infant baptism. What is more, such a ratification would be free of the element of pressure to complete one's round of basic sacraments (baptism, eucharist(!), confirmation). Instead the ratification could be done whenever the young person felt ready for it. It seems to me that all the pastoral benefits of linking confirmation with a school-leaving age can be obtained by making greater use of the Easter Vigil ceremony and its renewal of baptismal vows. Those on the brink of adulthood could form a special group at the front of the congregation and the preparation for that occasion could be for them a very special Lent and Holy Week, one in which prayer and even fasting could be a dominant feature.

Others have argued that the benefits of linking confirmation to the brink of adulthood outweigh the disadvantages. It is clear that I am not convinced of this, especially since the benefits could be obtained another way. However, my major problem is not the link with physical adulthood so much as the entrenchment of the contradiction that theoretically confirmation is the completion of baptism in preparation for participation in the eucharist, while in practice confirmation is effectively cut adrift from baptism by admitting an unconfirmed person to the eucharist. Such a practice really does admit a 'two-stage' doctrine into our lives. For those confirmed on the brink of adulthood have in all respects been fully initiated into the community. Seeing confirmation as a 'confirming' of what was done for one in infancy, as one's personal commitment, obscures even the remnants of the idea of completing one's initiation that was present in the older idea of confirmation as the achieving of spiritual adulthood. It is essential that confirmation, the gift of the Spirit, once again be seen to be part of Christian initiation.

Hence, those who would postpone confirmation to physical adulthood should follow the logic of their position by campaigning for the postponement of admission to the eucharist to that point too. This would once more set in relief the fact that confirmation completes one's sacramental initiation into the life of the Church, enabling one to share in the Church's celebration of the fact that it is one Body in Christ thanks to Christ's sacrifice. The Catholic Church is, to my knowledge, the only church that admits people to the eucharist before confirming them. This obstacle to ecumenism (for it is such) is a needless one and the sooner eliminated the better.

B.   EXPERIENCING THE SPIRIT

The Spirit is spirit and so cannot be seen, tasted or touched. Can the Spirit's presence really be *experienced* then? Note that I am not asking whether or not one can experience things that for a believer must clearly *be attributed* to the Spirit. I am asking whether or not one can actually experience the *Spirit*.

A major stream of Catholic thought has responded in the negative (see Rahner 1979:37). However, such an answer seems to clash with scripture and patristic and mediaeval tradition. A negative answer would rule out everything the New Testament witnesses to as regards the infant Church's experience of the Spirit. Indeed, the religious experience of the New Testament Church is part of the foundations of Christian faith. In patristic and mediaeval times there is a constant tradition that speaks of the soul as 'savouring' God, of having what has come to be called an experiential knowledge, a *cognitio experimentalis* of the divine. The Spirit surely can be experienced, therefore. But how? In what way can something non-spatio-temporal, something utterly transcending creation be experienced by created, spatio-temporal creatures?

To try and answer this is far from easy, and any serious attempt would demand a degree of analysis of the issues that goes far beyond the limits of this book. However, some comments can and should be made.

A start can be made by noting that the divine cannot be experienced in the same way as we experience spatio-temporal realities. These latter are not only experienced directly by our senses *but also as distinguishable from each other*. We are able (usually) to describe the limits of each experience we have of spatio-temporal realities: pain is distinguishable to a large extent from pleasure, roundness is distinguishable from squareness, etc. Moreover, we are able to distinguish within a single experience various elements: roundness, softness, warmth, etc.

However, the divine does not come to us in such a way as to clearly be distinguishable from spatio-temporal realities. I cannot distinguish within an experience between the God bit and the spatio-temporal bit. I cannot distinguish between an experience of God and an experience of beauty in the same way as I can distinguish between an experience of beauty and an experience of ugliness. Precisely because the divine comes to us and is experienced by us in spatio-temporal categories, and precisely because any such category can in principle be a vehicle for experiencing the divine, it is impossible to distinguish the divine element in any experience from the spatio-temporal one. It is, for the same reasons, impossible to distinguish in practice between the bread of the eucharist and the body of Christ that Catholicism believes it to become. To give another example, it is impossible to distinguish in practice between our bodies and their character as temples of the Spirit.

How then is the divine experienced? If the above is correct, then God's presence can only be experienced *in and through spatio-temporal realities and as a dimension of them.* There is no single reality that can be said to be sufficiently different from all other created things so as to mark off an area of the divine from the rest of what would then be beyond that area. This does not mean that the divine is not experienced as in no way different from spatio-temporal reality. Were that the case, then it is indeed questionable whether one could talk of an experience of the divine at all. At the most one could talk of *attributing to the divine* certain spatio-temporal experiences one has without being able to say that one has really 'touched' or 'tasted' the divine itself (needless to say, spatio-temporal words are all we have). However, the distinction between experiencing the divine and experiencing spatio-temporal reality is not to be found within spatio-temporal reality itself as though one item within it (e.g., love) was the specific locus of the divine to the exclusion of all else. Instead, the distinction is between the experience of a dimension to spatio-temporal reality and that reality as such, one that cannot clearly be marked off but is very real none the less.

Thus, from the viewpoint of a scientific observer a 'mountain-top' experience is simply a spatio-temporal experience. As such it is probably explicable in purely psychological categories and may be quite indistinguishable from other experiences (e.g., of joy or ecstasy) that others may have had without describing them as experiences of God. However, for those who do experience them as the presence of God, that presence is a dimension of the experience, not an added spatio-temporal element that could be detected empirically.

Rahner is famous for his work on this issue. Whether or not one agrees with him, one has to acknowledge the depth at which he tackled the problem. For Rahner, what we call experiences of God are ways in which a prior, pre-conscious experience of God becomes conscious to us in specific ways. Everyone can — and Rahner believes does — have a pre-conscious experience of God. What he means by that is itself not easy to convey in simple terms. But even at the risk of distorting his intricate thought, it will be worth attempting to do so.

Rahner would describe the essence of being human as openness to the infinite (see Rahner 1968:393ff.). By that he means that a human being is a bodily creature whose horizons stretch beyond any imaginable limit. We can always think of possibilities that lie beyond any particular situation. Indeed, our very experience of limitedness presupposes some awareness, some deep-down experience of unlimitedness. One cannot recognize limits if one is not already aware of the possibility of transcending them.

This awareness of the intrinsically unlimited character of existence is in all of us on a pre-conscious level. It is not totally *unconscious*, but *pre*conscious in the sense that it has not come to any clear focus in our minds. It only comes into focus, it only becomes something we are clearly conscious of, when we experience spatio-temporal reality and its limitations.

The primordial conscious experience of our openness to the infinite possibilities of existence is that of mystery (Rahner 1968:57ff.). Those who become reflexively conscious of the mysteriousness of all reality have brought into their consciousness something that was already there in an unfocused way: an instinctive experience of the infinite possibilities of reality, of the fact that existence has inexhaustible (and therefore inexplicable) depths. We are able to experience such depths precisely because we are more than simply spatio-temporal creatures. We are also what is called 'spirit'. We are not just in the world, but spirit in the world. We are that dimension of the world that is able to transcend its limitations. From within our spatio-temporal existence, therefore, we have some deep experience of reality that transcends it.

So far what is being described is a philosophy of being human — Rahner calls it a philosophical anthropology. However, Rahner the believer is convinced that since God has become part of our world and offers to all within it a share in the unity with God that was its purpose, the pre-conscious experience everyone has of the infinite is in fact an experience of God (Rahner 1968:126ff.). What we would have experienced naturally had God not become part of the world and were sin not a factor (the so-called state of 'pure nature') is something we do not know. All we do know is that we are part of a world called to unity with God. Hence our deepest experience of the infinite is not simply of the infinite possibilities of existence, but of a person: God. God is present to us and is experienced by us on a pre-conscious level, in an unfocused way. What we call 'experiences of God' are the spatio-temporal experiences that make us conscious of God's presence to us (see e.g., Rahner 1979:41–43).

Of course (and here I am no longer consciously following Rahner, though he may well have said something similar himself) for a variety of reasons the relationship existing between God and an individual, even on a pre-conscious level, can differ from individual to individual. Hence, the pre-conscious experience itself can be one of the reasons for widely differing appropriations of this on a conscious level. But that is to go beyond the main points I wish to make here: viz., that God is experienced as a dimension of all reality and not as one specific element within it; as such God is experienced as the 'mystery' dimension of reality; this experience can be pre-conscious and available to all; however we become conscious of the God dimension of our lives through specific spatio-temporal experiences.

As explained above, Rahner's views are subject to the sort of criticism Sullivan and others made of the sacramental interpretation of Spirit-baptism (see A (iv) above). However, just as that interpretation is easily adaptable to the integrative one, so too Rahner's views can be adapted to account for the sort of new 'sendings' of the Spirit appealed to by Sullivan. Rahner's main concern was to show how the divine can be truly experienced as a dimension of created reality.

Let me turn now to the question (which can be asked even if one does not accept Rahner's specific views): what spatio-temporal experiences are especially effective in mediating to us an experience of God, an experience of the Spirit?

It is normal in this connection to point to *unusual* experiences. Thus, when Pentecostals, charismatics and many others talk about 'experiencing the Spirit', they normally have in mind a *powerful* experience of the Spirit, an unusual experience, one that is quite overwhelming. It is the sort of experience that changes a person's life. 'All awareness of the men and their prayers, of the room, and even of myself was obliterated by the immense presence of God's power. He was unmistakably there, and my inner response was like the clatter of a bamboo wind chime in a gale; the very foundations of my soul shook violently' (a testimony quoted by Green 1975:142).

This is the sort of experience that many would call a 'baptism in the Spirit', though others would not, even though they would see it as an experience of the Spirit at work within them. However, it is not simply the strong emotions generated that enable such an experience to be an experience of the Spirit. As has often been pointed out, all experience is interpreted experience (see, e.g., Aagaard 1980:18). Hence there must be further elements in the experience that make the individual conscious of it as an experience of the Spirit.

These elements all have, I believe, some moral or religious dimension. Frequently such experiences take place within the context of a Christian prayer meeting, where explicit appeals to the Spirit have been made. This enables the 'mountain-top' experience to be an immediate experience of the Spirit, an experience which brings to consciousness in a vivid way the work of the Spirit within one. Another important element enabling the experience to be a religious one is the experience of newness and power, of the ability to break out of the confines of a sinful or meaningless past and move in a new direction towards God and neighbour. If a person's primordial experience of God is the experience of infinitude, of limitless possibilities, then the experience of being opened to new and perhaps undreamt-of possibilities can be an effective way of experiencing the Spirit.

The moral dimension is crucial. The Spirit can be experienced apart from unusual events. But there can be no experience of the Spirit that is not also an experience of the power of love in some form or other. In fact, the normal way in which a Christian will experience the Spirit will be most unspectacular, viz., in the very ordinary experiences of love, joy, peace, patience, kindness, goodness, trustfulness, gentleness, self-control. A Christian who experiences these virtues is experiencing the Spirit's presence — for they are the fruits of that presence (Gal 5:22). As Rahner has pointed out, the Spirit is experienced in the small, often hidden, acts we may perform, acts of forgiveness, obedience, self-denial, kindness, etc., where such acts are motivated by disinterested love (Rahner 1967:87).

Love, as Paul tells us, remains even after the spectacular has passed away (1 Cor 13:8). 'Mountain-top' experiences pass away. But love and the fruits of love remain as *the* way in which the Spirit is experienced. Of course, as with the experience all can have of God on the pre-conscious level, so too very often love is not actually experienced precisely as the presence of the Spirit. But this may be due to our stubborn tendency to identify experiences of God with the abnormal. If the Spirit dwells within us, then experience of the Spirit should be a habitual matter in the life of the Christian. If it is not, then more than likely the reason is either an absence of any meaningful prayer life or the limitation of prayer to specific times of the day. The old practice of constantly talking to God present within one in the middle of one's daily work is extremely important, if one is to create the milieu in which the ordinary becomes a constant experience of the Spirit's presence.

Finally, I would like to point out that what has been said here is not an attempt to provide *proofs* of the Spirit's presence. The very nature of the case precludes providing any proof that the Spirit-dimension of an experience is indeed that and not a delusion. To prove such a thing would necessitate being able to distinguish within the experience between the divine element and its spatio-temporal wrapping. As was pointed out, such an attempt is doomed to failure. However, the inability to provide proof does not mean that any individual cannot have complete certainty about the Spirit dimension of an experience. Rahner's theological anthropology has, I believe, demonstrated how and why such a certainty can exist. My only concern in this section has been to examine the way in which experience of the Spirit is in fact mediated to us.

QUESTIONS

Check questions

1 When does a person receive the Spirit for the first time?
2 What is meant by 'Spirit-baptism'?
3 What is the traditional Pentecostal view of Spirit-baptism and what arguments are used in its defence?
4 What are the three types of interpretation of Spirit-baptism found in the Charismatic movement?
5 What is the relationship between baptism and confirmation?
6 How does an experience of the Spirit differ from an experience of spatio-temporal realities?
7 In what way can we have a pre-conscious experience of God?
8 What role, for Rahner, does the spatio-temporal play in experiences of the Spirit?
9 Which spatio-temporal experiences are especially effective in mediating to us an experience of God, and why are they so effective?

Discussion question

Describe and discuss an experience of God's presence you have had. Analyse the elements of the experience, looking especially for the moral or religious dimension.

RECOMMENDED READING

On Spirit-baptism: Dunn 1970; Sullivan 1982; the first of the Malines Documents (the same viewpoint is to be found in McDonnell 1975); Congar 1983b. Highly recommended is the work by a colleague of mine, H. I. Lederle, referred to in the text (*Treasures Old and New* — see A (iv) above; a doctoral thesis, published in 1987 by Hendrickson Publishers, Peabody, Massachusetts).

As regards confirmation, for the historical aspect see above, Chapter 5, E. On its relationship to baptism and the issue of when it should be conferred, a brief discussion can be found in Küng 1974. Some useful material can also be found in Congar 1983c. The literature on the topic is very extensive and studies on the sacrament readily available.

As regards Rahner's views on religious experience, Rahner 1979 is a relatively digestible article on religious enthusiasm and the experience of grace (the whole of vol. 16 of the *Theological Investigations* is on the theme of experiencing the Spirit). On the other aspects of Rahner's theology relevant to the theme, the student can either plough through Rahner 1978, chs 1, 2 and 4, or use the somewhat easier work edited by G. A. McCool, *A Rahner Reader* (London: Darton, Longman & Todd, 1975), I, 3, IX, 1, 2, 4. Alternatively one can thumb through the *Theological Investigations* for articles on those aspects of Rahner's thought touched on in this chapter.

17

The Spirit transforms the whole of creation

The time has come to consider — in what will again be a brief chapter — the Spirit's work as regards the entire universe. The universe is humanity's environment and as such shares in humanity's sanctification. This will be the theme of the first section (A). However, like the sanctification of the individual, this sanctification occurs only with the co-operation of human beings, which raises the question of the relationship between being a Christian and striving for a just society (B). The final section (C) will deal with the contribution of people other than Christians to the world's sanctification.

A. THE SPIRIT CREATES HARMONY BETWEEN HUMANITY AND ITS ENVIRONMENT, THEREBY SANCTIFYING IT

The whole of creation and everything in it is humanity's 'environment'. Our environment therefore includes nature (the land, the sea, the sky, the trees, the animals, the stars, the entire physical universe), but also the structures we ourselves have created (countries, cities, families, cultures, work communities, play communities, shops, buildings, newspapers, radios, governments, schools, etc.). All this comprises our 'environment'.

Our environment is essential to us. We are bodily creatures — not angels unhappily imprisoned in an alien universe. This is why from the earliest days salvation was seen as embracing the whole of creation. It was seen as the restoration of paradise, the creation of a new universe, a new environment for humanity. Sin has turned our world into a place *that reflects our selfishness* and is therefore hostile to us, a place that frequently frustrates and hurts us as we struggle to live, especially to live happily. Sin has alienated us from our environment. Salvation, the overcoming of the effects of sin, involves bringing about the harmony that should exist between us and our environment. Hence, the Spirit not only brings about our unity with God, neighbour, and an inner harmony, all resulting in our transformation into the risen life; but also the harmony that should exist between us and our environment, resulting in the latter's transformation too.

What happens in the universe is, I believe, only the cosmic extension of a process that begins in the individuals who form Christ's Body. Inner harmony is achieved by pressing all one's faculties into the service of love. It is the Spirit that enables a person to do this. This bringing about of inner harmony is manifested in the fruits of love. The individual's new situation is a holy one — he or she belongs to God and reflects in his or her actions God's love, God's values. This creation of inner harmony — i.e. sanctification — is a process of growth. It does not happen all at once. It requires the co-operation of the individual. Even so, it is only after the old life has disappeared completely in death that the new, risen transformed life will be perfected. It is only after death that the individual's transformation will be complete.

Let me now apply this to the relationship between us and our environment. The Love that creates the community is meant to be reflected in the structures created by that community. The love that transforms the individual is meant to be reflected in actions that show the individual's concern for and unity with others. The Spirit's presence therefore is meant to result in the transformation not only of individuals but also of their environment. The presence of love should result in the creation of an environment in which people can feel loved and at peace, an environment that reflects the fact that people share in God's Spirit of love, an environment, therefore, that is holy. By sanctifying humanity the Spirit sanctifies humanity's world (see Rom 8:21). However — and, of course, it is a big 'however' — as with the individual, so, too, with the world as a whole, its sanctification is a growth process. It is not something that happens all at once. Moreover, this is not a mere theoretical statement. Christianity has reason to claim that for all its faults it has brought about social changes for the better in the world (for some examples, see Berkhof 1976:101–103). However, the sanctification of the world is a process of growth that requires our co-operation. It is therefore a growth that does not eliminate sin during the growth period (Mt 13:24–30). Our environment too is *simul justus et peccator* (see Chapter 14, D).

Already the world is being sanctified by the Spirit's presence, then. *Already* eternal life is part of the world's existence. For when Christ died and rose from the dead, the world's old situation died and a new life began for it. The transformation of Christ's dead body was the beginning of the transformation of the dead world of which his body was, is, and always will be a part. This is one of the reasons why the risen life inaugurated by the Spirit is truly the beginning of the 'last times' (see Chapter 2, A).

However, as with the individual, so too with the world as a whole, full transformation will only occur in the future. Even with our co-operation the world can only achieve its full glory through an act of the Spirit as mighty as that which transformed Christ on Easter day. It is beyond the scope of this book to deal with the question of this future of the world in any detail. All I wish to do here is to point out that the world's consummation will be, as Berkhof put it so well, 'the completion of the pneumatic process . . . the "pneumatizing" of the whole of creation' (1976:108). What awaits us and our world, is but the full flowering of a transformation that has already begun thanks to Love's presence in our midst. We so often think of the world as being destined for total destruction at the end of time. But only the worldly, only the *sinful aspects* of the world, only the world of *sin* will be destroyed. The world itself as a physical entity will be transformed. It may well pass through a cataclysm as dramatic for the universe as death is for the individual. But within the world there is a life, a Love that cannot die, cannot be destroyed, but will overcome even death. This life will give the world its resurrection, its glory (Rom 8:21). What exactly such a world will look like, no one can say (1 Cor 2:9; see also 1 Jn 3:2). But it will be a transformation as total as Christ's was on Easter day. Christianity's faith bids us to be sure at least of this: it will be a world in which there is no hindrance whatsoever to the exercise or the reception of love, to being totally one in the Spirit.

The virtues instilled in us by the Spirit, therefore, are not only the virtues of faith and love, but also the virtue of hope (Rom 15:13). What we possess already is but a foretaste of what is to come. The Spirit enables us, and with us the whole world to hope for a fulfilment yet to come (Rom 8:18–25). Of course, our hope is not a wishy-washy thing, a sort of 'I hope this will happen . . . but I realize it may not'. On the contrary, Christian hope is the firm anticipation of something we are *convinced* will happen. Our conviction rests on the guarantee we already have: the resurrection of Christ and the pouring out of his Spirit upon us.

Christians are people, therefore, who should take this world and its improvement extremely seriously. Moreover, they know that their attempts at improving the world are not doomed to failure. For the Spirit at work in those attempts is the guarantee of their success, a success that will come as the final demonstration of the power of God's love.

B.   THE RELATIONSHIP BETWEEN CHRISTIANITY AND STRIVING FOR A JUST SOCIETY

I would now like to take up the first of two questions that arise from the previous section. It is the relationship between Christianity and striving for a just society. As I said above, Christians must take this world and its improvement very seriously. Humanity's environment can only grow towards the sort of environment it should be with humanity's co-operation. Therefore, just as it is part of a Christian's calling to strive to be holy, so too is it part of that calling to establish a holy environment, which means a holy society, a just society, in the world. A 'just society' is one in which there is justice for all. It is a society based on the values that Jesus preached (see Nolan 1976:49ff.): sharing what one has with others (Mt 25:35; Mk 10:17–22); loving people more than social status (Lk 14:7–11) or one's own group identity (Mt 5:43–44; Lk 10:29–37); serving others (Mk 10:42–44). It is a society that creates an environment in which everybody can be a happy, fulfilled human being.

It is therefore right that Christians should, as Christians, take an interest in political, social and economic questions. It is right that they should do so and try to influence political, social and economic structures so that they reflect those values. It is, therefore, also right that Christians should, precisely because they are Christians, oppose all governments, laws, constitutions, structures, policies etc. that crush people and make a just society impossible. A Christian can do this, mindful of the fact that the Lord whose Spirit she or he shares said that laws (and therefore structures) were made to serve people, and not the other way round (Mk 2:27).

In doing such things Christians are enabling the Spirit to transform the world, for the power that transforms is the power of a Love that is not ours but God's. In doing such things Christians are allowing Christ's lordship over all creation to become a reality. For his lordship is the lordship of love and can only become a reality if through the power of his Spirit we create a world that reflects love.

The idea is still widespread that spiritual and political/social realities belong to different realms. However, if the divinity is a community and humanity is meant to be the created reflection of and sharing in that divine community (see Chapter 8, A), then spiritual reality is of its nature social. The idea is still widespread that to talk about the Holy Spirit is to talk about a religious reality that has nothing to do with socio-political issues. However, the Spirit's very identity is definable only in social terms — to be the way in which persons are present and united in love to each other (see Chapter 7, E).

Hence, it is wrong to see the Spirit's role in our unity with God as the primary one, relegating unity with neighbour and the social structures expressive of it to a secondary position. Jesus was condemned by the Jewish leaders precisely because he refused to accept that. He was condemned precisely because he made love of neighbour as important as love of God (see Chapter 9, C). As Rahner (1969a) has shown, love of God and love of neighbour are in fact one and the same activity. Or as 1 Jn 4:20 put it, it is impossible to love God if we do not love each other.

The very nature of the Spirit's role therefore is a social one, to build up society. From this it follows that to work for just social structures is to seek to give visible expression to the Spirit's work in the world. Granted, no secular structures, no matter how just, can ever function as sacraments of what God has called us to. Of their nature they cannot be explicit witnesses to the role of Jesus and the Spirit or even to the parent character of our God. But just secular structures are nevertheless structured expressions of love, and therefore expressions of the Spirit of Love.

It is worth nothing that, historically, Spirit-orientated movements were also very often movements for justice (see e.g., Chapter 7, C). Even the Pentecostal movement, which for many came to be *the* example of a Christianity divorced from social concern, has its roots in movements for social justice. Increasingly, charismatics are getting involved in matters of social justice (on this see Lederle 1986). Many approach it in a way that I would find theologically unsatisfactory: seeing it as carrying out a commandment of love rather than as expressive of the salvation Christians preach, of the Spirit's very nature. But at least the concern is there and, in Catholicism, has already formed the topic of the third of the Malines Documents. Indeed, in Germany the social dimension is very much to the fore: the title of an important charismatic publication there is *Erneuerung in Kirche und Gesellschaft*, 'Renewal in Church and Society' (Lederle 1986:72).

C.   THE SPIRIT AND THOSE WHO DO NOT BELIEVE IN CHRIST

From the above it is clear that the Spirit sanctifies the world by sanctifying people, builds human community by enabling people to love. This raises the question of the position of those who are not Christians. Which people does the Spirit sanctify, and, through them, the world as a whole: only Christians or also non-Christians?

Many Christians believe that the Spirit sanctifies only those who believe in Christ and (many will add) who are baptized. The reason is that the New Testament seems to demand belief in Christ and being baptized as a necessary condition for salvation. Read, for example, Acts 2:37–38 and 4:12. It can also be pointed out that the gift of the Spirit in the New Testament is always connected with belief in Christ. How then can we say that the Spirit sanctifies non-Christians and, through them, the world? Of course, many people who hold this viewpoint will agree that the Spirit continues to be active everywhere, also therefore within non-believers. But such action is seen simply as the necessary conservation of God's creation. Even though the social, cultural, political achievements evident amongst non-Christians are seen as gifts of the Spirit, they are viewed as gifts of the Spirit as creator, not as sanctifier (see, e.g., Chapter 6, B). In other words, the Spirit's action here is not a sanctifying one. It does not unite the world in love to God through non-believers.

However, Catholics together with many other Christians believe that God's Spirit is present to and sanctifies even those who have not heard or who honestly are not convinced by the Christian message (see Chapter 10, E). Of course, there is a proviso. Such people must have that attitude of obedience to and trust in the demands of truth and goodness that is at the heart even of a Christian's faith in Christ. But the point is that if the Spirit's saving, transforming activity occurs beyond the borders of the sacrament that is the Church, then non-Christians too can be part of the process of building up God's Kingdom. They can be part of the process of making the social dimension of salvation a reality in the world.

All social action contributes to the social dimension of salvation. As such it can be seen as a sort of *gratia gratis data* (see Chapter 15, introduction), the result of an impulse of the Spirit of love at work in the world. When such action flows from love, then there is also present (I believe) *gratia gratum faciens* — the grace that sanctifies. As a result, not only the structural dimension of salvation is fostered but also its living heart: love transformed by Love. It is such love that sanctifies the world.

The implication of the above is that salvation history, the history of the Spirit's work in the world, is a dimension of all world history. Salvation history is not limited to the history of a special group such as Israel or the Church. On the contrary, the role of such a chosen group is to be the place where the purpose of world history is revealed, to be the place where its purpose is visibly embodied. What used to be called salvation history is in fact the sacramental embodiment of world history. Whatever 'secular' activity down the ages was devoted to creating just structures, and to enabling human beings to experience unity in love, can be seen as part of salvation history.

It is such a vision that is at the heart of liberation theology. Liberation theology can, with justification, be regarded as a theology of the Holy Spirit, of the one whose presence throughout history moves people to love people, moves people to care for people, to respect their dignity, to work for their liberation. Granted, there are many critical remarks, serious critical remarks that need to be made of much of liberation theology. However, with the sure instinct given by the Spirit of love, liberation theology has exposed the hypocrisy of a Christianity in which the wealthy take the existence of the poor as a matter of course and see no reason to become unduly concerned about it. With the sure instinct given by Love, liberation theology has — whether it realizes it or not — retrieved the classic Augustinian tradition that only love gives full understanding of the things of God. In stressing the epistemological importance of praxis, liberation theology may be drawing immediately on contemporary insights, but it is in fact retrieving the patristic and mediaeval idea of the epistemological importance of love, love of God and love of neighbour. The love that gives us an insight into the things of God also gives us an insight into what fulfils human beings, for the latter is part of the former. Jesus and the Spirit have united God and humanity in such a way that the interests of the divine and the human can no longer be separated. Love is therefore crucial to liberation. No true liberation exists that is not experienced as love. No true liberation can be achieved that is not guided by love. The Spirit of love is the Spirit of true liberation.

QUESTIONS

Check questions

1 How has sin destroyed the harmony between humanity and its environment?
2 How does the Spirit create harmony between humanity and its environment?
3 What is meant by the phrase 'sanctifying the world'?
4 How does the Spirit sanctify humanity's world?
5 How can one integrate beliefs in the world's future total destruction with the belief that the world has been saved and is being sanctified?
6 What is the relationship between the Christian idea of salvation and the creation of just social structures?
7 Why is the creation of just social structures an expression of the Spirit's specific nature and role?
8 How can non-Christians sanctify the world and give structural expression to Christ's saving work?
9 What is the relationship between secular and salvation history and the role of the Spirit in that relationship?
10 In what way can liberation theology be seen as a theology of the Holy Spirit?

Discussion question

Liberation theology believes that God and therefore the Church must side with the oppressed. Is such a view compatible with the Spirit's nature as the one who overcomes divisions and unites people in love? Justify whatever position is adopted.

RECOMMENDED READING

On the cosmic dimensions of the Spirit's action see Congar 1983b:218–224 and, for a Reformed perspective, Berkhof 1976:94–108. Heron 1983:147–156 also has some useful material on the topic. On the involvement of charismatics in issues of social justice, see Lederle 1986; Malines Document 3; and, for an example of one author's approach, Christenson 1976.

18

The signs of the Spirit's presence

In Chapter 16, B, I pointed out that the Spirit's presence can be experienced, and also that it was impossible to provide strict proof that what was being experienced was in fact the Spirit. However, the inability to provide such proof does not mean that there are no criteria available for evaluating either one's own experiences or the claims of others to Spirit-induced experiences or Spirit-authorized activities. There are — for the believer — definite signs of the Spirit's presence that can serve as criteria. What are those signs? How are we to distinguish true from false signs of the Spirit's presence? Answers to these questions have already been given here and there throughout this book. However, it will be useful to deal in a unified way with the issue in this, the final and shortest chapter.

A.   THE SPECTACULAR SIGNS

Let me begin with what are regarded by many as the obvious signs of the Spirit's presence: prophecy, healings, visions, glossolalia, inspired worship, inspired insights into things, and so on. Spectacular phenomena such as the above are certainly regarded in the New Testament as gifts of the Spirit and, therefore, as signs of the Spirit's presence. This is an undeniable fact.

It is furthermore undeniable that in Acts we are repeatedly told of tongues appearing as a striking manifestation of the Spirit's presence. This is the New Testament grounds on which Pentecostalism bases its assertion that tongues are *the* sign of the Spirit's presence.

It is clear that in common with many other theologians I find such a claim unacceptable. Luke in fact was not interested in the question: what is *the* distinctive sign of the Spirit's presence? Hence it would be wrong to see him as intending to teach that tongues are *the* sign of the Spirit's presence. 'Luke certainly believes that the glossolalia was *a* manifestation of the Spirit's coming, along with praise of God in [Acts] 10.45 and prophecy in 19.6 (not to mention bold speech in 4.8ff., 31, and powerful speech in 13.9ff.). But it is equally certain that he has no intention of presenting glossolalia as *the* manifestation of the Spirit — otherwise he would have mentioned glossolalia in Acts 8 and made the point with greater force elsewhere' (Dunn 1975:191). It can be added that if one holds that Luke did see tongues as *the* sign of the Spirit, then he is in open contradiction to Paul. As was seen, Paul relegated tongues to a low place on the scale of gifts (Chapter 15, B (viii)). Moreover, while Paul clearly teaches that all Christians receive the Spirit, that all are temples of the Spirit (1 Cor 6:19), he asserts, by means of a rhetorical question, that not all Christians have the gift of tongues.

B.   THE PROBLEM OF DISCERNMENT

But let us leave the debate about tongues in particular and accept that tongues and other extraordinary phenomena were certainly viewed by the New Testament as signs of the Spirit. There is no doubt about this. What is interesting is that while Luke does not seem to have seen a problem with such an assertion, Paul did. Paul very soon became aware of the need to formulate certain criteria to enable Christians to distinguish between phenomena that were signs of the Spirit and phenomena that were not. The necessity of such criteria arose from the fact that phenomena existed outside the Christian Church resembling those which were regarded within the Church as extraordinary signs of the Spirit's presence. One could find people outside the Church who claimed to be able to prophesy and interpret things. And within the community there were false prophets. One could find people in ecstasy, similar to states believed to be induced by the Spirit, but who nevertheless cursed Jesus (1 Cor 12:3). One could find people who drove out demons and, apparently, performed many wonders in the name of Jesus but whom Jesus would reject (Mt 7:22). Even phenomena similar to tongues existed outside the Church (Chapter 15, B (i)).

All this means that even the extraordinary signs of the Spirit's presence are *by themselves* ambiguous. Taken by themselves, they may or may not be signs of the Spirit's presence. Something more is necessary in order to judge whether or not they are such, something that reflects the essential nature of the Spirit. A criterion is needed. What is that criterion?

C.   THE CRITERION FOR DISCERNMENT

Paul mentions several criteria: the criterion that Jesus is Lord (1 Cor 12:3), the criterion of building up the community (1 Cor 12:7, 14:12); the fruits of sanctification (Gal 5:22). However, these are all connected with each other. Paul's overriding concern with the unity of Christ's Body, a concern that flows from his vision of the Spirit's mission, enables us to formulate his basic principle, his basic criterion, as follows:

(a)   Anything that builds up the Christian community is a true sign of the presence of the Spirit;

(b)   anything that breaks down or mars the Christian community is not a sign of the Spirit.

D.   THE APPLICATION OF THE CRITERION

First of all, to curse Jesus is not a sign of the Spirit's presence, for it breaks down the unity forged by the Spirit of Jesus between him and us. It is impossible to be one with a person whom one curses. However, to confess and follow Jesus as Lord is a sign of the Spirit's presence, for Christian community is built around the risen Lord.

Secondly, suffering for Jesus' name is a sign of the Spirit's presence (1 Pet 4:14). Such suffering is a form of confession of the risen Lord. One can go further and say that suffering for the sake of justice (cf. Mt 5:10) is a sign of the Spirit's presence. Such suffering builds up the human community and therefore the Church in its broadest sense (see Chapter 10, E). In Old Testament times suffering was seen mainly as a sign of God's curse, a sign of sin's presence rather than God's. Jesus' death has revealed to us that God is present in suffering too. Christianity has no logical explanation of suffering. But it can and does proclaim that the God it believes in suffers too, has entered into our suffering. Jesus has therefore made suffering a sign of God's presence, of the presence of the Spirit of Love. Of course, this does not mean that suffering cannot be degrading, dehumanizing. On the contrary, suffering is the terrible reality it is precisely because its inner tendency is to dehumanize and degrade. But God's enduring of suffering has enabled it to be more than that. It has enabled it to be a sign of God's transforming presence in our midst, purifying people and enabling them to live out love, often on a heroic level. But this is one theme on which not I but those who experience suffering and God's presence in it must write.

Thirdly, the following are definitely not signs of the Spirit's presence: immoral, filthy and indecent actions, worship of idols and witchcraft, enmities, fights, jealousies, ambitiousness, separating into opposing parties and groups, envy, drunkenness, orgies and such like (Gal 5:19–21). These things destroy Christian community. Lives of this sort are signs of the Spirit's absence. But on the other hand, love, joy, peace, patience, kindness, goodness, faithfulness, humility, self-control — these are signs of the Spirit's presence (Gal 5:22–23). These things build up Christian community.

Even Pentecost Day was a true sign of the Spirit, mainly because it gave birth to the Christian community and broke down barriers between people — and not simply because of the wind and tongues of fire and strange languages spoken. The story of Pentecost stresses this breaking-down of barriers so that people can be one again. Unity is from the outset a sign of the Spirit's presence.

Fifthly, the Church itself is therefore meant to be a sign of the Spirit's presence. If anything that builds up Christian community is a sign of the Spirit's presence, then the Christian community itself is meant to be such a sign. Of course, the Church will only be a convincing sign if it can be *seen* to be a community of people truly united to each other in the love of the Spirit whose marvels it proclaims. Even in the early Church, remember, it was not just marvels and miracles that made it a sign of the Spirit's presence. More important was the love that the members had for one another (Acts 2:44–45).

It is because the Church itself is meant to be a sign of the Spirit's presence that belonging to the Church is meant to be a sign that individuals share in the Spirit.

Everything I have been saying about the signs of the Spirit's presence, really comes down to this in the end: *the* sign of the Spirit's presence is love (1 Cor 13:1–13). All the other marvels — prophecies, tongues, the faith that works miracles — all these are worthless without love. *The* characteristic of the Spirit is presence in love, Love. *The* sign of the Spirit's presence, therefore, is love. Where there is love, there, too, is the Spirit of love. 1 Jn 4:16 puts it beautifully: 'God is love, and whoever lives in love, lives in union with God and God lives in union with him'.

Moreover, together with many theologians (though others will disagree) I believe that wherever there is genuine love, there is the Spirit of Love, transforming, sanctifying, giving hope, as only Love can do. For all love is the gift of Love. People have often remarked on how much sin there is in the world despite all talk about a God of love. However, sin — distorted love — has its own power too. And the really remarkable thing is that love endures in the world even in the midst of so much sin. It continues to touch people's lives and transform them. Many a person has remarked on just how much love there indeed is in the world. Christians can see in this a sign of the Spirit's presence. Everything began with love — God's love for us (1 Jn 4:10). Love has been present with us ever since and will triumph over everything. The doctrine of the Holy Spirit is nothing more — and nothing less — than the doctrine of Love.

QUESTIONS

Check questions

1 Why are the accepted spectacular signs of the Spirit's presence ambiguous signs if taken by themselves?
2 What criteria does Paul give for distinguishing true from false signs of the Spirit's presence? What is his basic criterion?
3 Why are the following *not* signs of the Spirit's presence: cursing Jesus, immoral actions, enmities, fights, jealousies, ambitiousness, etc?
4 Why was Pentecost Day a true sign of the Spirit?
5 In what way can suffering be a sign of the Spirit's presence?
6 What is it about the Church that makes it a sign of the Spirit's presence?
7 What is presented in this chapter as *the* sign of the Spirit's presence, and why?

Discussion question

Love can be very demanding. Often what looks like love is not love. Discuss the problems this poses for the thesis so central to this book, viz., that *the* sign of the Spirit's presence is love.

RECOMMENDED READING

In the eighteenth century Jonathan Edwards, a Puritan theologian in America, was faced with the need to distinguish between true and false signs of God's presence at a time of religious emotionalism and appeals to the spectacular. His book on the topic, *A Treatise on Religious Affections*, is something of a classic. It has been republished recently (Grand Rapids: Baker, 1982). In Catholic theology one needs to look at works on the topic of the discernment of spirits. Hence the reader is referred once again to Guillet 1970, where further references can be found. In addition, Mühlen 1978 has two sections on the theme (pp. 167ff., 326ff.).

Bibliography and Abbreviations

The only works listed here are those referred to in the text. Moreover, the list is limited to modern works. Those from the patristic, mediaeval and Reformation periods are therefore excluded; the references to them in the text are adequate enough.

The few abbreviations used are inserted in their alphabetical place in the list.

Unless otherwise stated, all biblical quotations are from the Jerusalem Bible version (© 1966, 1967 and 1968 by Darton, Longman & Todd Ltd and Doubleday & Company, Inc.).

A. M. Aagaard, 1980: 'Die Erfahrung des Geistes' in O. Dilschneider (ed.), *Theologie des Geistes* (Gütersloh: Gerd Mohn), pp. 2–24.

W. M. Abbott (ed.), 1966: *The Documents of Vatican II* (London/Dublin: Geoffrey Chapman).

K. Aland (ed.), 1970: *Pietismus und Bibel* (Arbeiten zur Geschichte des Pietismus, vol. 9; Witten: Luther).

G. Alberigo and F. Magistretti, 1975: *Constitutionis Dogmaticae Lumen Gentium Synopsis Historica* (Bologna: Istituto per le Scienze Religiose).

R. Albertz and C. Westermann, 1976: 'Ruah Geist' in E. Jenni and C. Westermann (eds), *Theologisches Handwörterbuch zum Alten Testament* (Munich/Zürich: Kaiser/ Theologischer).

H. Urs von Balthasar, 1967: *Spiritus Creator. Skizzen zur Theologie* III (Einsiedeln: Johannes).

G. Bardy, 1957: 'Dons du Saint-Esprit. I. Chez les Pères' in *Dictionnaire de Spiritualité* 3 (Paris: Beauchesne), cols 1579–1587.

C. K. Barrett, 1966: *The Holy Spirit and the Gospel Tradition* (London: SPCK).
        1978: *The Gospel according to John* 2nd ed. (London: SPCK).

K. Barth, 1936: *Church Dogmatics* I/1: *The Doctrine of the Word of God* (Edinburgh: T. & T. Clark).

H. Bauch, 1974: *Die Lehre vom Wirken des Heiligen Geisten im Frühpietismus* (Hamburg-Bergstedt: Reich).

J. Behm, 1964: 'Glōssa' in G. Kittel (ed.), *Theological Dictionary of the New Testament* I (Grand Rapids: Eerdmans), pp. 719–727.

D. J. Bennett, 1975: 'The gifts of the Holy Spirit' in M. P. Hamilton (ed.), *The Charismatic Movement* (Grand Rapids: Eerdmans).

H. Berkhof, 1976: *The Doctrine of the Holy Spirit* (Atlanta: John Knox).

A. Bittlinger, 1967: *Gifts and Graces* (Grand Rapids: Eerdmans).

B. Bobrinskoy, 1981; 'The *filioque* yesterday and today' in Vischer 1981:133–148.

F. Bourassa, 1970: *Questions de théologie trinitaire* (Rome: Grégorienne).

A. de Bovis, 1967: 'Grâce d'état' in *Dictionnaire de Spiritualité* 6 (Paris: Beauchesne), cols 750–763.

D. Brown, 1978: *Understanding Pietism* (Grand Rapids: Eerdmans).

R. E. Brown, 1966: 'The Paraclete in the Fourth Gospel', *New Testament Studies* 13 (1966–67), 113–132.

    1971: *The Gospel According to John* 1 and 2 (London: Geoffrey Chapman/ Garden City, NY: Doubleday [1966, 1971]).

    1983: 'Diverse views of the Spirit in the New Testament', *Worship* 57, 225–236.

S. N. Bulgakov. 1946: *Le Paraclet* (Paris: Aubier).

S. T. Bunn, 1973: 'Glossolalia in historical perspective' in W.E. Mills (ed.), *Speaking in Tongues: Let's Talk about it* (Waco: Word Books), pp. 36–47.

J. P. Burns and G. M. Fagin, 1984: *The Holy Spirit* (Message of the Fathers of the Church 3; Wilmington: Glazier).

L. Christenson, 1975: 'Pentecostalism's forgotten forerunner' in Synan 1975:17–37.

    1976: *Social Action Jesus Style* (Minneapolis: Bethany).

D. M. Coffey, 1979: *Grace: The Gift of the Holy Spirit* (Faith and Culture Series, vol. 1; Sydney: Catholic Institute).

    1984: 'The "incarnation" of the Holy Spirit in Christ', *Theological Studies* 45, 466–480.

    1986: 'A proper mission of the Holy Spirit', *Theological Studies* 47, 227–250.

Y.-M. Congar, 1966: *Tradition and Traditions* (London: Burns & Oates).

    1968: *L'Ecclésiologie du Haut Moyen Age* (Paris: du Cerf).

    1971: 'Quelques problèmes touchant les ministères', *Nouvelle Revue Théologique* 103, 785–800.

    1983a: *I Believe in the Holy Spirit* I: *The Holy Spirit in the 'Economy'* (New York/London: Seabury/Geoffrey Chapman).

    1983b: *I Believe in the Holy Spirit* II: *'He is Lord and Giver of Life'* (New York/London: Seabury/Geoffrey Chapman).

    1983c: *I Believe in the Holy Spirit* III: *The River of the Water of Life flows in the East and in the West* (New York/London: Seabury/Geoffrey Chapman).

J. Coventry, 1968: *The Theology of Faith* (Theology Today Series, no. 3: Cork: Mercier).

R. H. Culpepper, 1977: *Evaluating the Charismatic Movement* (Valley Forge: Judson Press).

M. Damaskinos, 1974: 'La Disponibilité au Saint Esprit et la fidelité aux origines d'après les Pères grecs', *Istina* 19, 49–64.

W. D. Davies, 1970: *Paul and Rabbinic Judaism* 3rd ed. (London: SPCK).

D. W. Dayton, 1975: 'From "Christian perfection" to the "Baptism of the Holy Ghost" ' in Synan 1975:39–54.

M. E. Dieter, 1975: 'Wesleyan-Holiness aspects of Pentecostal origins: as mediated through the nineteenth-century Holiness Revival' in Synan 1975:55–80.

DS: H. Denzinger and A. Schönmetzer (eds), *Enchiridion Symbolorum* (Barcelona/ Freiburg/Rome: Herder, 1976).

J. D. G. Dunn, 1970: *Baptism in the Holy Spirit* (London: SCM).

    1975: *Jesus and the Spirit* (London: SCM).

E. Evans, 1948: *Tertullian's Treatise against Praxeas: The text edited, with an introduction, translation, and commentary* (London: SPCK).

Faith and Order Commission, World Council of Churches, 1981: 'The *filioque* clause in ecumenical perspective' in Vischer 1981:3–18.

E. J. Fortman, 1972: *The Triune God* (London/Philadelphia: Hutchinson/Westminster).

A. Gardeil, 1911: 'Dons du Saint Esprit' in *Dictionnaire de Théologie Catholique* 4 (Paris/Letouzey), cols 1728–1781.

J.-M. Garrigues, 1981: 'A Roman Catholic view of the position now reached in the question of the *filioque*' in Vischer 1981:149–163.

B. Gaybba, 1983: 'In what sense are the Scriptures "free from error"?' *Theologia Evangelica* XVI–I, 68–73.

1985: 'Love and know what you will: the epistemological role of love in Augustine' in C. Landman and D. P. Whitelaw (eds), *Windows on Origins: Oorspronge in oënskou* (Pretoria: University of South Africa).

J. Gill, 1982: *The Council of Florence* (reprint, with *corrigenda*, of the 1959 edition published by Cambridge University Press; New York: AMS Press).

M. Green, 1975: *I Believe in the Holy Spirit* (Grand Rapids: Eerdmans).

J. Guillet *et al.*, 1970: *The Discernment of Spirits* (Collegeville: Liturgical Press).

E. Haenchen, 1961: *Apostelgeschichte* (Göttingen: Vandenhoeck & Ruprecht).

G. Hasenhüttl, 1969: *Charisma: Ordnungsprinzip der Kirche* (Freiburg: Herder).

G. S. Hendry, 1965: *The Holy Spirit in Christian Theology* (London: SCM).

A. Heron, 1983: *The Holy Spirit* (London: Marshall, Morgan & Scott).

E. Hill, 1985: *The Mystery of the Trinity* (Geoffrey Chapman Theology Library [formerly Introducing Catholic Theology series] 4; London: Geoffrey Chapman).

W. J. Hollenweger, 1972: *The Pentecostals* (London: SCM).

A. M. Hunter, 1965: *The Gospel According to John* (The Cambridge Bible Commentary on the New English Bible; Cambridge: University Press).

M. E. Isaacs, 1976: *The Concept of Spirit. A Study of Pneuma in Hellenistic Judaism and its Bearing on the New Testament* (London: Heythrop College).

W. Jaeger, 1966: *Gregor von Nyssa's Lehre vom Heiligen Geist* (Leiden: Brill).

G. Johnston, 1970: *The Spirit-Paraclete in the Gospel of John* (Cambridge: University Press).

J. N. D. Kelly, 1977: *Early Christian Doctrines* 5th ed. (London: Black).

M. Kelsey, 1981: *Tongue Speaking: The History and Meaning of Charismatic Experience* (New York: Crossroad).

J. P. Kenny, 1967: 'Gifts, the seven' in *A Catholic Dictionary of Theology* 2 (London: Nelson), pp. 318–321.

J. P. Kildahl, 1975: 'Psychological observations' in M.P. Hamilton (ed.), *The Charismatic Movement* (Grand Rapids: Eerdmans).

R. A. Knox, 1950: *Enthusiasm* (Oxford: Clarendon).

R. Koch, 1970: 'Spirit' in J.B. Bauer, *Encyclopaedia of Biblical Theology* 3 (London: Sheed & Ward).

G. Kretschmar, 1968: 'La Doctrine du Saint-Esprit du Nouveau Testament à Nicée', *Verbum Caro* 22 (no. 88), 5–55.

R. Kugelman, 1968: 'The First Letter to the Corinthians' in R.E. Brown, J.A. Fitzmyer and R.E. Murphy (eds), *The Jerome Biblical Commentary* 2 (Englewood Cliffs: Prentice-Hall/London: Geoffrey Chapman [1969]).

H. Küng, 1974: 'Confirmation as the completion of Baptism' in P. Huizing and W. Bassett (eds), *Experience of the Spirit* (*Concilium* IX.10 [= 99]; New York/London: Seabury/Burns & Oates), pp. 79–99.

A. M. Landgraf, 1952: *Dogmensgeschichte der Frühscholastik* I/1 (Regensburg: Pustet).

J. Lécuyer, 1957: 'Docilité au Saint-Esprit' in *Dictionnaire de Spiritualité* 3 (Paris: Beauchesne), cols 1471–1497.

H. I. Lederle, 1986: 'The Charismatic Movement — the ambiguous challenge', *Missionalia* 14:2.

G. Leff, 1967: *Heresy in the Later Middle Ages* 2 vols (New York/Manchester: Barnes & Noble/University Press).

W. Lewis, 1978: *Witnesses to the Spirit: an Anthology* (Valley Forge: Judson Press).

M. Lienhard, 1965: 'La Doctrine du Saint-Esprit chez Luther', *Verbum Caro* 19, 11–38.

O. Lottin, 1949: *Psychologie et morale aux XIIe et XIIIe siècles* III: *Problèmes de morale* (Louvain/Gembloux: Mont César/Duculot).

1954. *Psychologie et morale aux XIIe et XIIIe siècles* IV: *Problèmes de morale* (Louvain/Gembloux: Mont César/Duculot).

P. Luislampe, 1981: *Spiritus Vivificans. Grundzüge einer Theologie Heiligen Geistes nach Basilius von Caesarea* (Münsterische Beiträge zur Theologie 48; Münster: Aschendorff).

D. Lys, 1962: '*Ruach*'. *Le souffle dans l'Ancien Testament* (Paris: Presses Universitaires).

K. McDonnell (ed.), 1975: *The Holy Spirit and Power. The Catholic Charismatic Renewal* (New York: Doubleday).

1980: *Presence, Power, Praise: Documents on the Charismatic Renewal* 3 (New York: Doubleday).

J. H. McKenna, 1975: *Eucharist and Holy Spirit. The Eucharistic Epiclesis in 20th Century Theology* (Alcuin Club Collections, no. 57; Great Wakering: Mayhew-McCrimmon).

J. P. Mackey, 1962: *The Modern Theology of Tradition* (London: Darton, Longman & Todd).

L. Malevez, 1932: 'La Doctrine de l'image et la connaissance mystique chez Guillaume de Saint-Thierry', *Recherches de Science Religieuse* 22:178–205, 257–279.

Malines Documents, nos 1, 2 and 3: see McDonnell 1980:13–70, 82–174, 291–357.

G. Martelet, 1972: *Résurrection, Eucharistie et genèse de l'homme* (Paris: Desclée).

W. M. Menzies, 1975: 'The non-Wesleyan origins of the Pentecostal movement' in Synan 1975:81–98.

A. Michel, 1922: 'Hypostase' in *Dictionnaire de Théologie Catholique* 7 (Paris: Letouzey), cols 369–467.

1950: 'Trinité (Missions et habitation des personnes de la)' in *Dictionnaire de Théologie Catholique* 15 (Paris: Letouzey), cols 1830–1855.

J. Moltmann, 1981a: *The Trinity and the Kingdom of God* (London: SCM).

1981b: 'Theological proposals towards the resolution of the *filioque* controversy' in Vischer 1981:164–173.

G. T. Montague, 1976: *The Holy Spirit: Growth of a Biblical Tradition. A Commentary on the Principal Texts of the Old and New Testaments* (New York/Paramus/Toronto: Paulist Press).

H. Mühlen, 1967: *Der Heilige Geist als Person* 2nd ed. (Münster: Aschendorff).

1968: *Una Mystica Persona. Die Kirche als das Mysterium der heilsgeschichtlichen Identität des Heiligen Geistes in Christus und den Christen: eine Person in vielen Personen* 3rd ed. (Munich/Paderborn/Vienna: Schonigh).

1978: *A Charismatic Theology* (London: Burns & Oates).

B. Neunheuser, 1964: *Baptism and Confirmation* (History of Dogma series: New York: Herder).

1982: *Handbuch der Dogmengeschichte IV/2: Taufe und Firmung* (Freiburg/Basel/Vienna: Herder).

A. Nolan, 1976: *Jesus Before Christianity* (Cape Town: David Philip).

F. Oakley, 1979: *The Western Church in the Later Middle Ages* (Ithaca/London: Cornell).

E. O'Connor, 1971: *The Pentecostal Movement in the Catholic Church* (Notre Dame: Ave Maria).

1975: 'The hidden roots of the Charismatic Renewal in the Catholic Church' in Synan 1975:169–191.

J. J. O'Rourke, 1969: 'I Corinthians' in R.C. Fuller, L. Johnston and C. Kearns (eds), *A New Catholic Commentary on Holy Scripture* (London: Nelson).

M. A. Orphanos, 1981: 'The procession of the Holy Spirit according to certain later Greek Fathers' in Vischer 1981:21–45.

A. C. Outler, 1961: 'Traditions in transit' in G.W.H. Lampe and D.M. Paton (eds),

Studies in Ministry and Worship: The Old and the New in the Church (London: SCM).

E. H. Palmer, 1958: *The Person and Ministry of the Holy Spirit: The Traditional Calvinistic Perspective* (Grand Rapids: Baker).

A. Palmieri, 1913: 'Esprit-Saint' in *Dictionnaire de Théologie Catholique* 5 (Paris: Letouzey), cols 676–829.

J. Pelikan, 1971: *The Christian Tradition. A History of the Development of Doctrine* I: *The Emergence of the Catholic Tradition (100– 600)* (Chicago/London: University of Chicago).

L. Pernveden, 1966: *The Concept of the Church in the Shepherd of Hermas* (Lund: Gleerup).

PG: J.-P. Migne (ed.), *Patrologia Graeca* (Paris, 1857ff.).

PL: J.-P. Migne (ed.), *Patrologia Latina* (Paris, 1844ff.).

G. L. Prestige, 1952: *God in Patristic Thought* (London: SPCK).

H. J. J. Th. Quistorp, 1964: 'Calvins Lehre vom Heiligen Geist' in Th. C. Vriezen, W. Foerster *et al.*, *De Spiritu Sancto: Bijdragen tot de leer van de Heilige Geest bij gelegenheid van het 2e eeuwfeest van het Stipendium Bernardinum* (Utrecht: Kemink), pp. 109–150.

K. Rahner, 1963: 'Membership of the Church according to the teaching of Pius XII's Encyclical "Mystici Corporis Christi" ' in K. Rahner, *Theological Investigations* 2 (London: Darton, Longman & Todd), pp. 1–88.

1966: *Theological Investigations* 4 (London: Darton, Longman & Todd).

1967: 'Reflections on the experience of grace' in K. Rahner, *Theological Investigations* 3 (London: Darton, Longman & Todd), pp. 86–90.

1968: *Spirit in the World* (London: Sheed & Ward).

1969a: 'Reflections on the unity of the love of neighbour and the love of God' in K. Rahner, *Theological Investigations* 6 (London: Darton, Longman & Todd), pp. 231–249.

1969b: *Hearers of the Word* (London: Sheed & Ward).

1970: *The Trinity* (London: Burns & Oates/Herder).

1974: 'Observations on the factor of the charismatic in the Church' in K. Rahner, *Theological Investigations* 12 (London: Darton: Longman & Todd), pp. 81–97.

1978: *Foundations of Christian Faith* (London: Darton, Longman & Todd).

1979: 'Religious enthusiasm and the experience of grace' in K. Rahner, *Theological Investigations* 16 (London: Darton, Longman & Todd), pp. 35–51.

D. Reed, 1975: 'Aspects of the origins of Oneness Pentecostalism' in Synan 1975:143–168.

A. Riaud, 1979: *The Holy Spirit Acting in our Souls* (New York: Alba).

D. Ritschl, 1981: 'Historical development and implications of the *filioque* controversy' in Vischer 1981:21–45.

W. J. Samarin, 1972: *Tongues of Men and Angels* (New York/London: Macmillan/Collier-Macmillan).

M. J. Scheeben, 1948: *Handbuch der katholischen Dogmatik* II, 3rd ed. (Freiburg: Herder).

M. Schmaus, 1958: *Katholische Dogmatik* III (Munich: Hueber).

1969: 'Holy Spirit, II: Gifts of the Holy Spirit' in K. Rahner *et al.* (eds). *Sacramentum Mundi* 3 (New York/London; Herder/Burns & Oates), pp. 59–61.

W. H. Schmidt, 1984: 'Geist/Heiliger Geist/Geistesgaben, 1. Altes Testament' in G. Krause and G. Müller, *Theologisches Realenzyklopädie* (Berlin/New York: Walter de Gruyter).

C. A. B. Stegman, 1979: *The Development of Tertullian's Doctrine of Spiritus Sanctus* (PhD thesis; Ann Arbor: University Microfilms International).

F. A. Sullivan, 1982: *Charisma and Charismatic Renewal. A Biblical and Theological Study* (Dublin: Gill & Macmillan).

1984: 'Pentecôtisme' in *Dictionnaire de Spiritualité* (Paris: Beauchesne), cols 1036–1052.

J. P. M. Sweet, 1966: 'A sign for unbelievers: Paul's attitude to glossolalia', *New Testament Studies* 13 (1966–67), 240–257.

H. B. Swete, 1912: *The Holy Spirit in the Ancient Church* (London: Macmillan).

1967: 'Holy Ghost' in W. Smith and H. Wace (eds), *A Dictionary of Christian Biography* 3 (AMS Press; New York: Kraus Reprint), pp. 113–133.

V. Synan (ed.), 1975: *Aspects of Pentecostal-Charismatic Origins* (Plainfield: Logos).

J. V. Taylor, 1972: *The Go-between God. The Holy Spirit and the Christian Mission* (London: SCM).

M. Thurian, 1961: *L'Unité Visible des Chrétiens et la Tradition* (Neuchâtel and Paris: Delachaux & Niestle).

F. Vandenbroucke, 1950: 'Le divorce entre théologie et mystique: ses origines', *Nouvelle Revue Théologique* 72, 372–389.

1957: 'Dons du Saint-Esprit. II. Le Moyen âge' in *Dictionnaire de Spiritualité* 3 (Paris: Beauchesne), cols 1587–1603.

L. Vischer (ed.), 1981: *Spirit of God, Spirit of Christ: Ecumenical Reflections on the Filioque Controversy* (London/Geneva: SPCK/WCC).

H. Vorgrimler (ed.), 1967: *Commentary on the Documents of Vatican II* 1 (London/New York: Burns & Oates/Herder).

1968: *Commentary on the Documents of Vatican II* 2 (London/New York: Burns & Oates/Herder).

G. Wainwright, 1971: *Eucharist and Eschatology* (London: Epworth).

H. Watkin-Jones, 1929: *The Holy Spirit from Arminius to Wesley. A study of Christian teaching concerning the Holy Spirit and his place in the Trinity in the seventeenth and eighteenth centuries* (London: Epworth).

B. Weber, 1985: 'Piétisme' in *Dictionnaire de Spiritualité* 12 (Paris: Beauchesne), cols 1743–1758.

C. Westermann, 1981: 'Geist im Alten Testament', *Evangelische Theologie* 41, 223–230.

C. G. Williams, 1981: *Tongues of the Spirit* (Cardiff: University of Wales).

J. C. Wilson, 1977: *Towards a Reassessment of the Milieu of the Shepherd of Hermas: its date and its pneumatology* (PhD thesis; Ann Arbor/London: University Microfilms International).

Indexes

INDEX OF BIBLICAL REFERENCES

NAME INDEX

SUBJECT INDEX